ECONOMIC BEHAVIOR

ECONOMIC BEHAVIOR

Jerry K. Rohacek
Associate Professor of Economics
University of Alaska, Anchorage

Prentice Hall
Englewood Cliffs, NJ 07632

Library of Congress Cataloging-in-Publication Data

Rohacek, Jerry K., 1945-
    Economic behavior / Jerry K. Rohacek.
        p.   cm.
    Includes index.
    ISBN 0-13-224148-X : $22.00
    1. Economics.   I. Title.
HB1715.R726   1989
330--dc19

Editorial/production supervision and interior design: **Maureen Wilson**
Cover design: **Lundgren Graphics**
Cover Photo: **Gabe Palmer, The Stock Market**
Manufacturing buyer: **Margaret Rizzi**

Printed in the United States of America

10 9 8 7 6 5 4 3 2 1

ISBN 0-13-224148-X

Prentice-Hall International (UK) Limited, *London*
Prentice-Hall of Australia Pty. Limited, *Sydney*
Prentice-Hall Canada Inc., *Toronto*
Prentice-Hall Hispanoamericana, S.A., *Mexico*
Prentice-Hall of India Private Limited, *New Delhi*
Prentice-Hall of Japan, Inc., *Tokyo*
Simon & Schuster Asia Pte. Ltd., *Singapore*
Editora Prentice-Hall do Brasil, Ltda., *Rio de Janeiro*

Contents

9   PRODUCTION AND ITS COSTS
131

10   SPECIALIZATION AND INDIRECT PRODUCTION
149

11 RESOURCE TRADE
165

12 BUSINESS FIRMS
185

13 COMPETITIVE AND MONOPOLY FIRMS
198

Preface

This is a short, friendly book about the principles of economics. It is not encyclopedic; rather, it presents economics as an evolving system of knowledge and contains a good balance between theories and applications. It also avoids mathematics and sophisticated economic apparatuses.

I wrote the book for both the one- and the two-term principles of economics courses, although my primary focus was on the one-term course. If you use the text in that course, but want to cover less ground, I recommend that you either skip the Application Questions at the end of each chapter or bypass some of the chapters. You can avoid Chapters 5, 6, 9–13 and 18 without a loss of continuity.

If you are using the text in a two-term sequence, then you have enough time to cover it all, and in-depth. For the micro-macro sequence, you can deal with the chapters in order. For the macro-micro sequence, the one employed at my school, I suggest you cover Chapters 1–4 and 14–19 in the macro class and then Chapters 5–14 and 20 in the micro class.

To present a gradually evolving system of knowledge, I organized the book around phenomena rather than economic concepts, and I followed the rule that simplicity should be sacrificed only when there is a sufficient gain in generality. Accordingly, the text presents an economic individual, perhaps a Robinson Crusoe, and then introduces the individual to increasingly more complex circumstances, those necessary to explain and predict additional sets of phenomena. As the complications are introduced, an economy is eventually built from scratch, an economy that approximates the one in which we live.

To obtain a good balance between theories and applications, I devoted about as much space to theories as I did to applications. As noted above, the division between theories and applications is close to 40 : 60.

I covered theories explicitly and in a very organized fashion. Theory presentations begin with an identification of some phenomena. The phenomena are then explained with concrete examples. Next, the explanations are used to generate various predictions. And finally, the theories are summarized.

After presenting the theories, I covered the applications as special topics. The applications are both various and brief. Variety gives perspective, while brevity provides simplicity and maintains interest. I chose the applications for their abilities to illustrate theories and for their entertainment value. The applications range from the standard variety to the unusual, as the following ten samples illustrate:

> Can the Old Compete With the New?
> The German Hyperinflation of the 1920s
> Industrialization and the Jeffersonian Embargo
> Head Hunters versus Want Ads
> Can Farmers Avoid Cyclical Unemployment?
> Adopting Children
> Parker Brothers' Monopoly
> Memory Money
> Chicken Little and Production
> Penny's Cooking

The applications are crucial. They help focus attention on the fundamental goal of the text and of economics: the explanation and prediction of economic phenomena—not the explanation of economic theories. The text is primarily concerned with recessions, not the Keynesian Cross. It focuses on consumer reactions to prices, not indifference curves. Theories shouldn't be and aren't ignored—almost all the standard ones are carefully and explicitly covered in the theory sections of the chapters. Theories are simply not ends in themselves. They are tools for the explanation and prediction of the phenomena contained in the applications and, more importantly, in the real world. The content of the material is fairly standard. Almost all the ideas are in one way or another contained in texts such as Samuelson and Nordhaus's *Economics* or Alchian and Allen's *University Economics*.

I owe a great deal to the many people who encouraged, tolerated, or directly aided the writing of this book. My debt to them is tremendous. Most of them helped me out of friendship or scholarship, and even the ones that were paid did far more than was necessary.

But my greatest debts are to my family: my mother, father, and stepfather, Rudolf Mikuta; my son, Don, my daughter, Lisa, and my wife, Penny. Penny deserves special thanks for reading and typing various versions of the manuscript as well as sitting in solitude, patiently and without complaint, while I wrote.

ECONOMIC BEHAVIOR

1

Introduction

What caused the Great Depression? How do some investors make millions on the New York Stock Exchange? Will a large increase in the U.S. national debt lead to an economic catastrophe? These are just some of the questions we will answer in this book on economics.

We will also deal with queries that you might expect to lie beyond our realm: Why do some people advertise for dates in the newspaper? Why does the World Series tend to go seven games? What roles do manners and customs play in American society? These questions will be within our focus because economics is much more than "the science of business." It is a study concerned with all economic behavior, behavior that occurs at play as well as at work, in our economy's public sector as well as in its private sector.

There are many reasons why you may want to learn about economic behavior. The most basic ones are that you will then know more about your environment, better understand what you read, and more intelligently discuss important social issues. After all, many of the things we see each day are economic in nature. And you can't read *Newsweek* or *Time* magazines without encountering discussions that involve economics in some way. Moreover, as a business or political person, almost all your conversations will center on economic issues, their meaning and their implications.

An understanding of economics can also improve your political decisions. Once you know what is likely to occur under various economic circumstances, you will be better able to decide which circumstances you want to exist.

Yet another reason for studying economics is that it can help you make better personal and business choices. With a knowledge of economics, you may be able to predict the consequences of various actions, effects that you might have otherwise overlooked.

However, you shouldn't expect that a knowledge of economics will radically change your behavior. For example, just because you may understand the economic effects of buying Japanese cars doesn't mean that you will be more or less likely to buy one. Rather than telling you how you should behave, economics tries to explain and predict how you do behave.

Before we begin to deal with economic behavior, in this first chapter we further discuss science and economics and also say something about theory, scope, and organization. You will then better know the nature of economics and be able to respond to some of the most common criticisms of the study. For instance, you will understand why economics is a science even though economists seldom conduct controlled experiments. You will also know why economic theories are useful even though they may yield imperfect results.

Our brief coverage of the nature and method of science, and specifically of economics, represents but one of many reasonable and useful approaches to the subjects. You can examine some of the other approaches by reading one of the many books on the philosophy of science.

SCIENCE AND ECONOMICS

Verifiable Predictions of Phenomena

Let's begin with science. **Science** is primarily an attempt to provide verifiable predictions of phenomena.

Specifically, a study has to pass two tests to be scientific. First, it has to focus on phenomena. The term **phenomenon** means any observable thing or event, unusual or not. Although scientists try to forecast the eruptions of volcanoes and the melting of polar ice, they also attempt to predict the most trivial of our daily individual and social activities.

Second, a study must present its predictions in a way that is directly or indirectly **verifiable**, in a manner that allows for the accumulation of observable evidence that can help support or refute the predictions. For instance, we can directly verify the prediction that lower prices will increase sales, since we can measure both prices and sales. However, we can't directly verify the prediction that more money will improve personal happiness. Although we can see if someone has more money, we can't see if the person is happier, since happiness is a nonobservable state of mind.

If a study passes the two tests, it is scientific even if it makes some wrong predictions. Science requires only an attempt at providing verifiable predictions of phenomena. All sciences—physics and chemistry as well as sociology and political science—predict phenomena with varying degrees of imperfection.

Economic Phenomena

The many phenomena that occur can be categorized into groups, creating areas of concentration for the various branches of science. One of the groups is within the purview of economics: the things and events that occur because people must deal with the fundamental problem of scarcity. **Scarcity** is a condition that exists when people want more goods than are available. We can define **economics** as the study of the phenomena that occur because people confront scarcity.

The phenomena caused by an attempt to deal with scarcity fall into two groups: phenomena related to the distribution of goods and those related to the production of goods.

The **distribution** of goods involves transferring goods from some people to others. Distribution can take many forms. We can sometimes obtain goods from other people by persuading them to give the goods to us. We can also sometimes coerce other people into surrendering goods to us, by using or threatening to use violence. Or we can obtain goods from others via exchange, giving up some of our goods for some of the ones other people own.

The **production** of goods involves combining things to form products. The things combined to form products are called **resources** or **factors of production**. Three types of resources, factors of production, exist:

a. **Land**—real estate and all other natural resources such as water, oil, and iron ore;
b. **Labor**—the natural unskilled abilities of people;
c. **Capital**—goods that have been produced only so that they can be used in subsequent production, items such as office buildings, machines, technology, and entrepreneurial ability (knowledge and skills used to direct and control other resources so that production can occur).

Although distribution and production can reduce scarcity, they can't eliminate it. The quantities of goods are limited and insufficient and so are the quantities of resources that can produce more goods.

Specific examples of economic phenomena are listed next. Some of these items may surprise you, but since they are all both observable and related to distribution and production, they fall within the scope of economics.

-Exchange	-Crime
-International trade	-Money
-Monopoly prices	-Wages
-Marriage	-Altruism
-Labor unions	-Prostitution
-Middlemen	-Cooperatives
-Price discrimination	-Racial discrimination
-Foreign exchange rate	-Pornography
-Banking	-Labor specialization
-Profits	-Conservation
-Unemployment	-Inflation
-Cartels	-Rent controls

-Government spending   -The national debt
-Pollution   -Drug distribution
-War   -Social manners

What Is, Not What Ought to Be

The various branches of science, including economics, ignore moral issues. They deal with what we can observe, not with what ought to be. For instance, a chemist can identify the effects of acid rain, but the chemist can't show that acid rain shouldn't fall on Toronto. Likewise, an economist may be able to predict how people will behave under capitalist conditions, but the economist can't prove that capitalism is either good or bad.

Nevertheless, Robert Oppenheimer, a physicist who directed the development of the atomic bomb, argued that the more powerful hydrogen bomb shouldn't be built. And economist John Kenneth Galbraith believes that more socialism should be introduced into the U.S. economy. These opinions reflect much more than objective predictions; they represent the subjective views of the associated individuals, their personal values. Whereas the sciences calculate what is, some scientists nevertheless also propose what should be.

Even when scientists try to remain impartial, it is impossible. For instance, neither a peace advocate nor a Pentagon warhawk can study the effects of disarmament in a totally unprejudicial manner. Each of us possesses a system of values and beliefs that influences us. Our choice of phenomena to study, our evaluation of data, and our use of theories are all affected by our personal views of the world.

Avoiding bias in economics is made more difficult by the fact that economic phenomena often directly affect our wealth and lie within our range of control. For instance, if you are renting an apartment, you may find it hard to analyze the effects of rent controls impartially. A limit on rents will then directly increase your wealth, and you may be able to help bring about the passage of rent-control legislation.

Still, we strive for objectivity. The material contained in this text does reflect views of what should be as well as what is, but an attempt has been made to keep bias to a minimum.

THEORY

Simplifications of Reality

So that we can predict economic phenomena, we will use the method of theory. That is, we will develop economic theories. Economic theories, like all **theories**, are simplifications of reality. They are but tools, instruments between us and our environments.

We will use theories to act as instruments for obtaining knowledge because the uniqueness of each phenomenon makes reality very complex. Each person, recession, business firm, market place, or inflation is somehow different. Predicting by dealing directly with complex reality is usually impossible. We need simplifications.

We develop theories by using the same method that we use when we first learn to see. For instance, when adults first gain their sight after being blind since birth, they see nothing because they observe everything. They can't identify a circle because they don't know where a line ends and its background begins. They recognize only colors. But gradually, these individuals learn to see by ignoring unique attributes of things and focusing on common factors. In much the same way, we build theories by ignoring unique aspects of phenomena and focusing on common elements. We see because our brains recognize only the essentials; our theories explain and predict because their components focus on just the fundamentals.

Explanations and Predictions

Theories have two parts: explanations and predictions. The **explanations** identify forces or factors that link the phenomena under study to other known things or events. Explanations are general. **Predictions**, on the other hand, forecast particular future or past phenomena. They are relatively specific.

For example, a theory of automobile movement may contain an explanation focusing on general factors such as kinetic energy, momentum, electricity, hydraulics and friction—forces that have already been used to predict other phenomena. In contrast, the theory's prediction may forecast specifically that an automobile in front of us will slow down after its taillights turn on.

One reason we want theories to have explanations as well as predictions is that predictions tend to be more accurate when explanations relate them to other known relationships or phenomena. For example, the nineteenth-century economist Stanley Jevons constructed a theory that used sunspots to predict changes in the output of the American economy. His theory may seem absurd until we hear its explanation, one that identifies already-known relationships: sunspots affect the weather, the weather affects farm output, and changes in farm output affect the output of an agricultural economy.

Sometimes we don't have theories; sometimes we lack explanations and possess only predictions. For instance, by using medical statistics, medical researchers can predict that smokers will contract lung cancer ten times more often than nonsmokers. But the researchers don't have a theory because they have failed to identify the forces that determine the relationships between smoking and cancer; they can't explain. As the American Tobacco Institute maintains, we would be more certain of the prediction if we had an explanation of how smoking causes cancer.

Judging Theories

Since theories are just tools, we must discuss how to tell a good theory from a bad one. How do we pick the best theories? We will select the theories that are most accurate, general, simple, and testable.

Accuracy

We certainly want theories that allow us to predict economic phenomena with the greatest possible success. Theories that predict 80% of the time are better than ones that predict only 70% of the time.

Notice that while it is important for theories to predict as accurately as possible, they need not predict all phenomena or even all phenomena of some chosen group. Economic and other scientific theories almost never yield perfect predictions. Nevertheless, as long as we gain more success with theories than without them, they remain useful.

We can usually increase the ability of a theory to predict accurately by developing specific formulations of it to deal with particular phenomena. Such formulations are called **models**. For instance, suppose we have a theory that deals with economic growth in capitalistic economies, but we are especially interested in the Canadian economy. In that case, we can obtain more accurate predictions by using the theory to construct a model that focuses specifically on Canadian economic growth, and then using the model to make our predictions.

Generality

When we say that we prefer **general** theories, we mean that we usually want theories that are able to deal with as many phenomena, or as many phenomena of a particular type, as possible. We aren't looking for theories that can predict only one thing or event. For example, we want a theory that predicts depressions rather than one that deals only with the Great Depression of 1929.

Simplicity

In addition to accurate and general theories, we want **simple** theories, ones with explanations and predictions that identify as few factors and relationships as possible. For example, we could propose two theories of how the solar system is organized. One theory can claim that the earth and other planets revolve around the sun in simple orbits. The other can assume that the sun and other planets move around the earth in very complex patterns. If both theories are equally accurate and general in predicting the locations of various heavenly bodies at different times of the year, then we can, nevertheless, judge the theory that places the sun in the center as superior. Its explanation is simpler.

In a sense, by preferring simple theories, we prefer unrealistic ones. Sometimes the very usefulness of a theory lies in its nonreality. Theories are simplifications, tools we find useful precisely because they are neither replicas nor detailed descriptions of the real world. We will avoid judging our theories by whether or not they are real.

Although we want simple explanations and predictions, accuracy and generality are usually more important than simplicity. As Albert Einstein said, "The purpose of science is to make the world as simple as possible . . . but no more than that." In other words, we will usually allow our theories to become more complex if we can thereby gain accuracy and generality.

For example, suppose that the Southern Bell Telephone Company hired you as an economic consultant to predict future telephone calls in the Atlanta area. Telephone companies want such forecasts so they can build facilities before telephone traffic expands, not after.

You might already have a theory that you developed to predict telephone calls in other areas, but to gain more accuracy, you would probably want to use that theory to construct a model for the Atlanta area. If you started to build the model by assuming that population changes cause certain changes in the number of calls, you would probably be able to forecast some of the changes in traffic. Your model would be simple and might yield some successful predictions. However, if you complicated your model (perhaps by including shifts in the business/residential ratio), you might predict the volume of calls more successfully. The sacrifice of simplicity might be worth the gain in accuracy. And perhaps the inclusion of more factors would give you even more success. But eventually, you would reach a point where adding more variables wouldn't improve the ability of the model to predict. You would then stop, since a loss of simplicity would occur without a gain in either accuracy or generality. You would obtain only a more complicated explanation or prediction and, therefore, an inferior model.

Actually, you would probably stop even sooner. The gain of only a small amount of accuracy is often not worth the sacrifice of a great deal of simplicity.

Testability

It has been said that the Greek philosopher Aristotle assumed both that inferior humans have fewer teeth than superior humans and that women are inferior humans. He then argued logically that women have fewer teeth than men. And for 200 years, people believed that women had fewer teeth than men. No one counted the teeth.

The story implies that in Aristotle's time, science was not yet upon us. Today, scientists would count the teeth. In fact, we will judge our theories by whether we can "count teeth"— by whether our theories are **testable**. We want to be able to make observations that tend to verify or reject our theories. We want our theories to be scientific.

Since economic theories deal with phenomena, we can usually test their validity. We can make observations of reality and see how well actual phenomena conform to the explanations and predictions of the theories.

Unfortunately, we generally can't conduct controlled experiments to obtain evidence. For instance, we can't hold everything in the United States constant and raise the money supply to see if prices increase—households, business firms, and governments are not white rats. However, our inability to conduct such experiments is a problem of degree rather than kind. Even when experiments are conducted very carefully, outside factors always affect results.

Controlled experiments would give us cleaner evidence rather than natural reality.

We also often can't obtain direct evidence to test the predictions of a theory. Nevertheless, testability can exist if indirect verification is possible.

Many of the predictions we will examine in this text don't lend themselves to direct verification, either because the predictions deal partly with non-observable factors, or because direct data to support or refute the predictions is unobtainable. Still, testability is generally possible because the predictions are logically derived from explanations, and we can usually obtain evidence to support the explanations or some of the other predictions of the explanations. In the specific case of Jevons' theory, if we couldn't obtain direct data about the relationship between sunspots and national output, we might nevertheless rely on indirect information, facts relating sunspots to the weather, the weather to agricultural output, and agricultural output to national output.

When we discussed the composition of theories, we noted that we want our theories to have explanations because predictions tend to be more accurate when explanations support them. Now we can cite another reason for having explanations: Explanations allow us to test predictions indirectly when direct verification is impossible.

SCOPE AND ORGANIZATION

An understanding of science, economics and theory is important for the comprehension of our last topic: the scope and organization of the material in this text. We can start by identifying the **scope** of our analysis, the range of phenomena that will lie within our study.

Behavior Caused by Circumstances

Economic phenomena emanate from interactions between people and the circumstances they confront. When either people or their circumstances change, different phenomena result.

In this book, we will focus on those economic phenomena that are caused by circumstances. We will relegate economic phenomena caused by differences or changes in people to later studies in economics, political science, psychology, and sociology. This concern with circumstances will allow us to concentrate our efforts.

From the Most Simple to the More Complex

The goal of explaining phenomena as simply as possible has dictated the organization of this text. We will begin in the next chapter by first identifying some universal and constant attributes of all individuals, people whom we will call **economic individuals**. Then, throughout the rest of the text, we will introduce our economic individuals to increasingly more complex economic circumstances, thereby gradually sacrificing simplicity to gain generality.

In Chapter 2, we will start by confronting our economic individuals with the simple circumstances of higher prices. This will allow us to explain and predict how individuals react to changes in the prices and the costs of goods. But with such simple circumstances, we won't be able to explain trade. To explain trade, we will, in Chapter 3, introduce more complex circumstances in the form of other economic individuals who value mutually desired goods differently. Next, to explain middlemen, cooperatives, markets, and money, we will have our economic individuals trade under circumstances where transaction costs are significant.

All these complications won't allow us to say much about price levels or price changes. Therefore, in Chapters 4 and 5 we will have our economic individuals exchange goods under more complex circumstances, those that exist in competitive and monopoly markets.

As indicated in Table 1.1, we will eventually include 30 sets of circumstances in our analysis, such circumstances as limited market information, the time-value of goods, and communal property rights. With each step, we will expand our ability to explain and predict by recognizing only the circumstances that are necessary for dealing with additional phenomena. When we have finished, we will have gradually built a complex economy from scratch, an economy that approximates the economic system in which we live.

TABLE 1.1   The Organization of the Text

> Economic individuals interact with increasingly complex circumstances to cause various sets of phenomena.

ECONOMIC INDIVIDUALS

Scarcity
Multiplicity of wants
Diminishing valuation
Substitutability
Rationality

CIRCUMSTANCES	PHENOMENA
1. Changes in prices and costs	Buying, selling, and choosing different quantities
2. Value differentials	Free trade and its effects
3. Transaction costs	Middlemen, cooperatives, markets, and money
4. A competitive market	Market-clearing prices and price changes

TABLE 1.1 The Organization of the Text (continued)

CIRCUMSTANCES	PHENOMENA
5. A monopoly market	Monopoly prices and quantities
6. Limited and costly market information	Surpluses, shortages, stable and slowly changing prices
7. Government and private price controls	Nonclearing prices and their effects
8. Future goods and their unknown values	Capital gains, losses, speculation, and conservation
9. Time-value of goods	Interest and the prices of capital goods
10. Scarce resources	Production
11. Substitutable resources	Responses to changes in costs
12. Comparative advantages	Specialization and trade
13. Indirect production	Economic growth
14. Mergers of resources initially owned by different individuals	Wages, rents, the prices of capital, and profits in competitive and monopoly resource markets
15. Cartels	Cartel prices and quantities
16. Team production	Business firms, costs, and production
17. Competitive product market	Prices and outputs of competitive firms and industries
18. Monopoly production	Monopoly prices and outputs
19. Private property rights	Capitalist production and distribution
20. Communal property rights	Socialist production and distribution
21. Government limitation of private property rights	Mercantilist production and distribution
22. Various transaction costs	A mix of monetary forms, limits on the money supply, and the effects of an increase in the money supply
23. Greater money supply and velocity, and fewer resources and products	Inflation and its effects
24. Price searching	Lagged inflation
25. Less money	Disinflation and deflation
26. Fixed resource prices	Classical unemployment
27. Price searching and demand shifts	Frictional unemployment
28. Price searching and aggregate demand decreases	
	Cyclical unemployment and the three stages of recession
29. More government spending, lower taxes, and more money	Recession, recovery, inflation, the national debt, interest rates, production and wealth changes, and supply-side effects
30. International comparative advantages and value differentials	International trade, balance of payments, exchange rates, and specialization in production

Our study will be cumulative. Although it is sometimes possible to deal with new phenomena by focusing on a few isolated circumstances, we will usually recognize many previous circumstances and add to them. As a result, rather than a set of independent theories, we will develop an internally compatible system of knowledge.

The Order of Phenomena

In terms of the phenomena covered, we will begin with a focus on exchange in Chapters 2–8. Subsequently, in Chapters 9–13, we will introduce production circumstances and deal with both exchange and production.

By covering exchange first and production later, we will go against what seems to be the natural order of things. After all, most goods are first produced and then exchanged. But there are two good reasons for discussing exchange before production. First, we can explain many exchange phenomena without saying anything about production. And second, since most goods are produced only so they can be later sold, a clear understanding of production requires some comprehension of subsequent exchange.

Although we will focus on exchange in Chapters 2–8, we will occasionally mention production. This is because some concepts apply to both exchange and production. Also, sometimes we can't ignore production when it strongly affects exchange.

After we have dealt with exchange and production on a fundamental level, we will discuss various economic systems in Chapter 14. We will see how capitalism, socialism, and other economic systems function.

Next, in Chapters 15–19 we will focus on money, inflation, and unemployment. We will start by looking closely at money and banking, and then examine the definitions, possible causes, and potential solutions to inflation and unemployment.

Finally, in Chapter 20 we will deal with international trade and phenomena related to it.

Micro- and Macroeconomics

Our organization of material separates the primarily microeconomics of most of the chapters from the macroeconomics of Chapters 15–19. **Microeconomics** deals with individual exchange and production choices whereas **macroeconomics** focuses on aggregated behavior of individuals. For instance, when studying microeconomics, we might be concerned with the determination of an individual price or with how much a particular firm produces. In contrast, when discussing macroeconomics, we might focus on the level of all prices or on the combined output of all firms in the economy.

Chapter Organizations

Most chapters discuss theory first, followed by special-topic sections. In the theory sections, we will identify the phenomena with which the theories are concerned. We will then explain the phenomena with the aid of specific and concrete examples. Next, we will derive the predictions of the explanations. And finally, we will summarize the theories.

The special-topic sections will generally contain applications of the theories to specific phenomena. However, some special topics will introduce new economic concepts such as elasticity and the mathematics of the multiplier. These concepts will expand the generalities of the theories. The concepts have been relegated to the special-topic sections because earlier coverage would have made the fundamental aspects of theories much more difficult to understand. Also, for some students, the gain in generality achieved by learning some of the less useful and more complicated concepts isn't worth the sacrifice of simplicity. When the concepts are treated as special topics, they can easily be skipped.

We have now finished our discussion of science, economics, and theory, and the scope and organization of this text. However, before we end, we can deal with one last question: Is economics complex? Well, as the late economist Alfred Marshall once said, "Every short statement about economics is misleading (with the possible exception of my present one)." Nevertheless, economics can be easy to learn if you:

    a. Study it systematically,
    b. Cover it in small components,
    c. Translate it into your own terms,
    d. Use it to explain your own experiences,
    e. Employ it to answer the chapter questions.

MAJOR AND MINOR POINTS

1. You may want to learn economics so you can understand economic phenomena and make better political, personal, and business decisions.
2. Science concerns itself with providing verifiable predictions of phenomena (observable things or events).
3. To be scientific, a study must deal with phenomena and present its predictions in a directly or indirectly testable way, a way that makes it possible to make observations that help support or refute the predictions. A study doesn't, however, have to be always successful to be within the realm of science.
4. Scarcity exists: There aren't enough goods to satisfy all human wants.
5. Economics is a branch of science that tries to explain and predict phenomena that occur because people confront scarcity.
6. To reduce scarcity, we distribute and produce goods.
7. Distribution moves goods from some people to others.

8. Production involves the combining of goods called resources or factors of production to form products.

9. Three types of resources or factors of production exist: land, labor, and capital.

10. Distribution and production can't eliminate scarcity because the supplies of goods as well as the supplies of resources that can produce goods are limited and insufficient.

11. Although science restricts itself to what is, some scientists are also concerned with what should be.

12. Even when we try, it is impossible to be totally impartial.

13. The objective study of economic phenomena is made more difficult when the phenomena have direct effects on our wealth and when we can control them.

14. Due to the complexity of reality, economists and other scientists use simple tools called theories.

15. Theories are comprised of explanations and predictions.

16. Explanations are general; they link the phenomena under study to other phenomena via fundamental forces.

17. Predictions are more specific; they forecast particular future and past phenomena.

18. We want accurate, general, simple, and testable theories. That is, we want theories that predict as successfully as possible, but we want to avoid theories that predict only one phenomenon, that have complicated explanations and predictions, or that predict nonobservable things and events.

19. Models are specific formulations of theories that deal with particular phenomena.

20. We don't expect our theories to predict perfectly since somewhat inaccurate theories can be useful. We also don't expect our theories to be real; we develop theories to simplify, not replicate, reality.

21. The explanations of theories provide opportunities for indirect verification when direct tests of predictions are impossible.

22. In this text, we will focus on economic phenomena caused by circumstances.

23. We will begin by identifying some universal attributes of human beings. We will call people with these attributes economic individuals. Then we will confront our economic individuals with increasingly complex circumstances, gradually sacrificing simplicity to obtain generality.

24. In Chapters 2–8 we will concentrate on exchange, whereas in Chapters 9–13 we will deal with both exchange and production. Then, in Chapter 14 we will examine various economic systems. Next, in Chapters 15-19 we will discuss money, inflation, and unemployment. Finally, in Chapter 20 we will look at international trade.

25. Microeconomics concerns itself with individual decisions, whereas macroeconomics deals with the aggregated behavior of individuals.

26. Chapters contain theory presentations followed by special topics. The theory presentations include identifications of phenomena, explanations, predictions, and summaries. Most special topics are applications of the theories to real phenomena, but a few deal with additional economic concepts that will expand the generalities of the theories.

QUESTIONS

If you can answer the following questions, you probably understand the funda-mental concepts covered in the chapter. If you want to check your ability to use those concepts, try to answer the application questions in the next section.

1. How are phenomena and science related?
2. How is scarcity related to economics?
3. How and why do people distribute and produce goods?
4. Why is science unconcerned with what ought to be?
5. What are theories, and why and how are they developed?
6. What are explanations and predictions?
7. Why do theories contain explanations as well as predictions?
8. What are the four criteria used to judge economic theories?
9. Economics isn't a science. Economic theories don't always work, the theo-ries are unreal, and we can't conduct controlled experiments to verify them. Evaluate.
10. Discuss the following terms and concepts:

Science	Theories
Phenomenon	Explanations
Scarcity	Predictions
Economics	Accuracy
Distribution	Generality
Production	Simplicity
Resources	Testability
The factors of production	Models
What is versus what should be	People versus circumstances
Scientists and bias	Micro- and macroeconomics

APPLICATIONS

The questions in this section require you to apply the concepts that were covered in the chapter. The questions are sometimes very difficult and you won't be able to answer them. Nevertheless, give them all a try and then check the answers in the back of the book.

1. Which of the following might science try to explain and predict?
   a. Happiness
   b. Stock market prices
   c. The disadvantages of more government
   d. Satisfaction
   e. The exploitation of labor
   f. Just prices
   g. Psychosis
2. Someone predicts that criminals who have found Jesus will commit fewer crimes. Is this a scientific prediction?

3. Sociology isn't a science because sociologists haven't learned much about group behavior. Comment.

4. Can you use economics to prove that it is better to go to college than to begin work after high school?

5. Why might it be more difficult to predict objectively the effects of minimum-wage laws than the effects of the moon on the tides of the earth?

6. Distinguish between theory and reality.

7. We learn to predict phenomena in much the same way that we learn to see and listen. Explain.

8. Examinations in economics courses predict student knowledge imperfectly. Should they be given?

9. Do you think Newton's laws of physics yield perfect predictions? Explain.

10. Which theory is more general, one that implies that Hitler caused World War II or one that claims a megalomaniac was responsible?

11. Why might a theory that predicts the effects of higher prices on consumer purchases be more useful than a theory that predicts the effects that higher oil prices have on oil consumption?

12. Can a theory that assumes the existence of perfect competition be useful even when some monopoly sellers are present?

13. Some students argue that the theories presented in this text are useless because they are unreal. Do you think those students explain and predict economic phenomena with theories that are duplicates of reality?

14. In what two basic ways can you go on a diet?

15. Freudian psychoanalysts try to deal directly with the minds of the insane when they want to cure psychotics. How else can psychologists change the behavior of the mentally ill?

2

Reactions to Changes in Prices and Costs

Why do basketball players perform better during championship games than in the regular season? After all, they always have both the ability and the desire to make spectacular plays, even in practice. And why is it that we have all told lies, yet we claim to be honest? Also, why do college freshmen go on so many dates if they consider good grades to be crucial to their well-being?

What is going on? Is human behavior inconsistent, random, unpredictable? As scientists, we assume that it isn't. The principle assumption of science is that nothing just happens; everything is caused and caused by a few fundamental forces. Once we have identified those forces, we can make sense out of what seems to be nonsense.

But what about the preceding apparent paradoxes? We can resolve them all with the law of demand, the theory we will develop in this chapter. The theory is called a **law** because it has been so strongly supported by observable evidence.

The law of demand is a logical place to begin. As we indicated in the preceding chapter, this book is concerned with the behavior of economic individuals under various circumstances. The law describes those individuals and confronts them with the most simple of circumstances, changes in prices and costs.

To cover the law of demand, we use the format that was mentioned in the introduction. We begin with a brief description of the phenomena that lie within the realm of the law. Then we explain the phenomena and derive predictions from the explanation. Next, we summarize the law. Finally, we look at seven special topics.

The special topics deal with the applicability of the law of demand to human needs, the apparent paradox that people who work at the worst jobs are often also paid the least, and the hypocrisy and corruption of some politicians. The topics also discuss rats and sports, why students drop classes early rather than late in the semester, and why it is rational to keep old cars when superior new ones are available. This time all the special topics involve applications of the theory to specific phenomena.

THE LAW OF DEMAND

The Phenomena

Since the law of demand concerns itself with our individual responses to changes in the prices and the costs of goods, we need to start by defining goods, prices, and costs.

We will define **goods** very broadly as any desired entities, any things that we may want. Goods include

    a. Material commodities such as food, shelter, labor, and machinery;
    b. Financial assets such as money, bonds, and common stocks;
    c. Nonmaterial items such as medical services, love, happiness, and friendship.

Of course, some goods, such as money, are desired only because they can later be used to obtain other goods. And it may be impossible to produce goods such as love, happiness, and friendship. Nevertheless, since all these items are desired by some people, they are goods.

Prices are rates of exchange; they identify the exact sacrifices that we make when we purchase goods and the gains we receive when we sell them. For example, if you trade $100,000 for a house, then $100,000 is the price; it is what you directly give to the seller and what the seller receives in exchange for the real estate.

When economists refer to the cost of a given action, the cost to which they refer is usually the **opportunity cost**. Opportunity costs are more general than prices: they are the values of the highest-valued alternatives that we sacrifice when we make decisions. For instance, if the highest-valued alternative that you could have obtained if you had not been reading this chapter is some fishing, then the value of the fishing is the opportunity cost of reading this chapter. It follows that if the value of fishing increases, the cost of reading this chapter rises.

When we buy goods, prices often reflect most of the costs that result—but not always. For example, to obtain three credits of economics, you must usually pay a price in the form of tuition, but you must also incur additional costs resulting from studying, attending lectures, and traveling to class.

To explain and predict our responses to changes in prices and costs, we can start by focusing on our responses to higher prices. With few exceptions, we have responded to higher prices by buying less. And we have bought less whether we were Vanderbilts or Joneses, whether we lived in socialist or capitalist economies, whether our cultures were primitive or modern.

An Explanation: Higher Pepsi Prices

The Example

To explain why we bought less when prices rose, let's focus on why you might buy fewer Pepsi-Colas at a higher price:

Suppose you want both more Pepsis and more money than you have. Furthermore, suppose you are willing and able to pay $1.20 for one Pepsi, $.80 for a second, $.60 for a third, and $.50 for a fourth.

This means that you value a Pepsi at $1.20 when you don't have one, but its value drops to $.80 after you obtain the first can, to $.60 with the purchase of the second, and to $.50 when you buy the third. We can say that these are your values because we define the **value,** or **worth,** of any good A as the amount of any other good B that an individual is willing and able to sacrifice for one more unit of A at a given point in time.

More generally, value is a marginal, personal rate of substitutability. The marginal unit is the next unit. Value is marginal in that it alludes to the value of the next unit of a good, not to all units. It deals with the next Pepsi, not with all Pepsis. Value is personal, since it varies among people. You may value another Pepsi much more than I do. And value is a measure of substitutability since it reflects only how much a person is willing and able to give up of some other good to obtain one more of the item in question. All we know is that you are willing and able to sacrifice $1.20 for the first Pepsi; we know nothing about how good it tastes to you or whether you will later be glad that you had purchased it.

Income strongly affects the values of goods, since no matter how vital some goods may be, we must be able to sacrifice other goods before we can value them. For example, a starving man in New Delhi may value a Pepsi much less than you do. The Pepsi may taste better and be more satisfying to the man than to you, but his poverty may force him to be willing to sacrifice very little.

Wants also affect our values. All other things the same, the more we want something, the greater its value. However, wants are different from values. I may want a Pepsi much more than you do, but if I want other things even more, such as a pound of rice, I may be willing and able to sacrifice only $.10 to buy a Pepsi.

Our income and our wants help determine our values. So do the quantities of goods that we already own. We have assumed that you value Pepsis less as you obtain more, as the columns in Table 2.1 indicate.

TABLE 2.1   *The Dollar Value of Pepsis*

Column (2) indicates how much you are willing and able to pay for the additional Pepsis in Column (1).

(1) PEPSI	(2) VALUE IN DOLLARS
1st	$1.20
2nd	.80
3rd	.60
4th	.50

Given these values, if you can buy Pepsis from a vending machine for $.60, you will purchase three. You will buy the first Pepsi since it is worth $1.20. You will also consume the second Pepsi worth $.80, since it is worth more than the price, even though the second is worth less than the first Pepsi. And you may or may not buy the third Pepsi worth $.60, but for simplicity, let's assume that you will. However, you certainly won't purchase the fourth Pepsi. Its $.50 value is less than the $.60 price.

Now, if the price rises, we can see that you will buy less. If the price of Pepsi rises to $.80, you will purchase only two Pepsis. The third Pepsi's value, $.60, will be below the new $.80 price. And at still higher prices, you will buy even lower quantities.

The Nature of Economic Individuals

At the core of the above example lies the assumption that you possess the five fundamental attributes of economic individuals. Let's look closely at each of these attributes:

The Scarcity Attribute.   Scarcity itself is not an attribute; it is a situation in which the quantity of a good isn't sufficient to satisfy human wants. The scarcity attribute, on the other hand, focuses upon scarcity from the perspective of the individual. The attribute reveals that for each of us, some types of goods are scarce. The attribute implies we aren't satisfied. In the preceding example, you wanted more Pepsis and more money than you had.

We can argue that all of us must deal with scarcity, partly because we defined a good as anything anyone wants, material or not. Maybe Nelson Rockefeller was satiated with material goods, but he found at least one nonmaterial good scarce: the U.S. presidency.

The Multiplicity of Wants Attribute.   The second attribute, multiplicity of wants, reveals that each of us wants additional units of more than one type of good. In the Pepsi example, you wanted more Pepsis as well as more money. Simply put, we aren't total fanatics who want more of just one category of goods.

The Diminishing Valuation Attribute.   The third attribute is diminishing valuation. It says that the more of any good any of us possesses, the lower its value. The value of Pepsis declined as you bought more.

The Substitutability Attribute.   The fourth attribute is substitutability. It means that each of us is willing to sacrifice some of any desired good for enough of any other desired good. You wanted more Pepsi and more money and were willing to sacrifice some of each good for enough of the other.

However, we may refuse to substitute one whole category of a good for another whole category. For example, you may have been unwilling to sacrifice all your money for Pepsi. Substitutability specifies the sacrifice of only *some* of any desired good for *some* of any other desired good.

Substitutability implies that we can express the value of every good we want in terms of every other good we want. The value of a pair of shoes may be some computer software, a kiss, or $62.

It follows that the shoes, software, and kiss are each worth $62. Once we want money, we can express the value of every good we desire in monetary terms. This is convenient, since money is the good we usually sacrifice in trade.

The Rationality Attribute.   The final attribute is rationality. It says that each of us is decisive and consistent.

Decisiveness requires that we know our values. In the Pepsi example, you preferred having $1.21 to a first Pepsi, you were indifferent between $1.20 and the first Pepsi, and you preferred the first Pepsi to $1.19.

Consistency mandates that our values don't contradict each other and also that we act according to the particular values that we have. If you prefer a Pepsi to $.60, then you must prefer a Pepsi to $.50. And if you are given a choice between a Pepsi and $.50, you have to select the Pepsi. In short, we will always give up less valuable goods for more valuable ones if given the opportunity. This fundamental motivation lies behind every economic decision.

This definition of rationality implies that irrational people choose arbitrarily. For instance, even when Pepsis cost the same, irrational people may pick Pepsis one moment and Cokes the next. Why? Perhaps because they are indecisive or inconsistent. That is, irrational people may be unable to make up their minds, they may possess contradictory values, or they may be ignoring the values they have.

Rationality doesn't require that we possess the "right" values. Children, criminals, dope addicts, and terrorists often reveal values that we think are inconsistent with their well-being. Nevertheless, to be rational, people need only obey whatever values they have.

Incidentally, rationality and the other attributes deal with individuals, not groups. Gangs, committees, and societies don't always behave the way we would have predicted from our knowledge of their members. We will continue to concentrate on individuals throughout this book, leaving the complexities of group behavior to other inquiries.

In summary, by assuming that you have the scarcity, multiplicity of wants, diminishing valuation, substitutability, and rationality attributes, we can explain why you will buy fewer Pepsis at higher prices.

The Predictions

Although our example deals directly with your reactions to higher Pepsi prices, the behavior results no matter which goods are involved or who the individuals are, as long as they are economic individuals. We can predict that if the price of any good rises, then we will buy less.

Since the explanation focuses on fundamental forces, we can make some additional predictions. First, if the price of a good falls, then we will buy more. In the Pepsi example, you were willing to purchase only three Pepsis for $.60 because the fourth was worth only $.50. If the price had fallen to $.50, however, you would have bought it. And you would have purchased still more if the price had fallen even further.

We can also predict that we will sell more of a good at higher prices than at lower ones. Imagine that you bought three Pepsis, sat down next to the vending machine, and suddenly the owner of the machine arrived and raised the price to $.80. If someone later came by who wanted to buy a Pepsi, what would you have done? If you didn't mind looking a bit strange, you would have offered to sell one of your Pepsis since its value ($.60) would have been below the new price ($.80). And had the owner of the machine raised the price to $1.20, you would have been willing to sacrifice two. The higher the price, the more you have been willing to sell. Conversely, if the price was reduced from $1.20 back to $.80, you would have offered to sell one less. And at lower prices, you would have been willing to sell even fewer units.

Next, we can predict that if the cost of a good rises, we will choose less; and if the cost falls, we will choose more. We can explain this by recognizing that we buy less of a good at a higher price because a greater payment means a higher cost. Higher prices increase the costs of buying.

The advantage of predicting our responses to costs rather than just our responses to prices is that we can thereby expand the generality of our theory to deal with a large variety of nonexchange decisions. For example, we can predict that

    a. Criminals will commit fewer crimes when prison sentences are long rather than short.

b. Religious people will attend church less often when they are on vacation than when they are at home.

c. People will jump into calm streams to rescue their friends more often than they will jump into raging torrents.

d. More high school graduates will go to college during recessions than during periods of prosperity.

e. Farmers will produce less wheat when the prices of the farm equipment they must buy are high than when the prices are low.

In each of these cases, when the cost of a good rises, economic individuals choose less.

Conversely, we can predict that

a. Students will study more on Wednesday night than on Saturday night.

b. Terrorists will strike unguarded airports more than well-secured ones.

c. Anglers will spend more time fishing near the road than in the wilderness.

d. Home-owners will mow their lawns more often on sunny days than on rainy ones.

e. The auto industry will produce more cars if steel prices are low than if they are high.

Here, when the cost of a good falls, economic individuals choose more.

When we make nonexchange decisions, we choose less at higher costs and more at lower ones for the same reasons that we buy less at higher prices. That is, we choose less because we are economic individuals, people who possess the scarcity, multiplicity of wants, diminishing valuation, substitutability, and rationality attributes. For example, when the cost of reading rises because better shows are on TV, we read less because we

a. Want both more reading and more TV than we have;

b. Want reading and TV rather than just one of the goods;

c. Value both reading and TV less as we obtain more of each good;

d. Are willing and able to substitute between reading and TV at some rate;

e. Are decisive and consistent in our values and behavior.

A Summary of the Law

We have now explained the law of demand. We have assumed that we are economic individuals who possess five fundamental attributes:

a. Scarcity

b. Multiplicity of wants

c. Diminishing valuations

d. Substitutability

e. Rationality

Given these attributes, we can predict that we will

a. Buy less at higher prices and more at lower prices;

b. Sell more at higher prices and less at lower prices;

c. Choose less at higher costs and more at lower ones.

SPECIAL TOPICS

The predictions of the law of demand are very general and therefore useful. They are also far from fascinating or even surprising. We can, however, use the law to explain some interesting phenomena, something we will do as we discuss the following seven special topics.

Human Needs

To survive, human beings must have certain minimal amounts of air, food, water, clothing, shelter, and medicine. These goods are called needs. The quantities of needs that are required differ among individuals and environments. Some people can't live without injections of insulin, some must have large quantities of water, and some—those living in cold climates—must have clothing and shelter.

Since we require minimum quantities of these categories of goods for survival, we may incorrectly argue that the law of demand does not apply to needs, that we will buy the same quantities of needs no matter what the prices. Nevertheless, when the prices of needs go up, people buy less; when the prices of needs go down, people buy more.

A number of reasons exist why the law of demand predicts even when the prices of needs change. First, we are generally consuming quantities of needs that exceed the quantities necessary for survival. Most people, even poor people, purchase more food, water, clothing, shelter, and medicine than they must have to live. Second, a variety of particular goods can fulfill most of our biological requirements, so that few particular goods are needed. We may need food, but if the price of wheat rises, we can buy more rice. Finally, we can change our survival requirements by changing our environments. If the price of clothing and shelter increases, we may be able to move south. If the price of insulin rises, we can be more careful with our diets.

Since the law of demand applies to most needs, the concept of a need is of little use in understanding human behavior; most behavior is unrelated to minimum biological requirements. We usually want more of most goods; we seldom need more.

So why is the term need so entrenched in our vocabulary? Partly because it is a powerful device in convincing people that more of some particular good should be chosen. For example, if you tell a politician that you need higher education, then you imply that no choice exists, that survival dictates more higher education, and that other goods will not suffice. This is why people argue that they "need" a Hawaii vacation, a second car, a larger home, and a yacht. If instead you were to claim that you wanted more higher education, the politician might respond by pointing out (correctly) that scarcity forces people to choose among many wanted goods.

Since we want more of most goods rather than need more, we encounter problems whenever we try to distribute goods according to what we think are needs of people. For example, during World War II, the International Red Cross tried to distribute goods to prisoners in prisoner-of-war camps on the basis of what was believed to be the needs of prisoners. What do you think happened immediately after identical parcels containing "necessities" were received? The soldiers started to trade. What seemed like necessary cigarettes and food to some were worthless to others. Some smokers and hungry prisoners even sold some of their cigarettes and food to obtain other goods they wanted more.

Hard Work, Low Pay

Why do professionals who earn high salaries also have the most pleasant jobs? After all, who has the more pleasant job, the president of Consolidated Coal or one of Consolidated's miners? And who gets the most pay?

Professionals receive more job satisfaction as well as more pay than nonprofessionals partly because they make more valuable contributions to production. This allows them to demand greater compensations in the form of higher salaries. As their salaries increase, however, diminishing valuation kicks in to reduce the values of the salaries relative to improved working conditions. The professionals then accept only part of their greater compensations in the form of higher salaries and the rest in the form of more pleasant jobs. They could demand even greater pay, but they choose improved working environments instead.

Other workers could also accept less pay and obtain more job satisfaction. Mexican immigrants, for instance, could eliminate sweatshops by accepting wage reductions. Nevertheless, they won't because their salaries are already so low that values of dollars are high relative to improved working conditions.

As the immigrants obtain more education, they will be able to demand higher wages. As their wages rise, the values of the wages will fall relative to other amenities of their jobs. Firms operating sweatshops will then be replaced by firms offering slightly lower wage increases but more enjoyable work. This is what has generally occurred throughout the Western world since the beginning of the Industrial Revolution.

Hypocritical and Corrupt Politicians

A number of years ago, a newspaper reporter questioned Henry Kissinger about the CIA's role in helping install a non-Marxist government in Chile. The reporter asked how U.S. politicians can simultaneously believe in nonintervention and also aid a government coup in a foreign country. Kissinger evaded the question by giving a very complex answer.

Kissinger could have used the law of demand to explain. The law implies that nothing is more important than anything else. There is no priority list of wants. American politicians want many things, including nonintervention and national security, and are willing to substitute among them. When the cost of nonintervention in terms of national security rises, as it apparently did in Chile, they opt for less nonintervention and more national security.

We can use this reasoning to explain the behavior of politicians during the ABSCAM dealings of the 1970s, in which undercover FBI agents offered members of Congress bribes for legislative favors. The law of demand predicts that all politicians can be bought. They may all want honesty, but they also desire other goods and are willing to substitute among them. What really upset us is the small amount that was required before some of the politicians sold out.

Actually, what we often admire most about our politicians is their willingness to substitute, to trade. They will often vote for laws they mildly dislike so they can "buy" the votes of other politicians in favor of legislation they think is extremely desirable. When they then succeed in getting legislation passed that we dearly want, we say that we admire their flexibility, their practicality, their willingness to compromise. Of course, when they make what we think are bad trades, they become hypocritical, immoral, and unethical traitors to their espoused beliefs.

Rats

So far we have focused on human behavior. We can, however, use the law of demand to explain the behavior of rats as well as humans.

In a paper presented at a meeting of the Southern Economic Association in November, 1976, "Demand Curves for Animal Consumers," John H. Kagel and Raymond C. Battalio described an experiment in which they "paid" a rat with cherry cola for pushing a bar. A computer controlled the amount of the cola dispensed and measured the daily consumption. The results showed that when the animal was paid 1 cubic centimeter of the soda per push, it consumed 200 cubic centimeters per day. When the amount was reduced to .5, daily drinking fell to 65, and at .025 cubic centimeter per push, cherry-cola consumption dropped to a bare 1 cubic centimeter.

Why did the rat choose less when the cost increased? Perhaps because it was an economic individual possessing the attributes of scarcity, multiplicity of wants, diminishing valuation, substitutability, and rationality. Human behavior may be more complex, but it is fundamentally the same as the behavior of other animals.

One reason for mentioning rats is that this case demonstrates the generality of the law of demand. We place more confidence in a theory that applies to all animals than in one that is special only to humans. Another reason is that it reveals that the usefulness of the theory doesn't rely on conscious thought. We don't need to consciously obey the law of demand—or any economic theory—to act according to its predictions.

Slippery Rock 21, USC 14

For that matter, are we ever really all that conscious? The law explains why, as athletes, we often unconsciously choose to perform inconsistently.

For instance, it is absolutely incredible how badly good football teams can play when they compete against weak opponents. They do so because high-quality performances require players to sacrifice personal glory, relaxation, and safety. When the players think they can win and still obtain personal glory, safety, and relaxation, they often unconsciously choose more of these goods and less quality play.

This gives football coaches nightmares by keeping games closer than expected. It also makes for great championship games in which the quality of play often exceeds everyone's expectations.

Dropping Econ 201

Have you noticed that you are more likely to drop a class earlier in the semester than later? We can use the law of demand to explain some of this behavior.

The reasons have nothing to do with the sacrifices you have already made. The sacrifices are irrelevant to your current decisions. You hesitate to drop classes late in the semester because the cost of credits falls as the semester progresses. That is, the highest-valued alternatives you have yet to give up decrease as there is less studying left to do. Since the cost is lower, you choose to stay in class.

Can the Old Compete with the New?

We can use the same reasoning to explain why you keep your old car even if you can buy a new, more fuel-efficient one. You drive the old car because the cost of a car falls after you buy it and continues to fall the longer you own it.

The costs associated with an automobile emanate from sacrifices related to acquisition, ownership, and operation. You incur an acquisition cost when you drive a new car off the showroom floor. It is the difference between the price of the car and its immediate resale value. Next, you incur an ownership cost from non-driving-related sacrifices: depreciation and the interest you could have earned had you left the money in the bank instead of buying the car. Finally, you incur operating costs from the additional depreciation caused by use and from the sacrifices associated with the purchases of gas, insurance, and maintenance services.

Relative to buying a new car, the old car has a zero acquisition cost (since that cost has already been incurred), and low ownership, driving-related depreciation, and insurance costs. These cost advantages more than compensate for the old car's poor looks, discomfort, bad handling, and greater maintenance requirements. You therefore continue to drive the old car.

We often own both new cars and old ones. When new cars have benefits that cover their costs, we buy the new cars. When the lower benefits of our old cars cover their lower costs, we keep them as well.

This reasoning also explains why American corporations using old plants can compete with modern Japanese firms. The zero acquisition and low ownership costs of the old American plants can offset their lower production efficiencies. New facilities may generate greater benefits, but they also cost more to buy.

More generally, managers in both nations are rational when they keep old and also buy new equipment. When the lower benefits of old equipment cover lower costs, the managers keep the old equipment. When the higher benefits of new equipment exceed their costs, the new equipment is also purchased. The only reason we have more old equipment in the United States is that we began sooner. We also drive proportionately more used cars.

By identifying the five fundamental attributes of economic individuals, we have been able to construct a theory that tells us how we will react to changes in prices and costs. We can't, however, explain and predict why and when we will trade. Nor can we explain and predict the involvement of middlemen, cooperatives, markets, and money in our exchanges. Our theory is too simple. To deal with these additional phenomena, we will, in the next chapter, complicate our theory by introducing our economic individuals to more complex circumstances, ones that include value differentials and transaction costs.

MAJOR AND MINOR POINTS

1. The law of demand explains and predicts our individual reactions to changes in the prices and the costs of goods.
2. The explanation of the law of demand identifies the nature of economic individuals, a human nature that is essential to all of the economic phenomena we will discuss in this book. The nature is described by the scarcity, multiplicity of wants, diminishing valuation, substitutability, and rationality attributes.
3. A good is anything anyone wants. This includes physical consumption commodities, resources, money, financial assets, and nonmaterial items such as love or medical services.
4. Price is the rate of exchange, it measures what is directly sacrificed and received when goods are bought or sold, respectively.
5. Opportunity cost is the value of the highest-valued alternative that we sacrifice when we make a decision.
6. The value of any good A is the amount of any other good B that we are willing and able to sacrifice for one more unit of A. It is a marginal, personal rate of substitutability. It isn't the satisfaction a good yields.
7. The value of a good can be changed by a change in our income, our wants, or the amount of the good that we own.
8. The scarcity attribute of economic individuals states that each of us wants more of some type of good.

9. The multiplicity of wants attribute assumes that each of us desires additional units of more than one type of good.
10. The diminishing valuation attribute claims that the more of any good any of us owns, the lower the value of each additional unit received.
11. The substitutability attribute states that each of us is willing to substitute some of any desired good for enough of any other desired good.
12. The rationality attribute maintains that each of us is decisive and consistent in our values and behavior.
13. The law of demand applies directly to individual behavior, not group behavior.
14. We can predict that economic individuals will
    a. Buy less at higher prices;
    b. Buy more at lower prices;
    c. Sell more at higher prices and less at lower prices;
    d. Choose less at higher costs and more at lower costs;
    e. Choose better working conditions at the expense of some salary increases;
    f. As politicians, sacrifice some things they want for other things they want more, often acting hypocritically and corruptly;
    g. As athletes, perform better against well-matched opponents and for bigger prizes;
    h. As students, drop classes early in the semester;
    i. Rationally own both old and new goods.
15. Past sacrifices aren't costs, they are irrelevant to present decisions. As a result, costs disappear as they are incurred.

QUESTIONS

1. The law of demand deals with individual reactions to changes in the prices and the costs of goods. What are prices, costs and goods? What are the attributes of economic individuals?
2. What is the definition of value that is used in economics?
3. Why will individuals buy less of a good when its price rises and more when the price falls?
4. Why will individuals sell more of a good when its price rises and less when the price falls?
5. Why will individuals choose less of a good when its cost increases and more when the cost decreases?
6. Discuss the following terms and concepts:

Law of demand	Rationality
Good	Irrationality
Price	Human needs
Opportunity cost	Priorities
Value	Hypocritical, immoral, unethical
The scarcity attribute	Flexible, practical, compromising
Multiplicity of wants	Animals and humans
Diminishing valuation	Past sacrifices and costs
Substitutability	Old versus new goods

APPLICATIONS

1. Distinguish among the price, the cost, and the value of this book.
2. Resolve this apparent paradox: The value of water is high whereas that of diamonds is low, and yet water has a low price while diamonds have a high price.
3. Are there any times when the values of goods rise with consumption?
4. Does substitutability imply that we will sacrifice all of our clean air for jobs?
5. Are economic individuals selfish in the sense that they want only commodities that directly benefit themselves?
6. Are patients in a hospital for the mentally ill rational?
7. Do we have the same specific values? Do we have the same value structure?
8. In 1986, the United States attacked Libya in retaliation for various terrorist attacks on U.S. citizens. Does the law of demand predict Libya's response?
9. Explain how we react to costs by using an example involving studying economics and watching TV.
10. Is the quality of food more important than the quantity?
11. Can we expect American workers to work as many hours as their grandparents?
12. Although we talk idealistically about honesty, we act practically and tell lies. Explain.
13. How might you be entrapped to commit a crime?
14. Does the law of demand explain and predict instinctive behavior?
15. Since basketball players want to win as well as to obtain personal glory, when is a team going to display more teamwork, when the score is 98–12 or 98–96? Why?
16. Why is it more likely that you will finish a job than that you will start it?

3

Trade, Middlemen, Cooperatives, Markets, and Money

Think about it: most of the things you own, you bought. Trade is a big part of our lives. And yet, most of us know little about it. Why and when will we exchange goods? Answering this question will be our first objective in this chapter; we explain and predict free trade.

We weren't able to deal with trade in the previous chapter because the law of demand focuses on the behavior only of one individual, perhaps a Robinson Crusoe trapped on a desert island. Trade quite obviously requires at least two people.

To explain and predict trade, we add a complication to the law of demand and thereby construct a theory of free trade. Specifically, we confront our economic individuals with others who value mutually desired goods differently. So that trade can occur, Robinson Crusoe meets his man, Friday.

Once we discuss free trade, we proceed to a second objective: the explanation and prediction of our use of middlemen, cooperatives, markets, and money. This goal requires us to tack a second specification to the law of demand so that we can develop the theory of transaction costs. We recognize that often before trade can occur, transaction services like transportation, packaging, refrigeration and information have to be produced at some cost, and that sometimes the cost can be reduced by middlemen, cooperatives, markets and money.

The special topics related to free trade deal with the economics of a POW camp, the adoption of children, and the distribution of transplantable human organs. Those related to transaction costs examine headhunters versus want ads, the cooperatives fostered by the utopian socialists of the 1830s, the existence of bars, and the difficulties of obtaining friends.

Our objectives remain scientific. We won't discuss whether we should trade, employ middlemen, create co-operatives, or use markets and money. We simply observe that we sometimes do these things and we want to know why and when.

THE THEORY OF FREE EXCHANGE

The Phenomena

Most of us begin life as the recipients of gifts. Our parents create our physical beings and then give us the food, clothing, shelter, money, and other goods that we consume in our early years. For a thank you here and there, we obtain an average of more than $150,000 worth of goods.

Upon reaching maturity, things begin to change radically as the flow of gifts from parents slows. To maintain life, we are forced to rely on people outside our families. But unfortunately, strangers don't automatically donate goods for our consumption.

We can obtain goods from strangers in a number of different ways: persuasion, coercion, and trade. Persuasion requires that we convince strangers to give us voluntarily the goods we want. With coercion, we threaten to take away or actually take away something that strangers value if they don't give us what we want. In effect, we confront strangers with a choice between being worse off if they give us what we want or being much worse off if they don't. Finally, trade causes us to give strangers something they want in exchange for something we want.

Actually, we seldom obtain goods by using persuasion or coercion. Persuasion is often ineffective and coercion is generally the province of thieves. That leaves us with trade. Throughout our adult lives, we get most of the goods we want by trading other goods for them. We usually sell our labor to obtain money, and then trade the money for food, clothing, shelter, transportation, and other items.

An Explanation: Purchasing Pepsis

To explain the nature of trade, let's go back to the example in which you were buying Pepsis with money. Your values are shown in Table 3.1 by columns 1 and 2.

Before you can trade, you must encounter another individual. So let's complicate the example with the values of an owner of a vending machine, illustrated by the columns 3 and 4 in Table 3.1. (The owner's values are structured in the same way as any individual's, except that they don't reflect dimin-

TABLE 3.1   A Value Differential

> The four columns contrast the values of Pepsis to you with those of the owner of a vending machine. Since you initially have no Pepsis, Pepsis are worth $1.20 to you; since the machine has 23, Pepsis are worth $.60 to the owner. A value differential of $.60 exists.

YOUR VALUES		THE OWNER'S VALUES	
(1) PEPSIS	(2) MONEY	(3) PEPSIS	(4) MONEY
1st	$1.20	20th	$.60
2nd	.80	21st	.60
3rd	.60	22nd	.60
4th	.50	23rd	.60

ishing valuation. This failure won't change results but will simplify our discussion.)

You have no Pepsis, so the value of Pepsis to you is the value of the first Pepsi, $1.20. The machine has 23, so its owner values Pepsis at $.60. Since a value differential exists, trade will occur.

But at what price will trade occur? You are willing to buy a Pepsi for $1.20 or less, whereas the owner of the machine is willing to sell for $.60 or more. We know that the price range will be $1.20 to $.60, but we can't predict the exact price. We can just assume the price is $.60. (We will begin to explain and predict prices in the next chapter.)

For $.60, you will certainly buy the first Pepsi worth $1.20 to you. The machine will sell its 23rd Pepsi since it receives what the Pepsi is worth to its owner. You will also buy a second Pepsi that you value at $.80, since you pay only $.60. The machine will give up the 22nd Pepsi worth $.60 to its owner to get $.60. Finally, you may or may not buy the third Pepsi, since it's worth $.60 to you, as much as the price, but for simplicity we can assume that you will make such a trade. For its part, the machine will relinquish its 21st Pepsi.

After you buy the third Pepsi, trade will stop. All value differentials will be gone; you and the owner of the machine will both think a Pepsi is worth $.60.

This explanation reveals that the general cause of trade is value differentials, not zero values. When you sacrifice money for Pepsis, it isn't because the money is worthless. Similarly, the machine doesn't sell the Pepsis because its owner places no value on them. Both you and the owner of the machine each place some value on both money and Pepsis before trade occurs; each of you simply places different values on the goods.

The Predictions

The explanation yields four predictions. First, when we encounter other economic individuals who value mutually desired goods differently, we will trade. Value differentials will give rise to exchange.

Second, the exchanges will distribute goods to those who value them more. In the Pepsi example, you valued the Pepsis more and you received them during trade, while the owner of the vending machine, who valued money more, received money.

Third, trade will increase the values of goods. In the example, both the values of the Pepsis and the money increased with trade. Since the first Pepsi was worth $.60 to the owner of the machine and $1.20 to you, its value rose from $.60 to $1.20 when you bought it. Similarly, the value of money increased since the owner of the machine valued money more. To you, $1.20 was only worth one Pepsi; the owner believed it was worth two Pepsis.

It may seem that since trade will increase the values of goods, it is always a good thing. This is wrong. High values aren't necessarily good values. For instance, consumers often buy products that they value highly but that yield very little satisfaction. Similarly, investors regularly purchase stocks that subsequently drop in value, and addicts commonly buy drugs that eventually kill them. Free trade may or may not be a good thing. It does, however, increase the values of goods at the time it occurs.

Finally, free exchange will move all parties to more preferred positions. Both you and the owner of the vending machine were happy to trade since you each obtained goods you valued more in exchange for ones you valued less.

The movement of both parties to more preferred positions explains why trade is voluntary, why it often involves the same people on an ongoing basis, and why it is so difficult to stop. If trade moved one of the two people involved to a less preferred position, people wouldn't generally trade voluntarily, and they wouldn't keep buying the same goods at the same stores. Moreover, illegal trades would be easier to stop since the police could obtain a great deal of information from buyers or sellers rather than from uninvolved third parties.

A Summary of the Theory

By assuming that we are economic individuals and that we encounter circumstances in the form of other economic individuals who value mutually desired goods differently, the theory of free trade predicts that

  a. We will trade.
  b. Goods will be distributed to people valuing them more.
  c. The values of goods will increase.
  d. Those who trade will move to more preferred positions.

SPECIAL TOPICS RELATED TO FREE TRADE

Now we can discuss three special topics involving barter, children, and transplantable human organs.

The Economics of a Prisoner-of-War Camp

In a classic article, "The Economics of a P.O.W. Camp," published in the November, 1945, edition of *Economica*, R. A. Radford described economic activity in a POW camp to which he was sent after being captured by the Germans during World War II. In the camp, economic activity revolved around the distribution of goods that were received at the beginning of each month in International Red Cross parcels.

The article is of interest to us at this point because Radford made certain observations that support or further explain our theory of trade. First, it wasn't necessary for prisoners to not want goods for them to be willing to sell goods. Prisoners often sold goods they valued, even cigarettes and food, if they were able to obtain other goods they valued more. Trades didn't occur so much because some soldiers placed a zero value on some goods as because soldiers valued mutually desired goods differently. Value differentials gave rise to exchange.

Next, money initially wasn't present and yet trade occurred. Although we used money in our explanation of exchange, this was only to minimize the complexity of that explanation. Money isn't necessary for the occurrence of trade, only value differentials are. Our theory of trade applies to barter economies as well as to monetary systems; it is general.

Another aspect of trade that the example underscores is that trade doesn't necessarily move goods toward the rich and away from the poor. Everyone in the prisoner-of-war camp initially received the same commodities, there were no income differentials. Value differentials nevertheless occurred and gave rise to exchange.

The argument that trade unfairly benefits the rich at the expense of the poor is an argument against poverty rather than against trade. If income in the United States were redistributed so that everyone had the same amount, trade would still occur, its effects would be the same, and it couldn't discriminate against the poor.

Finally, behavior in the POW camp revealed that trade isn't fundamentally a production phenomenon. There was little production in the camps. The parcels came as manna from the Red Cross. Incidentally, the article described the emergence of middlemen, markets, money, interest, and profits, making it clear that these phenomena also aren't primarily caused by production.

Adopting Children

Except under conditions of slavery, societies generally prohibit the sale of newborn infants. If parents don't want their children, then rather than being allowed to sell the children for cash, the parents must usually give the infants to adoption agencies. The agencies then normally ignore the willingnesses and abilities of prospective new parents to pay and instead give children to "deserving" couples, usually on a first-come, first-served basis.

What does our theory of free exchange predict would happen if free trade in children were made legal? First, exchange would occur between biological parents and adopting parents whenever the values of children and money differed.

Second, the babies and the money would be distributed to those people valuing each good the most. As a result, the distribution of the infants would change since the people now on top of adoption agency waiting lists wouldn't necessarily also be the ones valuing the babies the most. Some parents wishing to let their children be adopted would refuse to honor the order of the lists and instead would sell their children to the highest bidders.

Third, the values of money and the children would rise. The values of children would be higher to the new parents than to the natural ones. Also, to the extent that the children would be given to parents valuing them more than couples higher on adoption agency waiting lists, free trade would increase the values of the children more than adoption agencies would have.

Next, both the adopting parents and the biological parents would move to more preferred positions as a result of the transactions. Neither would move to a less preferred position.

Finally, in this case, the theory makes an additional and special prediction: It predicts that free exchange would increase the quantity of children being distributed. Why? Because adoption agencies not only refuse to sell children, they also won't buy them. The agencies accept only children that have no value to their parents. With free trade, biological parents would be paid a price. Being economic individuals, they would be willing and able to sell more. Specifically, the parents placing positive but very low values on their children would sell to buyers valuing the youngsters more.

If the price covered the cost of having babies, infants would even be produced for trade, as—in the case of surrogate mothers—some have. Some mothers would decide to become pregnant just to make money. And other mothers who were considering having abortions would change their minds. With a greater quantity supplied, childless couples would find it easier to adopt children.

Does all this mean that the theory claims that free trade rather than adoption agencies should be used to distribute children? No! The theory only predicts trade and its effects; it deals only with what will be, not with what ought to be. After all, the high bidders could be sexual perverts or farmers looking for good farmhands. You must decide for yourself what circumstances and resulting phenomena you think ought to occur.

The Distribution of Transplantable Human Organs

We can't usually buy babies in open markets. We also can't normally buy transplantable human organs.

Because there is an enormous scarcity of transplantable livers, kidneys, and hearts, doctors and hospital administrators must establish some criterion for distributing the organs. Usually they give the organs out on the basis of a modified first-come, first-served criterion. Recipients aren't allowed to bid for the organs, nor can they resell them to others.

What would happen if free trade were allowed in this area? Our theory predicts that

    a. To the extent that donors value their organs less than recipients, exchanges of money and the organs would result.

    b. Trade would increase the values of both goods since recipients would surely value the organs more and the donors would place greater valuations on the money.

    c. Both parties would move to more preferred positions.

    d. The quantity of available kidneys, livers, and hearts would rise.

The last prediction may seem unlikely, but the present system of distribution requires donors rather than sellers. For a price, more people would be willing and able to sell their organs.

Paying the suppliers would present some problems, since we tend to have little interest in trade when we are either dead or dying. We might, however, be able to sell our organs in advance to a business firm for a discounted price, a price that adjusts for the probability that we may never provide an organ. In the future, the firm could sell whatever organs it would receive to the highest bidders.

Under free trade conditions, some people wouldn't be able to obtain transplants. It is therefore tempting to conclude (wrongly) that trade causes scarcity and should therefore be banned. But trade only distributes existing, scarce goods in a particular way, it doesn't primarily determine how many goods are available. In fact, by raising the price that sellers obtain, trade indirectly can increase the quantity of a good that is available, reducing its scarcity. It is possible that if people were paid to donate their transplantable organs, the tremendous scarcity that now exists would be greatly reduced. In fact, the present scarcity isn't caused by a lack of potential donors but by the unwillingness of potential donors or their families to supply organs under the present distribution system.

Trade would also allow the poor to obtain some transplants that would have otherwise gone to the rich. At present, some rich people are receiving transplants because some hospital committees think that wealthy people are more deserving, even though some less wealthy or poor patients value the transplants more. In fact, markets sometimes distribute more of some particular goods to the poor than other methods of distribution.

Finally, the crime rate might fall. Crime is sometimes mistakenly blamed on trade because criminals usually steal goods so they can obtain money to purchase goods in trade. But crime is caused by scarcity, not trade. Actually, to the extent that free trade increases the supplies of goods and reduces their scarcities, less crime will occur. For example, a legalization of heroin might reduce the crime rate by making it possible for drug addicts to buy heroin at very low prices. It is possible that more illegal activity is associated with the present distribution of transplantable human organs than would occur under free trade conditions.

Free trade would cause different effects than the present distribution method. Which method is better? Once again, the theory of free trade fails to provide an answer. It says nothing about what should be; it tells us only what will be.

A THEORY OF TRANSACTION COSTS

The theory of free trade explains and predicts many exchange phenomena. To say more, however, we need a more complex theory; we need to confront our economic individuals with more complicated circumstances. We will do this as we develop a theory of transaction costs.

The Phenomena

When we observe trade in primitive societies, the exchanges are usually very simple: Two people interact in relative isolation, swapping one commodity for another. But when trades occur in our modern economy, the exchanges are often far more complex. People

a. Usually buy products from **middlemen** who purchase them from the original producers and sell to final consumers;
b. Sometimes deal with consumer and producer cooperatives that subsume the roles of middlemen;
c. Generally trade in markets;
d. Normally use money to facilitate their transactions.

An Explanation: Don the Middleman

To explain these phenomena, we can concentrate on why we use middlemen, and to explain our use of middlemen, let's take a look at another example. Imagine that your values of video movies and money are illustrated in Table 3.2 by columns 1 and 2, whereas the values of a store owner are shown by columns 3 and 4.

Since you value the movies at $7 and the owner values them at only $3, trade will take place. You will rent the movies until their value to you falls to equal their price. If the price is $3, you'll rent five. The movies and money will be reallocated to whomever values them more, the values of the goods will increase, and both the store owner and you will move to more preferred positions.

So far, we can use this example to illustrate why we trade, but it can't be used to explain middlemen. So let's complicate the circumstance.

Suppose you live on a hillside and that the store renting the movies is 5 miles away. Under these conditions someone has to make valuable sacrifices to

TABLE 3.2 Values of Rented Video Movies

The four columns identify the values of rented video movies to you and to a video-rental store owner.

YOUR VALUES		STORE OWNER'S VALUES	
(1)	(2)	(3)	(4)
VIDEO MOVIES	MONETARY VALUE	VIDEO MOVIES	MONETARY VALUE
1st	$7	496th	$3
2nd	6	497th	3
3rd	5	498th	3
4th	4	499th	3
5th	3	500th	3

transport the movies from the store to your house. The example now includes transaction costs.

Although transaction costs are involved, you may nevertheless rent some movies. Suppose you can only get one movie each trip and that what you must sacrifice to drive down the hill is worth $3 to you. Under these conditions, you would rent two movies—the first and second movies are worth $7 and $6, respectively, and each requires a $3 price plus a $3 transportation cost.

Other people need not value their travel sacrifices as much as you do. If the store owner values her sacrifices at only $2, she may offer to rent the movies for a delivered price of $5 each. You would certainly accept the offer and rent three rather than two films.

But suppose the lowest-cost producer of the transportation service is Don, a neighborhood teenager who has a motorcycle and little to do. If he values his sacrifices at $.50 and offers to get the tapes for that amount, you will hire him. Don will then be a middleman.

After some time, his middleman status might become more obvious. Don might simply rent the movies from the store owner for $3 and turn around and rent them to you and other hillside residents for $3.50. Unfortunately for Don, people might then believe that he is getting something for nothing. After all, he would be renting movies for $3.50 when everyone would know that the movies rent for only $3 at the local store. People might fail to understand that Don would be producing transportation at a cost to him of $.50, a cost that is lower than the one they would have had to incur if they had transported the tapes.

The Predictions

We can use the preceding explanation to predict that we will involve middlemen in our trades if we can thereby reduce our transaction costs. To behave rationally, we have to take advantage of any opportunity to reduce the sacrifices we make in obtaining goods.

We can also predict that we will do other things to reduce transaction costs. First, if consumer or producer cooperatives can reduce our transaction costs more than middlemen, then we will bypass middlemen and create the cooperatives.

Cooperatives are groups of consumers or producers that produce transaction services. For example, consumers may join together and form a consumer food cooperative to bypass their local supermarket. They will then sacrifice their labor to the cooperative rather than money to the supermarket.

The major reason for forming groups in the form of cooperatives to produce transaction services rather than producing the services individually is that the groups can produce the services at lower costs. This is because they can take advantage of mass-production technologies.

In addition to predicting our use of cooperatives, we can predict that we will trade in markets if we can reduce transaction costs. **Markets** are exchange institutions that bring buyers and sellers together for trade. They cut transaction costs by reducing the sacrifices associated with transportation and information. Markets can take the form of county fairs, trade shows, shopping centers, or newspapers.

Finally, we can predict that if we can reduce transaction costs, we will use money in our exchanges. **Money** is anything that acts as a generally accepted medium of exchange, although it also carries out some other functions that we will discuss in Chapter 15.

By acting as a medium of exchange, money lowers transaction costs by eliminating the "double-coincidence-of-wants" requirements of barter. For example, suppose you wanted to trade your old Ford for a used Apple computer. You would then encounter some difficulty because although there may be many sellers of Apples, the sellers would also have to want your Ford. You would find it easier to sell the Ford for money and then use the money to buy an Apple. The number of exchanges would double, but transaction costs would be much lower.

A Summary of the Theory

Our theory, by assuming that economic individuals encounter transaction costs, predicts that if the costs can be reduced, the individuals will

- **a.** Involve middlemen in their exchanges;
- **b.** Create cooperatives to bypass middlemen;
- **c.** Trade in markets;
- **d.** Use money as a medium of exchange.

SPECIAL TOPICS RELATED TO TRANSACTION COSTS

We can better understand the effects of attempts to reduce transaction costs by examining a few special topics.

Head Hunters versus Want Ads

For most of us, one of the most unpleasant tasks that we encounter in life is looking for a job. Not only do job searches tend to weaken our self-esteem, they can also be very costly in other ways. We usually have to spend a great deal of effort writing résumés, reading newspapers, calling friends, and "beating the pavement." Nevertheless, we can do all these tasks ourselves. Why then do we sometimes hire middlemen in the form of employment agents to find jobs? After all, these agents, often called "headhunters," are normally not free; we must usually pay for their services.

We employ the agents because they produce the transaction services associated with job hunting and charge us fees that are below the costs that we would have incurred in producing those services. The agents can charge less because they specialize in searching for jobs and can take advantage of mass production technologies. Also, they may already know more about the job market than we may ever learn, partly because they often possess special skills and partly because they sometimes have privileged relationships with various employers.

Employment agents are also sometimes more successful than unemployed workers in finding jobs because they provide services for employers as well as unemployed workers. Many small firms that don't have personnel departments fill jobs by using employment agencies. The agencies act as personnel departments for the firms, producing transaction services. It is simply less costly for employers to subcontract to employment agents than to screen the hundreds of applicants that would be obtained through want ads.

Some people deal with employment agents even though they think the agents make them worse off. Those people may believe that the agents and other middlemen create transaction costs rather than reduce them. When asked to explain why they still deal with the middlemen, they often can't explain their behavior. But people don't need to know why they use middlemen in order to do so.

The Rise and Fall of the 1830s' Cooperatives

In addition to explaining why we often hire employment agents to help us find jobs, we can use our theory to explain what happened to the many cooperatives that were created in the United States during the 1830s. These institutions came into existence with the propagation and popularity of various utopian socialist philosophies. The cooperatives bypassed middlemen and thereby increased the prices producers obtained and reduced the prices consumers paid. Nevertheless, although they were and continue to be legal, most of them failed.

Why? Because the values gained (the benefits) were less than the values sacrificed (the costs). For example, dairy farmers may have gained $1000 in revenues when they sold their milk to their cooperative rather than to a middleman, but they may have also incurred $2000 in additional costs. After all, while the farmers worked for the cooperatives, they couldn't simultaneously produce milk. Likewise, members of food cooperatives may have saved $50 on their monthly food bills, but they may have sacrificed $60 worth of alternative goods to work on weekends in the cooperative warehouses.

Some cooperatives have survived and our theory predicts which ones. The successful cooperatives have been those that have inflicted costs below the prices charged by middlemen. For instance, some farm cooperatives have remained because their members work between harvest and planting time, sacrificing little to produce transaction services. And some consumer grocery cooperatives have endured because many of their customers are unemployed or poor. People who are poor or unemployed usually also produce transaction services without sacrificing a great deal since their alternatives are limited.

Many nonprofit credit unions, mutual funds, and retail establishments have also done very well. They aren't, however, cooperatives in a strict sense because their members don't produce any transaction services. For example, Recreational Equipment Incorporated (REI) of Seattle, Washington, is called a consumer cooperative, but consumers don't work for the firm. REI is simply a corporation owned by consumers; its stockholders are its customers. The consumers share only the profits and losses, not the work. Much the same result is obtained when the residents of a small town buy their local general store.

Social Markets

In addition to dealing with employment agents and cooperatives, we can explain the survival of bars that charge high prices for drinks.

Although some people often frequent bars to consume alcohol, the high prices of drinks would drive most customers away if the bars didn't also act as social markets, cheaply bringing individuals into contact with other individuals who want to exchange ideas and friendships. For many lonely men and women, bars are the only institutions that allow them easily to meet a large number of other men and women wanting to exchange these items.

In recent years, dating firms using computers, video cameras, and video recorders have created a new market for those people wanting to meet members of the opposite sex. The firms have been especially successful in catering to "yuppies." These career-focused individuals have found the costs of drinking and talking in bars particularly high. By instead using the markets provided by dating firms, yuppies have been able to work longer hours, spend time shopping for BMWs, and still have dates on Saturday nights.

Not everyone believes it proper for people to find partners in bars or via computers and video recorders. Why? Perhaps because they simply feel that there are more tasteful ways to meet people. However, sometimes it is because markets foster competition. People providing very little beauty and personality may be better off when their potential competitors are difficult to find. While markets do move the parties actually trading to more preferred positions, they may reduce the opportunities that other people could have otherwise had.

Buying Friends with Your Personality

Finally, we can explain why it is so much easier to buy a car than to find a friend. We can buy a car with money, but we have to "sell" our own personalities to "buy" friends. While almost every seller of automobiles wants our money, many potential friends don't like our personalities. To find friends, we have to satisfy a double-coincidence-of-wants requirement. For example, you may want to "buy" the friendship of Heidi Donaldson or Tom Cruise, but they may not want anything to do with you.

Individuals who find it particularly difficult to find friends while they are single often find it almost impossible after they get married. The number of simultaneous personality exchanges rises geometrically when four rather than two people are involved. As a result, many married couples are relatively isolated from people outside their families. Family members become, for better or worse, forced friends.

In this chapter, by introducing our economic individuals to new circumstances in the form of value differentials and transaction costs, we have been able to explain and predict trade and the use of middlemen, cooperatives, markets, and money. In the next chapter, we will have our economic individuals trade under more complex and special circumstances—those that exist in a competitive market. We will then be able to explain and predict some of the prices at which trades occur. In subsequent chapters, we will deal with still other trade circumstances and thereby explain and predict other prices, sacrificing simplicity to obtain generality.

MAJOR AND MINOR POINTS

1. Individuals can often obtain goods from other people by using persuasion, coercion, or trade.
2. Trade occurs because individuals value mutually desired goods differently.
3. Trade distributes goods to people who value them more and increases the values of goods. Trade also moves both parties to more preferred positions.
4. The effects of trade occur in barter as well as in monetary systems. The effects don't depend on the distribution of income or on production.
5. If markets distributed babies and human organs, the goods would be distributed to people valuing them most, the values of the goods would be increased, and all parties to the exchanges would move to more preferred positions. Also, more babies would be born and adopted, and more organs would be transplanted.
6. Markets can reduce the scarcities of some goods, shift some goods to the poor, and reduce crime rates.

7. We must usually produce transaction services before we can trade. These services are costly to produce, but we can often reduce the costs by using middlemen, cooperatives, markets, and money.

8. We sometimes create buyer or seller cooperatives to bypass middlemen. When the gains from the cooperatives exceed their costs, the cooperatives survive. When they don't, they fail.

9. Markets are institutions that bring buyers and sellers together. We trade in markets because they reduce our costs of transportation and information.

10. Money is a medium of exchange that reduces our transaction costs by eliminating the double-coincidence-of-wants requirement of barter, the need to find someone who wants what we have to sell and also has what we want to buy.

11. To obtain transaction services cheaply, we often hire employment agents to find jobs for us.

12. Many 1830s' cooperatives failed because they raised the costs of transaction services above the prices charged by middlemen.

13. Bars and computer dating firms can act as markets reducing the costs of trading ideas and friendship.

14. Rather than using money, we usually "buy" friends by "selling" our own personalities, but then we have to fulfill the double-coincidence-of-wants requirement of barter. This raises our transaction costs and reduces the extent of trade.

QUESTIONS

1. How does free trade compare and contrast with coercion and persuasion?
2. When and why will trade occur?
3. How does trade affect the values of goods, the distribution of goods, and the parties involved?
4. When will people involve middlemen, cooperatives, markets, and money in their trades?
5. Discuss the following terms and concepts:

Persuasion	Less preferred position
Coercion	Poor versus rich
Trade	Crime
Zero values	Middlemen
Value differentials	Cooperatives
The distribution of goods	Markets
Increased values	Money
More preferred positions	Double-coincidence-of-wants

APPLICATIONS

1. Before the Mediterranean and the Baltic could trade, the Baltic had to have more food than it could consume. Is this true?
2. It was necessary for us to satisfy our desire for food before the Industrial Revolution could begin. Is this true?

3. I buy a lamp that I later discover doesn't work. Has trade increased the values of goods?

4. Suppose your 5-year-old daughter wanted to purchase a stick of chewing gum for $10, a stick she values at more than $10. Would you allow the trade to occur? Why?

5. Trade is necessarily an exploitative phenomenon. People get rich by selling us goods with low values and buying from us goods with high values. Is this true?

6. Both trade and coercion can be used to distribute goods. Distinguish between the effects of each.

7. Is war irrational?

8. When politicians trade votes on various pieces of legislation, the practice is known as logrolling. Why does logrolling occur?

9. Politicians aren't allowed to take explicit bribes. What types of implicit bribes might they accept?

10. Farmers receive only about one-fourth of the final retail price of peaches. Why don't they usually set up fruit stands so they can obtain more revenue?

11. In the United States, the number of farmers, manufacturers, and builders is small compared to the number of wholesalers, retailers, and shippers. In many industries, people growing, producing, and building goods receive less total income than middlemen. What is going on?

12. If you want to buy a used car, why might you be willing to pay more to a used-car dealer than to a private party?

13. Because of the Germany hyperinflation of the 1920s, many Germans eventually refused to accept money in payment for goods. How did this affect the German economy?

14. Why do some wholesalers want Chicago's commodity market to be eliminated?

4

Competitive Prices

If I'm willing to buy a Nikon camera for $300 and you're willing to sell one for $200, we will trade, but at what price? It will be somewhere between $300 and $200, but where?

The answer depends on the circumstances surrounding the exchange. Many different circumstances can exist: we may trade in isolation, in a fairly competitive market, or under monopolistic conditions; we may possess relatively good information about prices and products, or we may have very little of such information; we may be free to trade at whatever price we mutually desire, or government may dictate a price to us.

In this chapter, we focus on only one set of exchange conditions, those that exist in a competitive market. We do this as we examine a theory of competitive exchange. The theory allows us to explain and predict competitive market prices and changes in those prices.

In the process of examining competitive markets, we discuss supply, demand, and other market concepts. These tools are crucial to our study of economics. In fact, it has been said that, if you teach a parrot to say supply and demand, you have an economist. This isn't true.

You will find that the theory of competitive exchange is much simpler than reality. The theory ignores real world complications such as monopoly power, limited information and government price controls. It ignores these complications because their inclusion would only make the theory more complex and not improve its ability to explain and predict the particular phenomena with which it is concerned. Theories should be as simple as possible.

To help explain the theory of competitive exchange, we examine six special topics. The topics deal with the determination of prices at auctions and the effects that changes in demands and supplies have on the prices of medicine, Seattle real estate, computers, and cigarettes.

THE THEORY OF COMPETITIVE EXCHANGE

The Phenomena

The theory of competitive exchange can be used to explain and predict prices in highly competitive markets, markets in which there are many buyers and sellers. Examples of highly competitive markets are the world commodity exchanges for wheat, corn, and pork.

When we look at highly competitive markets, we see that the **equilibrium prices** (stable prices that have little tendency to change unless circumstances change) vary a great deal. But the equilibrium prices do have one thing in common: they are **market-clearing prices**, prices that "clear the markets" of all offers to buy and sell at the going rates of exchange. For instance, every buyer in the world corn market can buy the quantity of corn he or she desires at the equilibrium market price. Likewise, every farmer can sell his or her crop at that price. No one willing and able to trade at the equilibrium market price is frustrated. By definition, market-clearing prices are at levels where neither shortages nor surpluses exist. This is because of the way shortages and surpluses are defined.

Shortages are circumstances where buyers are willing and able to buy larger quantities than owners want to sell at existing prices. Shortages are defined relative to prices and are different from scarcities. For example, there is no shortage of land in North Carolina, since anyone willing and able to pay the market price for land can buy. But a scarcity of land exists; there isn't enough land for everyone who wants it.

Surpluses are conditions where owners are willing and able to sell more than buyers want to purchase at existing prices. Surpluses are also defined relative to prices and they differ from overabundances. For instance, the price of food can be so high that a surplus exists because people aren't willing and able to buy as much as farmers want to sell. At the same time there may be no overabundance of food. It is possible for people to starve while a surplus of food exists.

Once market-clearing equilibrium prices are established in highly competitive markets, everyone trades at those prices. Negotiation doesn't occur. All buyers and sellers usually "take" the market-clearing price as their rate of exchange.

An Explanation: The Used Nikon Market

To explain why equilibrium prices in highly competitive markets are at market-clearing levels and why all buyers and sellers take those prices as their rates of exchange, we can examine an imaginary, perfectly competitive market in which used Nikons are traded. By dealing with a used product rather than a new one, we can avoid the complications of production.

A Perfectly Competitive Market

To understand how price is determined in the used Nikon market, we need to start by defining the nature of the market. A **perfectly competitive market** is a trade condition characterized by the presence of many buyers and sellers, each buying and selling an infinitesimally small proportion of the amount exchanged. Relative to the market, individual buyers and sellers are insignificant.

Demand

Consumers in the used Nikon market want the cameras, but how many they are willing and able to purchase depends on price. As the law of demand predicts, they are willing and able to buy fewer Nikons at higher prices and more at lower ones.

Demand is the amounts of a good that consumers are willing and able to buy at various prices in a given time period. We can illustrate demand with a schedule of prices and quantities. Let's assume that the two columns in Table 4.1 represent the demand in the used Nikon market during one week.

TABLE 4.1 Demand Schedule for Used Nikons

> The demand schedule indicates the various quantities demanded at the various prices. The whole schedule is demand.

Price	Quantity Demanded
$350	120
300	140
250	160
200	180
150	200

Quantity Demanded

Notice that demand is represented by the whole schedule, not just a part of it. For instance, demand isn't simply that consumers are willing and able to buy 120 Nikons at $350 but also that they are willing and able to purchase 140 at $300, 160 at $250, etc. This creates a problem: If demand is all the prices and their associated quantities, then when price decreases from $300 to $250, we can't claim that demand increases from 160 to 180. Demand doesn't change; the schedule remains the same. We simply move from one combination "on demand" to another.

To resolve this difficulty, we will use the term **quantity demanded** to refer to a particular amount on demand. Demand refers to all the quantities and prices. Given these definitions, price movements change quantity demanded. According to the law of demand, a lower price will increase quantity demanded and a higher price will reduce it.

Supply

While demand for the used Nikons comes from consumers, the supply emanates from present owners. **Supply** is the amounts owners are willing and able to sell at various prices in a given time period. As the law of demand predicts, the quantity supplied increases with price.

Supply, like demand, can be illustrated by a schedule. The supply schedule for the used Nikons is shown by the two columns in Table 4.2.

Quantity Supplied

A price change won't change the schedule, which reveals that it won't affect supply. A price change will change only the **quantity supplied**, the specific amount that owners are willing and able to sell.

TABLE 4.2   Supply Schedule for Used Nikons

> The supply schedule indicates the various quantities supplied at the various prices. The whole schedule is supply.

Price	Quantity Supplied
$350	200
300	180
250	160
200	140
150	120

TABLE 4.3   Combined Demand and Supply Schedules for Used
Nikons

Price	Quantity Demanded	Quantity Supplied
$350	120	200
300	140	180
250	160	160
200	180	140
150	200	120

Supply and Demand Curves

Table 4.3 summarizes the circumstances that exist in the market for used Nikons. It reflects the quantities demanded and supplied at the various prices.

We can see the relationships contained in Table 4.3 better with the curves shown in Figure 4.1. You can derive the curves yourself: Simply plot the various combinations of price and quantity demanded as points on a graph containing price on the vertical axis and quantity on the horizontal. Do the same for the combinations of price and quantity supplied. Then just connect the points.

More specifically, the price of $150 and the quantity demanded of 200 is one price-quantity combination on demand. You can plot it as a point by first moving vertically to the price of $150 and then moving horizontally to the point

Figure 4.1   Supply and Demand Curves

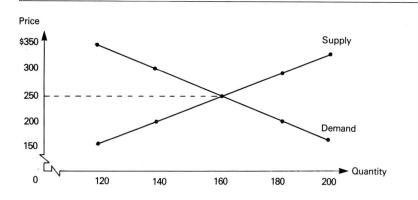

Supply and demand curves represent supply and demand in the used Nikon market. The equilibrium price in the market is the price at which the supply and demand curves cross, the $250 price. That price clears the market; 160 cameras are both demanded and supplied.

above the quantity of 200. That point represents both the price $150 and the quantity 200. Do the same for all the other combinations of price and quantity demanded. After you have plotted all five points, connect them with a straight line. This line is the demand curve for the used Nikons. Next, plot the combinations of price and quantity supplied and connect them to obtain the supply curve.

The Market-Clearing Price

Now we can see why the equilibrium price in the perfectly competitive used Nikon market will be the market-clearing level of $250, the level where quantity demanded and quantity supplied both equal 160. We can show that the price will be at $250 by explaining why it can't be anywhere else. That is, it can't be lower or higher than $250.

The price of the used Nikons can't be lower than the market-clearing level because a shortage would exist. If the price were only $150, a shortage of 80 cameras would be present, since the quantity demanded would be 200, whereas the quantity supplied would be only 120.

The shortage would make many consumers unhappy and they would react. If, for instance, I couldn't buy at $150, I would offer more. After all, I am willing to pay as much as $300 for a camera. I would compete with the other consumers for the 120 used Nikons by raising the price.

If frustrated consumers offered $200, two things would happen. First, some of the buyers who were willing to pay $150 would decide not to buy and the quantity demanded would fall to 180. Second, some of the owners of used Nikons would decide to sell more. This would cause the quantity supplied to rise to 140. The higher price would pinch out the shortage by both decreasing quantity demanded and increasing quantity supplied.

The $200 price would cut the shortage, but it wouldn't eliminate it. As long as the shortage persisted, competition among consumers would continue and price would rise further. Eventually, at $250, the shortage would disappear. Everyone willing and able to pay $250 could then buy. Competition among consumers would cease and the price would stop rising.

We have shown that the price can't be below the market-clearing level of $250. It also can't be above it. If the price were above the market-clearing level, a surplus would be present. For instance, if the price were $350, the 200 quantity supplied would exceed the 120 quantity demanded, causing a surplus of 80 cameras. The surplus would create competition between the sellers who couldn't sell and those who could. Frustrated sellers would then force the price downward and this would cause a decrease in the quantity supplied and an increase in the quantity demanded. The market would eventually clear at $250. Once the market cleared, competition among the sellers would stop and the price would stabilize.

Now we can explain why you and I will trade at the market price of $250. We will trade at that price because if I tried to pay less, you would simply sell to my competitors, other buyers. On the other hand, if you attempted to charge more, I would deal with your competitors, other sellers.

The Predictions

The preceding explanation allows us to predict that prices in perfectly competitive markets will be at market-clearing levels. Shortages or surpluses at other levels would create competition and the competition would then move the prices back to the market-clearing levels. The explanation also allows us to predict that all buyers and sellers will accept the market prices as their rates of exchange. Competition prevents exchanges at any other prices.

We can also make some other predictions. Since supply and demand determine price in a competitive market, we can predict that

    a. An increase in demand will raise price.
    b. A decrease in demand will lower price.
    c. An increase in supply will lower price.
    d. A decrease in supply will raise price.

The Determinants of Demand

To explain why an increase in demand will raise price, we need first to identify the **determinants of demand**, factors that determine and therefore can change demand, causing consumers to be willing and able to buy different amounts at the same prices.

The determinants of demand include items that modify the number of consumers or the values that consumers place on a good. The major determinants of demand are

    a. The number of consumers in the market;
    b. The incomes of consumers;
    c. The prices of other goods;
    d. Consumer price and income expectations;
    e. Consumer tastes.

Increases in the numbers of consumers will increase the demands for almost all goods. An increase in population growth in Texas, for example, will increase demand for Texas land. At the same prices, higher quantities of land will be demanded.

Next, increases in the incomes of consumers will change the demands for goods, but not always in the same direction. Goods for which demand rises when incomes increase are called **normal goods**. Most goods are normal goods. Goods for which demand decreases when incomes increase are called **inferior** goods. Only a few goods are inferior goods. Possible examples of inferior goods are used cars, potatoes, and used Nikon cameras.

How changes in the prices of other goods will change the demand for a good depends on whether the other goods are substitutes or complements. **Substitutes** are goods that a consumer can buy to replace a good. Almost all desired goods are substitutes (according to the substitutability attribute), but some are much better substitutes than others. For example, tennis can be easily substituted for racketball, train transportation can readily replace bus transportation, and apple juice can be easily substituted for orange juice. When the price of a substitute for a good increases, demand for the good increases. **Complements** are goods that tend to be purchased together—ham and eggs, cars and tires, shirts and pants. When the price of a complement to a good increases, demand for the good decreases.

Price and income expectations directly affect the demands for goods. When consumers expect the price of a good to rise in future, they are willing and able to buy more of the good in the present. Likewise, when consumers expect an increase in income, they immediately increase their demands for normal goods and reduce their demands for inferior goods.

Finally, consumer tastes also directly affect demands. When consumers shift their tastes towards football and away from basketball, demand for football increases, whereas demand for basketball decreases.

An Increase in Demand

Now we can explain why an increase in demand will raise price. Suppose demand for Nikons in the market increases following an increase in the number of consumers. The greater demand means that at the same prices, consumers want to buy more cameras. Imagine that at every price, consumers are willing and able to buy 40 more. This increase in demand shifts the demand curve to the right by 40 units, as shown in Figure 4.2.

Figure 4.2 An Increase in Demand

Demand increases by 40 units at each price. The demand curve thus shifts 40 units to the right, from D to D'.

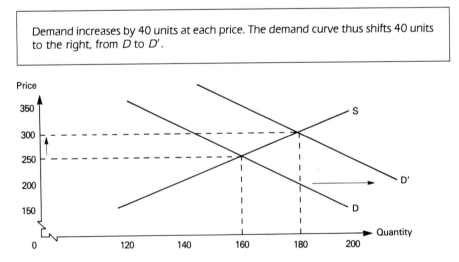

The price will then rise to $300. At the old price of $250, the quantity demanded would have been 200 rather than 160. Supply wouldn't have, however, changed; quantity supplied would have stayed at 160. The shortage of 40 cameras would have created competition among buyers. The competition would have continued until the shortage was eliminated by a price increase to $300.

A Decrease in Demand

We can also use the used Nikon market to explain why a decrease in demand will reduce price. For instance, if the prices of used cameras other than Nikons fall, then demand for used Nikons will decrease, and this will cause the price of the Nikons to decrease. If the demand for the Nikons decreases to the extent that 40 fewer Nikons are demanded at each price, then the price of the cameras will decrease to $200.

Why? Graphically, as shown in Figure 4.3, the demand curve will shift to the left by 40 units. A surplus would have existed at the old price of $250 and the surplus would have created competition among the sellers. That competition would have forced the price to fall. The lower price would have increased quantity demanded and reduced quantity supplied until the market cleared at $200.

The Determinants of Supply

Of course, supplies as well as demands can change. Increases in supplies will reduce prices, and decreases will raise them. We can again explain this by looking at the used Nikon market, but first we need to discuss what might cause supply to change.

Figure 4.3 A Decrease in Demand

Demand decreases by 40 units at each price. The demand curve therefore shifts 40 units to the left, from *D* to *D'*.

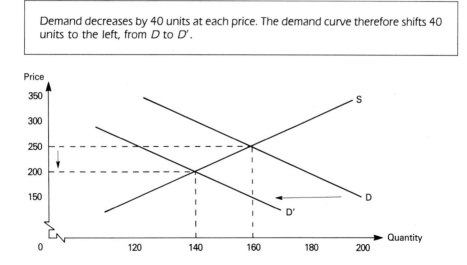

Supply will change when the **determinants of supply**, the factors that determine the quantities supplied at the various prices, change. When dealing with already produced goods such as the used Nikons, the determinants of supply are similar to those of demand: They include items that modify the number of sellers or the values of sellers.

Unlike used Nikons, most goods are new products that are sold by business firms to consumers. Let's also take a quick look at nature of product supplies and their determinants. (We examine product supplies in depth in Chapter 13.)

Like the supplies of other goods, product supplies contain direct relationships between prices and quantities. That is, business firms are willing and able to supply greater quantities only at higher prices. This causes the supply curves of products to slope upward. (We don't have to say upward and to the right because the point of reference when discussing a curve is always the origin. The supply curve slopes upward when we look at it from the point where the two axes intersect.)

Firms are willing and able to supply greater quantities only at higher prices because, although mass production technologies often reduce the cost of additional units when output is initially increased, the cost eventually rises once low-cost resources are used up. Since the cost of additional units rises, firms must obtain a higher price to cover the higher cost.

The determinants of product supplies are different from those of already produced goods. The determinants of product supplies include factors that change the number of suppliers or the profits that suppliers obtain from production. The major determinants of product supplies are:

    a. The number of producers;
    b. The costs (including taxes) that producers incur;
    c. Government payments or other subsidies that producers receive.

If the number of producers increases, supply will rise. For example, an increase in the number of producers of camcorders has greatly increased the supply of camcorders; at the same prices, more camcorders are available for sale.

Reductions in the costs of production increase the supplies of goods while increases in the costs reduce the supplies. For instance, if taxes or resource prices fall or if technology advances, production costs will decline and supplies will increase; producers will be willing and able to sell larger quantities of products at the same prices. Conversely, if taxes or resource prices rise or if the best technology can no longer be employed, costs will rise and supplies of products will fall; producers will be willing and able to sell smaller quantities at the same prices.

Governments can affect supplies not only by changing taxes but also by using subsidies to change the rewards from production. For example, if the federal government subsidizes small farmers by granting them low interest loans, then the supplies of farm products will increase. At the same prices, more farmers will produce and larger quantities of agricultural products will be for sale.

An Increase in Supply

To understand why an increase in supply will decrease price, suppose some of the owners of Nikon cameras purchase camcorders and decide to sell their old cameras in the used Nikon market. As a result, the supply in the market increases. If it increases by 40 Nikons at each price, we can predict that the price of the cameras will fall to $200.

Graphically, the supply curve will shift to the right by 40 units, as shown in Figure 4.4 by the shift from S to S'. At the old price, a surplus of cameras would have existed and this would have created competition among sellers and forced the price to fall. As the price fell, quantity demanded would have increased and quantity supplied would have decreased until the market-clearing price of $200 was reached.

A Decrease in Supply

Next, if supply falls, price will rise. For instance, if the owners of used Nikons change their tastes in such a way that they value the cameras more, the supply of the Nikons will fall. If the supply decreases by 40 units at each price, then the price will rise by $50 to $300.

Graphically, as shown in Figure 4.5, the lower supply will shift the supply curve to the left by 40 units at each price, from S to S'. At the old price of $250, a shortage of 40 units would have existed. This would have created competition among buyers and the price would have risen. With the rising price, quantities demanded would have fallen and quantities supplied would have risen until the market cleared at $300.

Figure 4.4 An Increase in Supply

Supply increases by 40 units at each price. The supply curve therefore shifts to the right by 40 units, from S to S'.

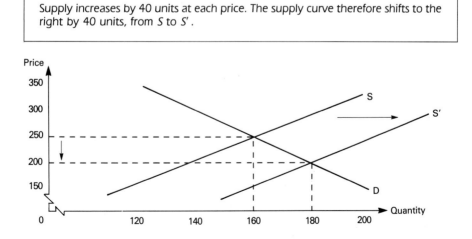

Figure 4.5   A Decrease in Supply

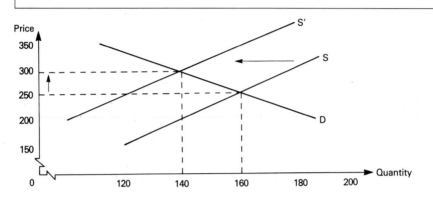

Supply decreases 40 units at each price. The supply curve therefore shifts to the left by 40 units, from S to S'.

A Summary of the Theory

Our theory of competitive exchange is complete. We have shown that if we, as economic individuals, interact in a perfectly competitive market with others who value mutually desired goods differently, then the market price will

a. Be in equilibrium at the market-clearing level
b. Be the one that we will use in trade
c. Rise if demand increases
d. Fall if demand decreases
e. Fall if supply increases
f. Rise if supply decreases

SPECIAL TOPICS

Now that we have presented and explained the theory, we can look at six special topics, the first two dealing with market-clearing equilibrium prices and the remaining four focusing on changes in those prices.

Prices at Auctions

The theory of competitive exchange explains why the equilibrium price at an auction is the market-clearing price, the price that equates the quantity demanded to the quantity supplied.

At most auctions, the auctioneer begins by calling a low price. After the price is called, many hands often go up simultaneously, indicating a large quantity demanded, but the quantity supplied is only one. A shortage exists.

We usually can't tell the exact size of the shortage because many of the people willing and able to pay don't bother raising their hands. They know the auctioneer will raise the price anyway and they will have to bid more in later rounds if they want to buy the good which is being sold.

The shortage creates competition among the consumers, a competition that manifests itself as a willingness and ability to pay higher prices. Although the consumers could announce higher prices themselves, the auctioneer does the calling and the consumers respond. As the price rises, the quantity demanded falls. Eventually, the price at which only one buyer remains is reached. At that price, the quantity demanded equals the quantity supplied, exchange occurs, and the market clears.

The auctioning process is illustrated in Figure 4.6. The supply curve in the figure is vertical because the quantity supplied remains one at all prices. At the below-clearing price P', a shortage exists, since quantity demanded exceeds the quantity supplied. Competition among buyers causes the price to rise and quantity demanded to fall until the market clears at the price P. At P, quantity demanded and supplied both equal one.

Figure 4.6 Market-Clearing Price at an Auction

Supply at an auction is represented by a vertical line since the auctioneer offers one unit at all prices. Demand is downward sloping since consumers are willing and able to buy less at higher prices. The auctioneer raises the price until the market clears at price P.

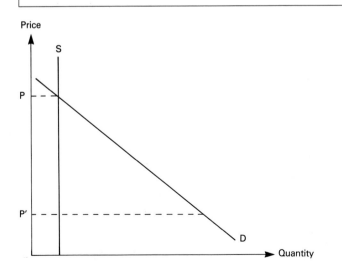

Auctioning Paintings

Auctioneers normally start at low prices where shortages exist, but they sometimes begin at high prices where surpluses are present. Very expensive items such as paintings and apartment houses have been auctioned off this way.

When auctioneers start high, the results are nevertheless market-clearing prices. The prices clear markets because at initial levels, surpluses cause the auctioneers to reduce prices. Eventually, at the lower prices, quantities demanded rise to one, hands go up, and the markets clear.

Why do sellers of very valuable goods want the auctioneers to start high? Because they can then get the highest possible prices rather than prices slightly above the second highest bids. For example, if the two highest values on a painting are $250,000 and $200,000, trade is likely to occur at $250,000 if the auctioneer starts high. But if the auctioneer starts low and raises the price, then after the $200,000 bidder drops out, trade may occur at only $201,000.

At most auctions, the differences between the highest and the next highest bids are so small that starting high would fail to yield significantly higher prices. In fact, the prices might be lower: When auctioneers begin low, the auctioning process itself can raise the values consumers place on goods. The excitement of an auction along with the revelation that other people are willing to buy can cause people to offer more than they would have otherwise. This is why good auctioneers are well paid.

Although auctions demonstrate some of the forces at work in competitive markets, they inaccurately represent those markets to the extent that quantities supplied are fixed. In competitive markets, quantities supplied increase with prices; supply curves slope upward—they aren't vertical. As a result, rising prices in competitive markets eliminate shortages by increasing quantities supplied as well as by reducing quantities demanded. Similarly, falling prices eliminate surpluses by cutting quantities supplied as well as by raising quantities demanded.

Wealthy Doctors

In the 1970s and 1980s, demand for medicine increased because of expansions in employer-supplied medical insurance and government Medicaid and Medicare programs. During the same periods, the supply was relatively fixed, and therefore the price of medicine increased. The price increase prevented shortages that would have otherwise occurred.

Graphically, the increase in demand shifted the demand curve from D to D', as shown in Figure 4.7. At the old price, a shortage caused competition among patients, competition that pushed the price upward. As the price increased, it forced some people out of the market until quantity demanded fell. The remainder of the surplus was eliminated by the expansion of quantity supplied.

Figure 4.7 Increase in the Demand for Medical Services

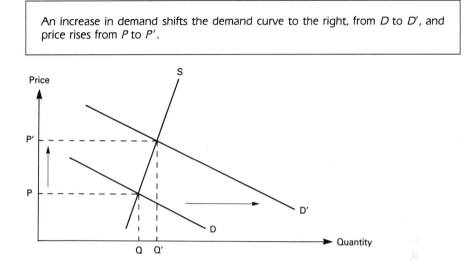

> An increase in demand shifts the demand curve to the right, from *D* to *D'*, and price rises from *P* to *P'*.

The increase in quantity supplied accounted for only a small part of the reduction of the shortage. Why? Largely because the supply of doctors, nurses, and hospitals was restricted by government regulations. Although government restrictions were aimed at maintaining a high quality of medical services, they also limited the supply of those services.

Many politicians and businesspersons thought that they could eliminate the scarcity of medical services by giving money to people who otherwise weren't able or willing to buy. But this only let some people out-compete others for the limited quantity of services. A higher price simply forced some to do without medicine so that employees with medical insurance, the poor covered by Medicaid, and the old receiving Medicare could buy more. Different people remained ill or died while doctors prospered.

Lower Prices of Seattle Houses

Many real estate agents will tell you that the price of homes can only rise. Nevertheless, the price of homes in Seattle, Washington, fell in the early 1960s after a drastic reduction in demand.

The decrease in demand occurred following a major reduction in U.S. military spending. The Boeing Company of Seattle, a major defense contractor, was forced to lay off so many engineers and production workers that the city lost population. With people leaving town, the number of consumers fell and the demand for homes declined.

The lower amounts demanded at the same prices created a surplus. Competition among sellers then ensued, causing price to fall. The lower price then increased the quantity demanded and reduced the quantity supplied.

It was difficult to get consumers to want to buy more and sellers to want to sell less just by reducing the price of the homes. Since both the quantities demanded and the quantities supplied were relatively insensitive to the market price, the price plunged. But a market-clearing level was eventually found. Former renters purchased homes and some speculators bought, thinking that better days were to come.

Graphically, the demand curve for houses shifted to the left as shown in Figure 4.8 by the movement from D to D'. The surplus at the old price P caused competition that reduced the price to P'.

Cheaper Computers

With the progress of the electronic revolution, the price of computers has fallen dramatically. The price has decreased because the supply of computers has greatly increased. The supply increased because firms were able to earn far more at the same prices due to a reduction in the cost of producing computers—technological advances allowed firms to replace expensive vacuum tubes with cheap microchips. The greater supply temporarily created a surplus. The surplus caused price competition that subsequently forced the price downward.

The reason the price fell isn't because individual firms reduced their price to pass lower costs to consumers. Instead, the price fell because competition among the firms forced each producer to accept a lower price.

Graphically, lower costs increased market supply, as indicated in Figure 4.9 by the shift of the supply curve to the right. The greater supply created a surplus, which in turn created competition that forced the price downward until the market cleared at the new P' price.

Figure 4.8   Decrease in the Demand for Seattle Homes

Demand decreases causes the demand curve to shift to the left, from S to S', and price falls from P to P'.

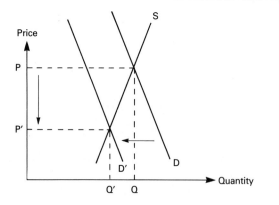

Figure 4.9 Increase in the Supply of Computers

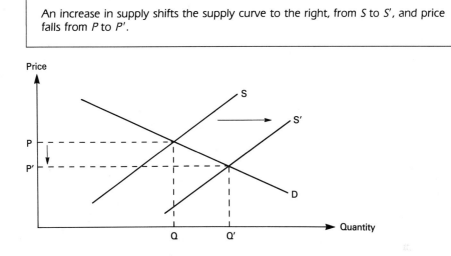

An increase in supply shifts the supply curve to the right, from *S* to *S'*, and price falls from *P* to *P'*.

Although the cost of production is a major determinant of the market supply, the cost that only particular computer firms incur isn't. Each firm is such a small part of the market that its production is relatively insignificant. As a result, the cost reductions that accrued only to individual firms didn't cause much of an increase in supply. With little change in supply, market price stayed about the same. Graphically, isolated cost reductions had little effect on market supply, so the supply curve stayed put, preventing a significant price decrease.

It should seem reasonable that individual cost reductions don't reduce prices very much. After all, if lower individual costs reduced prices, what incentives would firms have to reduce their costs? The gains from lower costs would then be offset by lower prices. Conversely, if higher individual costs raised prices, why would managers ever worry about higher costs?

Who Pays Corporate Income Taxes?

If the president and Congress decided to increase government spending and fund the increase by placing a tax on the tobacco industry for each package of cigarettes sold, how would the tax affect the price of cigarettes?

Initially, not at all. Higher taxes would have little effect on either supply or demand, so the price would remain the same. The tobacco industry would simply pay more taxes.

In time, however, the greater taxes would reduce the production of cigarettes. Lower profits would force some firms into bankruptcy and others to reduce output. Supply would then fall, and shortages of cigarettes would result. The shortages would create competition among consumers, and this would force price upward until the market cleared. Eventually, the price would rise until it compensated the remaining firms for the higher taxes. Instead of tobacco manufacturers, smokers would wind up paying the taxes.

Graphically, an increase in taxes on tobacco producers wouldn't have any immediate effect on price, since the supply and demand curves wouldn't change. Only after firms cut production or left the industry would supply decrease, shifting the supply curve to the left. This is shown in Figure 4.10 by the movement of supply from S to S'. A shortage of cigarettes would subsequently be prevented by a price increase from P to P'.

It is possible that under some competitive market conditions the price might not rise as much as the tax per package. In fact, the graph in Figure 4.10 depicts just such a situation. The price wouldn't rise by the amount of the tax if the reduction in output caused a reduction in production costs. The lower production costs would partly offset the higher taxes, and prices would rise by less than the taxes. But this doesn't mean that the producers would effectively be paying some of the taxes. All the tax increases would still indirectly accrue to the consumers. The extent by which prices wouldn't rise as much as the taxes reflects lower production costs, not the payment of taxes by the industry.

The preceding explanation implies that personal income taxes accounted for only a portion of the taxes you paid last year. In addition to the money you sent the IRS, you paid some corporate taxes via higher prices. For instance, of the $10,000 you may have paid for a Chrysler last year, only $9500 may have been for the car, while the remaining $500 may have compensated Chrysler for the corporate income taxes that it paid.

Although consumers eventually pay most corporate taxes, politicians still have an incentive to raise corporate taxes rather than individual income taxes. Corporate taxes tend to be hidden.

Figure 4.10 Decrease in the Supply of Cigarettes

The supply curve shifts to the left, from S to S', and the price increases from P to P'.

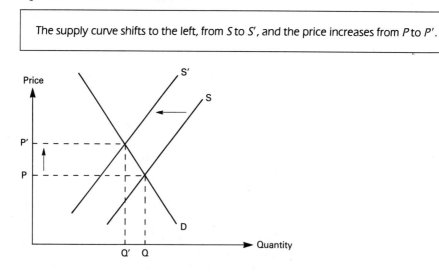

WHEN TO USE THE THEORY

The theory of competitive exchange doesn't claim that perfectly competitive markets exist. It only predicts and explains what will happen if they exist. Actually, there are no perfectly competitive markets in the real world. Even in the world wheat market, each farmer produces more than an infinitesimally small proportion of the market supply and therefore affects the market price, even though the effect is so small that we can't, as a practical matter, measure it.

Does this mean the theory is useless? No. We can successfully employ the theory to predict prices in less than perfectly competitive markets, as long as sufficient competition is present. Like all theories, the theory of competitive exchange is a useful tool even though it is a simplification of reality.

Sufficient competition is often present in markets that initially seem to be far from competitive. For example, if you ask building subcontractors how their bids on various jobs are determined, they will often claim that the bids are based on a cost-plus formula. Rather than claiming that supply and demand determine price, they will claim that cost determines price.

Nevertheless, if you then ask them why they don't charge more or less, they are likely to cite the pricing behavior of other subcontractors, their competitors. For example, they might point out that if they have more business than they can handle because other subcontractors are bidding higher prices, then they will raise the percentage added to costs. Conversely, if business falls off because other subcontractors are biding less, then they will reduce the percentage added to costs. All this implies that supply and demand determine price, not cost.

Sometimes it is even more difficult to recognize the effects of supply and demand and resulting competition. For instance, many small towns have only one local golf club. When the clubs are privately owned, we might expect them to charge a higher price than similar clubs in large cities. After all, the city clubs have to compete. Nevertheless, the prices charged by many golf clubs in small towns aren't much higher. Why? Maybe because the prices are primarily determined by competitive forces. Although golf clubs in small towns are the only sellers of golf, they aren't the only sellers of recreation nor, more generally, of entertainment. Therefore, the managers of the clubs often avoid higher prices because they fear that many golfers will defect to tennis, hunting, skiing, or the movies. The clubs have to keep their prices competitive.

We can use the tool we have developed to explain and predict many more prices than we might initially expect, but we can't use it to deal with all prices. Some prices can be explained and predicted only if we recognize more complex trade circumstances. In the next chapter, we will begin to recognize some of these circumstances—those that involve monopoly power.

MAJOR AND MINOR POINTS

1. Competitive exchange conditions are special trade circumstances; they aren't universal.
2. In a competitive market, there are many buyers and sellers.
3. In highly competitive markets, equilibrium prices, those that stay the same unless underlying conditions change, are at market-clearing levels. Market-clearing levels are those where the quantities demanded by buyers equal the quantities supplied by sellers. In other words, the equilibrium prices are at levels where neither shortages nor surpluses are present.
4. Shortages exist when the quantities demanded exceed the quantities supplied at existing prices.
5. Surpluses are present when the quantities supplied exceed the quantities demanded at existing prices.
6. In a perfectly competitive market, there are so many buyers and sellers, each buying or selling such a small amount of the total quantity exchanged, that no one can affect the market price by buying or selling a higher or lower quantity.
7. Demand is the amounts of a good that consumers are willing and able to buy at the various prices in a given time period.
8. Quantity demanded is the amount consumers are willing and able to buy at a given price. Price changes cause changes only in the quantities demanded; they don't change demands.
9. Supply is the amounts of a good that owners are willing and able to sell at various prices in a given time period.
10. Quantity supplied is the amount owners are willing and able to sell at a given price. Price changes change only the quantities supplied, not supplies.
11. Demand curves illustrate demand, whereas supply curves illustrate supply.
12. Prices in a competitive market will be in equilibrium at market-clearing levels because at higher or lower prices, surpluses or shortages would have occurred. The surpluses or shortages would have created competition among sellers and buyers, respectively, causing the prices to move to the market-clearing levels.
13. In a perfectly competitive market, we trade at the market price because we can't sell for more due to competition from other sellers and we can't buy for less because of competition from other buyers.
14. Since prices in perfectly competitive markets are at levels determined by supply and demand, the prices change when supplies or demands change, preventing shortages or surpluses that would have otherwise existed.
15. Changes in demand are caused by changes in the determinants of demand, factors that change either the number of consumers or the values of consumers.
16. The major determinants of demand are the number of consumers, the incomes of consumers, the prices of other goods, consumer tastes, and the price and income expectations of consumers.
17. An increase in demand will raise price. A shortage would have existed at the old price, causing competition among buyers until the price increased to the new market-clearing level.
18. A decrease in demand will cause a lower price.
19. Changes in supply are caused by changes in the determinants of supply. If we

ignore production, the basic determinants of supply are factors that can change the number of sellers and the values of the sellers.

20. Product supply curves slope upward (relative to the origin) because production costs eventually rise with output and higher prices must cover the higher costs.

21. The basic determinants of product supplies are the number of producers, the costs (including taxes) of production, and government payments and subsidies.

22. Increases in supplies will lower prices, whereas decreases in supplies will raise prices.

23. Costs don't determine competitive market prices. But when costs change supplies, the changes in supplies can change prices. If the costs that many producers incur rise, supplies will fall and prices will increase. If those costs decline, supplies will increase and prices will fall.

24. Higher taxes on products are at first primarily borne by sellers. In time, however, supplies fall and prices rise to shift the burden to consumers.

25. The theory of competitive exchange doesn't claim that perfectly competitive markets exist.

26. Supplies and demands determine prices in many markets that aren't perfectly competitive.

QUESTIONS

1. Use the various concepts covered in this chapter to explain why the equilibrium price in a competitive market will be the market-clearing price.

2. Why will buyers and sellers in a competitive market be price takers?

3. If demand for a good sold in a competitive market increases, what will happen to the price? Why?

4. If demand for a good sold in a competitive market decreases, what will happen to the price? Why?

5. If supply of a good sold in a competitive market increases, what will happen to the price? Why?

6. If supply of a good sold in a competitive market decreases, what will happen to the price? Why?

7. For the theory of competitive exchange to be useful, does a market have to be perfectly competitive?

8. Discuss the following terms and concepts:

Competitive market	Determinants of demand
Equilibrium price	Change in demand
Market-clearing price	Normal goods
Shortage	Inferior goods
Surplus	Substitutes
Perfectly competitive market	Complements
Demand	Determinants of supply
Quantity demanded	Change in supply
Supply	Price and taxes
Quantity supplied	Cost and price
Demand and supply curves	Perfectly competitive versus
Price takers	actual markets

APPLICATIONS

1. Why do economists often call buyers and sellers in competitive markets "price takers"?
2. Did a shortage of food exist during the 1985 Ethiopian famine?
3. Which of the following will fail to cause an increase in demand for dental services?
    a. Less fluoride in water
    b. Greater consumption of candy
    c. A lower price of dental services
    d. An increase in the price of toothpaste
4. Following are the supply and demand schedules representing supply and demand for lobsters in a Denver fish market. Derive the supply and demand curves from the schedules.

PRICE	QUANTITY DEMANDED	QUANTITY SUPPLIED
$25	2,000	8,000
20	4,000	7,000
15	6,000	6,000
10	8,000	5,000
5	10,000	4,000

5. How do the supply and demand curves associated with the Denver fish market illustrate the law of demand?
6. What will be the equilibrium price of the lobsters in the Denver fish market? Show graphically.
7. The market price for my house is $100,000. Why wouldn't I sell for less? Why wouldn't you buy for more?
8. What would happen to the price of lobsters in the Denver fish market if demand increased by 3000 at each price? Explain and show graphically.
9. Explain and show graphically how the elimination of Medicare would affect the prices of medical services.
10. Do patients pay for the increased prices of medical malpractice insurance?
11. If the wages of carpenters declined, how would the rental rates of apartments be affected?
12. How would the price of beef be affected if a disease killed half of the cattle in the United States? Explain and show graphically.
13. Some years ago in California, voters passed Proposition 13. Among other things, the proposition reduced the taxes landlords had to pay. Many people predicted that rents would fall as a result. Rents not only failed to fall, but in some cases, they rose. What happened?
14. Wilson is the only seller of Wilson tennis balls. How is the price of Wilson tennis balls determined?
15. Both building subcontractors and small-town golf clubs can charge higher prices and still sell some quantities. Would we better understand their prices and price changes if we included this in our analysis?

Monopoly Trade

You have probably played the Parker Brothers' game of Monopoly. To win, you must purchase various groups of properties, build hotels, and charge high rents, depleting the wealth of other players before they have had a chance to absorb yours. The game shows us that we may get rich if we become **monopolists**, single sellers of goods. It doesn't, however, explain, real monopoly, the game the Parker Brothers Corporation plays when it sells its product. Real monopoly is far more interesting and a bit more complex.

In this chapter, we study the actual game. We present, explain, and use a theory of monopoly exchange, a tool that allows us to explain and predict monopoly exchange phenomena.

To help explain monopoly behavior, we look at six special topics. After comparing the Parker Brothers' game to real monopoly, the topics discuss monopoly trades between husbands and wives and the sale of drugs by the Mafia. The topics also deal with the monopoly effects that farmers sometimes obtain, the question of whether monopolies cause inflation, and the elasticity of demand concept.

A THEORY OF MONOPOLY EXCHANGE

The Phenomena

We play the real game of monopoly when we encounter monopoly circumstances. Under the competitive conditions of the preceding chapter, many buyers and sellers, valuing mutually desired goods differently, exchange goods. Under monopoly conditions, although many buyers and value differentials are still present, there is only one seller, the monopolist.

When we look at monopolists in our economy, we see that the monopolists charge higher prices than sellers in competitive markets. Also, when competitors are eliminated and only monopoly sellers remain, prices rise. Conversely, when monopolists suddenly encounter competition from other sellers, prices fall.

An Explanation: A Monopoly Seller of Ski Wax

To explain why monopolists charge more, suppose you arrive at a ski area on an unseasonably warm day and are the only one with silver ski wax, the type used for wet snow. You have ten sticks of the wax and value the wax less than other skiers. Given these conditions, you decide to become a monopoly seller of ski wax.

Monopoly Demand

The law of demand predicts that your monopoly won't let you sell all you want at any price. Since skiers possess the five attributes of economic individuals, they will buy less wax at higher prices and more only at lower ones. This is shown by the demand schedule in Table 5.1.

Total and Marginal Revenue

To you, demand represents a source of revenue. When skiers buy wax, you receive money. **Total revenue** is all the money you receive by selling the wax. It equals the price of the wax times the quantity sold. **Marginal revenue** is the change in total revenue that you receive when you sell one more unit. The total and marginal revenues associated with the sales of various units of wax are indicated by columns 3 and 4 in Table 5.2.

As the columns in Table 5.2 reveal, the marginal revenue will be below price for all but the first unit. This is because to sell additional units, you will have to reduce the price not only of the additional units but also of the previous units you could have sold for more.

For example, since you can sell the first stick for $10, your total revenue will rise from 0 to $10. Therefore, the marginal revenue of the first unit will equal its $10 price. But the marginal revenue of the second and all subsequent units will be below the price. The second unit will have a marginal revenue of

TABLE 5.1 Demand for Ski Wax

> The demand for ski wax, like any good sold by a monopolist, contains an inverse relationship between price and quantity demanded.

PRICE OF SKI WAX	QUANTITY DEMANDED
$10	1
9	2
8	3
7	4
6	5
5	6
4	7
3	8
2	9
1	10

only $8 and a price of $9. This is because to sell the second unit, you must not only reduce the price of the second unit to $9, but you also have to cut the price of the first from $10 to $9. The $1 loss on the first unit cuts into the $9 received from the sale of the second, causing the marginal revenue of the second unit to be $8 rather than $9. The third stick of wax will have a marginal revenue of $6 although it will sell for $8. The marginal revenue will be only $6 because the sale of that unit will require that the first two units be sold for $8 rather than $9.

TABLE 5.2 Demand, Total Revenue, and Marginal Revenue

> Total and marginal revenues are derived directly from demand on the assumption that all units are sold at the same price.

(1) PRICE	(2) QUANTITY	(3) TOTAL REVENUE	(4) MARGINAL REVENUE
$10	1	$10	$10
9	2	18	8
8	3	24	6
7	4	28	4
6	5	30	2
5	6	30	0
4	7	28	−2
3	8	24	−4
2	9	18	−6
1	10	10	−8

Uniform Pricing

Marginal revenue will be less than price because of the assumption that all units are to be sold at the same price. If the prices of previous units were unaffected as the prices of additional units were reduced, marginal revenue would always equal price. For instance, the marginal revenue of the second unit would equal its $9 price, since total revenue would rise by $9 if you could sell the first stick for $10 and the second for $9.

In effect, one of the rules of our monopoly game is **uniform pricing**. We assume that you must charge the same price for all units you sell and, therefore, that you must worry about the effects of "spoiling the market," losing revenue by reducing the price on initial units to sell additional ones.

Is the uniform-pricing rule realistic? Usually. No doubt every monopolist would try to avoid spoiling the market by using **price discrimination**, a pricing method involving the charging of higher prices for some units than for others. But price discrimination is difficult to carry out. If, for example, you tried to charge more for some units of ski wax than for others, you would probably have to identify and separate the skiers willing to pay more from those willing to pay less. Also, you would have to keep those charged less from reselling to those charged more. A skier charged $1 might have an incentive to buy 10 sticks of wax and resell 9 of them.

In Chapter 13 we will examine other problems of price discrimination. We will see that while all the problems can sometimes be overcome, this is not the general case. Uniform pricing by monopolists is far more common than price discrimination.

Monopoly Costs

When selling ski wax, in addition to gains in the form of money received, you will incur costs in the form of ski wax sacrificed. To obtain the money that you want, you must give up ski wax that you also want.

In Chapter 2 we defined the opportunity cost of an action as the value of the highest-valued alternative sacrificed. When you are selling ski wax to obtain money, the opportunity cost of selling the wax is the value you place on the wax being sacrificed.

If we are specifically focusing on the sale of one more unit of a good, the marginal unit, we become concerned with the cost associated with the sale of that unit: the **marginal cost**. The marginal cost of selling one more unit of wax is the value of that wax to you. When you have many units, the value of wax will be low, so the marginal cost will be low. But the more units you sell, the higher will be the value of the units you have left, and therefore, the greater will be the marginal cost. The last column in Table 5.3 identifies the marginal cost that you incur as you sell various units of wax. The marginal cost is measured in terms of dollars (remember, the substitutability attribute implies that we can measure the value of any good in monetary terms as long as we want both that good and money).

TABLE 5.3 The Monopoly Price and Quantity : Marginal Revenue and Marginal Cost

> The monopolist equates marginal revenue to marginal cost, charging
> a $7 price and selling four units.

(1) P	(2) Q	(3) TR	(4) MARGINAL REVENUE	(5) MARGINAL COST
$10	1	$10	$10	$1
9	2	18	8	2
8	3	24	6	3
7	4	28	4	4
6	5	30	2	5
5	6	30	0	6
4	7	28	−2	7
3	8	24	−4	8
2	9	18	−6	9
1	10	10	−8	10

Maximization of Net Gain From Trade

Faced with the marginal revenues and costs in Table 5.3, what price will you charge and how many units will you sell?

To answer, we first need to define the net gain from trade. The **net gain from trade** is the value of the total gains from trade minus the value of the total sacrifices. The net gain from trade that accrues to a seller is sometimes called a seller surplus. When resources are purchased and their products are sold, the net gain is generally called a profit. In the case of selling ski wax, the value of the total gains is reflected in the total revenue while the value of the total sacrifices is reflected in the total cost. If you obtain $28 in cash by sacrificing $10 worth of ski wax, you receive an $18 net gain from the trade.

Given the definition of net gain from trade, the five attributes of the law of demand imply that you will behave so as to maximize that net gain. And to maximize your net gain, you will charge the price and sell the quantity of ski wax related to the equality of marginal revenue and marginal cost; you will equate marginal revenue to marginal cost. Why? Because you could obtain a greater net gain by selling more if marginal revenue exceeded marginal cost or by selling less if marginal cost exceeded marginal revenue.

As the monopoly seller of ski wax, to equate marginal revenue and marginal cost, you will charge $7 and sell four units of wax. You will certainly sell the first stick of wax. It has a marginal revenue of $10 and a marginal cost of only $1. You would have to be irrational to turn down $10 for a stick of wax worth only $1 to you.

The sale of the second stick won't be as good a deal. It will sell for $9, bring in $8, and require you to sacrifice $2 worth of wax. Nevertheless, you will sell it. Your net gain might increase only $6, but it will still increase.

The third unit will generate $6 in additional revenue at a cost of $3. You will therefore also sell that unit. Finally, the fourth unit will generate $4 of marginal revenue at a $4 marginal cost. You might or might not sell it; however, to keep things simple, let's assume that you will. But that's it. You will reduce the price to $7 and sell 4 units; marginal revenue will then just equal marginal cost.

You definitely won't sell the fifth stick of wax. Although it could sell for $6 and cost only $5, its marginal revenue would be $2, not worth the $5 marginal cost. The sale of the fifth stick of wax would reduce your net gain.

Total Revenue, Total Cost, and Net Gain

To decide what price and quantity will maximize your net gain from trade, you don't need to know the levels of your total revenue and total cost. When making real-world decisions, we in fact usually don't know these levels. You need only know if an additional unit has a marginal revenue that exceeds its marginal cost. If it does, then you also know that the value of the gain from that unit will exceed the value of the sacrifice and, therefore, net gain will rise with the sale of the unit. Being rational, you will reduce price and sell it.

Nevertheless, let's use the ski wax example to show that the marginal-revenue-equals-marginal-cost rule results in a choice that maximizes the extent to which total revenue exceeds total cost, thereby maximizing the net gain from trade. To do this, we first need to derive the total cost and the net gain associated with your sales of various units of the wax.

If we assume that the values of particular units are unaffected by sales, then we can simply add up the marginal costs of the various units to obtain the total cost of selling those units. For example, since the marginal cost

TABLE 5.4 The Monopoly Price and Quantity : Net Gain From Trade

> The monopolist charges $7 per unit and sells four units, the price and quantity at which the monopolist's net gain from trade is maximized.

(1) P	(2) Q	(3) TOTAL REVENUE	(4) MR	(5) MC	(6) TOTAL COST	(7) NET GAIN
$10	1	$10	$10	$ 1	$ 1	$ 9
9	2	18	8	2	3	15
8	3	24	6	3	6	18
7	4	28	4	4	10	18
6	5	30	2	5	15	15
5	6	30	0	6	21	9
4	7	28	−2	7	28	0
3	8	24	−4	8	36	−12
2	9	18	−6	9	45	−27
1	10	10	−8	10	55	−45

of selling the first unit is $1 and the marginal cost of selling the second is $2, the total cost of selling two units is $3. Computing in this manner, we obtain the total cost column in Table 5.4.

Next, we can obtain the net gain from the sales of various units by subtracting the total cost from the total revenue. For example, since the sale of two units generates $18 in total revenue and $3 in total cost, the sale will generate $15 in net gain to the seller.

Now we can see that the net gain is greatest at the $7 price and the four-quantity combination, the combination at which marginal revenue equals marginal cost. Net gain reaches the same maximum at the $8 price and three-unit quantity, but again, we assume that you will sell a unit if it doesn't change your net gain.

Graphing Monopoly Price Determination

We can get still more insight into monopoly price determination by examining the graph in Figure 5.1. The curves were derived directly from the schedules in Table 5.4. The downward-sloping demand curve illustrates the demand for your wax. The line below the demand curve is marginal revenue curve. Except for the first unit of sales, it lies below the demand curve because, with uniform pricing, marginal revenue is less than price. Finally, the upward-sloping curve is the marginal cost curve. It reveals the marginal costs you will incur should you increase sales.

Your monopoly price and quantity are $7 and four units, respectively. At any quantity below four units, the marginal revenue curve lies above the marginal cost curve. This reveals that the value of the money you will receive from the sale of those units will exceed the value of the wax that you will sacrifice. You will therefore sell those additional units. At more than four units of sales, the marginal cost curve sits above the marginal revenue curve, indicating that the marginal value of the wax that would be sacrificed exceeds the marginal gain in revenue that would be obtained. You therefore avoid the sale of more than four units. To trade away fewer or more than four sticks of wax, you would have to be irrational.

Comparative Prices

Now that we have used an example and graph to identify the monopoly price of the ski wax, let's conclude our explanation by showing that the monopoly price is greater than the price that would have existed under competitive conditions.

The monopoly price is greater than the competitive price because the competitive price would have been only $6 rather than the monopoly price of $7. This is because under competitive conditions, there would have been no market-spoiling effect, since you would have been such a small factor in the market that your sales wouldn't have reduced the market price. Without a market-spoiling effect, your gain from selling each additional unit would have been the price. As

Figure 5.1   Graph of Monopoly Price and Quantity

The monopoly price is $7 and the quantity is four units. It is the price and quantity associated with the equality of marginal revenue and marginal cost, as identified by the intersection of the marginal revenue and the marginal cost curves.

Price, Marginal Revenue, or Marginal Cost

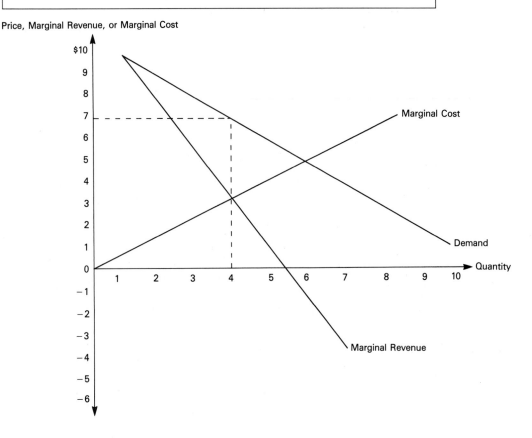

a result, you would have kept selling as long as price exceeded marginal cost. Since the price of the fifth unit would have been $6 and the cost would have been only $5, selling it would have been rational.

The competitive price wouldn't have fallen below $6. For the price to have fallen to $5, you would have had to sell another unit, but to sell a unit worth $6 for $5, you would have had to be irrational.

The Predictions

Higher Prices, Smaller Quantities

From the preceding explanation, we can predict that monopolists will charge higher prices than competitive sellers. Monopoly prices will exceed competitive prices.

We can also predict that monopolists will sell smaller quantities than would have been sold under competitive conditions. In our ski wax example, rather than selling the five units that you would have sold under conditions of competition, you will sell only four.

In making either the price or the quantity decision, you will be making the other: You can set the price of ski wax at $7 and sell as much as possible, which will be four units, since consumers value only the first four units at $7 or more. Or you can put four sticks of wax up for sale and try to get the highest possible price. Consumers will then force the price up to $7. This is because at a lower price, a shortage would have existed, causing competition among consumers and a higher price. For example, at a price of $6, quantity demanded would have been five and the one-unit shortage would have driven the price to $7. In the real economy, some monopolists charge more and wind up selling less, whereas others supply less and eventually charge more.

Shifts in the Net Gains From Trade

We can also predict that a monopolist will obtain more net gain than if he or she had sold at the competitive price. For example, your net gain as the single seller of ski wax will be greater than if you had to compete with other sellers. This is because, under competitive conditions, you would have sacrificed five sticks at a total cost to you of $15 and received $30, for a net gain of $15. In contrast, with monopoly power, you will trade four sticks at a total cost of $10 for $28 in total revenue, yielding a net gain of $18, $3 more than under competition.

We can also say something about the net gain that consumers obtain from trade. Consumers as well as sellers gain and sacrifice goods that they value during trade. We can predict that the net gain of consumers will be lower under monopoly circumstances than under competitive ones.

In our ski wax case, the net gain from trade to consumers is $4 lower under monopoly conditions than it would have been under competitive conditions. This is because under competitive conditions, skiers would have paid a total of $30 for five units. They think the units are worth $40, so their net gain would have been $10. (You can derive the $40 value from the demand schedule by adding how much the skiers are willing and able to pay for individual marginal units. For instance, they are willing and able to pay $10 to buy the first unit. Therefore the first unit must be worth $10. Since the price must be reduced to $9 to sell a second unit, the value of the second unit must be only $9, and so on.) On the other hand, under conditions of monopoly, skiers will spend $28 for goods worth $34. Their net gain will be only $6 rather than $10.

Reduction in the Combined Net Gains From Trade

The conclusion that, as a monopolist, you will charge more and sell less, increasing your net gain and reducing the net gain of consumers, isn't surprising. Common experience tells us as much. What is more difficult to recognize is that the net gain to consumers falls more than the net gain to monopolists increases. The combination of the net gains from trade to society, which includes sellers and buyers, will fall under monopoly relative to competitive conditions. For example, while your monopoly of ski wax will allow you to obtain $3 more in net gain than you could have obtained under competitive conditions, the net gain of other skiers falls by $4.

The reduction in combined net gains occurs because monopolists will hold goods that are more valuable to consumers than to themselves. They will do so to avoid spoiling their markets.

For instance, the $1 reduction in net gains from the trade of ski wax will occur because you will refuse to sell the fifth unit of wax, an item that you would have sold under competitive conditions. That item is worth $6 to consumers and only $5 to you. By keeping it, you will keep the value of the wax $1 lower. You will be willing to keep the value of wax lower because you wouldn't obtain $6 in revenue by selling the fifth unit. You would have to spoil your market for the other four units and lose $4 from the necessary price reduction. Rather than $6, the marginal revenue of the fifth unit would be only $2, insufficient to cover its $5 value to you.

Monopolists are willing to shrink the combined net-gains pie because their share of the smaller pie is substantially larger. Conversely, they are unwilling to increase the combined net-gains pie by selling the competitive quantity because their share of the larger pie would be substantially smaller.

A Summary of the Theory

By assuming that a single seller trades with many buyers, we have been able to predict that relative to competitive conditions

a. The monopoly price will be higher;
b. The monopoly quantity will be lower;
c. The monopolist will obtain a greater net gain from trade;
d. Consumers will receive a lower net gain from trade;
e. The combination of the net gains from trade to society will be lower.

SPECIAL TOPICS

Parker Brothers' Monopoly

How does the real game of monopoly compare and contrast with the Parker Brothers' game?

The two games are similar to the extent that once sellers obtain a monopoly, they raise their prices and increase their net gains at the expense of consumers. But that's as far as the similarities go.

The two games differ in three very important respects. First, in the real world, when a monopoly price is too high, you can buy something else. In contrast, in the Parker Brothers' game, if you happen to fall on your opponent's property, you must pay the price. You can't leave Park Place and go to Mediterranean Avenue if you don't have or don't want to pay $1500 for a hotel room. Real-world monopoly demand curves slope downward; in the Parker Brothers' game, demand curves are vertical.

Second, in reality, monopolists select their prices and can thereby change their sales as well as their revenues. In the Parker Brothers' game, players can charge only what the rules allow and sell the quantities that chance dictates.

Finally, in actuality, the combined net gains of society fall under conditions of monopoly relative to those of competition. In the Parker Brothers' game, the net gains are constant since all gains and sacrifices are represented by the fixed amount of money and property in circulation. What one player obtains, another player directly or indirectly loses.

Marriage and Monopoly

Monopoly effects don't depend on the use of money. The effects occur under barter conditions as well as where money is employed as a medium of exchange.

To explain, suppose Elizabeth and John get married. Liz is a liberated woman who marries John because she loves him a great deal. John, on the other hand, is a male chauvinist who marries Liz because of the high quality of her home cooking.

As soon as Liz discovers why John has married her, she decides not to give away her home-cooked meals; she sells the meals to John in exchange for him doing various chores around the house. To keep John off guard, Liz sells the meals only implicitly. That is, if John does the dishes, she fixes his favorite casserole. If he doesn't vacuum the carpets, she fixes frozen TV dinners or has pizza delivered to the house.

After some time passes, Liz begins to realize that she has monopoly power. She is the only seller of her quality cooking. Having little sympathy for John, she decides to maximize the gains from her position and quickly reduces the supply of home-cooked meals.

Why does Liz benefit from selling less? Because the value of home-cooked meals to John—and, therefore, the price John is willing and able to pay—depends on the value of the marginal unit. The value and therefore the price of meals rises as she sells fewer units because John values marginal units more when he obtains less. With lower sales and a higher price, Liz increases her net gain from trade and reduces John's.

Another effect of the monopoly restriction on sales is that the combination of the net gains from trade related to the marriage falls relative to what the combination would have been under competitive conditions. This becomes obvious when Liz keeps John dissatisfied even though she wants more home-cooked meals. John might not comprehend why Liz is creating an artificial scarcity of a good that both of them want, but Liz might understand: By restricting supply and not spoiling John, Liz can obtain a higher price for all of the units she sells.

If you asked Liz to explain her behavior, she might not claim that she is trying to increase her net gain. She might instead argue that she is trying to maintain the value of the cooked meals, a value that would be lost should supply suddenly rise. This is how the producers of French Champagne justify turning tons of excellent grapes into vinegar when they harvest unexpectedly large amounts. Nevertheless, while the values of the marginal units do decline with greater sales, the values of previous units need not fall. The value of a particular home-cooked meal or bottle of Champagne is not diminished by the fact that the value of the next unit is lower.

The example with Liz and John has one major flaw. Although the theory of monopoly exchange can be used to explain how some couples trade within a marriage, it can't be used to predict. For one thing, married individuals often value the welfare of their spouses so much that they will make personal sacrifices and not take advantage of monopoly power.

More importantly, although there may be only one seller in a marriage, there is also only one buyer. The theory's ability to predict depends on the presence of many buyers. This is because when only one buyer is present, he or she may refuse to buy unless price is reduced and offers to sell are increased. John, for instance, might start negotiating with Liz, threatening to do no chores unless she reduces the price and increases the supply of home-cooked meals. Marriages are actually examples of the more complex circumstances of isolated interpersonal exchange or bilateral monopoly, rather than the simple conditions of monopoly exchange for which our theory was designed.

The Mafia, a Monopoly Seller of Drugs

In the book and movie, *The Godfather*, Don Corleone, the boss of the Mafia in New York, initially refused to let the various New York crime families deal in illegal drugs because he believed that drugs were extremely detrimental to society and because he thought society would not tolerate extensive drug trade. But he was later overruled.

Today, like the fictional Mafia, the real Mafia is heavily involved in drug traffic. It is reasonable to assume that it has sometimes been able to eliminate competition and become the only seller. What does our theory predict about the behavior of the Mafia under the resulting monopoly circumstances?

First, the prices of drugs are higher than if many competitors were present. As a monopoly seller, the Mafia raises the price. Also, the quantity sold is smaller. To keep the price higher, the Mafia must restrict the supply. Next, the Mafia's net gain from trade is greater, and the net gain of addicts is smaller, relative to competitive conditions. Finally, the combined net gains from trade (the net gain of the Mafia plus that of the addicts) is smaller. Drugs that are more valuable to consumers are kept by the Mafia to avoid spoiling the market.

The desire of society to reduce drug sales may be consistent with the wishes of organized crime. The legalization of drugs would be a disaster for the Mafia, since massive competition would drive the price of drugs down until it equaled their very low cost of production. As a special interest group, the Mafia might work harder to oppose drug legalization than the Baptist Church.

Bad Harvests, Happy Farmers; Good Harvests, Sad Farmers

Farmers sometimes obtain monopoly effects even though they generally sell in very competitive markets. They obtain the effects when natural events reduce supply under conditions where the quantity demanded of food is very insensitive to price. For instance, if harvests fall off 30% and this causes prices to rise 50%, farmers will receive greater revenues. A poor harvest year will become a terrific profit year.

Although farmers may benefit, the combined net gains from trade that accrue to society will fall. Less food will be available for consumption. The combined total net gains pie will shrink as farmers receive their substantially greater share.

During a good harvest year, results may be reversed. A good harvest year may be a poor profit year for farmers. Large crops will create a greater market supply. If the quantities of food that consumers demand are relatively insensitive to food prices, farmers may have to accept radically lower prices, spoiling the market for previous units so much that revenues will decline. A 30% increase in the quantities sold will not increase revenues if prices fall 50%.

There is little doubt that individual farmers would prefer higher prices and lower sales. They might even be willing to destroy some of their crops to keep prices high. But so many farmers usually exist that they individually have no such option. Even if an individual farmer reduced production to zero, world agricultural prices would remain the same.

If farmers could act together and reduce supply simultaneously, they could obtain monopoly results. However, so many farmers exist that effective collusion is very difficult. We will see why in Chapters 11 and 13.

Monopoly and Inflation

Do monopolists cause continuous general increases in prices, **continuous inflation**? No. Monopolists charge higher prices than competitive sellers, but whereas prices may be higher, monopolists don't continually raise prices.

The creation of a monopoly would cause a once-and-for-all price increase to the level at which marginal revenue equals marginal cost, but that's it. Once a monopolist has increased price to the level where the net gain from trade is maximized, he or she will raise price further only if either demand or cost subsequently increases. When demands or marginal costs remain the same, monopoly prices also remain the same.

Elasticity and Monopoly Prices

We have discussed how monopoly prices are determined by using the concepts of marginal as well as total revenues and costs. We have also examined monopoly price determination with the help of graphical analysis. We can shed still more light on monopoly price determination by using the concept of elasticity to explain what happens when monopolists raise their prices.

Elasticity of demand measures the relative sensitivity of quantity demanded to changes in price. When a monopolist raises the price, quantity demanded always falls—it is always sensitive to price, but at some points on demand the quantity falls much more than at other points. In other words, the demand for a good can vary in its elasticity.

Demand is **elastic** when a given percentage change in price causes a larger percentage change in quantity demanded. For example, demand for travel on an airline is elastic if a 10% price increase results in a 20% reduction in the quantity demanded.

Demand is **inelastic** when a given percentage change in price causes a smaller percentage change in quantity demanded. Demand for medicine, for instance, is inelastic if a 40% price increase causes only a 5% decline in the quantity demanded.

Finally, demand is **unit elastic** when a percentage change in price equals the resulting percentage change in quantity. Demand for automobiles is unit elastic if a 30% price increase causes a 30% quantity decrease.

When monopolists start raising prices from low levels, they usually find that demands are inelastic. Consumers are initially very unresponsive to price increases, in part because at low prices, relative price increases absorb a comparatively small amount of money. For instance, even if price rises 50%, consumers may tend to ignore the increase if the initial price is only .10¢; .05¢ doesn't mean much to most buyers. Things might be different if price rose by 50% from a base of $5000 since few consumers would ignore a $2500 price increase.

Since monopolists find demands to be inelastic when prices are low, they can raise prices and obtain greater total revenues. The price increases cause total revenues to rise more than quantity declines force total revenues to fall. For example, when the monopolistic Arab oil cartel OPEC first raised its price by 400%, quantity demanded fell only 1%, causing revenues to increase greatly. In addition to greater revenues, monopolists incur lower total costs when they raise prices, since they sacrifice less when they sell less. When faced with inelastic demands, the combinations of greater revenues and lower costs induce monopolists to raise prices.

As monopolists keep charging more and consumers respond by buying less, the monopolists eventually encounter portions of demand curves that are elastic. Prices can rise so high that further increases greatly affect consumers. When demands become elastic, revenues fall because gains in revenues from higher prices are more than offset by losses in revenues from lower sales. For example, a 5% price increase will fail to offset a 10% drop in sales. Total revenues will decline. Nevertheless, monopolists will continue to raise prices. This is because total costs continue to fall as fewer goods are sold, and for limited ranges, total revenues decline less than total costs.

Eventually, however, total revenues fall as much and then more than costs. Once revenues fall as much as costs, the monopolists reach points at which net gains are maximized. They then stop raising prices and sell.

Both the competitive and the monopoly prices we have discussed have been at market-clearing levels, although the monopoly prices have been higher than the competitive ones. In the real world, however, prices are often at levels where markets do not clear, levels where shortages or surpluses exist. To explain why, we will in the next chapter have our economic individuals trade under more complex circumstances.

MAJOR AND MINOR POINTS

1. A monopolist is a single seller.
2. Monopoly exchange conditions exist when there are one seller, many buyers, and a value differential.
3. Monopolists will sell less at higher prices and can sell more only at lower prices.
4. Total revenue is the total gain from sales; it equals the price times the quantity sold. Marginal revenue is the change in total revenue that occurs with the sale of one more unit.
5. A monopolist must usually sell all units at the same price, employing a uniform-pricing policy. This means that the sale of additional units spoils the market for previous units. As a result, marginal revenue is less than price for all units except the first.
6. A monopolist usually sells all units at the same price because price discrimination, charging different prices, is usually impossible.
7. When a person gives up an additional unit of a good by selling it, the value of the additional unit to the seller is the marginal cost of the sale.
8. Marginal cost rises with sales because as a monopolist has fewer units, the value of the remaining units to the monopolist is greater.
9. A monopolist, or any seller, will try to maximize the net gain from trade, the difference between the value of the total gains and the value of the total sacrifices associated with trade.
10. So as to maximize the net gain from trade, a monopolist, or any seller, will charge the price and sell the quantity associated with the equality of marginal revenue and marginal cost. If marginal revenue were greater than marginal cost, greater sales would increase net gain. If marginal revenue were less than marginal cost, the sale of the associated units would reduce net gain.
11. The quantity at which marginal revenue equals marginal cost is the quantity at which total revenue exceeds total cost by the greatest amount, and, therefore, the quantity at which the net gain from trade is maximized.

12. The monopolist will charge the price and sell the quantity associated with the intersection of the marginal revenue and the marginal cost curves.

13. Compared to competitive conditions, the monopoly price will be higher, the monopoly quantity will be lower, the monopolist's net gain will be greater, the net gain of consumers will be lower, and the combination of the net gains to society will be lower.

14. The Parker Brothers' game of Monopoly differs from the real game. In the real game, monopolists select prices, control quantities, increase their net gain, reduce the net gain of consumers, and reduce the combined net gains to society.

15. Monopoly trade theory explains and predicts economic phenomena related to barter exchanges.

16. Monopoly trade theory can both explain and predict economic phenomena related to illegal exchanges in drug markets.

17. Farmers often obtain monopoly effects when crop yields rise or fall. If consumers are insensitive to price changes, then smaller yields can cause prices to rise so far that they offset the lost revenues from smaller sales, and vice versa.

18. Monopolists don't cause continuous inflation. Monopolists charge higher prices than competitive sellers, but they don't continually raise prices.

19. The elasticity of demand is the relative sensitivity of quantity demanded to price. Monopoly sellers will raise price as long as demand is inelastic. When demand becomes elastic, they will continue to raise price only until gains from lower costs fail to offset revenue decreases.

QUESTIONS

1. With which set of monopoly circumstances is the theory of monopoly concerned?

2. What happens to price, total revenue, and marginal revenue as a monopolist sells larger quantities?

3. Why is marginal revenue less than price for all units sold by a monopolist save the first?

4. What happens to marginal cost as a monopolist sells larger quantities?

5. What price will a monopolist charge and what quantity will be sold? (Answer from the perspective of marginal revenue and marginal cost, and from the perspective of net gain from trade. Also show the results graphically.)

6. Why is the monopoly price above the price that would have been charged under competitive conditions?

7. How are the net gains of sellers, buyers and society affected by monopoly as opposed to competitive conditions?

8. What is elasticity of demand and how can it be used to explain the determination of the monopoly price?

9. Discuss the following terms and concepts:

Monopoly circumstances	Marginal revenue curve
Monopoly demand	Marginal cost curve
Total revenue	Net gain

Marginal revenue
Marginal revenue < price
Uniform pricing
Spoiling the market
Price discrimination
Marginal cost

Combined net gains
Inflation and monopoly
The elasticity of demand
Elastic, inelastic, and unit
    elastic demand
Elasticity and monopoly

APPLICATIONS

1. There are no pure monopolists. All monopolists must compete with the sellers of other goods. Explain.
2. If monopoly demand curves were vertical, what prices would monopolists charge?
3. If price discrimination were possible, what would be the relationship between marginal revenue and price?
4. The Roxie Theater is sold out of tickets to a special movie about Africa. Should the owners be happy or sad?
5. If Louisiana fishermen were granted monopoly power, their wealth would increase and so would the wealth of Louisiana. Is this true?
6. What is good for General Motors is good for America. Would this apply to the granting of monopoly power to General Motors?
7. Does Liz need to know economics to restrict her sale of home-cooked meals?
8. Distinguish between total value and marginal value.
9. During a drought, the price of food rises. Does this mean that the total value of food increases?
10. A crop failure reduces the California grape harvest and farmers make more money. Explain why.
11. When questioned about his monopoly power, a monopolist argues the he charges only what his goods are worth—no more, no less. Evaluate.
12. How did nature allow Elvis Presley to obtain monopoly power?
13. Distinguish between the elasticity of demand for gasoline and the elasticity of demand for gasoline sold by a particular gasoline station.
14. If the demand curves of monopolists remained inelastic as the monopolists increased prices, how would the monopolists behave?

6

Nonclearing Prices

The prices we have discussed so far have all been at market-clearing levels, at levels where neither shortages nor surpluses exist, although the monopoly prices were higher than the competitive ones. Nevertheless, when we look at trade circumstances in our economy, nonclearing prices often occur. Surplus bales of tobacco, store inventories, and vacant apartments often go unsold. And tickets to the Orange Bowl, parking places in downtown Boston, and good looking men and women are frequently in short supply.

It would be nice if we could follow our usual format to explain a theory of nonclearing prices. But in this case, the presentation would be too complex, since the possible causes of nonclearing prices are very diverse. We can, however, achieve almost the same results if we simply say that nonclearing prices occur because buyers, sellers, or governments want one or more of ten possible effects of nonclearing prices and then identify and explain those effects.

We cover the 10 possible effects of nonclearing prices in this chapter. We first identify each effect and see how it manifests itself in apartment rental markets. Then we further discuss the effects by analyzing retail store inventories, minimum-wage laws, and consumers in the Soviet Union. We will also look into the allocation of A's in economics courses, the economic effects of gift-giving, and the distribution of land by the Homestead Act of 1862.

TEN POSSIBLE EFFECTS OF NONCLEARING PRICES

Surpluses for Inspection or Immediate Purchase

One possible effect of nonclearing prices is that they can bring about surpluses of goods that consumers can inspect or immediately purchase.

In unregulated apartment-rental markets, for example, rents are generally at levels such that 6% surpluses in the form of vacancies exist. The excess supplies are worthless to landlords, are costly to maintain, and can be eliminated by rent reductions. It would be irrational for landlords to keep these vacancies unless tenants compensated them by eventually paying sufficiently higher rents. But tenants do just that. Tenants will usually pay landlords to keep surpluses because vacancies eliminate a great deal of costly shopping, planning ahead, or waiting.

For instance, rather than paying rents of $470 per month and having no vacancies, prospective tenants will often prefer rents of $500 per month that create 6% vacancies. With the vacancies, tenants may eventually pay $30 per month extra, but the vacancies allow easy inspection and thereby reduce the cost to tenants of producing information about quality and price. Without empty apartments, tenants would have to get their information either by quickly inspecting new vacancies or by examining occupied units, both of which are costly alternatives. In addition to providing apartments for inspection, the vacancies act as inventories for immediate purchase. As a result, prospective tenants incur lower costs, since they don't have to search for apartments as long, rent in advance, or wait for empty apartments.

Stable and Gradually Changing Prices

Another effect of nonclearing prices is that they make it possible for prices to remain stable in the face of fluctuating demands and supplies. Consumers possess limited price information, and that information is costly for them to produce. This makes price stability valuable. Relative to constantly fluctuating prices, stable and gradually changing prices reduce the amount and the cost of the price information that consumers have to produce.

For example, in unregulated rental markets, landlords could obtain greater revenues and suffer lower costs by raising rents every time shortages of apartments occurred and lowering rents during slack periods. Average rents could then be lower. But landlords generally avoid constantly changing rents. It appears that tenants prefer higher but stable payments. Why? Because fluctuating rents would force tenants to do more shopping. The tenants appear to think that the costs of constantly moving and searching the rental markets for reasonably priced places to rent would generally exceed the sacrifices associated with slightly higher, nonfluctuating rents.

When demands or supplies permanently shift rather than just fluctuate, nonclearing prices also make it possible for prices to change gradually.

Gradual changes can be beneficial because if sellers want to change prices gradually, they can produce price information slowly, and price information, like most goods, is less costly to produce when it is produced slowly.

A good example of gradually changing prices in the face of rapid changes in demands occurred in Anchorage, Alaska, during and after the construction of the trans-Alaska pipeline. Landlords in Anchorage usually keep rents at levels such that 6% vacancies exist. Prospective tenants pay the higher rents to cover the costs of these vacancies because the empty apartments facilitate inspection and immediate rental. However, when demands for apartments rose during the construction of the pipeline, vacancy rates fell below 6% because landlords didn't immediately raise rents. They didn't initially know that the demand increases had occurred.

They could have found out sooner. They could have hired real estate consultants to monitor the markets, read the want ads more carefully, kept a closer eye on rents and vacancies, or interviewed other landlords about their recent rental experiences. But all this would have been costly. They instead produced the market information more slowly, typically by seeing how long it took to rent apartments. As a result, they increased rents only after they observed that apartments were renting quickly.

Once landlords learned that demands were rising, they didn't know how much. They therefore raised rents gradually. In fact, the gap between rents and demands increased because demands kept rising faster than rents. As a result, vacancy rates continued to fall, eventually reaching a 1% level.

In time, demand stopped growing. This gave landlords a chance to catch up, and rents gradually rose until vacancies increased to 6%.

After pipeline construction, the population of Anchorage fell by 10,000. Demand for apartments declined with it, but landlords again adjusted rents gradually. The vacancy rate rose to 15% before the rent reductions finally forced it back to 6%.

Throughout the period, supply as well as demand changed. Nevertheless, the basic response of landlords was to change rents gradually.

In summary, limited market information creates conditions in which nonclearing prices may coincide with the maximization of net gains. By creating excess supplies for immediate purchase and inspection and by allowing stable prices that change slowly, nonclearing prices can reduce the cost and the amount of market information that buyers and sellers desire.

In preceding chapters, we were able to predict and explain the prices both competitive sellers and monopolists charged by ignoring limited market information. We assumed that buyers and sellers could "see" supply, demand, and costs, and could simply pick the optimal rates of exchange. There was little harm in this, since a recognition of limited information would have made things much more complex and wouldn't have greatly improved our understanding of price levels and price changes.

Nevertheless, if we want to predict and explain some deviations of prices from clearing levels, the sacrifice of simplicity is worth the gain in generality. Most buyers and sellers are in fact **price searchers**, individuals who have limited market information and must produce market information at some cost. Unlike price-taking competitors and price-setting monopolists, price searchers may want prices to be at nonclearing levels if the resulting shortages, surpluses, stable prices, or gradually changing prices either allow them to cheaply produce information or eliminate the need for it.

In-Kind Wealth Transfers

Sometimes limited information has nothing to do with nonclearing prices. Many nonclearing prices occur because sellers, buyers, or governments want some of the other effects that the prices can create.

Perhaps the most sought after effect of nonclearing prices is that they can change the wealth of buyers and sellers. When prices are reduced, buyers usually benefit at the expense of sellers, and when prices are increased, sellers usually gain while buyers lose. For example, rent controls in New York City increase the wealth of tenants and reduce the wealth of landlords by reducing rents.

Wealth changes related to nonclearing prices are **in-kind** rather than monetary since the gains are tied to specific goods. This makes a big difference because the total of all losses may be greater than the total of all gains. Nonclearing prices can reduce the total wealth of society.

For example, when rent controls in New York reduce the rent of an apartment from $500 to $200 per month, the landlord loses $300. However, to a particular tenant who would have been willing and able to pay only $300 per month for the apartment, the gain is only $100, far less than the landlord's $300 loss.

Unhappy Buyers and Sellers

Although buyers may benefit from lower prices and sellers may gain from higher ones, the presence of shortages or surpluses implies that all prospective buyers or sellers aren't better off. Prospective buyers and sellers gain only if they can actually buy or sell at the nonclearing prices. If fact, buyers or sellers who can't trade are worse off, since they must accept less preferred alternatives.

For instance, shortages of apartments in New York City reveal that rent controls have failed to improve conditions for all potential tenants. Only people able to rent apartments have benefited. The prospective tenants who couldn't rent are in less preferred positions, since they must live elsewhere.

Nonprice Discrimination

Nonclearing prices also create **nonprice discrimination**, the use of criteria other than price to decide who buys or sells. To understand this, we need to recognize only that when supplies are scarce, sellers must discriminate among consumers and decide who will receive the goods. Scarcity forces discrimination.

Under market-clearing conditions, sellers discriminate in favor of buyers willing and able to pay the highest prices and against those willing and able to pay lower prices. On the other hand, below market-clearing prices create shortages—more people are willing and able to buy than can do so—and this forces sellers to select some additional nonprice criteria for choosing among consumers.

In the case of New York with its rent controls, more than one person wants to rent each apartment. Landlords therefore have to select some criterion in addition to rent for choosing among tenants. The criteria include first-in-line, friendship, age, number of children, race, or the applicant's income (even though landlords obtain the same rent, they may prefer rich tenants to poor ones if they feel that the rich tenants will do less damage, pay the rent sooner, etc.).

If rent controls cause the use of race and income as criteria for discrimination, various minorities and the poor may find that they gain little or lose because of rent controls. In their effects, rent controls may be antiminority, antipoor statutes. If minorities and the poor can't rent apartments, it does them little good to know that rents have been reduced.

From a different perspective, if landlords in free markets want to discriminate among prospective tenants by using nonprice criteria, they must reduce rents to below clearing levels. The rent reductions make nonprice discrimination costly. As a result, landlords in free markets will usually avoid nonprice discrimination; they will avoid renting exclusively to their friends, relatives, Caucasians, or adults. However, when rent controls are imposed, landlords have no choice. They must accept the lower rents and deal with the resulting shortages by nonprice discriminating among prospective tenants.

In contrast to individuals selling goods in free markets, governments have a tendency to sell goods at below clearing prices and practice nonprice discrimination. This is because when revenues accrue to the state, government agents and politicians personally sacrifice little by picking "deserving" buyers rather than selling to the highest bidders. This explains the claim that the incidence of racial discrimination in the South has historically been greatest in the public sector. In the past, blacks had little trouble buying automobiles, clothing, and food from white-owned private businesses. However, when public swimming facilities, transportation, and education were allocated, "whites only" signs were in clear view.

Nonprice Competition

Another closely related effect of nonclearing prices is that they cause nonprice competition. Once a criterion for discrimination is chosen, we compete to fulfill it. When the criterion is price, we compete by trying to buy at a high price or sell at a low one. But when nonprice criteria are employed, nonprice competition results. Since nonclearing prices create nonprice discrimination, they also create nonprice competition.

For instance, when landlords in New York discriminate among potential tenants on the basis of first-in-line, good looks, or friendship, tenants compete by trying to arrive first, cutting their hair, or making many friends, respectively. Of course, potential tenants can't easily compete to fulfill criteria such as age or race. But they can still compete politically to change the criteria, perhaps eventually bringing about the passage of laws forcing landlords to ignore age or race when choosing among applicants.

Higher Transaction Costs

Subsequent to the establishment of nonclearing prices and the consequent nonprice competition, transaction costs generally rise, creating yet another effect of nonclearing prices. To obtain an apartment at an auction, you have to only raise your hand. But to find a place to live in New York, you may have to drive around town for 3 weeks.

The sacrifice of money differs from that of driving. When you pay more, your wealth loss accrues to the landlord—wealth is simply redistributed. But when you drive around town, no one benefits.

Black Markets and Kickbacks

Nonclearing prices also often cause secondary trades. When sellers use criteria other than price to pick among buyers, the new owners will usually value their purchases less than some other potential buyers. Some value differentials will continue and the opportunities for further trade will therefore exist.

When the subsequent exchanges occur, they are secondary trades. When the subsequent exchanges are illegal, they are called **black-market** trades.

For instance, suppose you obtained a New York apartment at a regulated rate of $200 per month and you valued the unit at $300 (if you had to pay more than $300, you would have moved to the city's suburbs). If a friend later arrived in town and couldn't find an apartment for her family at the regulated rent, she might offer you $500 per month for yours. Would you sublet the unit and move out of town?

Greater Shortages and Surpluses

After nonclearing prices have existed for some time, shortages and surpluses often increase. Shortages increase because sellers react to lower prices by cutting sales and shifting goods to other markets.

In the case of rent controls, governments can force landlords to reduce their rents, but governments generally can't force landlords to build new apartments, or keep landlords from converting apartments into condominiums. As a result, apartment shortages increase.

Quality Changes

Finally, nonclearing prices can cause changes in quality. An easy way to create a ghetto in a large city is to control rents. Once 50 people want to rent an apartment, a landlord no longer has to paint the walls or fix the plumbing.

SPECIAL TOPICS

Now that we have discussed the effects of nonclearing prices and looked specifically at nonclearing rents, we can examine some other examples.

Store Inventories and Inventory Analysis

Retail stores normally keep prices above clearing for much the same reason that landlords often keep rents where vacancies exist: Above-clearing prices create surpluses for inspection and immediate purchase and allow prices to remain stable or change only slowly. The surpluses take the form of store inventories.

However, consumers aren't always willing to pay for inventories. And even when consumers are willing to pay, they will pay only the limited amount that supports an inventory of the optimum size. As a result, inventory decisions are complex.

Many factors determine the size of inventories. One of the most important ones is the cost of the inventory. When the items displayed and available for sale are more expensive, inventories cost more and consumers want less. Not surprisingly, inventories of gasoline station attendants and shoes tend to be far greater than inventories of doctors and Boeing 757 jets.

Inventory costs can be greatly reduced if they are spread over more units of sales. As a result, more inventories will exist when sales volumes are large. For example, when a town is small, residents may have to order cars from a wholesaler, sight unseen. But as sales expand, a retail outlet may be created that maintains an inventory of automobiles for inspection. And when the town grows to become a city, inventories may increase to allow for both immediate purchase and inspection.

Another factor affecting the size of inventories is the cost of rapidly producing the products making up the inventories. If products can be quickly produced at a low cost, inventories may be unnecessary. For example, if you want to buy a suit, you may have to wait only a day or two for production to be completed. The wait may cost very little compared to the price you would have to pay to cover the cost of an inventory that has your size, color, and style.

The costs that consumers incur when they shop, plan ahead, or wait also affect inventory sizes. When consumers shop or plan ahead, those who earn high income sacrifice more than those who earn less. As a result, stores catering to high-income customers generally find it profitable to raise prices and maintain greater inventories, facilitating inspections and immediate purchases.

Consumers typically find that their transaction costs differ over time. This causes the same consumers to sometimes buy goods from a retail store such as Sears and at other times to buy lower-priced goods from the catalogue. In general, if the benefits of inventories exceed their costs, sellers will find that inventories and higher prices will yield greater earnings. Otherwise, they will reduce inventories and prices.

When retail stores sell products, the other eight effects of nonclearing prices generally don't occur. Nonclearing retail prices clear markets in the sense that the sellers produce information and charge extra for it by raising their prices above normal levels. The other effects of nonclearing prices are best illustrated by other nonclearing prices, such as minimum wages.

The Effects of Minimum-Wage Laws

When governments pass minimum-wage legislation, they do so to keep wages above normal levels. At those levels, the ten effects of nonclearing prices occur:

1. Above-clearing wages create labor surpluses that act as inventories of unemployed workers. Employers have many applicants from which to choose and search costs are lower.

    The surpluses of workers also imply shortages of jobs. This causes unemployed workers to incur higher search costs, since inventories of jobs for inspection and immediate "purchase" become nonexistent. Want ads are few and far between and job vacancies fill quickly.

2. Minimum wages also reduce some information costs by reducing the need for both workers and employers to obtain wage information. A minimum-wage rate is generally known to everyone, and it changes only when the law is changed.

3. Minimum-wage laws are generally passed to help workers, and this is partially accomplished. Some workers, those who had productivities above the minimum wage but—perhaps because of limited information—were paid less, are paid more. The higher labor prices shift wealth from employers to such employees.

    However, the wealth shifts are in-kind, not monetary. As a result, employers may lose more than employees gain. When a minimum-wage law raises the wage of a worker from $2 to $4 per hour, the employer will suffer a $2-per-hour loss. But if the employee would have taken the job only if the job had paid at least $3 per hour, then the gain to the employee will equal only $1 per hour, not $2 per hour.

4. Some workers fail to benefit from the minimum-wage statutes. This is because higher wages reduce the number of workers employers want to hire. The surplus workers, the unemployed, gain nothing from the law except the knowledge that their working friends earn more. In fact, they are worse off, since they have to find less desirable jobs. A minimum wage of $500,000 per year would surely do little for you except to leave you unemployed.

5. With many unemployed and equally qualified workers seeking each job, nonwage discrimination occurs. Business firms must choose among workers using nonwage criteria, since applicants can't compete with each other by offering to work for less. The criteria for employment include first-in-line, friendship, grades in school, test scores, appearance, age, sex, and race.

   If the nonwage criteria become age and race, teenage and black unemployment rates may rise after the passage of minimum-wage laws. Not only will the laws cause employers to layoff workers who can't produce enough to cover the minimum wage, but the statutes will force employers to use nonwage criteria to choose among many equally qualified applicants.

6. Since minimum wages force employers to select workers on the basis of first-in-line, friendship, appearance, age, sex, race, etc., they also create competition among employees to fulfill those criteria. Workers compete with each other by trying to arrive first when a job opens up, making friends with employers, and being more neatly dressed and groomed.

   Of course, workers can't do much to meet criteria such as age, sex, or race. Nevertheless, they still compete politically to have only the most advantageous criteria chosen.

7. Labor market transaction costs increase, since workers must expend greater effort to find jobs. It is insufficient for them to simply want to work at the going wage; they must also be nice to their employer, dress well, have their hair cut often, and go to political meetings to support the passage of laws forcing employers to fill jobs with the "right" people.

8. Since a shortage of jobs is created by minimum-wage laws, union officials, company supervisors or owners of business firms sometimes either demand kickbacks from employees or illegally sell the jobs to the applicants bidding the most.

9. Unemployment tends to rise as more workers enter the market seeking to obtain the jobs that pay minimum wages. For instance, Mexicans are attracted by the high wages and more of them may enter the United States illegally if they think that they will be able to find work.

10. Finally, with more applicants than jobs, the quality of workers increases while that of jobs declines. Employees try to improve themselves. At the same time, due to the surplus of applicants, employers treat workers worse, in some cases creating sweatshops. If anyone quits, others can easily be hired.

The Life of a Consumer in the Soviet Union

Although governments sometimes set prices above market-clearing levels, as in the case of minimum-wage laws, this isn't the general practice. Usually governments set prices at lower than market-clearing levels. In the Soviet Union, where government administrators determine most prices, below-clearing prices are very common. By looking at the ten effects of those prices, we can get some idea of what life is like for a consumer in the Soviet Union:

1. The below-clearing prices cause shortages, eliminating surpluses. Since surpluses in the form of inventories don't exist, consumers must incur high costs of shopping, planning ahead, or waiting.

2. Prices are stable and change only when the government wants them to. Knowledge about prices is cheap to buyers and sellers.

3. Some consumers benefit and the government obtains less revenue. But the benefits to consumers are in-kind rather than monetary. As a result, the values of the gains can range all the way down to zero. For example, a Communist party official may be able to buy a car for 20,000 rubles, a car that might have had a market value of 50,000 rubles. But if the car is worth only 20,000 to the official, he or she gains nothing while the government, the society, loses.

4. Many consumers become frustrated because—while they may be willing and able to pay for products—the products may be unavailable. Low prices benefit only those actually able to buy. People who can't buy are worse off.

5. Shortages force distributors to discriminate by using criteria in addition to price. Distributors often sell to those willing to wait in line, friends, members of the Communist party, etc. In fact, special stores have been established that cater to only Communist party members.

6. Nonprice discrimination creates nonprice competition as people compete to be the first to arrive, befriend the "right" individuals, join the Communist party, etc.

   This effect is particularly interesting because many Communists claim that markets cause competition and that after markets have been eliminated, competition will cease. Nevertheless, scarcity causes competition. When markets distribute goods, price criteria are used and price competition occurs. Without markets, nonprice criteria for discrimination must be chosen and nonprice competition follows. A basic difference between a socialist and a capitalist economy is the form rather than the existence of competition.

7. Transaction costs are enormous. It has been estimated that the average Soviet citizen spends 20 hours each week standing in a line. In addition to waiting, consumers must try to make friends, attend party meetings, search for black-market alternatives, etc.

8. Many buyers who can't get goods through normal channels resort to black-market exchanges. They offer sellers additional money or other goods in exchange for the products in short supply.

   Barter is common in these markets. Why? Because the value of money is determined by what it will buy, and when most commodities are in short supply, money seems to buy very little. To Soviet citizens, commodities are harder to obtain than money, so sellers in black markets want commodities.

9. Shortages often get worse. Even though the government doesn't respond to low prices by producing less, many products find their way into black markets, reducing the supplies available for legal trade.

10. Finally, product quality tends to be low. Low prices reduce quality partly because distributors divert the highest quality goods to black markets and partly because producers don't have to worry about selling low-quality products since enormous shortages are present.

Getting an A in Econ 201

Some of the most interesting examples of below-clearing prices are zero prices, cases where scarce goods are distributed free of charge—but not necessarily free of sacrifice. This occurs when professors allocate A's to students in economics courses. Because the zero prices are below clearing, the following effects often occur:

1. Inventories of A's don't exist for inspection. The surpluses are only of students wanting the grades.
2. The prices are zero and don't change.

These first two effects are uninteresting. The third isn't.

3. The giving of A's shifts wealth from teachers to students. Students can keep their money in their wallets since they get the grades at a zero price.

   However, the shifts of wealth are in-kind and not monetary. Therefore the value of the A's received by students may be far below the market values of the A's. A's that would have had very high market values may be given to students taking classes for fun. Those students may gain nothing from the grades.
4. The shortages mean that all students don't gain from the fact that A's have market prices of zero. Only those able to "buy" benefit. Those who can't get A's are worse off.

   The students adamantly opposed to the sale of the grades may be those with the most money as well as the poor. If the wealthy students think that they would easily get the highest exam scores, they may prefer to use their money to buy other goods, items being sold at market-clearing prices. Similarly, wealthy tenants may want rent controls if they think that they will be able to rent at the controlled rates and retain a great deal of money, funds they can use to buy other goods.
5. The shortages also force the teachers to nonprice discriminate among students. A's may be given on the basis of examination scores, attendance, appearance, or courtesy to the teacher.
6. With the selection of nonprice criteria for discrimination, nonprice competition results as students compete by studying for exams, going to classes, having a nice appearance, or showing their teachers the proper amount of respect.
7. Transaction costs rise. It would have been much less costly for some students to buy the grades than to study and attend class.
8. Although it appears to be rare, black-market trade can occur when students bribe professors with money or other goods.
9. Shortages increase over time as more students register for classes where grades are given away rather than sold at positive prices, and professors cut back on the number of A's to reduce their class sizes.
10. The "quality" of the grades decreases as professors, realizing that a surplus of students exists, are less concerned with the welfare of their pupils. Prompt, well-dressed, and courteous students are sometimes taught by tardy, sloppy, and rude instructors.

A Theory of Gifts: The Homestead Act of 1862

Gifts, in addition to grades, are scarce goods "sold" at below-clearing zero prices. When the government provides free camping spaces in Yellowstone or when parents subsidize their children's education, donors are charging zero prices as they "sell" goods to recipients. When donors distribute gifts, the ten effects of nonclearing prices occur.

This was certainly the case when the United States gave land to farmers via the Homestead Act of 1862. The following 10 effects occurred:

1. Inventories of land were nonexistent. Instead, there were shortages.
2. Prices were stable and didn't change.

These two effects were insignificant. The third wasn't since it was largely responsible for the passage of the law.

3. Since farmers had to pay next to nothing for their land, wealth shifted toward them. Of course, someone had to lose. In this case it was the public at large. Land that belonged to all was given to a few.

   The gains to the recipients of the act didn't generally equal the values sacrificed by the public. If a farmer was willing and able to pay $1000 for 160 acres that had a market value of $100,000, society lost $100,000 in wealth. But the farmer nevertheless increased his wealth by only $1000. As is often the case with in-kind gifts, the farmer would have preferred cash to the in-kind gift.

   This explains why recipients are sometimes so ungrateful when they receive in-kind gifts. When Native Americans, the poor, college students, and foreigners receive in-kind food and education, the value of these goods to them may be close to zero even if the goods cost the donors millions.

   The only times recipients value in-kind gifts as much as cash is when they would have purchased the same goods had they instead received money. For example, the Homestead Act gave some farmers land worth $10,000 that they would have otherwise bought for that price had they received $10,000. In those cases, the values of the gifts were the same as $10,000 in cash.

   When donors give recipients goods that the recipients would have purchased otherwise, the donors don't necessarily control what is, in effect, received. By releasing money that would have been used to buy land, the act may have in effect given some farmers liquor and gambling money rather than land.

4. Since there were shortages of homestead land, not all farmers benefited from the zero prices. Those who couldn't obtain land were, in fact, worse off.

5. Nonprice discrimination was used to distribute the land. Property wasn't given to those willing and able to pay the most but to those who were first to file claims.

6. With the nonprice discrimination came nonprice competition as people tried to be first by riding the fastest horses, obtaining the best knowledge of the land, etc.

7. Transaction costs were significant. It would have been easier to buy land at a government land auction than to race for it on opening day.

8. Secondary transfers were eventually legal, after 5 years. As a result, many farmers sold their land to those valuing it more. In many cases, the act failed to put land in the hands of the poor. It gave land to some poor people, but many of them subsequently traded it for cash.

   Since secondary trades are likely to occur when goods are distributed to other than the highest bidders, donors usually make in-kind gifts nontransferable. The recipients of food stamps, low-income housing subsidies, and holiday gifts may not always be allowed to sell to other people who value the goods more.

9. Shortages of land increased as knowledge spread of the ability of farmers to get land at a zero price via homesteading.

10. Finally, and in this case this isn't very interesting, the quality of land fell as the best property was taken first and less desirable land was opened to homesteading.

We have now completed our discussion of the 10 effects of non-clearing prices. In the next chapter, we will expand our body of theory by examining some of the effects that time has on our trades.

MAJOR AND MINOR POINTS

1. Nonclearing prices often
   a. Provide surpluses for inspection and immediate purchase;
   b. Allow prices to remain stable or change only slowly;
   c. Shift wealth among buyers and sellers;
   d. Frustrate some buyers and sellers, and make them worse off;
   e. Force nonprice discrimination;
   f. Institute nonprice competition;
   g. Raise transaction costs;
   h. Cause secondary transfers, black markets and kick-backs;
   i. Increase shortages and surpluses over time; and
   j. Reduce or increase product quality.

2. Nonclearing prices can make surpluses available for inspection and immediate purchase and allow prices to be stable or change only slowly. As a result, they can reduce the amount and the cost of price information.

3. Wealth transfers caused by nonclearing prices are in-kind (tied to specific commodities) rather than monetary. In-kind transfers may have little or no value to recipients even if they cause high losses to donors.

4. Wealth gains accrue only to those buyers and sellers able to trade at the non-clearing prices.

5. Markets discriminate on the basis of price. When we eliminate markets, we must choose other criteria for discrimination.

6. It is costly to nonprice discriminate because nonprice discrimination requires price changes that cause wealth shifts.

7. Nonprice discrimination is more likely to occur in the public sector of the economy, where it is less costly.

8. Price discrimination creates price competition. Nonprice discrimination creates nonprice competition.

9. Transaction costs are increased by nonprice competition. Money payments represent losses to some but gains to others. The incurring of transaction costs represents losses only to some.

10. Secondary transfers, black-market trades, and kickbacks often accompany or follow the nonprice distribution of goods.

11. After the institution of nonclearing prices, shortages and surpluses often increase over time as sellers and buyers react to higher or lower prices.

12. When prices are fixed at levels such that shortages exist, quality tends to fall. Inner-city ghettos and sweatshops sometimes result. Conversely, when prices are pegged at levels such that surpluses exist, quality tends to rise.

13. The effects of nonclearing prices occur when stores keep prices at above-clearing levels, when governments pass minimum-wage laws, when governments in socialist countries set prices, when teachers give away grades, and when donors distribute gifts.

QUESTIONS

1. What are nonclearing prices?
2. How does limited and costly market information cause nonclearing prices?
3. Relative to market-clearing prices, how do nonclearing prices shift wealth between buyers and sellers?
4. Why don't all buyers and sellers benefit from below- or above-clearing prices, respectively?
5. How do nonclearing prices affect discrimination and competition?
6. Why do nonclearing prices increase transaction costs?
7. Why do nonclearing prices create secondary trades and kickbacks?
8. What happens to shortages and surpluses over time when prices remain at nonclearing levels?
9. How do nonclearing prices affect the qualities of goods?
10. Discuss the following terms and concepts:

Nonclearing prices	Nonprice competition
Inspection	Transaction costs
Immediate purchase	Secondary transfers
Stable prices	Black markets and kickbacks
Gradually changing prices	Quality changes
Price searching	Ghettos and sweat shops
In-kind wealth shifts	Minimum-wage laws
Frustrated buyers or sellers	Government prices
Nonprice discrimination	Monetary versus in-kind gifts

APPLICATIONS

1. Distinguish among price takers, price setters, and price searchers.
2. The Soviet Union's economy is much more efficient because wasteful inventories aren't present on store shelves. Comment.

3. Even when the Bureau of Indian Affairs gives Native Americans goods having high market values, why are the Native Americans sometimes ungrateful?

4. Rent controls make it possible for the poor to obtain apartments. Is this true?

5. Would price controls on kidney-dialysis machines make it possible for everyone to buy them? Who would benefit from the controls?

6. If racial discrimination in the selling of homes exists, how might you get rich?

7. When socialism replaces capitalism, cooperation will replace competition. Discuss.

8. Does the law of the jungle determine who receives goods in competitive markets?

9. Why are black markets and kickbacks so difficult to eliminate?

10. Secondary exchanges make it difficult to keep goods away from people of a particular sex, race, or creed. Explain.

11. If price controls were imposed on automobiles, what would happen to their durability?

12. Why do we wait for dentists, whereas grocery clerks wait for us?

13. At J.C. Penny's, why do some customers pay higher store prices while others pay lower catalogue prices?

14. Congressional seats are sold at the below-market price of zero. What are the economic effects of these below-clearing prices?

15. What are the 10 effects of distributing desirable men and women in Newport Beach at zero prices?

Capital Gains, Losses, Risk Allocation, and Conservation

Okay, here's what you've been waiting for. This is the chapter that deals with how people get rich by trading on the New York Stock Exchange, investing in real estate, or gambling on commodity futures.

Unfortunately, we explain and predict only that some people will obtain capital gains from their investments. We are not able to predict exactly who they will be, nor do we find out how to join them. If economists knew how to make millions predictably, they would spend less time teaching, writing, and doing research.

Of course, the bookstore has a whole shelf of books on how to get rich, most of them written by successful retired millionaires. Why don't we simply look at their advice? People who have gotten wealthy can surely tell us how to do likewise—right? Wrong. If they knew how they made their first million, they would be billionaires, not talk-show guests trying to advertise their manuscripts.

Explaining and predicting capital gains is only a subsidiary objective of this chapter. Our primary goal is to develop a theory of capital goods. The theory allows us to deal not only with capital gains, but also capital losses, selective risk allocation, and the economics of conservation.

We construct the theory by specifying that we can buy **capital goods**, goods we define very generally as any items that are expected to yield a flow of future goods. By defining **income** as a flow of goods, we can say that capital goods are items that are expected to yield future income.

We won't distinguish between physical and financial capital goods because our theory works equally well in either case. We need only recognize that future income can take a non-monetary form. According to our definition, homes, cars, land, shares of common stock, treasury bonds, and labor are all examples of capital goods. These items are expected to generate income in the form of streams of future shelter, transportation, crops, earnings, interest, and wages, respectively.

Notice that capital, which we defined as a produced resource, is a special case of a capital good. A unit of capital yields future income in the form of a stream of future productive services.

To explain the theory of capital goods, we revert to our usual format. We cover the theory with a description of selected phenomena, an explanation, some predictions, and a summary. Subsequently, we discuss some special topics.

The special topics will deal with some common theories of stock market values, why some landlords and bosses are nasty, capital losses at holiday time, and paper versus actual capital gains. The topics will also examine whether capital gains are a result of brains or luck, how monopolists make capital gains, and the occurrence of capital gains in socialist economic systems. And finally, the special topics will look into the economic effects of commodity futures markets, the economics of conservation, and the economic effects of land speculation.

A THEORY OF CAPITAL GOODS

The Phenomena

When we examine our market purchases, it is clear that in addition to present consumption goods, we buy capital goods, items that are expected to yield future income (future flows of goods). Not only do we buy goods for present consumption, but when we buy capital goods, we also purchase goods for future consumption.

After our initial purchases of capital goods, we also often sell some of them only so we can buy others. On the New York Stock Exchange, for example, investors often buy shares to replace others they just sold. Likewise, in real estate markets, commodity futures markets and the markets for still other capital goods, buyers sometimes make initial purchases, but at other times they only change the composition of their holdings.

An Explanation: Buying and Selling IBM Stock

We can explain our initial purchases of capital goods by first defining wealth. **Wealth** is the market value of all of the goods we own, the sum of the price times the quantity of each good in our possession.

Now suppose that your wealth is initially in the form of $500,000 in cash. What would you do? You would begin to trade the cash for other goods.

First, you would probably buy consumption goods such as food and clothing. These items would fulfill your present desires for survival and well being.

However, you would not spend all your money on consumption goods, since you would be concerned with the future as well as the present. As you bought more goods for immediate consumption, their values would fall below the values of some future goods. Perhaps after spending $10,000 on consumption goods, you would start buying some future goods in the form of capital commodities such as a car or a house. These commodities would give you streams of future consumption services.

Eventually, maybe after spending $200,000, you would become concerned with your ability to buy other future goods that were as yet unknown or unobtainable. You could keep the remaining $300,000 in cash for this purpose, but money is a barren asset. Instead, you would probably buy some financial capital goods such as common stocks, bonds, or treasury notes. You could expect to obtain future income in the form of a stream of future money from these assets, funds you could use to buy future consumption or capital commodities.

We have now explained our purchases of capital goods by pointing out that we want both present and future goods and can obtain future goods by purchasing capital goods. We have yet to explain why we later trade some capital goods for others. The reason is not obvious. After all, isn't $300,000 worth of IBM stock worth as much as $300,000 worth of land, bonds, commodity futures, or General Electric stock?

To explain why we sell some capital to buy others, let's focus on the purchase of a share of IBM common stock, starting with an examination of its value to investors. If you were an investor, the value of a share of IBM to you would depend on your present valuation of the future earnings that you would expect the share to generate. Your expectations of the future earnings, in turn, would be based on your interpretation of present, limited information about the future. The higher your expectations, the greater the value of the share; the lower the expectations, the smaller the value.

Suppose that, based on your interpretation of limited information, the stream of future earnings of a share of IBM stock had a present value to you of $100. Other investors would also interpret their present limited information and it is likely that they would reach different conclusions, causing their expectations to differ. If they valued the future earnings (and thus the share) of IBM at less than $100, you would be the one to buy.

After you bought into IBM, why might you later want to sell your share and buy other stock? Because as new information became available, you might interpret it differently than other investors, just as you interpreted the original information differently. If the new information made you more pessimistic than other investors, you would move out of IBM and into money. You could subsequently use the money to buy stock about which you were relatively sanguine, perhaps shares of General Electric. In short, we sell some capital goods to buy others because we often interpret new information about the prospective income of capital goods differently than other investors.

The Predictions

Buying and Selling Capital Goods

From this explanation, we can predict that if we value capital goods more than present consumption goods and also value capital goods more than other people, we will buy capital goods. If we later obtain new information that lowers our valuations of some of the capital goods we own below the values that other investors place on them, then we will sell those capital goods and may subsequently buy others which we value more.

Capital Gains and Losses

We can also make predictions that identify some of the effects of trading in capital goods. First, as a result of our purchases of capital goods, we will make capital gains and losses.

To explain, we first need to define capital gains and losses. **Capital gains** are unexpected increases in the prices or quantities of the capital goods we own. For example, if you own a pear tree and the price of pears unexpectedly doubles, you obtain a capital gain as the price of the tree increases.

The increases in the prices or quantities of capital goods must be unexpected for them to be capital gains. There are two reasons for this. First, we want to ignore saving. When people save their income, they can increase the quantities of capital goods that they own, but such increases in quantities are not capital gains.

Second, as we will see later in this and the next chapter, the prices of many capital goods will automatically rise because of time-value or other costs of conservation. The resulting increases in prices reflect compensations for predictable sacrifices rather than capital gains.

In contrast to capital gains, **capital losses** are unexpected decreases in the prices or quantities of the capital goods that we own. Thus, if the price of pears unexpectedly falls and reduces the price of your pear tree, you will incur a capital loss.

Like capital gains, capital losses must be unexpected. Expected reductions in the prices or quantities of capital goods are not capital losses. For instance, if the value of your pear tree falls as the tree ages or if you sell the tree, the reduction in price and quantity is not a capital loss.

The prices of capital goods are based on values. The values are based on expectations of future income. And, in turn, the expectations of future income are based on limited information. Therefore, when new information becomes available, it will unexpectedly change the values, which will unexpectedly change the prices. The unexpected price changes will be capital gains or losses.

For instance, if you own shares of IBM stock and it is unexpectedly revealed that IBM will be allowed to sell computers in Japan more freely, you and other investors will predict that IBM's future earnings will rise. The price of the IBM shares will then rise, giving you a capital gain. Conversely, if IBM unexpectedly loses an antitrust suit, you will incur a capital loss as the price of IBM shares falls.

Inability to Predict Capital Gains or Losses

We can also predict that we will be unable to successfully predict future capital gains or losses unless we have either

a. Secret information;
b. A special method of evaluating existing information;
c. A unique skill in predicting future prices.

This is because the prices of capital goods already reflect public information, the known methods of evaluating information, and the predictive abilities of most individuals. These three factors determine market expectations and, in turn, they determine market supplies, demands, and prices. Only extremely secret information, very special evaluation methods, and unique predictive skills are possessed by a small number of investors and thus have insignificant effects on market expectations and therefore market prices.

Selective Allocation of Capital Gains and Losses

Next, we can predict that we will obtain capital gains and losses selectively. We will make just the capital gains and losses that are associated with the particular capital goods that we happen to own. If the prices of other capital goods change, the capital gains and losses that result will accrue to other people.

It is impossible to avoid capital gains or losses. At any point in time, we have to hold our wealth in the form of some capital goods whose future incomes are never known with certainty. We can, for instance, avoid the capital gains and losses incurred from owning IBM stock by selling our shares, but we will then have to hold our wealth in the form of other capital goods, items also subject to price changes.

Even if we choose to hold money, we will obtain capital gains if deflation (a general decrease in prices) unexpectedly occurs. We will also incur capital losses if we encounter unexpected inflation.

Although we can't eliminate capital losses, we can reduce future capital losses (and capital gains) by purchasing capital goods whose prices fluctuate less. For instance, rather than holding IBM stock, we can buy 6-month treasury notes that have more stable prices.

We can also cut down on fluctuations in our wealth by purchasing many different types of capital goods rather than one type. If we own a greater variety of capital goods, then our wealth will be more stable. We can even buy some financial assets that already represent a portfolio of many capital goods. For example, the prices of mutual funds that own shares of different corporations, or holding companies that control various firms, will fluctuate less than the prices of their individual possessions.

Yet another way for us to cut down on our wealth fluctuations is to pool our wealth with others. Instead of investing $1 million in one small business, we may want to invest $500,000 in each of two partnerships.

Finally, if we want to retain the ownership of capital goods temporarily without accepting the capital losses that may result from future price changes, we may want to sell the goods in advance at presently determined prices. That way we will accept the risk of unexpected inflation rather than the risk of decreases in the future prices of those goods.

For example, if you were going to retire next year and move to Maine and if you did not want to gamble on the real estate market, you might want to sell your house 1 year in advance. That way you could live in the house and still be guaranteed a future price. If the market folded, you would not lose.

We can, of course, increase the fluctuations of our wealth by reversing the above tactics. We will obtain more capital gains and losses if we

a. Buy capital goods whose prices fluctuate a great deal;
b. Purchase one capital good rather than many;
c. Buy shares of one corporation rather than shares of mutual funds or holding companies;
d. Avoid pooling our wealth with other investors;
e. Not sell volatile assets in advance.

Shifting Goods Into the Future

Our purchases of capital goods will also shift consumption goods out of the present and into the future. For instance, if the capital goods we purchase are orange trees, then an increase in our demand for those trees will cause producers to reallocate resources away from the production of present consumption goods and into the planting of more orange trees. Fewer present consumption goods will then be available and more future oranges will be supplied.

From this perspective, our purchases of capital goods represent a greater demand for future consumption goods. Producers will respond by producing more of the future goods and fewer present ones.

As a special case, we can predict that we will convert some present consumption goods into capital goods by storing them for later consumption, as long as we expect that their future prices will cover the costs of holding them. We will conserve goods like wheat, corn, oil, and land for the future when we expect their future prices to exceed their present prices plus the costs of conservation.

Higher Present and Lower Future Prices of Consumption Goods

Next, our purchases of capital goods will tend to raise the prices of present consumption goods relative to the prices of future consumption goods. For instance, if we buy oil for future consumption, present demand for oil will increase and this will raise present oil prices. And since more oil will be available later, future oil prices will be lower.

Costs of Conservation

Finally, when we purchase capital goods, we will incur the costs of shifting goods into the future. The most significant of these costs will often be the sacrifices of present goods.

A Summary of the Theory

By recognizing both our desires for capital goods and the uncertainty of their future incomes, we can predict that we will

a. Buy capital goods and later sell some of them so we can buy other capital goods;

b. Obtain capital gains and losses from our ownership of capital goods;

c. Fail to predict capital gains without secret knowledge, special evaluation methods, or unique predictive skills;

d. Receive capital gains and incur capital losses selectively;

e. Reallocate consumption goods into the future;

f. Raise the present prices of consumption goods relative to the future prices of consumption goods;

g. Incur the costs of shifting goods into the future.

SPECIAL TOPICS

Common Explanations of the Values of Common Stock

If you asked most investors what determines the values of shares of common stock, few would cite the values of expected future earnings. Some common explanations are

a. Supplies and demands;

b. Psychological forces;

c. Price/earnings ratios;

d. The prices paid for physical facilities as revealed by the financial reports of firms.

Each of these claims is either wrong or limited in its usefulness. The allegation that the supplies and demands for the shares of common stocks determine the values of the shares is incomplete and backwards. Expected future earnings determine the values of the shares, and those values determine supplies and demands (which in turn determine the prices of the shares). When expected future earnings decline, for instance, the values of shares fall. This causes demands to decrease and supplies to increase. As a result, the prices of shares decline. Conversely, if expected future earnings rise, share values increase. Supplies then contract and demands expand, forcing share prices upward.

Next, psychological forces do seem to play a role in determining stock values, but we're left to wonder what determines the psychological forces. The psychological forces often reflect expected future earnings. Lower expected future earnings, for example, can put investors into a state of depression, pessimism, and panic. Stock values can then decline causing supplies to increase, demands to decrease, and prices to fall. If psychological forces were definitely not rooted in expectations of future incomes, we could get rich by purchasing shares each time the market was falling because of strictly emotional factors.

Price/earnings ratios are the current prices of shares divided by their current earnings. For instance, if a stock is selling for $100 per share and this year's earnings are $10 per share, the ratio is 10 to 1.

The ratios are only loosely related to stock values. Some stock market analysts, however, use price/earnings ratios to search for good buys. These analysts usually consider shares with low price/earnings ratios to be undervalued. But if this were true, the shares of all stocks on the New York Stock Exchange would have the same price/earnings ratio, since everyone would buy stocks with lower ratios and sell stocks with higher ones. This would change the prices of shares until all of the ratios were equal. Nevertheless, price/earnings ratios differ.

The problem with using price/earnings ratios to find undervalued stocks is that the ratios focus on the present, whereas the values of stocks depend primarily on the future. For example, suppose one stock is selling for $100 per share and has present earnings of $100 per share, yielding an incredible price/earnings ratio of 1:1. Suppose also that another stock is selling for $100 per share but has no current earnings, and therefore has an undefined ratio. Which stock is the better buy?

It may seem to be the first stock, but why would anyone sell $100 in earnings for $100, giving away all future earnings? Only if he or she believed there would be no future earnings. The first stock may be of a corporation that is about to go bankrupt or is already in the process of liquidation. On the other hand, why would anyone buy the second stock? Only if its expected future earnings were worth at least $100 per share. The second stock may be in a company that is developing a gold mine but has not yet begun to extract minerals. Present earnings are zero, but expected future earnings are significant.

Finally, financial records showing what was spent to purchase factories and other capital facilities do not reveal the values of stocks. For instance, an electronics firm may have originally sold $50 million worth of stock and spent the money to buy various physical assets. This does not, however, mean that the stock of the firm is now worth $50 million. If expected future earnings are presently worth only $500,000, then the stock is worth only $500,000. On the other hand, if the expected future earnings of the firm are presently worth $500 million, then the stock is worth $500 million.

Nasty Landlords and Bosses

Why are apartment houses not usually operated by the same people who volunteer to help the poor live through rent strikes? To explain, suppose an apartment house comes up for sale and two people are thinking of buying it. One is a scrooge who plans on collecting the rent on time. The other is a social worker who anticipates letting some tenants pay late or not at all. Who will pay more for the apartment house? The scrooge. To him or her, the value of the apartment will be greater since the expected future income will be greater.

Of course, if the scrooge eventually behaves too far out of line, tenants will move. The scrooge might then have to reduce rents drastically to attract and keep other tenants. In that case, the scrooge might sell the apartment to a more moderate landlord. Capital markets provide limits on how nasty as well as how nice landlords can be.

The markets also limit the behavior of bosses who buy and run small businesses. Bosses who treat employees too nicely (in the opinion of the market), will lose money; so will bosses who treat employees too harshly, since employee turnover will cause increases in recruitment and training.

Capital Losses at Holidays

Have you noticed that we're sometimes disappointed at Christmas, Hanukkah, or some other holiday even when we receive presents. Why? Because long before the holidays, most of us expect to obtain gifts from our friends and family. The expected gifts are capital goods, and we include their expected values in our wealth calculations. Then when we actually receive the gifts, we incur capital losses if they are less valuable than we had expected. Our wealth declines, and we have to work hard to appear delighted.

On the other hand, young children do not know what to expect and therefore their wealth does not totally include the future gains they will receive. As a result, they almost always obtain capital gains as they open presents. They are seldom anything but ecstatic.

If friends or relatives wanted us to feel as happy as children, they would find it very difficult. They would have to constantly give us more than we expected. Not only would this mean that they would have to provide us with more than the previous year, but, since we would soon expect more, they would have to give us even more than that. In the end, the only way they could provide us with capital gains would be to make us incur capital losses occasionally by giving us nothing or far less than we had expected.

Instant Versus Paper Capital Gains and Losses

When will the price of a capital good change—in the future when a different income is actually received or the moment new information about prospective income is obtained? The price will change the moment new information is obtained.

For example, the instant information indicates that IBM's earnings will be lower than previously expected, the price of IBM shares will fall, reflecting their lower value. As an owner, you will immediately incur a capital loss. On the other hand, if additional information subsequently indicates that future earnings will not fall, the price of the shares will rise and you will obtain a capital gain.

If the price of a share of stock that you own falls from $100 to $50, you may be tempted to say that the capital loss is only a "paper loss," since you have not sold the stock. Conversely, if the price subsequently rises from $50 to $100, you may want to call the capital gain only a paper gain. Nevertheless, you have incurred an actual capital loss and an actual capital gain; the prices of the capital goods you owned have unexpectedly fallen and then risen. After all, if you had sold the stock for $100 per share and used the money to later purchase twice as many shares for $50 per share, you could have avoided the capital loss and made only a capital gain.

Capital Gains: Brains Versus Luck

Evidence shows that very intelligent, diligent, and knowledgeable investors have done no better on the New York Stock Exchange than dull, lazy, and ignorant investors. Why has this happened? Because the prices of stocks already reflect the interpretations of present information by the most brilliant, hard-working, and knowledgeable security analysts. When individuals with these characteristics think that a stock is underpriced, their purchases cause the price to rise quickly until any expected gain is eliminated. Conversely, when these people believe a stock is overpriced, they sell their shares. The price then falls to reflect the lower expected future income.

From the evidence, it seems that to make capital gains with certainty, we have to have unique information or be smarter, harder working, and better informed than almost all professional investors. This is difficult to achieve, as evidenced by all the corporate presidents, stockbrokers, security analysts, and financial advisors who work for a living.

What about the millionaires? Perhaps they were simply the lucky ones. After all, people make millions in Las Vegas and this does not mean that they are wise, persistent, and knowledgeable. If millionaires knew how to get rich, they would be getting far richer and doing so faster.

Although many of us choose to gamble in the stock market, some of us have opted to take our chances in other arenas of trade, hoping to do better. However, studies of investors in bond, real estate, and commodity markets have yielded the same results: There is no observable characteristic that we can use to predict in advance who will make or lose money. Markets use existing information so well that beating the markets appears to be a game of chance. Although we may like to distinguish between gambling and investing, on close observation, it all looks like gambling.

If you can't beat organized markets, why not try to make capital gains by shopping at garage sales? At these sales, single sellers often do not know the market value of what they are selling. If you are the first and only buyer, you may be able to make a real killing. But be careful, many sellers at garage sales know more about what they're selling than you do. If capital gains could be made easily at garage sales, wouldn't we all be driving around town early on Saturday morning? Perhaps what many people consider to be capital gains earned at such sales are compensations that cover enormous shopping costs.

Monopoly Capital Gains

Next, we can predict that we also can't predictably earn capital gains by buying monopoly rights. To explain, we need to first define monopoly profits. By charging higher prices and selling lower quantities than competitive sellers, monopolists can increase total revenues and reduce total costs and thus increase their net gains from trade. Net gains from trade accruing to sellers under conditions of production are usually called **profits**. The proportion of net gains from trade that monopolists receive strictly because of their monopoly power are called **monopoly profits**. (Incidentally, because monopoly profits emanate from a fixity of supply, they are sometimes called **monopoly rents**.)

Although monopoly profits can be earned if monopoly rights are purchased, capital gains need not occur. This is because monopoly profits are predictable and are therefore included in the prices paid for monopoly rights.

For example, suppose information leads you to believe that you will obtain future monopoly profits now worth $1 million by having next year's exclusive concession rights at Miami International Airport. How much will you have to pay for the rights? Probably close to $1 million. This is because other vendors will also expect the future profits and bid against you as long as they expect to increase their wealth by buying the concession rights.

Next year, if expectations equal realizations, you will earn revenues above your additional costs. But such revenues will only compensate you for the $1 million you paid for the monopoly rights.

In all likelihood, however, you will earn some unexpected revenues and incur some unforeseen costs. As a result, you will make either capital gains or losses on your monopoly investment, just as you would from the purchase of any other capital good.

Socialist Systems

Do capital gains and losses occur in socialist economic systems? If we adopt a more general definition of capital gains and losses, yes.

In socialist systems, most capital goods are not traded in markets and therefore price changes will not yield capital gains and losses. But capital gains and losses will occur if we think of capital gains and losses as unexpected changes in the values rather than the prices or quantities of capital goods. Our theory argues that unexpected changes in the values of capital goods occur because of differences between expectations and realizations. Since differences between expectations and realizations exist under socialist as well as capitalist conditions, the theory predicts that capital gains and losses, in the form of unexpected changes in the values of capital goods, will occur under socialism.

The basic difference between capitalist and socialist circumstances lies in the way property is held. Under capitalism, property is owned by individuals; under socialism, it is owned collectively by a group. When individuals own property, they obtain capital gains and losses selectively. In contrast, when groups own property, individuals obtain capital gains and losses proportionately.

For example, in the capitalistic United States, people usually own only selected shares of the wealth of the nation, depending on which capital goods they buy. They can therefore concentrate their gambling according to their preferences. In contrast, the wealth of the Soviet Union is mostly held in common, as if the country were one huge corporation and each citizen had one share of stock. As a result, when the value of the nation unexpectedly rises, all citizens obtain a capital gain; when the value unexpectedly falls, they all incur a capital loss.

Of course, under capitalist conditions, individuals can form groups and own property together. Corporations and families are associations that, among other things, allow individuals to combine their ownership of capital goods and thereby share capital gains and losses. These are, however, voluntary cooperatives. Under socialist conditions, communal wealth holding is involuntary. When individuals are forced to own property collectively, they can't personally avoid the ownership of some capital goods and concentrate their wealth on other capital goods.

Commodity Wheat Futures

Our next special topic is one of the most interesting and important. We can use our theory to explain the economic effects of **commodity futures' markets**, institutions in which trades of future commodities are arranged in the present.

For example, rather than waiting until the September crop is harvested, farmers can sell their wheat in advance, in May, in a wheat futures market. They might want to sell their wheat in advance because although they might be willing to accept the risks related to growing and harvesting wheat, they may prefer to avoid gambling on September prices. If information available in May yields a general expectation of a $2-per-bushel September price, some farmers may want to sell immediately at the $2 price rather than risk a lower rate. Their expertise may lie in farming, not in understanding the world wheat market.

By selling the wheat in advance, the farmers shift their wealth out of future wheat and into future money. If the September price is above or below $2, capital gains or losses will accrue to the new owners of the wheat. The farmers will earn only the capital gains and losses associated with unexpected inflation or deflation, since they will receive the $2-per-bushel price.

What happens in September when the wheat is harvested? Do the owners of the wheat take delivery from the farmers? Not usually. The farmers normally sell the wheat at the market price and use the money to settle the futures' contracts. For example, if September wheat sells for $3, then rather than giving the wheat to the buyers for the prearranged $2 price, the farmers can sell the wheat on the market for $3, let the buyers of the futures' contracts keep their $2, and pay those buyers an additional $1. In contrast, if the September price is $1, the farmers can sell for $1 and receive another dollar from the buyers of the futures' contracts.

The presence of futures' markets erodes the claim that the government needs to intervene in the agricultural sector of the economy to protect farmers from radical shifts in prices. Where futures' markets exist, farmers can sell at known stable prices before they plant so much as one seed. In effect, futures' markets allow farmers to sell the capital gains and losses associated with future price fluctuations to others and bear only the capital gains and losses associated with unexpectedly large or small harvests.

Land Speculators

A final special topic is the explanation of the effects of land speculation. The effects illustrate each of the predictions of the theory. That is, if we speculate in land, we can predict the following:

a. We will buy land for speculation as long as we value its expected future yield more than its present price.

b. We will earn capital gains if new information indicates that the future value of the land will be greater than previously thought, and incur capital losses if new information implies a lower future value.

c. We will generally be unable to make more capital gains than losses from our purchases of property, unless we have either secret information, a special method of predicting the future, or a unique ability to find underpriced land. The prices of the land will already reflect present limited information as evaluated by the most intelligent, diligent, and knowledgeable real estate analysts, investors, and land owners.

d. We will make capital gains and losses selectively from the land that we purchase. Other investors will make the capital gains and losses associated with other capital goods that we choose not to buy.

e. We will conserve land for future buyers and consumers. As buyers, we will act as middlemen, representing future consumers in present markets. Market allocations will therefore reflect future as well as present consumers. In a sense, speculators are the conservationists of capitalism.

How much land will we conserve? Will we conserve too little or too much? There is no way to know. We can say only this: We, as speculators, will have an incentive to shift land into the future until future prices just cover present prices plus conservation costs. If we conserve too much, we will incur capital losses from low future prices. If we conserve too little, future prices will be high, implying that we could have earned greater capital gains had we conserved more.

f. We will force present land prices upward with our demands but reduce future land prices when we later sell.

g. We will incur the costs of shifting land into the future. That is, we will be the ones who make the present sacrifices. Higher future prices will therefore not always represent capital gains. Prices will have to be higher to compensate for interest and other storage costs.

Given these effects, why are speculators so disliked by many people? One reason is that many people fail to recognize that capital gains are unpredictable. When speculators earn capital gains, it may seem that they made no sacrifices. Nevertheless, they took the risk that capital losses would occur. As we have seen, capital losses occur as often as capital gains in normally functioning markets.

Second, present consumers may resent speculators because the speculators increase the demands for present goods and raise present prices. On the other hand, sellers may dislike speculators because speculators increase supplies and reduce prices when they sell goods that were purchased in the past.

Finally, some of the earnings of speculators will erroneously appear to be capital gains simply because future prices will generally be above past prices. However, the higher prices will often be expected and will often just compensate speculators for conservation costs.

So far, we have concentrated on some of the basic determinants of the prices of capital goods: expectations regarding their eventual incomes. We have not, however, said much about the actual prices of capital goods. In the next chapter, we will be able to discuss actual prices by introducing another complicating circumstance to our body of theory: We will recognize that present goods are more valuable than the same goods in the future.

MAJOR AND MINOR POINTS

1. Capital goods are items that are expected to generate future income (future flows of money or nonmoney goods).
2. Wealth is the market value of all of the goods we own.
3. We buy capital goods whenever we value their expected incomes more than present consumption goods.
4. The values of capital goods are determined by our valuations of the incomes that we expect them to generate. Our expectations of future incomes are in turn based on our personal interpretations of present limited information regarding the future.

5. We trade some capital goods for others because our interpretations of new information regarding the future incomes of capital goods differ. We will sell the capital goods about whose future incomes we're more pessimistic (relative to other investors) and buy the ones about whose incomes we're more optimistic.

6. Capital gains are unexpected increase in the prices or quantities of capital goods that we own.

7. Capital losses are unexpected decreases in the prices or quantities of the capital goods we own.

8. We will generally obtain capital gains and losses after we purchase capital goods because the values of capital goods are based on present limited information about prospective income, information that will change as the future becomes the present.

9. We will generally be unable to predict future capital gains with certainty unless we have secret information, special and superior methods of evaluating information, or unique predictive skills. Market prices will reflect public information, known methods, and rare (but not necessarily unique) predictive skills.

10. When we choose to own some capital goods and not others, we are selectively choosing to obtain particular capital gains and losses.

11. We can't totally eliminate the risk of capital losses, but we can reduce capital losses (and capital gains) by
    a. Purchasing capital goods whose prices fluctuate less;
    b. Buying many types of capital goods;
    c. Holding shares of mutual funds and holding companies;
    d. Pooling our assets with other investors;
    e. Selling volatile assets in advance.

12. Goods will be shifted into the future when we buy capital goods because the purchases will either increase in the production of capital relative to present goods or cause the conservation of present goods.

13. By buying capital goods, we tend to raise the prices of present goods relative to future ones.

14. When we buy capital goods, we incur the costs of conservation.

15. Supplies and demands, psychological forces, price/earnings ratios, and the amounts spent to buy capital do not determine the values of common stocks. Stock values are determined by the present values of expected future earnings.

16. The buyers of apartments and business firms will tend to be those who expect the greatest future income. As a result, landlords or bosses will eventually be neither too nasty nor too nice. Rather, they will respond to the dictates of the markets.

17. We make capital gains during the holiday season only if we receive more than we expected.

18. Capital gains and losses occur the instant that market values change. They also occur whether we sell our holdings or not; paper capital gains and losses are actual capital gains and losses.

19. There is no known characteristic or system that can allow someone to predict capital gains successfully. People who make millions seem to be lucky.

20. We can't generally knowingly obtain capital gains by purchasing monopoly rights. The prices of monopoly rights will equal the value of the future profits

from monopoly power. Capital gains and losses will, however, result when expectations and realizations differ.

21. When capital gains and losses are defined generally as unexpected changes in the values or quantities of capital goods, then socialism doesn't eliminate capital gains and losses since it fails to eliminate the existence of limited information about the future. Socialism only causes capital gains and losses to be borne communally rather than individually.

22. Futures' markets allow farmers to sell their crops in advance and avoid the capital gains and losses resulting from unanticipated future price changes.

23. Speculation in land causes the same economic effects that the purchases of other capital goods generate.

QUESTIONS

1. What are capital goods?
2. When do individuals buy capital goods?
3. When will individuals sell some capital goods only so they can buy other capital goods?
4. What are capital gains and losses?
5. Why do individuals incur capital gains and losses from their ownership of capital goods?
6. How can individuals reduce their risks of capital losses?
7. What requirements do individuals have to fulfill before they can knowingly obtain capital gains by buying capital goods?
8. How do the purchases of capital goods represent conservation?
9. How do the purchases of capital goods affect the present and future prices of consumption goods?
10. Who generally incurs the costs of conserving goods for the future?
11. Discuss the following terms and concepts:

Capital goods	Anticipating capital gains
Income	Paper versus actual capital gains
Wealth	Socialism and capital gains
The values of capital goods	Profits
Capital gains and losses	Monopoly profits
Supply, demand, and capital values	Selective risk-bearing
Psychological factors	Commodity futures' markets
Price/earnings ratios	Speculation
Expenditures on capital	Conservation

APPLICATIONS

1. Distinguish among money, capital, and capital goods.
2. What determines the value of an apple tree?
3. Would capital gains and losses occur in a world of unlimited information? Would there still be exchange and production?

4. If you hear that the earnings of National Steel are going to rise next quarter, why can't you buy the stock now and make a capital gain?
5. If you strike oil on your land, when will you obtain the capital gain, immediately, after the oil is sold, or when you sell the land?
6. Why do stockbrokers, bookies, security analysts, corporation presidents, and horse trainers get up in the morning and go to work?
7. What two conditions have to be fulfilled before you can knowingly buy some land and make a capital gain?
8. There are no known bad or good deals in the Wall Street Journal. Is this true?
9. What might be the easiest way to determine the value of the future earnings of Mobil Oil Company stock?
10. The Alaska Native Land Claims Settlement Act forces Alaska natives to hold wealth in the form of shares in native regional corporations. In what sense do the corporations represent socialism?
11. Explain all the economic effects of commodity trades in oil futures.
12. Conservationists just talk, speculators put their money where their mouth is. Evaluate.
13. In what sense are labor markets futures' markets?
14. Since people live only 80 years or so, future generations can't depend on speculators to conserve goods for them. Is this true? Explain.
15. Since land will be present in the future with or without speculators, land speculation results in a wasteful withdrawal of present land. Is this true? Explain.

8

Interest Rates and the Prices
of Capital Goods

In the preceding chapter, we introduced the complication of time into our body of theory. In particular, we recognized our desires for the future goods that capital goods can yield. By focusing on the uncertainty of those future goods, we were able to explain and predict capital gains, capital losses, and other related phenomena.

In this chapter, we specify that future goods are not only uncertain, but they are also less valuable than the same goods in the present. This complication makes our theory of capital goods more general by allowing it to predict that commodity and money interest rates will be positive and that the current prices of capital goods will lie below their future yields.

After the theory is presented and explained, the special topics are examined. The topics deal with the time-related behavior of children, the effects inflation has on money interest rates, the value of winning the New York lottery, and the prices of common stocks. The topics also examine how capital gains are made on bonds, the methods used in determining the values of capital projects, and the economics of solar energy.

THE THEORY OF CAPITAL GOODS (EXPANDED)

The Phenomena

To deal with the values of present and future goods, let's examine the direct exchanges of present and future goods under barter conditions. By focusing on barter trades, we avoid monetary complications.

Trades of present and future goods are commonly called **loans**. When loans occur under conditions of barter, debtors buy present commodities from creditors with promises to repay future commodities. Conversely, creditors buy future commodities by giving up present ones.

We can explain the occurrence of loans by arguing that whereas debtors and creditors usually want both present commodities and future commodities, they value them differently. Relative to future commodities, debtors value present commodities more than creditors. Loans occur because of value differentials.

This is hardly surprising, since our theory of free trade predicts that trade will occur when value differentials exist. What more can we observe? We see that across time and space, to buy present commodities, debtors have had to pay back more than an equal amount of future commodities. In other words, the prices of present commodities in terms of future commodities have universally exceeded one. For instance, to borrow one present apple, debtors have had to pay back more than one future apple.

We reveal the price of present in terms of future goods by citing the **interest** paid by the borrower to the creditor, the extra amount of future goods that must be repaid for the purchase of given present goods. For instance, if 100 present apples require a repayment of 105 apples next year, then the interest is 5 apples. We also usually identify interest as a yearly percentage of the quantity borrowed. In the case of the 100-apple loan, the interest rate is 5% per year.

Using interest terminology, we can say that real interest rates, rates reflecting the prices of present in terms of future commodities, have been positive (greater than zero).

An Explanation: Present and Future Apples

To explain why real interest rates have been positive, suppose you're a subsistence farmer who owns some very young apple trees. You expect the trees to yield both present and future apples, but they provide you with so few present apples and will yield so many future apples that present apples are worth more. Specifically, the distribution of the apples over time is skewed toward the future so much that you value today's apples 15% more than next year's apples.

You can't make the trees produce more apples now and less later, but suppose you can borrow from a neighbor who also has apple trees, but older ones. He has so many apples now and expects so few next year that he is initially willing to lend you apples at a zero interest rate, swapping an apple today for one next year.

Since both you and your neighbor are rational, you start borrowing and he begins lending. Although the trees still produce apples at the same times, you consume more present apples because your neighbor cuts today's consumption, but he will eat more future apples because you will reduce next year's consumption.

As he lends you more present apples, the values to him of the remaining apples he has rise (due to diminishing valuation in reverse). Eventually, present values rise to equal future values, and he refuses to lend any more apples at a zero interest rate.

Since you have simultaneously increased the quantity of present apples that you own, their value to you has also changed. The value has fallen to less than 15% more than next year's apples. Suppose he hasn't, however, satisfied your desire for present relative to future apples. To you, today's apples are still 10% more valuable than next year's apples.

Although further trade doesn't occur at a zero interest rate, it continues at rates between 0% and 10%. You buy more present apples and sell more future apples as long as your valuation of present apples exceeds that of future apples by more than the interest rate. Conversely, your neighbor sells more present apples and buys more future apples as long as his valuation of present apples exceeds that of future apples by less than the interest rate.

In time, the loans stop. Diminishing valuation eventually causes both you and your neighbor to value present apples at, say, 5% more than apples the next year.

Why have the loans stopped at an interest rate showing that present apples are more valuable than future apples? Because in combination, you and your neighbor have too few present relative to future apples given the values you place on apples over time. Trades have been able to eliminate interpersonal value differentials, but they have not eliminated **time-values** (values of goods that exist strictly because of the time in which the goods are available). Despite the greater values of present goods, the trees won't increase their present and reduce their future production, and you and your neighbor won't adjust your wants to fit the particular streams of apples that the trees yield.

The Predictions

Positive Real Interest Rates

From this example, we can derive the general prediction that if present commodities are scarce relative to future commodities, then real interest rates will be positive. The rates will be positive because they reflect prices and prices reflect values. If present commodities are scarce relative to future commodities, then present commodities will be more valuable than future commodities. As a result, the prices of present commodities in terms of future commodities will be greater than one. That is, to obtain some present commodity, the buyer will have to give more of a future commodity.

If we had more present and fewer future commodities, or if we changed our desires so that we wanted more future and less present commodities, the values of present and future goods could be brought to equality. Nevertheless, we have too few present commodities relative to future commodities given our values, and this makes present commodities more valuable.

Positive Money Interest Rates

Next, we can predict that if money is used in an economy, then money interest rates will be positive. This is because when we use money, exchanges of present and future commodities take the form of monetary loans. Debtors buy present dollars only so they can purchase more present commodities, whereas creditors buy future dollars only so they can obtain more future commodities. Since present commodities are more valuable than future commodities, present money is more valuable than future money. If, for example, present commodities are 5% more valuable than future commodities and if prices in the economy stay constant over time, then present money is 5% more valuable than future money. Finally, since prices reflect values, the greater present values of money show up in positive money interest rates in much the same way that the greater present values of commodities are reflected in positive real interest rates. For instance, if present money is 5% per year more valuable than future money, then the money interest rate will be 5% per year.

The Prices of Capital Goods

Finally, we can predict that the prices of capital goods will be less than the income that the capital goods yield. For example, if an apple tree will yield $100 worth of apples next year and then die, the present price of the tree will be less than $100.

Why? Because positive interest rates reveal that present goods are worth more than future goods, and this means that future goods are worth less than present ones. If $100 now is worth more than $100 next year, then $100 next year is worth less than $100 now. How much less? Since the interest rate tells how much more present goods are worth than future goods, we can use that rate to discount (reduce) future values to obtain present values. If the interest rate is 5%, then next year's goods are 5% less valuable than present ones. Specifically, discounting at 5% per year, $100 next year is worth only $95 now. This means that the value of an apple tree that we expect to yield $100 worth of apples next year is $95. As a result, the price of the tree will be $95, not $100.

A Summary of the Theory

Our expanded theory of capital goods, by recognizing the greater values of present relative to future goods, predicts that

    a. Interest rates on commodity loans will be positive.

    b. Interest rates on money loans will be positive.

    c. The prices of capital goods will be less than the income that the capital goods yield.

SPECIAL TOPICS

Lisa's Behavior

We can use our expanded theory of capital goods to explain why children sometimes behave differently than adults.

For instance, my 7-year-old daughter, Lisa, is a member of the Coho Swim Team. For well over 2 years, she has spent 1 1/2 hours per day, 4 days a week, swimming the butterfly, backstroke, breaststroke, and freestyle.

Lisa is motivated by daily rewards: Daddy's praise, new goggles, Orange Crush sodas, the fun of the locker room, etc. Her incentives don't include the prospect of an Olympic Gold Medal in the year 2000. That's far away and for Lisa, future goods are almost worthless.

If Lisa is like most of us, then, as she matures, the value she places on future goods will rise, although they will stay below the values of present goods. For now, however, she, like most children, places extremely high values on present relative to future goods.

A few weeks ago, to get some idea of just how much more Lisa values present goods, I gave her the option of either receiving one Orange Crush soda immediately or two the following week. She quickly picked the one present soda. I then offered her three future sodas and again, she opted for the present one. Eventually, Lisa, after much thought, barely accepted a promise of four future sodas. To her, four Orange Crushes one week later were apparently worth only one present Orange Crush. And a soda one year later was probably worth next to nothing.

By recognizing the enormous value that Lisa places on present relative to future goods, we can explain and predict a great deal of her behavior: For one thing, Lisa is not a good prospect if you want a loan. To borrow an Orange Crush from her, you would have to pay 300% interest per week. The baby loan shark wouldn't settle for much less, given the low value she places on the future interest plus principal.

Also, its hard to get a loan from Lisa because she has little to lend. She doesn't save. Moving goods out of the present and into the future is irrational, given her values. Whatever Lisa has, she tries to consume as fast as possible. Saving, a form of conservation, is inconceivable.

In fact, to the extent that she can, Lisa will consume more now by borrowing and promising to give her creditors future goods. She makes an excellent target for a loan shark. After all, Lisa is willing to pay almost 300%

weekly interest to obtain present Orange Crushes. For her, there is almost no tomorrow.

The relatively low values Lisa places on future goods also cause her to place relatively low values on capital goods, since capital goods generate future income that Lisa largely ignores because of her orientation toward the present. For instance, when Lisa buys toys, she is more interested in immediate gratification than in durability. When she purchases candy, her only concern is with how good it tastes, not how long it will last.

When I try to get Lisa to do something that she would prefer to avoid, time-value plays a vital role. The only effective rewards are the ones she will receive soon, since she will heavily discount distant gains. It would take four of next week's Orange Crushes to provide the same incentive generated by one of today's Orange Crushes.

The low value of future rewards means that Lisa won't necessarily go to school on her own accord, even if she knows the benefits of an education. Many of the benefits lie far in the future and consequently have a low present value.

Furthermore, threatening Lisa with a loss of next Saturday morning's cartoons if she doesn't clean her room is far less effective than an immediate reduction of viewing time. Present TV is worth much more than future TV, and therefore its loss has a greater significance. Lisa discounts future costs heavily relative to present costs.

Finally, the fact that future costs are lower partly explains why Lisa will procrastinate at every opportunity. If she has to clean up her room, tomorrow is always a better time than today. Even if tomorrow's sacrifices will be the same, their value will be lower because they lie in the future.

Money Interest Rates and Inflation

Some accountants believe that money interest rates are strictly monetary phenomena that are caused by inflation. But this is untrue. Let's explain why.

Inflation is a general increase in the money prices of nonmoney goods over time. Since more money must be used to buy the same nonmoney goods, the value of money falls during inflationary periods. This means that future money is less valuable than present money. For example, if the inflation rate is 25% per year, then future money will buy about 25% fewer goods than the same money a year earlier. Future money is therefore about 25% per year less valuable than present money. A borrower who wants present money and is willing to sacrifice future money will consequently have to promise to repay at least 25% more future money each year; the yearly money interest rate will be at least 25%.

Although inflation makes money interest rates positive, the rates tend to stay above the rate of inflation. This is because future dollars are not only less valuable than present dollars, but the future commodities that future dollars buy are less valuable than the present commodities that present dollars buy. Money interest rates will therefore include two compensations to lenders: one for the lower value of future money and another for the lower value of future commodities. For example, if, by itself, future money is 25% less valuable than present money and future commodities are 4% less valuable than present commodities, then the money interest rate will be 29%.

The adjustments for the lower value of future commodities make money interest rates a real as well as monetary phenomena. The money interest rate will be the sum of the real interest rate and the rate of expected inflation.

Winning the New York Lottery

In recent years, the state of New York has run a lottery. It claims that winners receive a $20 million prize, but the prize is worth much less. Let's see why.

The lottery pays the winners only $952,380 immediately. It then gives them $952,380 per year for the next 20 years. The twenty-one $952,380 payments sum to $20 million dollars, but since 20 of the payments are made in the future, the present value of the 21 payments lies far below $20 million.

How far? To answer, we have to deal with a few computation problems that we have so far ignored because we have focused on concepts.

The prize, like most capital goods, is expected to yield a complex multiyear stream of future goods. To compute the present value, otherwise called the **capital value**, of each of the future values within such a stream, we can use the present value formula below. The formula uses the interest rate to discount future values to their present values.

$$P = \frac{F}{(1 + i)^t}$$

where: P = present value
F = future value
i = the interest rate
t = the number of periods

If F = $952,380, t = 1, and i = .10, then P = $865,800. That is, the present value of a $952,380 payment made at the end of the first year, when the interest rate is 10%, is $865,800. In other words, the value of $952,380 obtained after 1 year, discounted at a 10% interest rate, is $865,800. Next, if we use the formula to compute the present value of a payment 2 years from now, we obtain a present value of only $787,091. The longer we have to wait for the money, the lower its present value.

Table 8.1 shows the present values of all 21 payments. Only the first is worth $952,380; the others are worth increasingly less.

TABLE 8.1   The Capital Value of the New York Lottery

> The capital value of the New York Lottery at a 10% discount rate is the present value (PV) of the various future values (FV) to be obtained in (*t*) years—that is, $9,060,205.

t	FV	PV		FV	PV
0	$952,380	$952,380	11	$952,380	$333,817
1	952,380	865,800	12	952,380	303,499
2	952,380	787,091	13	952,380	275,862
3	952,380	715,537	14	952,380	250,824
4	952,380	650,533	15	952,380	228,006
5	952,380	591,173	16	952,380	207,264
6	952,380	537,460	17	952,380	188,441
7	952,380	488,651	18	952,380	171,415
8	952,380	442,207	19	952,380	155,719
9	952,380	403,893	20	952,380	141,456
10	952,380	367,147			
				FV = $20,000,000	PV = $9,060,205

After computing the present values of all of the future payments, we see that at a 10% interest rate, the lottery prize is worth only $9,060,205, not $20 million.

We can avoid using the formula and make computations in our heads when we deal with the present values of perpetual, constant streams of dollars and a 10% rate of interest. We then have to figure out only how much we would have to put in a savings account paying 10% interest so that we could get a given stream of interest. For instance, we would have to deposit $1000 in a bank at 10% interest to get the bank to perpetually pay us $100 per year. Therefore, the present value of a perpetual $100 per year (a $100 per year perpetuity), when the interest rate is 10%, equals $1000.

Stock Market Prices

The shares of many stocks traded in the various exchanges around the world have generally yielded (total) incomes that were greater than the previous prices of the shares. Does this mean that the owners of such stocks made capital gains?

Not always. Since the prices were paid earlier and the incomes were obtained later, the differentials between the prices and the incomes were often expected and were necessary to compensate buyers for the higher-valued present dollars they gave to obtain relatively lower-valued future dollars. For capital gains to occur, earnings had to exceed past prices by more than the going rates of interest.

For example, if everyone knew that a share of General Motors stock would yield a perpetual $20 per year in income, then although the income would eventually sum to infinity, the present value of the (total) income would be a far smaller, finite amount. At a going interest rate of 10%, the income would have a present value of only $200, and this would cause the price of the share to be $200. By buying the share for $200, you would change only the form of your wealth. You wouldn't make a capital gain even though your income would be infinite.

Speculating on Bonds

Why do people earn capital gains and losses in bond markets, even though **bonds** are promises of debtors that guarantee creditors fixed streams of future dollars in the form of interest and principal? Part of the explanation is that there are no real guarantees. Borrowers often make promises that they can't keep.

Since there is a chance that bonds won't be paid off, the interest rates on bonds usually reflect not only a discount for time-value but also a discount for the possibility of default. For instance, although the time-value of present money may be 8% relative to future money, particular debtors may have to pay 10%. If the extra 2% is just the amount necessary to compensate creditors for the possibility of nonpayment, then the creditors as a group will receive the time-value of 8%. However, some creditors will make capital gains when they don't encounter their share of defaults, whereas others will incur capital losses when defaults are greater than normal.

Unanticipated repayments and defaults generate some capital gains and losses, but most capital gains and losses on bonds are unrelated to repayments and defaults. They emanate from unexpected changes in the time-values of money, changes that manifest themselves in new unforeseen money interest rates.

For example, suppose you can buy a $1000 perpetuity bond, a promise on the part of the seller to pay you $1000 per year, forever. Since future dollars are worth less than present dollars, you don't have to pay an infinite amount for the asset. The finite price you have to pay depends on what the "market" believes future dollars will be worth relative to present dollars. If, based on present limited information, the market thinks that dollars will be worth 10% less than the year before, then the bond will sell for $10,000. Printed on the bond may be a price of $10,000, an interest yield of 10%, and a promise to pay the bearer $1000 per year, forever.

Suppose you buy the bond for $10,000. What will happen on the following day if new information indicates that future dollars will be worth only 5% less per year than present dollars, rather than 10% less per year? Under these conditions, everyone will want to buy the bond. The bond will give its owner future dollars suddenly worth twice as much. You and other bond holders will, however, refuse to sell for the bond's printed $10,000 price. You will demand and be able to receive up to $20,000. As a result, your wealth will unexpectedly increase as you make a $10,000 capital gain.

Of course, the values of future dollars can unexpectedly fall as well as rise. If the values of future dollars fall to where future dollars are worth 20% less per year than present dollars, the rate of interest in the economy will rise to 20% per year and the value of your bond will fall to $5000. Your wealth will unexpectedly fall as you incur a $5000 capital loss.

Bonds are clearly risky investments. Not only is there always a chance that they won't be repaid, but the future values of their yields can fall to reduce the capital values of the bonds.

As with all capital goods, to avoid predictable capital losses and make only capital gains on bonds, we must have either some secret information, a unique method of evaluating information, or some special ability to predict future values. The bond market has already taken present limited information about future defaults and interest rates into account, and that information is already reflected in bond interest rates. We should therefore be leery of any economist who claims that interest rates will be different in the future, except to the extent that the markets already indicate the future changes. If anyone knew better than the bond market where interest rates were going to be, he or she could become very wealthy.

Should We Build a Dam to Generate Electricity?

Economists, accountants, and engineers are often asked to provide capital valuation studies that estimate the values of various proposed capital projects. Using our capital theory, we can explain how such studies are done.

For example, suppose the owners of a private corporation in Tennessee are thinking of building a dam across the Mississippi River to provide electricity in future decades and they commission an engineering firm to determine if the future values of the electricity will be sufficient to cover the costs of building and operating the dam. Although the engineers assigned to do the study will make many complex assumptions, they will use a relatively simple methodology: First, they will predict future streams of revenues and costs. Revenue projections will be based on factors such as the expected future prices and the demand for electricity, whereas cost projections will be based on other variables like the prices and quantities of resources necessary to construct and operate the dam. Then the researchers will attempt to determine when revenues will accrue and when costs will be incurred. Next, the future values of revenues and costs will be discounted to obtain their present values. And finally, the two totals will be compared. If the present values of revenues cover the present values of costs, the dam will be declared valuable (profitable or feasible).

The importance of discounting future values to their present values prior to making final judgements can't be underestimated when project costs will be incurred early and perpetual yields will be obtained late. Perpetual streams of future revenues will always cover construction costs if time-value reductions aren't made.

To be more specific, suppose the projected revenue and cost streams for the Mississippi dam are those shown in Table 8.2. Since the revenues go to infinity, they exceed the early costs. But whether the project is valuable depends on the present rather than the future values of the revenues and costs. Since the revenues generally occur far later than the costs, discounting for time-value reduces revenues much more.

If the researchers discount the future values in Table 8.2 at 10% per year, they will obtain the present values that the table reveals. At 10%, the project will have a projected capital value of about $66 million.

Two important questions usually arise whenever capital valuation studies like the preceding one are done. First, what interest rate should be used for discounting, and second, how should inflation be dealt with?

The choice of the interest rate is crucial. If higher interest rates are chosen, the values of capital projects will fall. The revenues of these projects occur much later than the costs and higher interest rates discount them more. On the other hand, if lower interest rates are selected, capital projects will rise in value. For instance, if the interest rate fell from 15% to 10%, and then from 10% to 5%, the value of the Mississippi dam project would rise from about −$200 million to $66 million and then from $66 million up to around $1 billion.

In our examples, we have chosen 10% only to simplify computations. When predicting actual present values, other interest rates are usually more appropriate. The most objective and often the most dependable rate is the market interest rate of bonds that have a similar risk and duration as the project being evaluated. For instance, the Mississippi dam project may be fairly risky and of long duration. The corporate BB long-term bond rate (the interest rate yield on fairly risky long-term corporate bonds) may therefore be the most appropriate rate for discounting.

The question of how to deal with inflation also has to be answered. It is important to remember that inflationary expectations are already reflected in money interest rates. Projected revenues and costs should therefore also include those expectations. And once they do, it is necessary to discount only by the

TABLE 8.2   *The Capital Value of a Dam*

At a 10% discount rate, the total present value of the future revenues of a dam exceeds the total present value of the future costs by $66 million. The dam therefore has a capital value of $66 million.

YEAR	0	1	2	3	(4 TO INFINITY)	TOTALS
Future revenues	—	—	—	$100M	$100M ...	Infinite
Present values	—	—	—	$75M	$683M	$758M
Future costs	$250M	$250M	$250M	$1M	$1M ...	Infinite
Present values	$250M	$227M	$207M	$.8M	$6.8M	$692M

money rates. Discounts to reflect both money interest rates and rates of inflation are redundant. They inaccurately and drastically reduce future values.

Solar Versus Gas Heat

Why don't we replace our gas heating systems with solar systems? Advocates of solar heating argue that the solar systems eventually and easily pay for themselves and that we are irrational for not installing them. Nevertheless, most of us continue to choose natural gas heating.

Our theory can help explain why we stay with natural gas. Even if the total expenditures on natural gas eventually add up to infinity, the present values of the expenditures generally fall below the costs of new solar systems.

For example, if natural gas were to cost you $600 per year, forever, and a solar heating system were to cost $10,000 to buy and install, then at a 10% interest rate, you would still keep the gas system. The future gas payments would eventually equal and then exceed $10,000, and in time, the payments would become infinite. However, at 10%, the present value of the $600-per-year payments is only $6000. If you bought the solar system, you would be spending $10,000 to save $6000. Buying the system would be irrational.

Some people think that the only reason they don't buy the solar system is that they lack the necessary cash. But if they could borrow the money, the irrationality of the solar system would become even more apparent. The people wouldn't have to pay the gas company $600 per year if they borrowed money and used it to install solar heat, but at 10% yearly interest, they would have to pay the bank $1000 per year on their $10,000 loan.

Many of the choices we face require us to compare stocks of benefits or costs to flows of benefits or costs. Our capital theory allows us to make such comparisons. The trick is to convert both options either to stocks or to flows. For instance, we can compare the $10,000 stock cost of solar heat to the savings flow of $600 per year by converting the $600 per year flow to a stock value of $6000. The $10,000 expenditure obviously doesn't cover the $6000 savings. Or, we can convert the stock cost of $10,000 to a perpetual flow of $1000 per year. The $1000 yearly flow cost clearly exceeds the $600 flow savings.

For simplicity, we have in this and previous chapters focused on exchange, assuming that all goods come as "manna from heaven." Nevertheless, we can understand many economic phenomena only if we introduce the complexities of production. Most goods must be produced before they are exchanged and consumed. In the next chapter, we will turn our attention to the production of goods from scarce and substitutable resources.

MAJOR AND MINOR POINTS

1. Loans represent trades of present and future goods.
2. Loans occur because, relative to future goods, debtors value present goods more than creditors.

3. Since prices reflect values, positive real interest rates reveal that present commodities are more valuable than the same commodities in the future.

4. Goods can have a time-value, a value that results because of the time in which the goods are available.

5. Present commodities are more valuable than future commodities because a scarcity of present commodities exists relative to future commodities.

6. Since present money can purchase present commodities and future money can purchase future commodities and since present commodities are worth more then future commodities, present money is worth more than future money.

7. Because prices reflect values and present money is more valuable than future money, money interest rates are positive.

8. Capital goods are items that are expected to yield income (a flow of future goods). Since present goods are more valuable than future goods, future goods are less valuable than present goods. Consequently, we can predict that the prices of capital goods will be less than the incomes that the capital goods are expected to yield.

9. When interest rates are positive, we must discount (reduce) future values to obtain present values.

10. Because children usually value future goods less than we do, they will tend to:
    a. Respond to present rather than future rewards;
    b. Be debtors rather than creditors;
    c. Charge high interest rates on loans;
    d. Pay high interest rates to borrow;
    e. Avoid saving;
    f. Buy very few capital goods;
    g. Respond to present costs and ignore future ones;
    h. Procrastinate.

11. Money interest rates reflect both the higher present values of commodities and the expectations of inflation.

12. To compute the present value, the capital value, of a future value, we can use the following present value formula:

$$P = \frac{F}{(1 + i)^t}$$

where: P = present value
F = future value
i = the interest rate
t = the number of periods

13. We can also compute the value of a perpetuity (a fixed amount of money received each year, forever) at 10% by simply calculating in our heads how much money we would have to put into a bank savings account to have the bank pay us that amount forever at a 10% interest rate. A $5000 perpetuity is worth $50,000, since at 10% interest, a bank will pay us $5000 every year in interest as long as we leave the money in the account.

14. The prices of shares of common stocks are less than the incomes that the shares are expected to yield. The prices equal the present values of the expected future incomes.

15. Capital gains and losses can be earned on the bond market. They can occur when default rates are unexpectedly low or high. They can also occur when the present values of future goods unexpectedly change. If interest rates suddenly fall, bond prices will rise, generating capital gains for creditors. But if interest rates unexpectedly rise, creditors will incur capital losses as bond prices fall.

16. Capital valuation studies usually compare the present values of future streams of revenues and costs.

17. The capital costs of solar heat usually exceed the present values of the infinite streams of natural gas payments we expect to pay. As a result, we don't often buy and install solar heating systems.

18. Capital theory allows us to compare stocks and flows by converting stocks to flows or vice versa.

QUESTIONS

1. What is the nature of a loan?
2. Why is the real interest rate positive?
3. Why is the money interest rate positive?
4. Why are the prices of some capital goods below the incomes that they will yield?
5. Discuss the following terms and concepts:

Loans	Discounting
Interest	The present value formula
The real interest rate	Capital gains and losses on
Money interest rates	bonds
Inflation	Capital valuation studies
Prices of capital goods	The choice of discount rates
Capital values	Stocks and flows

APPLICATIONS

1. All of us value future goods less than present goods by the degree reflected in the rate of interest. In what sense is this true?
2. What would happen to the rate of interest if a nuclear war was suddenly expected in the near future? Why?
3. Are present goods more valuable than future goods in socialist as well as capitalist economies?
4. Are capital gains and interest rates phenomena that arise from production?
5. All other things the same, why might college students be less likely to borrow money?
6. Are interest rates monetary phenomena?
7. If the interest rate is 10%, what is the present value of a car that will yield $1000 per year in transportation services for 5 years?
8. You expect to earn $40,000 per year, forever. If the interest rate is 10%, how much is your labor worth now? What if the interest rate rises or falls while your expected income remains the same?

9. If the interest rate is 10%, how much is a share of common stock that will perpetually yield $40 per year in dividends worth now? What if the interest rate rises or falls and the yield remains the same?

10. Relative to the price you paid for shares of Chrysler Corporation stock, your yearly rate of return is 2%. Have you increased your wealth by buying the shares?

11. Suppose a criminal can obtain $10,000 by committing a robbery and the cost of being caught is $15,000. How can a rational criminal still commit the crime?

12. How will higher anticipated inflation affect the price of a home mortgage? A hotel? A common stock? Why?

13. If you were asked to determine the value of a small business so that a divorced woman could get her half of community property, how would you go about it?

14. The U.S. Army Corps of Engineers builds capital projects. Why do you think the corps has historically used a low interest rate to determine the feasibility of these projects?

15. Suppose you could drop a well for a total present cost of $3000. If you also had the option of hooking up to the public water utility for $30 per month, forever, which would you choose?

Production and Its Costs

Newton's physical law of the conservation of matter states that matter can be neither created nor destroyed. Its value can, however, be increased. So far we have seen how we can increase the values of goods by moving them among us as we trade. We can also often increase the values of goods by combining them into products during **production**.

In this chapter, we examine and then apply a general theory of production. By recognizing that economic individuals confront circumstances that include limited and substitutable resources, we are able to explain and predict many phenomena related to production and its costs.

After we have discussed the theory, we look at some special topics. This time the special topics deal with the effects of war on an economy, the extent to which government subsidies can increase national output, the trade-offs between work and leisure, the story of Chicken Little and production, and the economics of procrastination. The topics also deal with purchases of bankrupt ski areas, the liquidation of profitable farms, the cost of a mercenary army relative to a draft army, why panics occur, and the problems of motivating chief executive officers (CEOs) of business firms.

A THEORY OF PRODUCTION

The Phenomena

On any given day, most of us usually go to work, combine our labor with other resources, and generate limited quantities of a variety of products. In fact, we often spend more time producing goods than consuming them.

An Explanation: Eric the Subsistence Farmer

To explain why we produce, why we produce limited amounts, and why we produce a mix of products, let's discuss an example involving Eric, a subsistence farmer who resides in Montana. Eric lives by himself on 50 acres of land and produces almost everything he consumes.

Resources: Land, Labor, and Capital

Although Eric lives off the land, he produces goods the same way that we all do; he combines goods called **resources** into final products. Eric's resources, also called **factors of production**, fall into three groups: land, labor, and capital.

Land includes all natural resources. The most significant attribute of land is that it is fixed in supply. Eric's land comprises 50 acres and everything under and over it.

Labor is the unskilled natural ability of people. It is the basic human resource. Eric's labor supply consists of his personal efforts.

Finally, **capital** consists of goods that have been produced so that they can be used to produce other goods. Eric has purchased capital in the form of tools, a chain saw, seeds, a rifle, animal traps, a fishing pole, and other equipment so he can build, farm, hunt, trap, and fish.

Eric also owns one intangible capital resource: capital in the form of **technology**, knowledge of how to combine goods into other goods. Eric has learned how to hunt from his father, knowledge that has been produced by a combination of his efforts, his father's advice, rifles, and other equipment.

Eric obtained his hunting knowledge as a by-product of his past hunting trips. This is, however, unusual. We normally obtain technology as a result of explicit decisions to shift resources away from the production of other goods and toward education, research, and development.

Another intangible capital resource that Eric owns is **entrepreneurial ability**, the skills and knowledge used to direct and control other resources so that production can occur. Eric must determine which goods to produce, how to produce them, and accept the risks associated with production. Some economists refer to entrepreneurial ability as a distinct resource, the fourth factor of production.

Eric also has some money. Money is, however, a resource only in a very special way. By serving as a medium of exchange, it allows Eric to reduce his transaction costs on the few occasions when he purchases goods in town. But money is useless otherwise; it is incapable of producing anything.

We can say even more about money if we look at it from a national perspective. In the United States, money acts as a resource to produce transaction services, and it thereby reduces transaction costs. Once money is present, however, an increase in its supply will not reduce those costs further nor will it allow more goods to be produced. Unfortunately, an increase in the supply of money tends to inflate only prices, not abilities to produce.

Many businesspersons refer to money as capital because they must have money before they can produce goods. Nevertheless, they don't produce with money. They produce with the resources that money can buy.

Limited and Substitutable Resources

Eric realizes that he has a limited number of resources. Consequently, he also knows that he can produce only a given total quantity of products. His finite resources constantly constrain his total output. However, he does have many production choices because his resources are substitutable; they can each be used in the production of a variety of products. For example, to cut more spruce, Eric can shift resources from his vegetable garden; to hunt more elk, he can reallocate resources from fishing.

For simplicity, let's focus on two products, wood and vegetables, and assume that Eric's production options are as depicted in Table 9.1. The schedule in the table is called a **production possibilities schedule**, since it identifies various possible combinations of goods that can be produced with existing resources at a given moment of time. The particular schedule shows five possible combinations of cords of wood and pounds of vegetables.

TABLE 9.1   A Production Possibilities
Schedule

> Eric can produce various combinations of wood and vegetables. If all his resources are employed as efficiently as possible, he can produce more wood only by sacrificing vegetables, and vice versa.

(1) WOOD	(2) VEGETABLES
20	0
15	150
10	300
5	450
0	600

The columns reveal that since resources are scarce and substitutable, production possibilities are limited and various. Eric can't produce as many vegetables or as much wood as he wants, but he can increase his production of one of the products if he is willing to forgo the production of some of the other. For instance, he can produce 300 pounds of vegetables instead of only 150 if he is willing to reduce wood output from 15 to 10 cords.

We can graphically illustrate the production possibilities available to Eric with the **production possibilities frontier** shown in Figure 9.1. You can construct the frontier in the same way that we derived previous curves: Plot the various combinations of wood and vegetables as points on the graph and then connect the points. The resulting line is called a frontier because any point on or inside it can be produced, but combinations beyond the frontier require more resources than are available and hence represent presently unattainable combinations.

Product Values Equal Costs

So far we have identified only Eric's options. What can we say about his actual production decisions? If Eric is an economic individual concerned with maximizing his net gains from production, we can make two claims. First, Eric will choose a combination on his frontier. He could select one inside and let some of his resources go either unused or used in a way that would not yield maximum possible production, but this would be irrational. Eric always prefers valuable products to idle or wasted resources.

Second, Eric will pick the combination of wood and vegetables on the frontier such that the value of each good is equal to its cost, which is the value of the quantity of the other good that is sacrificed. (Remember, value refers to the value of the next unit of a good, not to the total value of all units chosen or sacrificed.)

To explain, let's look at one of many possible ways by which Eric could find the optimal combination. Suppose that cords of wood were initially

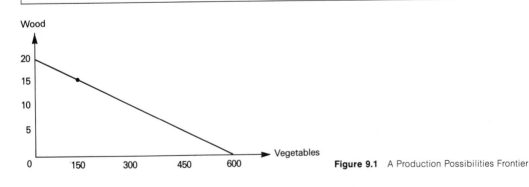

Eric can produce any combination of resources on or inside the production possibilities frontier. But Eric can't produce a combination beyond the frontier.

Figure 9.1   A Production Possibilities Frontier

more valuable than pounds of vegetables. As a result, he would begin by pro-ducing the wood. The opportunity cost of cords of wood would be the value of the pounds of vegetables sacrificed. As long as the value of cords of wood exceeded the value of the pounds of vegetables sacrificed, as long as the value gained exceeded the cost, Eric would continue to produce more wood.

However, due to diminishing valuation, as he opted for additional cords of wood, the value of wood would fall. Once the value of additional cords of wood dropped below the value of the pounds of vegetables sacrificed, Eric would begin to select vegetables. But the value of vegetables would also fall as he selected more, forcing him to eventually shift back to wood. Eric might flip back and forth between the two goods, choosing more of each until he ex-hausted his resources.

Once he ran out of resources, Eric would be producing the combina-tion of cords of wood and pounds of vegetables (say, 15 cords of wood and 150 pounds of vegetables) such that the value of cords of wood would equal the cost, the value of the sacrificed vegetables. At any other combination, cords of wood would have been either more or less valuable than the sacrificed vegetables and this would have caused Eric to shift production toward the more valuable product.

The Predictions

Producing Limited and Various Products

From this explanation, we can predict that we will produce, produc-ing limited quantities of products and a variety of products. We will produce because products are more valuable than unused resources. We will produce limited quantities of products because we have limited resources. And we will produce a variety of products because our substitutable resources give us the option and being economic individuals will make us exercise that option.

Higher Cost, Lower Production

If our explanation is correct, then we can say more about our behav-ior: We can also predict that we will produce less of a product if its cost rises and more if its cost falls.

For example, if the cost of wood rose because of an increase in the value of vegetables, Eric would reduce his production of wood and increase his production of vegetables. The reasoning is simple: To be rational, Eric had to equate the value of wood to their cost, the value of sacrificed vegetables. An increase in the cost of wood would imply an increase in the value of sacrificed vegetables above the value of produced wood. As a result, Eric would reallocate his resources away from wood and toward vegetables.

As he gave up more wood and gained more vegetables, the value of wood would rise and that of vegetables would fall. Eventually, the value of wood would again equal the value of the sacrificed vegetables. Eric would then stop shifting his resources and produce the associated combination of the two products.

Indicators of Opportunity Costs

The costs we have been referring to are the opportunity costs of production, the values of the highest-valued alternatives sacrificed as goods are produced. When we look at Eric's simple circumstances, opportunity costs are fairly easy to determine. But under more complex conditions, opportunity costs are less apparent. As a result, we are sometimes forced to use indicators that only approximate those costs.

Many indicators for opportunity costs exist. Let's take a close look at five of the most common ones and, in each case, examine both how they are related to costs and how they can sometimes be misleading.

A first indicator is the use of resources. It is useful because, all other things the same, if more resources are used to produce a given product, more alternative goods are sacrificed, and this means that the cost of production rises.

However, the use of resources can sometimes inaccurately reflect the cost of production, because even when the same resources are employed, costs can vary if the resources are used at different times. For example, although it takes Eric just as long to cut wood in the summer as in the fall, he is nevertheless able to reduce his cost of wood by cutting in the fall. In summer, he would have to give up more vegetables for the same cords of wood.

A second indicator is historical cost. It refers to the sacrifices that have already been made. The indicator predicts future costs whenever past sacrifices are indicative of future sacrifices.

Past sacrifices are, however, gone and are not the opportunity costs of present production. Only present and future sacrifices determine production costs. If future sacrifices are higher or lower than past ones, historical costs will be misleading cost indicators.

For instance, suppose Eric wants water for his cabin and can obtain it only by digging a well. If the value of water is $1000 and he expects to sacrifice less than that, he will begin to dig the well. If he sacrifices $1000 worth of goods and still doesn't strike water, will he keep digging? Not if the past sacrifices imply that future costs will exceed $1000.

However, if he still values water at $1000 and expects that it will cost him less than another $1000 worth of goods to find water, he will continue. Although he may have already sacrificed $1000 worth of other products, those sacrifices are gone. He will incur those costs whether he digs further or not. In the end, Eric may seem irrational if he winds up sacrificing goods worth $5000 for water worth $1000. Nevertheless, he would have still behaved rationally as long as the expected future cost remained below $1000 each step of the way.

A third indicator for opportunity costs is the price paid for resources. Even though the prices of resources are the opportunity costs of buying the resources, the prices can also reflect the opportunity costs of production if the prices reflect the values of the alternative products that the resources can produce. Land that has a price of $10,000 can usually contribute $10,000 to the values of products. Otherwise it wouldn't sell for $10,000.

However, if resources are held for a long time and if the values or quantities of the alternative products that the resources can produce radically change, then past resource prices will greatly over- or understate production costs. For instance, if a company buys an office building for a price of $3 million, that price will probably reflect the opportunity cost of occupying the building at that time. But if economic expansion subsequently occurs and the value of office space doubles, then the opportunity cost of occupying the building will be $6 million, not just $3 million.

A fourth indicator is the price of a product. It directly reveals the opportunity cost of buying the product, but it can also reflect the opportunity cost of production. For example, if the price of wheat is $3 per bushel and if it tends to remain $3 per bushel, we can be fairly certain that wheat costs farmers $3 per bushel to produce. If the cost were greater than the price, farmers would produce less and thereby reduce the supply and cause the price to rise. Conversely, if the cost were lower than the price, farmers would produce more, increase the supply, and drive the price downward.

Nevertheless, the price of the product will often fail to reflect the costs of production when goods are produced by governments or by nonprofit firms unconcerned with revenues. For instance, a school system may provide school lunches at a zero price, but the costs will be far from zero. Like everyone else, the system will have to employ resources to produce the lunches, resources that could have produced other valuable products. As the saying goes, there is no such thing as a free lunch.

Finally, we can often use the average group cost of production as an indicator for the cost that the individuals in the group incur. When costs are spread evenly, a high average cost means that the individuals in a group incur a high individual cost; a low average cost means a low individual cost.

But there are many cases where group costs are not spread evenly among group members. In these circumstances, the average group cost can be high even though many individuals within the groups have an individual cost that is low or zero.

Since individuals make decisions based on the personal cost that they incur rather than on the basis of the average group cost, average group costs can be poor predictors of group behavior. For example, suppose that 90% of an army of soldiers will lose their lives if a given battle is fought and won. The soldiers would probably argue that the cost of the battle isn't worth the victory. However, a general might nevertheless order the fight to begin. Even if the group's average cost exceeds the average value of the gain, the general's personal cost may be below the value of his gain. The general may stand only a small chance of being killed, may place a small value on the lives of his soldiers, and may value victory a great deal.

All the preceding indicators can reflect opportunity cost under some conditions. When they fail, however, they give rise to some incredible misunderstandings, some of which we discuss when we look at our special topics.

A Summary of the Theory

Our theory assumes that we are economic individuals who have limited but substitutable resources. It predicts that we will

    a. Engage in production;
    b. Produce a limited total output;
    c. Produce a mix of products;
    d. Produce less of a product if its cost rises and more if its cost falls.

SPECIAL TOPICS

Wars, Government Spending, Taxes, and Money

Although we have developed the production possibilities frontier to help us understand the production decisions of individuals, we can also employ the tool to analyze the production choices of groups. After all, groups also have scarce and substitutable resources.

For example, we can use the frontier to explain what happened in the past when the United States went to war. Many people believe that war has always caused an increase in production, but we can show that this has only occurred sometimes.

Whether national output expanded depended on the combination that had been produced before the war. When the economy was operating on its production possibilities frontier, a war was able to only modify the composition of total output; more war goods were produced because some consumption and capital goods were sacrificed. We can illustrate this on the frontier shown in Figure 9.2 as a movement from A to B.

This happened during the Civil War. The impression that the war increased output was probably given by the expansion of war-related industries. Nevertheless, since the economy was operating at almost full employment prior to the war, the expansion of those industries was made possible by the contraction of other industries.

World War II was a different case altogether. Prior to the war, the U.S. economy was in the depths of the Great Depression, well within its frontier, as illustrated by point C. As a result, that war was able to stimulate the employment of formerly unemployed resources, causing total output to rise. The economy was then able to move to a point such as B.

We can use the same logic to analyze the effects of more government spending, lower taxes, or a greater money supply. Any of these factors can

Figure 9.2 War versus Consumption and Capital Goods

If a nation is producing on its production possibilities frontier, then a war can only change to composition of total output, as the movement from *A* to *B* indicates. But if the nation is inside its frontier, then a war can increase total output, as the movement from *C* to *B* indicates.

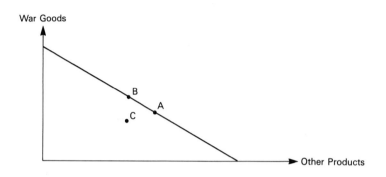

sometimes stimulate output if our economy lies inside its frontier. Formerly unemployed resources can then be put to work. But if output is already at a maximum, only the composition of total production can change.

Government Subsidies to Increase Production

How can the government increase the production of an industry? Since goods are produced by resources, the government can increase the productive ability of an industry only by either giving it more resources or providing it with money to buy more resources.

If the government helps an industry during a period when unemployed resources are available, it can increase the productive ability of one industry without reducing the productive ability of another. On the other hand, if full employment exists, all the government can do is reallocate resources, helping one industry and hurting another.

Although government industrial subsidies during periods of full employment tend to merely redistribute production rather than raise it, politicians may nevertheless recognize only the positive effects. One reason is that while the help that industries receive and their expansions are fairly visible, the harm done to other industries tends to be more subtle. When a government helps an industry, a law is usually passed earmarking funds that are then given directly to the firms within the industry or to the consumers of the products of the firms. The law, the money, and the resulting expansion of the industry are easy for everyone to identify. In contrast, no law is passed saying that other industries must sacrifice resources. Other industries are only indirectly forced to buy fewer resources because they either pay more taxes or can't compete with subsidized firms for resources.

Also, although the beneficial effects of government aid are usually concentrated, the adverse effects on other industries tend to be dispersed. As a result, the adverse effects often seem insignificant, even unmeasurable, although they may add up to enormous absolute amounts.

Work, Leisure, and Unemployment

One of the basic choices we must all make involves work versus rest and relaxation. We can use our theory to explain and predict which combination of work and leisure we will select.

To explain the work-leisure decision, we need to divide possible products into two groups: leisure and other products. We can then illustrate the options available with the production possibilities frontier in Figure 9.3.

Using this frontier, what can we say about our choices? First, we will select a combination on the frontier. If we selected a combination inside, we would either be unemployed or underemployed. **Unemployment** is a condition wherein some resources are unused. **Underemployment** occurs when resources are employed, but in a physically inefficient way, in a manner such that it is possible to increase the production of one good without reducing the production of another. In either case, we would be irrational to produce inside the frontier and thereby sacrifice valuable products or leisure for nothing.

Second, we will choose the particular combination of leisure and other products on the frontier such that the values of the goods chosen will equal their costs. If we began on the frontier by looking at the combination giving us only leisure and no other products, the value of leisure would be below that of other products. We would then move along the frontier, selecting more of the other products and less leisure until the value of the other products equalled the value of the leisure sacrificed. Eventually, we would not only pick a combination on the frontier that is physically efficient, we would also choose the

Figure 9.3 Other Products versus Leisure

If leisure is considered a product that can be produced by labor, then a production possibilities frontier can illustrate the trade-off between leisure and other products.

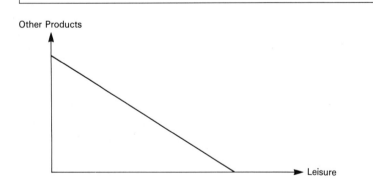

one combination that is **economically efficient**, the combination that wouldn't let us produce more of one product without sacrificing a more valuable alternative.

Chicken Little and Production

In recent years, many people have expressed a fear that the prosperity of United States is at an end. They cite the existence of the huge national debt, competition from foreign producers, the balance of payments deficit, the low price of the dollar, the rise and fall of the Roman Empire, and so forth. Without discussing any of these arguments specifically, our theory allows us to analyze these claims by revealing the foundation of our prosperity. The reason we have so much is that we have many resources and those resources can produce large quantities of valuable products. As long as we have those resources, the sky is not going to fall, at least not all the way.

What about the exhaustion of natural resources? Such an exhaustion seems unlikely in the near future. Natural resources are fairly abundant and easy to acquire. In fact, less than 10% of total wealth can be attributed to natural resources. This explains why Switzerland, Israel, and Japan can have high standards of living even though they have few natural resources. The resources that seem to be most important to production are educated labor and other capital. It is the abundance of these resources in developed countries like the United States, Sweden, and West Germany that explains why these nations produce so much.

This and the preceding three special topics have dealt directly with the allocations of resources among alternative products. The remaining five focus on the superiority of the opportunity cost concept over the various indicators of opportunity costs.

Why Procrastinate?

Is it rational for us to procrastinate, to put off until later what we can do now? Yes. Although procrastination can't usually reduce the quantity of resources used in production, it can often reduce the cost of production.

For example, it may always take you half an hour to do the dishes, but you may still prefer to do them at 7 P.M. rather than at 6 P.M. By washing them later, you may be giving up an almost worthless television program rather than an evening news program.

Using the same reasoning, we can explain why automobile mechanics often want to keep your car for 3 days to do a 1-hour tune-up. They can then delay and prolong production so that they work during the hour that results in the lowest sacrifices. If you want your car tuned immediately, they may be happy to do it, but only if you cover their higher cost with a higher price.

Finally, we can explain why building subcontractors often show up and finish jobs later than promised. It is because the contractors try to work on many jobs at one time, stretching out each one so they can do it when it costs the least.

Buying a Bankrupt Ski Area

After creditors have attached the assets of a bankrupt firm, the creditors often choose to continue production. Why? Not because they can thereby retrieve past costs. Past costs are gone. It is usually because future expected opportunity costs are covered by future expected revenues.

For example, suppose an entrepreneur expects that by building a ski area in Wyoming, she will have to incur $10 million of construction costs to build a chair lift and a lodge plus an additional $1 million of operating and maintenance costs each year. To cover these costs, suppose she expects to obtain $20 million per year in revenues. The venture certainly looks profitable. She decides to invest $1 million of her own money and borrows $10 million from various creditors at 10% interest. She then uses the $11 million to buy resources to build and operate the ski area for one year.

Unfortunately, at the end of the first year, she discovers that revenues have only been $1,100,000, not $20 million. Since her operating costs are $1,000,000 and her interest payments are another $1,000,000, she's in trouble.

If she had used her own money instead of that of creditors to build the facility, she would have accepted the loss and continued to operate. The costs of the lodge and lift would have been gone and irretrievable. Since the $1,100,000 in revenues would have covered the operating and maintenance costs of $1 million, she would have been left with $100,000 more by operating than by closing down.

Nevertheless, since she has borrowed the money to finance construction, she has to pay out both the $1 million in operating costs and the $1 million per year in interest. Since she can pay only $100,000 of the interest, she declares bankruptcy.

The bankruptcy court gives the ski area to the creditors. What will they do with it? They will operate it. They can't retrieve the $10 million they sacrificed to help finance construction, but they can obtain $100,000 more in revenues than they incur in additional costs.

The creditors can also choose to sell the area. How much would you pay for the bankrupt ski area? A lot. If you expected the area to yield perpetually $100,000 per year, you might be willing to pay $1 million for it.

Liquidating a "Profitable" Orange Grove: Accounting Costs

According to their accountants, many farms in southern California have earned profits by growing oranges. Why then have the farms gradually gone out of business? Because, contrary to the accounting records, the costs of producing oranges on southern California land has increased rapidly in recent years. Accountants use the prices paid for land as indicators of opportunity costs because the prices are objective, measurable, and usually accurate estimates of costs. However, in southern California, the opportunity costs of land have risen above the original purchase prices of the land. As a result, the old prices greatly understate the current opportunity costs. The opportunity costs are so high that some farms are unprofitable.

The prices paid for resources can be inaccurate estimates of opportunity costs in other cases. As indicated in the ski area example, when a firm produces resources for future specialized production, the opportunity costs of using those resources once they are in place are far below the money that was spent to obtain them.

Also, if resources are given to a firm, the zero purchase prices of these gifts fail to reflect the appropriate opportunity costs. For instance, if the owner of a firm gives the firm entrepreneurial services at a zero price, the cost of the services may nevertheless be $50,000 per year if the owner could have earned that amount by working elsewhere. A profit of $10,000 reported by the firm's accountant may conceal a $40,000 loss.

The Costly Draft Army

Which army produces military services at a lower cost, a mercenary army or one comprised of draftees? The mercenary army.

The opportunity cost of producing an army of soldiers is not the price that we pay for the soldiers. The cost is the value of the highest-valued alternatives that the soldiers could have otherwise produced. If, for example, a man can produce $30,000 worth of goods in the economy and if he is drafted and paid only $2000, the opportunity cost of the military services he produces is nevertheless $30,000.

A mercenary army produces military services at a lower cost because the mercenary army will try to hire qualified workers who are willing to work for the lowest wages, and those workers will be the ones who can produce the least valuable alternative products. In contrast, a draft army will produce at a higher cost because its workers tend to be chosen arbitrarily. Sometimes the draft selects low-cost workers, but it also selects high-cost ones.

What about the argument that a mercenary army can't attract quality soldiers? This is simply untrue. Quality depends on price. All that the military has to do to get quality is to pay enough to cover quality's higher opportunity cost. This is how the Boeing Company, Humana Hospitals, and Mobil Oil purchase high-quality "mercenary" engineers, doctors, and production workers. In fact, the most educated and qualified members of the military, the officers, have always been mercenaries.

If a mercenary army is less costly to produce, then why is the draft army so appealing to many people? Perhaps because many people are taxpayers and the draft shifts wealth toward taxpayers and away from the individuals drafted. The imposition of a draft may raise the costs of production, but it keeps taxes from rising.

The Rationality of a Panic

Many people are killed each year by human stampedes during public panics. The panics are sometimes caused by fires or explosions, but at other times they are caused simply by fear. If panics were avoided, many lives would be saved. This is why so much time is spent educating people on the virtues of orderly behavior during emergencies. Nevertheless, the next time a deadly fire breaks out in a public building, a panic is likely to occur. Why? Because panics are caused by individuals who respond to their personal opportunity costs rather than to the average cost that accrues to their group.

To explain, suppose you were in a theater and a fire broke out. At first, everyone might start to march out in an orderly manner. But what if it soon became obvious that some people would not survive? Under these conditions, even if order would save lives, a panic would be more likely. The average cost to the group might be greater as a result of a panic, but only individual costs count, and a panic would reduce some individual costs. For instance, if you were among the last people that would exit if order were maintained but one of the first if you raced for the door, you might opt for a quick exit, reducing your cost even if the average cost to the group would rise. In fact, if you suspected that other people were about to panic, you might race for the door even if you thought that you would survive under orderly conditions.

Controlling CEOs

Not only are individuals concerned with their personal costs rather than average group costs, they are also concerned with their personal welfare rather than the welfare of a group to which they may belong. If we recognize this, we can explain some of the problems that the owners of business firms have in controlling their chief executive officers (CEOs). Although the owners may want CEOs to consider only profits when decisions are made, the CEOs may not always do so. If CEOs don't maximize their personal welfare when they maximize the profits of the firm, then they will not pursue maximum profits. They will sacrifice profits to increase their own welfare.

If you're one of the owners of a firm, how can you motivate the chief executive to be concerned with profits rather than with just himself or herself? How can you get the CEO to worry about sales rather than the installation of a new executive bathroom? Simple. Make the individual's welfare coincide with the success of the firm by instituting a profit-sharing plan. This will reward the manager if the profits of the firm rise and provide a penalty otherwise.

What motivates corporate executives may not motivate individual workers in large firms. Profit sharing will be ineffective if individual workers have virtually no effect on the profits of a company. For example, a teller working for the National Bank of California will not be motivated to work harder by a profit-sharing plan. After all, the bank will earn about the same amount of money and the teller will share in the profits whether the teller works hard or not.

So far, by recognizing that economic individuals confront circumstances that include scarce and substitutable resources, we have been able to predict and explain various production phenomena. In the next chapter, so that we can explain and predict more, we will also recognize that resources have comparative advantages and that some indirect production techniques can often generate more products.

MAJOR AND MINOR POINTS

1. We can increase the values of goods by moving them around via trade and by combining them via production.
2. We produce goods, we produce limited total quantities of goods, and we produce a variety of goods.
3. We produce goods by combining other goods called resources or factors of production.
4. There are three types of resources: land, labor, and capital.
5. Land is everything on, under, and next to real estate. Labor is the unskilled natural ability of people. Capital is a product used to produce other goods.
6. Capital includes skilled labor, technology, entrepreneurial ability, and the existence of money. An increase in the supply of money, however, doesn't represent an increase in capital.
7. Our resources are limited and substitutable. As a result we can produce only a limited number of products, but we can produce a variety of products.
8. We can show our production options with a production possibilities frontier.
9. We will produce a combination on the production possibilities frontier because we want products, not unused or wasted resources.
10. We will produce products such that their value equals their cost because we are economic men and women who exercise all options that allow us to sacrifice less valued goods to obtain more valued ones.
11. We will produce less at a higher cost and more at a lower cost.
12. Indicators of opportunity costs include
    a. The use of resources
    b. Historical sacrifices
    c. The prices of resources
    d. The prices of products
    e. The average group costs of production
13. By using the same resources at different times, we can often reduce the opportunity costs of production.

14. Historical sacrifices are gone and can't be retrieved. They are relevant only to the extent that they can indicate future costs.

15. If resources were purchased a long time ago, the prices of the resources are unlikely to reflect the opportunity costs of production. The prices will also not reflect opportunity costs if the resources were donated to the firm.

16. Product prices are unlikely to reflect opportunity costs if the products are sold by governments or by nonprofit firms.

17. Actions that reduce the average cost to individuals in a group may increase the costs that some individuals incur, and vice versa.

18. Wars, government spending, taxes, and money will cause an increase in output only if they stimulate the employment of formerly unemployed resources. But if full employment exists, only the composition of output can change.

19. Government can increase the production of a given industry only by allowing that industry to obtain more resources. If full employment exists, then one industry can obtain more resources only if some other industry obtains fewer resources.

20. We will produce a unit of a product only if it is at least as valuable as the leisure or other goods we must sacrifice.

21. Unemployment is the nonuse of resources. Underemployment is the physically inefficient use of resources, use in a manner such that more of one product can be produced without a reduction in the production of another.

22. We will produce not only on a production possibilities frontier where physical efficiency occurs, but we will produce the particular combination that is economically efficient, the combination that contains the goods that have values equal to their costs.

23. As long as resources produce products and as long as the United States has many resources, we will be able to produce a great deal.

24. By putting off until later what we can do now, we can often reduce production costs.

25. Firms may go bankrupt by not earning enough to cover historical costs, but as long as they can generate revenues sufficient to cover additional costs, someone is likely to operate them.

26. Accountants use prices paid for resources as indicators of opportunity costs. These prices over- or understate costs when
    a. Specialized resources were purchased or produced;
    b. Opportunity costs of resources have fallen since the resources were acquired;
    c. Inflation raises the opportunity costs of resources;
    d. The firm uses donated resources.

27. The draft army reduces the cost to taxpayers of buying soldiers, but the opportunity cost of production to society is higher than that of a mercenary army.

28. Panics represent attempts to reduce individual opportunity costs, even though they may raise average group costs.

29. A manager will do what an owner wants only if the personal welfare of the manager is thereby improved.

30. Profit-sharing plans only motivate workers if the workers can individually affect the profits significantly by working faster or more slowly.

QUESTIONS

1. What is production and how does it occur?
2. Why are production possibilities limited and various?
3. Which goods will economic individuals produce?
4. Why are each of the following indicators of opportunity costs useful but also sometimes misleading?
   a. The use of resources
   b. Past sacrifices
   c. The prices of resources
   d. The prices of products
   e. Average group costs
5. Discuss the following terms and concepts:

Production	Historical costs
Resources	Resource prices
Factors of production	Product prices
Technology	Average group costs
Entrepreneurial ability	Production and war
Money	Unemployment
Limited resources	Underemployment
Substitutable resources	Physical versus economic
Production possibilities	efficiency
schedule	Procrastination
Production possibilities	Mercenary versus a draft
frontier	army
Opportunity cost of	Panics
production	Profit sharing
Use of resources	

APPLICATIONS

1. Do the physical characteristics of goods have to change before production can occur?
2. Undiscovered natural gas is land. Is discovered natural gas land? Is exploration a productive process? Explain.
3. There are really only two basic resources, labor and land. Capital is but a manifestation of a way of combining labor and land to produce products. Is this true?
4. Money is capital. In what sense is this true? In what sense is it false?
5. Since we can't see if we are producing the most valuable goods, how do we know that we do so?
6. When the government helps small farmers by subsidizing food prices, what are the economic effects of this aid?
7. How does an increase in production by one of Eric's neighbors affect Eric? How does an increase in production by Japan affect the United States?
8. Why does it often cost more to do a job within a more limited time period?

9. How could someone have spent $2000 to repair a Toyota Landcruiser worth only $1500?
10. Why do new oil taxes affect prospective wells more than old wells?
11. Do generals continue battles so that the dead will not have died in vain?
12. Why might you liquidate your small business even though it gives you an accounting profit of $10,000 per year?
13. Can the government produce goods at a lower cost than a private firm?
14. The benefits of a revolution in Poland would be far greater than the costs, and yet, the majority allows itself to be controlled by a few Communists. This shows that people are irrational. Explain how it is possible for the majority to be rational under such circumstances.
15. Why are government employees often unwilling to do things that benefit other people more than they cost those people?
16. How can the Soviet Union motivate managers to focus on group costs of production?

10

Specialization and Indirect Production

Throughout most of human history, we consumed what we personally produced, and we produced by combining labor directly with land. Eric, the Montana subsistence farmer, was the rule, not the exception. And like Eric, we produced and consumed relatively little. But since the Industrial Revolution, we have abandoned simple subsistence production. To raise our living standards, most of us have focused on two production processes: specialization and indirect production.

In this chapter, we explain and predict our use of the two processes by developing the theories of specialization and indirect production. The theories recognize two technological factors:

    a. Almost every resource has a comparative advantage in the production of some good.
    b. Some indirect methods of production yield more products than direct methods of production.

The special topics related to specialization examine household specialization, the Old South and King Cotton, the Jeffersonian Embargo, whether developing nations should industrialize, and the economic effects of barriers to international trade. The special topics related to indirect production deal with economic growth and how Andrew Carnegie became wealthy.

THE THEORY OF SPECIALIZATION

The Phenomena

Although resources are substitutable in production and can therefore produce many different products, we **specialize**, or concentrate our resources in the production of one or at most a few goods. This specialization is a phenomenon that is common in both primitive and advanced economic systems.

An Explanation: Jack's Farm

To explain specialization, let's examine the production options on a hypothetical farm owned by Jack. Suppose Jack has 40 acres of land that can be used to produce either wheat or corn. Nevertheless, each piece of land is different. If Jack avoids specialization by using the north and the south 20 acres to produce both wheat and corn, the north 20 will produce 15 bushels of wheat and 10 bushels of corn, while the south 20 will produce 15 bushels of wheat and 5 bushels of corn. As shown in Table 10.1, Jack's farm will produce a total of 30 bushels of wheat and 15 bushels of corn. (The $\frac{1}{2}$s indicate that half of the productive capacities of the land are being used on the particular commodities.)

These production options mean that the acres have comparative advantages in the production. If two resources can each produce products A and B, the resource that can produce a given quantity of A at a lower sacrifice of B has a **comparative advantage** in the production of A.

In the case of Jack's farm, the north 20 has a comparative advantage in corn. To produce 10 bushels of corn on the north 20, Jack must sacrifice 15 bushels of wheat. To do so on the south 20, he would have to sacrifice 30 bushels of wheat. This is because it takes one-half of the north 20 to produce 10 bushels of corn and that half could have otherwise produced 15 bushels of wheat. In contrast, Jack must use all the south 20 to produce 10 bushels of corn and those acres could have otherwise produced 30 bushels of wheat.

On the other hand, the south 20 has a comparative advantage in wheat. To produce 15 bushels of wheat on the south 20, Jack has to sacrifice 5

TABLE 10.1 Jack's Production Without Specialization

The table shows outputs when the north and the south 20 produce both wheat and corn, each using one-half of their productive capabilities on each product.

	WHEAT		CORN	
North acres	15	$(\frac{1}{2})$	10	$(\frac{1}{2})$
South acres	15	$(\frac{1}{2})$	5	$(\frac{1}{2})$
Totals	30		15	

bushels of corn. In contrast, he would have to sacrifice 10 bushels of corn if he produced the wheat on the north 20. This is because while it takes half of both the south 20 and the north 20 to produce 15 bushels of wheat, half of the south 20 could have otherwise produced 5 bushels of corn, whereas half of the north 20 could have otherwise produced 10 bushels.

If Jack specializes his resources in production by concentrating his resources on the commodities in which they have comparative advantages, total production will rise. By growing only corn in the north and only wheat in the south, Jack will be able to produce an additional 5 bushels of corn, as indicated by Table 10.2. Output increases because sacrifices decrease.

Jack, as an economic individual who values products, will always choose more production rather than less. Since specialization will increase production, Jack will specialize his resources.

The Predictions

Specialization

From this explanation, we can predict that if some of our resources have comparative advantages in production, then we will specialize the resources in production according to those comparative advantages. We won't distribute our resources evenly over the production of a variety of products.

The Law of Increasing Cost

We can also make a prediction called **the law of increasing cost**: The incremental cost of producing additional units of any product will rise as we produce more.

The cost of producing additional units will rise because as we exhaust resources that require the smallest sacrifices of other products, we will have to start using resources that require greater sacrifices. We can see this if we examine Jack's farm. If Jack produces only 20 bushels of corn, he can do so with the north 20 acres and sacrifice only 15 bushels of wheat. But if he wants to produce more than 20 bushels, he has to shift the south 20 into corn production and sacrifice more wheat to produce each bushel of corn. To produce just 10 additional bushels of corn, he has to sacrifice 30 additional bushels of wheat.

TABLE 10.2 Production With Specialization

> With specialization, production rises by 5 bushels of corn.

	WHEAT		CORN	
North acres	0		20	$(\frac{2}{2})$
South acres	30	$(\frac{2}{2})$		
Totals	30		20	

We can sometimes temporarily offset the effects of the law of increasing cost by using mass production technologies. Nevertheless, eventually the employment of resources that require greater sacrifices of alternative products forces production costs to rise.

Interpersonal and Interregional Specialization and Trade

We can also predict the occurrence of interpersonal and interregional specialization and subsequent trade if we recognize that resources aren't spread evenly among people and regions.

If Jack, for example, gave the north 20 acres to his son and the south 20 to his daughter, interpersonal specialization by his children could then increase production by 5 bushels of corn. Or if the north 20 were in Canada and the south 20 were in the United States, international specialization could yield 5 extra bushels of corn. Specialization is a technological phenomenon that is independent of who owns resources or where they happen to lie.

Once resources are dispersed among various people and regions, trade becomes a likely and often necessary prerequisite to specialization. This is because a concentration of production results in lower values to producers.

For example, if Jack's son were to produce only corn, diminishing valuation would drive the value of corn to him to a low level, even zero. He would therefore be willing to specialize in corn production only if he could subsequently sell some of his corn to his sister. And it is likely that she would want to trade if she concentrated her production on wheat, since the value of wheat to her would also be driven down by diminishing valuation.

What can we say about the rate of trade, the price? Under isolated interpersonal exchange conditions, we can only identify the possible price range. Since Jack's son could produce a bushel of wheat by giving up $\frac{2}{3}$ bushel of corn, the most that he would be willing to pay for a bushel of wheat is $\frac{2}{3}$ bushel of corn. Conversely, since his sister would give up $\frac{1}{3}$ bushel of corn to produce a bushel of wheat, she would demand at least $\frac{1}{3}$ bushel of corn for a bushel of wheat. Therefore, the price range for a bushel of wheat would be between $\frac{2}{3}$ and $\frac{1}{3}$ bushel of corn.

Although we can't identify the exact price, our analysis does make one thing very evident: Specialization and trade will occur only if both parties move to more preferred positions. If the price is such that one party won't benefit from trade, resource substitutability will allow him or her to stop trading, despecialize, and produce the products that are no longer purchased.

A Summary of the Theory

Our theory assumes that

a. We are economic individuals.
b. Resources have comparative advantages in the production of some products.
c. In terms of quantities and qualities, resources are unevenly distributed among us.

These assumptions allow us to predict that

a. We will specialize our resources according to their comparative advantages.
b. The costs of production will rise as we produce more of a given product.
c. Interpersonal and interregional specialization and trade will occur.

SPECIAL TOPICS RELATED TO RESOURCE SPECIALIZATION

Penny's Cooking

In many households, husbands and wives specialize in producing various goods. For instance, the husbands often spend time tuning up the car while their wives cook dinner. Why? It's not because of tradition. Nor is it because women can't work on cars. It's because wives usually have a comparative advantage in cooking while their husbands have a comparative advantage in automobile maintenance and repair.

Take the example of Penny and Jerry. If Penny is a good cook and a poor mechanic, she may sacrifice only part of a tune-up to cook dinner. If her husband Jerry is a bad cook and good mechanic, he may sacrifice many tune-ups to cook the same meal. Under such conditions, Penny has a comparative advantage in dinners.

Conversely, since Jerry is a good mechanic and poor cook, he may sacrifice very few meals while tuning up the car, whereas Penny, a poor mechanic and a good cook, may sacrifice many meals. Jerry can produce tune-ups at a much lower sacrifice than Penny; he has a comparative advantage in tune-ups.

By specializing their resources according to comparative advantages, Penny and Jerry sacrifice fewer alternative products during the production of any given product, and therefore their total production rises. Since Penny and Jerry want more products, they specialize in production.

During the past century, attitudes toward the roles of men and women have changed greatly. Many women are now brought up to do tasks and obtain jobs that were traditionally the exclusive provinces of men. Increased education, improved skills, and different attitudes have allowed many wives to obtain comparative advantages in goods that used to be almost always produced by their husbands.

This doesn't mean, however, that specialization will no longer increase production possibilities. If wives produce tune-ups at a lower sacrifice than their husbands, they will still specialize; they will simply tune up the cars while their husbands do the cooking.

Incidentally, one resource doesn't have to be absolutely better at one task while another is absolutely better at some other task in order for specialization to increase production. Even if one resource is better at producing everything and another is worse at producing everything, comparative advantages exist if the resource that is better at everything has a greater advantage in some product than in others, whereas the resource that is worse at everything has a smaller disadvantage in some product than in others. Where such comparative advantages exist, specialization of resources will increase production.

For example, if Neanderthal women were both better rabbit hunters and root diggers than men, they nevertheless could have had comparative advantages in producing roots. If the women were only slightly better hunters and much better foragers, then they would have had to sacrifice more roots to catch a rabbit than men. On the other hand, if the men were worse at both hunting and foraging, but almost as good at hunting and much worse at foraging, then they would have had to sacrifice more rabbits to obtain roots than women.

The Old South and King Cotton

Some historians claim that the Old South retarded its economic expansion by specializing in cotton to such a large extent. Why did the South do so? More specifically, why didn't the Old South concentrate more on the production of clothing? Because the South had a comparative advantage in the production of cotton. Compared to England, the South gave up very few garments to produce a bale of cotton. Similarly, England had a comparative advantage in the production of garments. Relative to the Old South, England's cotton sacrifices were small. The Old South and England increased their combined outputs by specializing in cotton and manufacturing, respectively, producing each product at a lower sacrifice of the other.

Industrialization and the Jeffersonian Embargo

The example of the Old South and England reveals that maximum production doesn't require industrialization. Although our theory predicts that efficient production requires industrialization by those nations and regions that have comparative advantages in the production of manufactured items, it also calls on others to concentrate on agriculture. If New Zealand, Kansas, and many developing nations industrialized, total world production would fall.

Governments can force industrialization even if sacrifices are great. They cannot, however, change the productivities of resources. For example, in early American history, relative to England, the Northeast had a comparative advantage in the production of agricultural goods. It therefore specialized in agriculture, whereas England specialized in manufacturing. However, after the Jeffersonian embargo restricted the importation of English industrial products, a significant number of manufacturing firms in the Northeast successfully initiated production. They continued to produce throughout the term of the embargo. But once the embargo was lifted, most of the new firms were bankrupted by the flood of low-cost, English-manufactured items. The Northeast reverted to agriculture and England again focused more on manufacturing.

Some years later, the Northeast developed a comparative advantage in the production of manufacturing products because energy, natural resources, and high-quality labor became more important. Industrialization then flourished naturally.

Producing and Simultaneously Importing Oil

Although specialization can increase production, individuals and regions seldom totally concentrate on the production of one good. This is because the law of increasing cost implies that as more is produced by an individual or region, the cost will increase. Once the cost increases above the costs that other individuals or regions incur, it becomes cheaper to buy than to produce still more.

For example, some oil in Texas is so close to the ground that we can extract it with only a few sacrifices. As we expand production, however, we are forced to go both deeper and offshore. More resources are necessary and the cost rises. Eventually, the cost of producing more exceeds the price of Saudi crude and we begin to import oil. We wind up both producing and buying oil because we are the lower-cost producers only up to some given level of production.

We can't explain all limits to specialization by citing the law of increasing cost. Many limits occur because specialization sometimes leads to a loss of job satisfaction. Work can become boring if it relegates us to repetitious tasks. It can also become alienating if our small contribution keeps us from identifying with the final product. Most of us would be driven to distraction by the boredom and alienation of tightening 14-millimeter bolts on a Buick production line 4000 times each day.

We also sometimes limit specialization because we want to maintain our independence. The more we produce of the products we consume, the more independent we become of other people's outputs.

Independence seems to be particularly important on a group scale. Nations often strive for independence by trying to produce domestically. Mao and Mussolini, for example, both tried to make their nations independent of the world.

Of course, the despecialization necessary to attain job satisfaction and independence reduces the production of other goods. We will despecialize only when the values gained exceed those sacrificed.

Trade Barriers: Producing Automobiles in Oklahoma

Barriers to trade will prevent specialization and therefore reduce total production. For example, fishermen aren't about to eat all of the fish they catch. If they aren't allowed to sell their outputs, they won't specialize even if it causes a decline in total personal, regional, or national production.

Why do societies erect barriers to trade if the restrictions force greater sacrifices and therefore reduced output? Primarily because the barriers simultaneously increase the wealth of some politically powerful individuals. For instance, suppose that you wanted to produce automobiles in Oklahoma. It could be done. You could simply buy resources that are now being used for oil and shift them to the production of automobiles. However, oil workers don't necessarily make good automobile designers; resources vary in their abilities. As a result, the cost of each car might approach $20,000. Your basic problem would be obvious: How could you compete with Michigan Fords costing only $10,000?

One possible solution could be to fly to Oklahoma City and make a passionate plea to the legislature: We must limit the importation of cheap Michigan vehicles. We simply can't compete against Michigan automobiles that are being produced below cost. By restricting trade, we will save the jobs of Oklahoma workers and protect the dividends of Oklahoma stockholders. Just think of the tax revenues that auto production in Oklahoma will bring, not to mention the savings from lower unemployment and welfare expenditures.

Since the Constitution keeps states from interfering with interstate commerce, Oklahoma couldn't restrict the imports of Michigan cars. But let's assume that you succeeded in obtaining the restrictions anyway. You could then produce and sell your cars.

Since people in Michigan couldn't obtain "Oklahoma dollars" to buy oil from Oklahoma, exports would fall and the oil industry would be forced to release resources. You could employ those resources to produce the Oklahoma automobiles (and prevent unemployment). In the process, real production would be greatly affected. Resources would be producing cars instead of oil, and they would produce very few cars at a sacrifice of a great deal of oil.

Nevertheless, as a producer of automobiles you might favor the restrictions on trade. Even if it were very costly to everyone else, you might become very wealthy, as might some of your auto workers and stockholders.

Trade and Transportation Costs

Finally, we can explain some of the tremendous increase in world production that has occurred in the last two centuries. Much of the increase has been made possible by more efficient transportation networks. By allowing products to move cheaply, greater specialization of resources has resulted, and with more specialization, world output has increased dramatically.

THE THEORY OF INDIRECT PRODUCTION

The Phenomena

In addition to using specialization, we usually increase output by replacing direct methods of production with indirect ones. **Direct production methods** involve the combination of labor with natural resources to generate consumption goods. **Indirect methods** require the initial synthesis of labor and natural resources into capital, and then the subsequent merging of the capital with more labor and natural resources to produce final products.

An Explanation: Fencing in Cattle

To explain why we use indirect production methods, suppose that you can produce cattle directly by combining your labor with natural resources while hunting the wild. But you can also obtain the animals indirectly by first constructing a fence and then using the fence to help raise the cattle. Which method would you choose? The answer depends on the values of the expected gains and sacrifices.

Suppose you expect that each method will require the same labor but that the direct method will yield 5 cattle each year, whereas the indirect method will generate no cattle the first year (as the fence is being built) but 6 cattle each year for the following 6 years (after which the fence will be worn out). As Table 10.3 shows, with the indirect method you expect to gain an extra steer each year for 6 years by sacrificing 5 cattle the first year.

Is the indirect method superior? Certainly the gain of 6 future cattle is worth the sacrifice of 5 present cattle if future goods are worth as much as present ones. But future goods are generally less valuable. To obtain their present values, the values of the future cattle have to be discounted.

The value of the 6 extra future cattle equals the value of 5 cattle in year 1 if future cattle are discounted at about 8% per year. If future cattle are less valuable, you will have to hunt in the wild. On the other hand, if future cattle are more valuable, you will build the fence, engaging in indirect production.

The Predictions

Using Indirect Production

The preceding explanation allows us to predict that we will use indirect production methods whenever the present values of their yields exceed the present values of the yields of direct production methods. If we engage in

TABLE 10.3   *Indirect versus Direct Production*

> Direct production yields 5 more cattle in year 1, but indirect production yields 1 extra steer in years 2–7.

YEAR	1	2	3	4	5	6	7	TOTAL
Direct	5	5	5	5	5	5	5	35
Indirect	0	6	6	6	6	6	6	36

indirect production under these conditions, we will obtain more valuable goods than we sacrifice.

Higher Interest Rates, Less Indirect Production

We can also predict that if interest rates rise, we will engage in less indirect production and vice versa. Why? Because higher interest rates imply that the values of future goods have fallen relative to the values of present goods. This means that the values of the products of indirect production methods have declined relative to the values of the products of direct production methods. We will therefore increase our use of the direct production methods.

For example, in the case of cattle production, if interest rates were to rise from 6% to 10%, you would change your decision from building the fence to hunting cattle in the wild. The extra future cattle that the fence would yield would then be worth less than the present cattle that you would have to sacrifice to build the fence. The fact that you could obtain cattle earlier would more than make up for the smaller amount produced.

Product and Resource Trades

Finally, the theory's explanation predicts that indirect production will increase the number of exchanges related to time-value and uncertainty.

Let's look at time-value trades first. In the cattle example, if the extra 6 future cattle that you can obtain by building the fence are worth less than the 5 present cattle you have to sacrifice, then you will avoid the indirect production method. But what if I think that the future cattle are more valuable? If I offer you 5.1 present cattle for the extra 6 future cattle, would you then be willing to build the fence and engage in indirect production? Of course. You would have to be irrational to give up .1 present cattle at no sacrifice to you.

I wouldn't necessarily make a capital gain by buying 6 future cattle for only 5.1 present ones. The extra future cattle might compensate me only for their lower time-value.

Trades related to uncertainty would also occur. They are associated with indirect production because we have limited knowledge of future products.

For example, if you decided to engage in indirect production, you would make a capital gain if you produced 8 rather than 6 extra cattle with the fence. But if you raised only 3 extra cattle, you would incur a loss. Now, what could you do if you expected the yield of the fence to be lower than I did or didn't want to take the chance of a loss? You could sell me your unspecified extra future output for 5.1 present cattle. Then if you produced 8 extra cattle with the fence, I would make a capital gain, and if the fence yielded only 3 extra cattle, I would incur a loss.

Unspecified future products are usually not sold directly. Instead, resources are sold. Rather than selling the extra future output of your resources, you might simply sell me your labor and natural resources for a price of 5.1

present cattle plus 5 cattle per year for the following 6 years. I would then employ you to produce the fence and the cattle. As a result, I would make a capital gain if 8 extra cattle were produced and incur a loss if output rose by only 3 cattle. And if just 6 extra cattle were produced, I would break even, just covering my time-value sacrifices (assuming an 8% time-value discount).

A Summary of the Theory

The theory we have developed specifies that we, as economic individuals, confront circumstances in which we can combine our resources in indirect ways that yield more products at later periods of time. It also recognizes that the extra future products are sometimes quantitatively sufficient to offset their lower time-value and that we vary in the values we place on the future products. Given these assumptions, we can predict that

a. We will combine our resources in indirect ways that yield more goods, though later.
b. We will engage in more indirect production at lower interest rates and less at higher ones.
c. We will trade present and future products or resources.

SPECIAL TOPICS RELATED TO INDIRECT PRODUCTION

Economic Growth

If interest rates decrease, **economic growth** (an expansion of production possibilities) will increase. Let's see why by using the production possibilities frontier and our theory of indirect production.

Production possibilities are determined by the available resources. When we engage in indirect production, we shift from the production of present consumption goods and toward the production of capital. This is shown by the movement from point A to point B on the production possibilities frontier in Figure 10.1. More capital then becomes available in subsequent periods and production possibilities expand as reflected by the shift of the curve to the right.

If real interest rates (interest rates adjusted for inflation) decrease, this implies that future products are even more valuable relative to present products than was the case previously. We will respond by shifting production toward more capital, away from direct and toward indirect production processes. As a result, the frontier will shift even farther to the right.

We can't say that economic growth is a good thing. Our theory states only that we must sacrifice some present goods to obtain economic growth. The theory does not predict that the values of the future gains will be worth the present sacrifices.

Indirect production increases the supply of capital available for future production, causing the production possibilities frontier to shift outward.

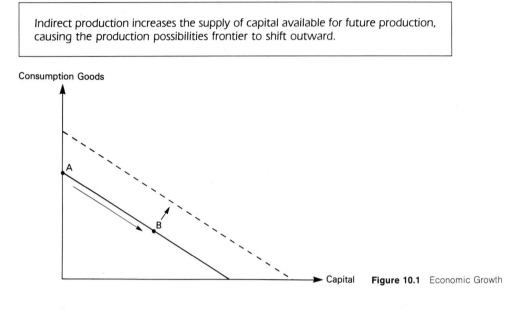

Figure 10.1 Economic Growth

How Andrew Carnegie Became Wealthy

How did Andrew Carnegie and other industrialists become so wealthy? They might have claimed that they did so by building the factories they owned. But clearly, workers built the factories, not industrialists. Some history texts give us the impression that the industrialists became wealthy by using corrupt practices and monopoly power. However, although some of the industrialists did obtain their wealth from these sources, many of them were honest and sold their goods under competitive conditions.

Most of the industrialists who became wealthy did so by using voluntary exchange and production. Specifically, the industrialists purchased factories from various resource suppliers in advance by buying resources. The resources were manifestations of the future factories. The wages paid workers plus the prices paid other resources suppliers represented the prices the industrialists paid for the future factories.

How much did the industrialists who became wealthy pay for future factories via wages and other resource prices? Less than the expected future values of the factories. Future goods were less valuable than present goods, and therefore the industrialists had to pay only the present values of the expected future values of the factories. Had realizations equaled expectations, the industrialists would have broken even. Even though the future values of the factories would have exceeded the prices of resources, the workers and other resource owners were given money early while the industrialists obtained the factories late.

Realizations, however, far exceeded expectations; the particular factories that the wealthy industrialists had purchased were eventually worth far more than what was generally predicted. The industrialists therefore benefited because they shifted their wealth into more valuable future factories and out of less valuable present money. In the process, they allowed workers and other resource owners to shift their wealth into present money and out of the future factories. Retrospection indicates that the various resource suppliers would have been better off had they decided to not sell factories in advance.

Of course, workers and other owners of resources often don't have the means to build factories and wait for the future income that will be earned as the factories produce products or are sold. Nevertheless, it's unlikely that they would have opted to build the factories even if they had sufficient wealth. After all, besides the industrialists, other capitalists had the means and, by not building the factories, the other capitalists revealed that they thought the prices paid resource suppliers exceeded the expected values of the future factories by more than going interest rates. The industrialists were risking a great deal by purchasing the factories in advance.

In fact, not all industrialists prospered; many eventually declared bankruptcy. In such cases, the workers and other resource suppliers had charged more for the future factories than the factories were eventually worth, fortuitously shifting their wealth out of the future factories and into present money. Indirect production, a time-consuming phenomenon, had capital losses as well as capital gains associated with it.

Although we often buy and sell resources to either change our consumption over time or selectively bear the risks of production, we also trade resources in order to increase output by combining our resources with those of other people. In the next chapter, we discuss such resource trades.

MAJOR AND MINOR POINTS

1. We have gradually eliminated subsistence production with increased use of specialization and indirect production.
2. Resources generally have comparative advantages in the production of some goods. A resource has a comparative advantage, relative to some other resource, in the production of a product if it can produce that product by sacrificing less of another product.
3. Specialization according to comparative advantages reduces sacrifices and therefore increases production.
4. As we produce more of a product, the incremental cost of additional units will rise. This proposition is called the law of increasing cost. The cause of the law is that we must employ higher-cost resources after we have used up lower-cost ones.
5. Since resources are distributed unevenly among people and areas, interpersonal and interregional specialization and trade occur because they increase production and consumption.
6. When members of a household specialize, they can increase production.
7. Even when one set of resources is better or worse in producing everything relative to another set, specialization where advantages are greatest or disadvan-

tages are smallest, where comparative advantages are present, will increase output.

8. The Old South and England increased their combined outputs by specializing in cotton and manufacturing, respectively.

9. Industrialization increases output only if it results in the production of manufacturing items by resources that have comparative advantages in manufacturing.

10. Individual and regional concentration in production is often limited because individuals and regions have different resources. As they increase the production of any product, they encounter increasing costs. Once costs exceed those of other producers or regions, production shifts to other products.

11. Specialization is often limited because it can require the sacrifice of job satisfaction and independence.

12. Specialization is limited by the extent of the market. Barriers to trade reduce specialization.

13. People often want barriers to trade if their personal wealth is increased even if regional or national production falls.

14. As transportation and information costs fall, trade will become easier and the extent of specialization will rise.

15. Goods can be produced directly by combining labor and natural resources. They can also be produced indirectly by first producing capital and then using the capital with labor and natural resources to produce consumption goods.

16. Indirect production often yields more goods but at a later point in time. If we value the greater quantity of goods in the future more than the smaller quantity of goods sacrificed now, we will produce goods indirectly.

17. Indirect production will be used if its productivity exceeds the rate of interest.

18. By selling future goods now, we may be willing to engage in indirect production even when we don't personally value the extra future goods as much as the present sacrifices.

19. By selling our resources now, we can sell future potential capital gains and losses as well as future goods.

20. Economic growth, an expansion of production possibilities, can occur if we engage in indirect production.

21. At lower real interest rates, we will engage in more indirect production because future products will become more valuable relative to present products.

22. When we pay now for products we will obtain later, we will usually pay less than the values of the future products because present goods are more valuable than future goods.

23. We can become wealthy by buying resources. If resource prices underestimate the actual future values of products, we can make capital gains by buying. However, if resource prices overestimate the values of future products, we can incur losses.

QUESTIONS

1. What is specialization?
2. Why will resources be specialized in production according to their comparative advantages?

3. Why will specialization according to comparative advantages increase output?
4. Why will the unit cost of production increase as more units of a product are produced?
5. Why will specialization increase trade?
6. When will specialization in agriculture increase output?
7. Why will restrictions on trade reduce output?
8. Why is specialization limited?
9. Why will a reduction in transaction costs increase output?
10. What is indirect production?
11. When will indirect production occur?
12. Why will a rise in the real rate of interest reduce investment?
13. Why will interest and capital gains be associated with indirect production?
14. Discuss the following terms and concepts:

Specialization	Transportation costs
Comparative advantage	Indirect production
Law of increasing costs	Time-value
Trade and specialization	Economic growth
South and King Cotton	Interest rates
Industrialization	Capital gains
Trade barriers	Resource trades

APPLICATIONS

1. Given the conditions shown in Table 10.4, which nation's resources have a comparative advantage in the production of guns? Butter? What will be the gains from specialization according to comparative advantages?

TABLE 10.4

	GUNS		BUTTER	
United States	30	$(\frac{2}{3})$	40	$(\frac{1}{3})$
Australia	15	$(\frac{2}{3})$	30	$(\frac{1}{3})$

2. What does the law of increasing cost do to the shape of the production possibilities frontier?
3. Opposites attract. In what sense are marriages between opposites more productive?
4. Restrictions on foreign trade are necessary to stimulate industrial development and protect small developing firms from foreign competition. Evaluate.
5. To the extent that West Virginia specializes in the production and sale of natural resources (coal), does the rest of the world represent an imperialist power exploiting the state for its resources?
6. When will farmers quit producing corn and get jobs with IBM?
7. Why does the United States both produce and import steel?

8. Is alienation caused by the separation of a worker from his or her tools, or by the insignificant nature of the contribution the worker makes to a final product?
9. Economics reveals that people should specialize. Does it?
10. Economics shows that trade barriers shouldn't be erected. Does it?
11. What argument could oil producers in Michigan make for restricting Oklahoma oil imports?
12. If you were not allowed to buy anything, how would your output be affected?
13. Does foreign trade create jobs? Does it destroy them?
14. What is the relationship between the real interest rate and the level of investment? Why?
15. Suppose the anticipated value of your total future sacrifices from going to college was $150,000 and the anticipated value of your total future gains was $200,000. Under what conditions would avoiding college nevertheless be rational?
16. If the early industrialists had not been willing to accept many of the risks associated with building factories, would the factories have been built?

Resource Trade

About 100 years ago, Karl Marx argued in *Das Kapital* that under the conditions of free enterprise, capitalists exploit workers. His theory provided the ideological foundation for numerous communist revolutions and is part of the rationale for most of the socialist economies of the world today, nations that encompass well over one-third of the population of the earth.

But do capitalists exploit workers? Whether we can answer this question using economics depends on how we define exploitation. We can't answer the question if exploitation is a form of injustice. However, in this chapter we define exploitation as an event; then we can see if and when the event occurs. You can subsequently decide for yourself if the event is just or not.

To deal with exploitation and various phenomena related to the prices of resources, we examine a theory of resource trade. The theory explains exchanges involving resources by recognizing that we can often increase the productivities of our resources by combining them with the resources of other people. Before such resource mergers can take place, however, we must either sell our resources to other individuals, or they have to sell their resources to us.

After we examine the theory of resource exchange, we look at some special topics. The topics first deal with the possibility of exploitation in various markets. Then they examine the NCAA, the validity of class exploitation theories, the effects of labor unions, and the nature of the American Medical Association. The special topics also discuss what happens when large unions negotiate with large companies; how resource monopolies affect production; and whether rent, interest, and profit represent the exploitation of labor.

165

A THEORY OF RESOURCE EXCHANGE

The Phenomena

Although many of us may envy Eric on his Montana subsistence farm, we nevertheless choose not to produce goods with the resources we just happen to own. Instead, we usually either sell our resources to other people who combine them with their resources, or we buy resources from other people and merge those resources with ours.

Our exchanges of resources are, however, limited. We are seldom willing to sell all our resources or purchase all the resources other people want to sell.

An Explanation: Hiring Restaurant Servers

To explain why we buy and sell resources and why our resource trades are limited, let's see if we can explain the employment of servers (waiters or waitresses) by an imaginary restaurant in Jackson, Mississippi, and start by discussing the value of the servers. (As with all goods, the value of a resource refers to the value of the marginal unit, not to the value of all units.)

The Value of Servers

If a prospective server, Dave, wants a job at the restaurant, how much is he worth to the owner, Janet? Dave might argue that Janet should place an infinite value on his life or his soul, but no matter how disconcerting, the value of his labor is far less.

Like all resources, the value of Dave's labor depends on its **marginal revenue product**. The marginal revenue product equals the marginal product times the marginal revenue (of the units within the marginal product).

The **marginal product** is the change in total output that occurs as a result of the employment of one more unit of a resource. If the restaurant serves 10 more meals per hour as a result of Dave's employment, then his marginal product is 10 meals per hour.

Just because a resource is responsible for a given marginal product doesn't mean that the resource produces the marginal product. Dave's marginal product is 10 meals per hour, but he alone doesn't produce those meals. The meals are produced by combining Dave's labor with other resources such as the restaurant, the cook, and tables. Without the other resources, Dave wouldn't produce anything.

It's impossible even to identify a resource's proportional contribution to the marginal product. For example, if Dave weren't hired, all 10 served meals would be sacrificed, not just the ones that would reflect his fractional contribution.

In addition to the marginal product, the marginal revenue product depends on the marginal revenue that the items within the marginal product yield. If each meal adds a net of $1 to total revenue, then the marginal revenue of each unit within Dave's marginal product is $1.

Since Dave's marginal product is 10 meals per hour and the marginal revenue of each meal is $1, Dave's marginal revenue product is $10 per hour. Dave is worth $10 per hour to Janet.

Dave's labor is worth $10 per hour to Janet, but what is the labor worth to Dave? If the best paying alternative job that Dave could obtain pays $1 per hour because his marginal revenue product in that job would be $1 per hour, and if $1 per hour exceeds the value of leisure, then the value of Dave's labor to himself is $1 per hour. Dave therefore values his labor at $1 per hour.

Dave's labor is worth more to Janet than to him because Janet can combine the labor with other resources to produce served meals worth $10 per hour. Dave doesn't have the other resources, and his best alternative is a job that pays $1 per hour.

Since Dave's labor is worth $10 per hour to Janet and only $1 per hour to him, Dave and Janet will trade. At some wage between $10 and $1 per hour, the money and the labor will be redistributed, the values of the money and the labor will increase, and both Dave and Janet will move to more preferred positions.

Incidentally, the mergers of labor and other resources don't always have to be formed by the owners of capital; instead of capital buying labor, labor sometimes buys capital. Sometimes servers buy restaurants, farmers purchase small farms, laborers invest in small businesses, and fishermen buy fishing boats.

Diminishing Valuation of Resources

Because of the value differentials that exist, Janet hires Dave and other servers. But she hires only a finite number of servers and the servers refuse to sell all of their labor to the restaurant. This is because as more servers are bought and sold, Janet values their services less while the servers value their services more, and this eventually eliminates value differentials.

To Janet, the value of the servers falls because their marginal revenue product falls. And the marginal revenue product falls because both the marginal product of the servers and the marginal revenue of the meals fall.

We can explain the decline of the marginal product by referring to a proposition known as the **law of diminishing returns**. The law states that as more of a resource is added to a fixed set of other resources, the marginal product of the resource will eventually decrease. The reason marginal product eventually decreases is that added resources have fewer fixed resources to work with. In the case of Janet's restaurant in Jackson, although the number of servers increases, the amount of floor space, the number of tables, and the number of cooks remain the same. This causes each additional server to add less to total output than the previous server.

The marginal revenue generated by the meals falls because of diminishing valuation. As customers buy more meals, diminishing valuation reduces the values of the meals. To induce more sales, Janet must reduce price, and therefore marginal revenue declines. In the case of competitive selling, the marginal revenue falls as much as the price (since marginal revenue equals the price); in the case of monopoly selling, marginal revenue falls faster than the price (due to the market-spoiling effect).

While the value of labor to Janet falls as she hires more servers, the value of labor to the workers rises. Since the marginal revenue product of labor falls as more labor is employed, it rises when less labor is employed. When Janet hires more servers, fewer workers are employed in alternative employments and therefore the marginal revenue product of labor in those employments increases. Since the workers have a higher marginal revenue product in alternative employments, the workers value their labor more. Moreover, if the same servers are asked to work longer hours, the value of their leisure rises; this also makes them value their labor more.

Since the value of labor to Janet falls as more servers are hired and since the value of labor to the servers rises as more servers are sold, trade eventually eliminates value differentials. When all differentials are gone, the exchanges of labor stop.

The Predictions

Limited Resource Trades

From the preceding explanation, we can predict that we will trade when we value resources differently. However, we will limit our trades, seldom buying or selling all of the resources available.

Competitive Resource Prices

The explanation also lets us make some predictions about the price of resources under various market conditions. First, when exchange conditions are competitive, the equilibrium price will be the market-clearing price determined by the impersonal forces of supply and demand.

For instance, suppose the market for servers in Jackson is highly competitive. That is, suppose many servers in Jackson want work and many restaurants want their labor. Under these conditions, if the first worker is worth $10 per hour to the restaurants, then the restaurants are willing and able to hire that worker for a $10 hourly wage. If subsequent workers are worth less, then the restaurants are willing and able to employ additional workers only at a lower wage rate. This gives rise to a demand curve for servers that slopes downward.

On the supply side, if the marginal revenue product in alternative employment of the first worker is $1 per hour, then the supply curve will begin at the one unit of quantity and the $1 wage, well below the demand curve. Because the marginal revenue product in alternative employment increases as more servers are sold to the restaurants, the wage must rise to induce additional workers to sell their labor. The supply curve therefore slopes upward.

Since the demand curve slopes downward and the supply curve slopes upward, and since the supply curve begins below the demand curve, then the curves eventually cross. This is illustrated in Figure 11.1.

Given the competitiveness of the market, the equilibrium wage rate will lie where the curves cross, at the rate where the market clears. Specifically, the wage will be $5.50 per hour. At that wage rate, 5.5 servers will be willing and able to work and the restaurants will be willing and able to hire the 5.5 servers. At any higher wage rate, a surplus would have caused competition among workers, causing the wage rate to fall; and at any lower wage rate, a shortage would have caused competition among restaurants, causing the wage rate to rise.

Monopsony Resource Prices

Trade conditions aren't always competitive. Sometimes **monopsonists** (single buyers) exist, and the monopsonists often trade with many sellers. Under these circumstances, we can predict that both the prices and the quantities of resources employed will be less than under conditions of competition.

To explain why the prices and quantities will be lower under monopsony conditions, suppose that Janet's restaurant is the only one in Jackson, and that columns 3 and 5 in Table 11.1 identify the marginal revenue products of potential servers when they work in Janet's restaurant or in alternative employments. Under these conditions, how many servers will Janet hire and what wage will she pay? She will hire 4 and pay them $4 per hour.

The first server's marginal revenue product in alternative employment is only $1 per hour, so Janet can hire that server for $1 per hour. The **marginal resource cost** is the increase in the total cost caused by the employment

Figure 11.1 The Competitive Wage Rate

The equilibrium wage in a competitive market is the market-clearing wage, $5.50. It is the wage at which the downward-sloping demand curve for labor (D) and the upward-sloping supply curve of labor (S) cross.

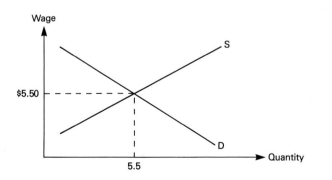

TABLE 11.1   Monopsony Price and Quantity

Because of the market spoiling effect, a monopsonist incurs a marginal resource cost that exceeds the wage. Equating marginal revenue product to marginal resource cost results in a wage of $4 per hour and the employment of 4 workers.

(1) WAGE	(2) QUANTITY OF LABOR	(3) MARGINAL REVENUE PRODUCT	(4) MARGINAL RESOURCE COST	(5) MARGINAL REVENUE PRODUCT OF ALTERNATIVE EMPLOYMENT
$ 1	1	$10	$ 1	$ 1
2	2	9	3	2
3	3	8	5	3
4	4	7	7	4
5	5	6	9	5
6	6	5	11	6
7	7	4	13	7
8	8	3	15	8
9	9	2	17	9
10	10	1	19	10

of one more unit of a resource. The marginal resource cost of the first server to Janet will therefore be $1 per hour. If hired, the server will generate a marginal revenue product for Janet worth $10 per hour. Janet will certainly hire the first server since she can obtain the marginal revenue product of $10 per hour for a marginal resource cost of only $1 per hour.

A second server will require a higher wage. Since the marginal revenue product in alternative employment is $2 per hour, Janet will have to pay the server $2 per hour. But the employee will cost her more. Janet will probably have to pay all the servers the same wage for the same work, especially in a small town. Therefore Janet will have to raise the wage of the first server to $2 per hour to hire the second. The second server's marginal resource cost will be $3 per hour, not $2 per hour. Nevertheless, the marginal revenue product of $9 per hour will cover the $3 per hour marginal resource cost. Janet will employ at least two servers.

The third server will force the wage level to $3 per hour. The server's marginal resource cost will be $5 per hour and the server will yield an $8 per hour marginal revenue product. To receive the $3 per hour net gain from trade, Janet will hire the third server.

Finally, Janet will hire the fourth. That server will raise the wage rate to $4 per hour, have a $7 per hour marginal resource cost, and generate a marginal revenue product of $7 per hour. She will just break even with that server's employment.

Janet certainly won't hire a fifth server. Even though the marginal revenue product would be $6 per hour and the wage only $5 per hour, the marginal resource cost would be $9 per hour. It would be irrational for her to sacrifice $9 to obtain $6.

Under competitive labor market conditions, no market-spoiling effect would have occurred, since each restaurant would have been insignificant in the market. As a result, the marginal resource cost would have equaled the wage. Since Janet would have continued to hire servers until the marginal revenue product fell to equal the marginal resource cost, she would have continued to hire until the marginal revenue product equaled the wage. As a result, she would have hired 5.5 servers rather than 4 servers and paid a wage of $5.50 per hour rather than $4 per hour. Under competitive conditions, both the wage and the level of employment are higher than under conditions of monopsony.

Monopoly Resource Prices

Resources can also be traded under conditions of monopoly. If we specify a monopoly resource market, one in which only one seller of a resource deals with many buyers, then we can predict that the price will be higher and the quantity employed lower than under competitive conditions.

To explain how monopoly resource prices are determined, let's assume that a single seller of servers exists in Jackson, the Jackson Restaurant Servers Union, that the union deals with many restaurants, and that the various marginal revenue products are the same as before (as shown in columns 3 and 5 in Table 11.2).

TABLE 11.2 Monopoly Price and Quantity

> The monopolist obtains marginal earnings that are less than the wage due to a market-spoiling effect. Equating marginal earnings to the marginal revenue product of alternative employments results in a $7-per-hour wage and the employment of 4 workers.

(1) WAGE	(2) QUANTITY OF LABOR	(3) MARGINAL REVENUE PRODUCT	(4) MARGINAL EARNINGS	(5) MARGINAL REVENUE PRODUCT OF ALTERNATIVE EMPLOYMENT
$10	1	$10	$10	$ 1
9	2	9	8	2
8	3	8	6	3
7	4	7	4	4
6	5	6	2	5
5	6	5	0	6
4	7	4	−2	7
3	8	3	−4	8
2	9	2	−6	9
1	10	1	−8	10

The union is a **monopolistic cartel**, a group that can act as a monopoly seller. It's relevant to look at a cartel because while Michael Jackson, Steven King, and Larry Bird possess significant monopoly power, individual monopoly sellers of resources are comparatively rare. If we assume that the union wants to maximize the net gain from trade of its members, then we can predict that the union will charge $7 per hour and sell 4 servers to the restaurants.

The union will certainly be willing to sell the first server. It can charge $10 per hour for that worker since the worker's marginal revenue product is $10 per hour. If we define the **marginal earnings** of a resource as the change in total earnings that occurs when one more unit of a resource is sold, then the marginal earnings of the union from the sale of the first server is $10 per hour. The sale of the worker will require the union (its members) to sacrifice alternative employment worth $1 per hour, assuming that the wage in alternative employment would be equal to the marginal revenue product in that employment. Since the marginal earnings of $10 per hour exceed the union's $1-per-hour sacrifice of alternative earnings, the union will sell the first server to receive the $9 net gain from trade.

The union will also be willing to sell a second server. Although it will spoil its market for the first server by reducing the wage level to $9 per hour, the resulting marginal earnings of $8 per hour will still exceed the $2-per-hour loss of alternative earnings.

Three servers will also be sold. The marginal earnings of $6 per hour at the $8-per-hour wage will cover the loss of an additional $3 per hour worth of alternative earnings.

Finally, the union will break even with the sale of a fourth member. The $4 per hour in marginal earnings at the $7-per-hour wage will just equal the $4 per hour worth of alternative earnings sacrificed.

Under competitive conditions, the wage rate would have been $5.50 per hour and 5.5 servers would have been employed. In contrast, under monopoly conditions, the wage rate is a higher $7 per hour and the quantity employed is a lower 4 servers. Monopoly resource prices are higher and quantities are lower.

A Summary of the Theory

Our theory makes four assumptions:

a. The value of resources to buyers is determined by their marginal revenue products.
b. The value of resources to sellers is determined by the marginal revenue products in alternative employment.
c. Resources have greater productivities when they are combined with the resources of other individuals.
d. The value of marginal products falls to buyers as more resources are purchased and rises to sellers as more are sold.

These assumptions imply that

   a. We will sell or buy resources.
   b. In a competitive market, the price of a resource will be in equilibrium at the market-clearing level.
   c. In a monopsony market, both price and quantity exchanged will be lower than in a competitive market.
   d. In a monopoly market, price will be higher and quantity employed lower than in a competitive market.

SPECIAL TOPICS

Labor Exploitation and Competitive Markets

Do capitalists exploit workers? As indicated in the introduction, we can't deal with this question if exploitation relates to the fairness of a situation. However, we can define exploitation as an event and then see if and when the event occurs.

Let's define **exploitation** as the payment of a price below or above the value of a resource to either a buyer or a seller. For instance, if a worker is worth $100 to an employer and is paid only $10, exploitation results. Similarly, exploitation occurs when the value of a worker's labor to the worker is only $10 and the worker charges $100 for that labor. (Again, value or worth refers to the last unit purchased or sold, not to the total of all units.)

Given our definition of exploitation, we can show that exploitation of labor by employers doesn't occur in competitive labor markets. In those markets, the wages of workers equal the values of the resources to employers since the wages equal the marginal revenue products of labor. For example, in the competitive market for servers in Jackson, the servers were worth $5.50 per hour because their marginal revenue products were $5.50 per hour and the servers were paid a wage of $5.50 per hour.

Exploitation of labor fails to occur because competition among employers increases the wage when the wage is less than the marginal revenue product of labor. For instance, the restaurant owners in the competitive server market would prefer to hire servers for $1 per hour rather than $5.50 per hour. But if the wage were $1 per hour, all the restaurants would be able to increase their net gain from trade by hiring additional servers. One server would be willing to work for $1 per hour but the quantity of servers demanded would be 10. The shortage would cause competition and the competition would raise the wage rate, eventually to $5.50 per hour.

Not only are workers in competitive labor markets not exploited by capitalists, but capitalists also aren't exploited by workers. Workers charge a wage that just reflects the value of the labor to themselves, its marginal revenue product in alternative employment. For example, in the competitive server market, the marginal revenue product in alternative employment was $5.50 per hour and the servers charged just $5.50 per hour for their time.

Like the restaurant owners, the employees would prefer to do better; they would like to be paid more than the value of their sacrifices. But competition from other workers for jobs paying more than the values of sacrifices makes this impossible. For example, if the wage in the market for servers were $10 per hour and their sacrifices were worth only $1 per hour, one server would certainly be happy. But a surplus would occur since 10 servers would be seeking work and only 1 would find a job. Competition from the other servers would then force the wage to drop to the $5.50 rate, a wage just equal to the value of the marginal revenue product of the servers in alternative employment.

Exploitation by a Monopsonist

Competitive exchange conditions aren't universal. Although exploitation, as we have defined it, doesn't occur in competitive labor markets, it can occur in other markets. Specifically, when monopsony conditions are present, our theory implies that workers will be exploited. For example, if Janet owned the only restaurant in Jackson, she would pay $4 per hour for a $7-per-hour marginal revenue product and hire only 4 servers. She wouldn't hire more servers because it would then be necessary to pay higher wages, not only to the additional servers, but also to all of the others.

When Karl Marx lived in England at the beginning of the Industrial Revolution, it is likely that the case of monopsony was more prevalent than now. Aided by significant labor immobility and high market information costs, some large firms in small towns may have exploited workers to a significant extent.

Monopsonistic Cartels: The NCAA and the NFL

In the labor markets of today, monopsonistic circumstances are rare because many firms generally compete for the same workers. Once in a while, however, firms join together and form a **monopsonistic cartel** so they can act as one employer. That way they can increase their profits by paying lower wages and hiring fewer workers. For instance, even if many restaurants serve food in Jackson, the owners may nevertheless be able to obtain monopsonistic gains from trade by forming a Jackson Restaurant Association and using it to regulate wages and employment. Our theory predicts that such a cartel would exploit labor if it acted the same way as a single buyer would have.

A contemporary example of a monopsonistic cartel in the labor market is the National Collegiate Athletic Association (NCAA). The NCAA is a combination of colleges that has, among other things, decided to pay college football players compensation that is far below their marginal revenue products. The association keeps compensation low by establishing upper limits on scholarships, jobs, bonuses, and almost every other type of benefit players may receive.

Since monopsonistic cartels increase the net gain from trade of their members, why aren't they universal? One reason is that they are generally illegal. But even when they are legal, the cartels are seldom formed and when they are, they seldom succeed. This is because while a monopsonistic cartel may increase the net gain of its members, once such a cartel is in place, each of the members can increase its net gain even further by violating the restrictions of the cartel. Such violations of the rules can eventually destroy the cartel.

For example, if the Jackson Restaurant Association set the wage of servers at $4 per hour, member restaurants obeying the rules of the cartel could increase their net gain from trade relative to competitive conditions by hiring 4 employees for $4 per hour, servers that could generate a $7-per-hour marginal revenue product. However, individual restaurants could obtain even more net gain if they violated the rules of the cartel by hiring additional servers for slightly more than the $4 wage rate, servers that would generate marginal revenue products worth slightly less than $7 per hour. With enough members violating the restrictions of the cartel in this way, the cartel would collapse into a competitive condition. With the resulting competition, the quantity hired would rise to 5.5 servers, the wage would rise to $5.50 per hour, and the marginal revenue product would fall to $5.50 per hour.

To survive, cartels must constantly police their members, penalizing members if they try to increase net gain by hiring more workers at prices higher than cartel prices. For example, hardly a year passes when the NCAA doesn't place some schools on probation for giving athletes more than a scholarship.

Even when cartels succeed in holding their members in check, they still have to contend with competition from the outside. For instance, some restaurant owners might realize that by not joining the cartel, they would be able to avoid its restrictions. Outside the cartel, they would be able to hire all the workers they wanted at slightly more than the cartel rate. For a cartel to be successful, it not only has to avoid competition from within, but it must also prevent competition from without.

Sometimes restrictions on outside competition come easily and naturally. The NCAA, for example, encounters only limited outside competition partly because another monopsonistic cartel, the National Football League (NFL), has found it in its interest not to compete with the NCAA for high school graduates. The NFL uses the NCAA as a cheap training ground for future players.

Because of the problems cartels encounter, their success often depends on government intervention: The government must prevent competition from non-cartel members. The Jackson Restaurant Association, for instance, might be able to get the city council to require that all establishments serving food must join the association, and then the association could limit its membership. Also, the NCAA might have politicians sponsor legislation regulating college sports.

Class Exploitation Theories

Some class exploitation theories implicitly assume the existence of monopsonistic cartels among the buyers. We can use our theory to predict that if men, whites, or capitalists get together, they can indeed increase their net gain from trade by lowering both the wages and the employment levels of women, blacks, and workers, respectively.

Nevertheless, the probability of so many buyers getting together is very low. The problems of preventing competition from within and without would be mind-boggling. If women, blacks, and workers, for instance, were ever paid $5 for producing $10 worth of goods, any man, white, or capitalist could make millions by paying slightly more and hiring enormous quantities of the exploited workers. For extensive class exploitation to continue, every person in the exploiting group would not only have to want to be a member of the conspiracy, but he or she would have to want it so much as to be willing to forego opportunities to get rich.

Furthermore, even if all members of the exploiting group joined and obeyed the rules of the cartel, this wouldn't assure success. The survival of the cartels would still require that members of the groups being exploited join the cartels whenever they obtained enough wealth to become employers. Once women, blacks, and workers could become employers, they would have to join the cartel and pass up opportunities to increase their net gain from trade by hiring members of their group at slightly more than the cartel wages.

All this doesn't mean that people are always paid what they are worth. The problems of cartels can and have been overcome. We have said only that the creation of a successful cartel is difficult for a number of reasons.

Monopolistic Exploitation

So far, we have seen that exploitation will not occur in a competitive market, but that under monopsony, it is likely. Exploitation is also likely under conditions of monopoly. Our theory predicts that monopoly sellers of resources will restrict sales and charge more than they value the resources.

For example, the reason many of us envy the wealth of Johnny Carson, Lee Iaccoca, and Magic Johnson is that we think they receive wages that exceed the values of their sacrifices. If these workers had to give up alternative products worth $1 million to obtain $1 million, few of us would be impressed. Making a million by mowing one million lawns just isn't what most of us have in mind when we say that we want to get rich.

Monopoly sellers of labor exploit buyers because the monopolists spoil their markets if they sell too much. If they can earn another $1 million by sacrificing only $10,000 worth of leisure, they may nevertheless prefer not to sell if they have to reduce the price of previous units significantly. In the process, they will exploit buyers because the price of their services will exceed the marginal revenue products in alternative employments.

A Carpenter's Union
and the American Medical Association

As we indicated, cases of monopoly in resource markets are fairly rare. However, monopolistic cartels in the form of labor unions are fairly common. Our theory predicts that if the cartels act the same way as individual monopolists, then the cartels will exploit buyers, charging prices above the marginal revenue products of resources in alternative employments. For example, our Jackson Restaurant Servers Union charged $7 per hour for labor that can only yield $4 per hour in marginal revenue product in alternative jobs.

Not all unions of workers succeed in extracting exploitative wages. In fact, some studies indicate that unions have only raised wages a bit more than 10% above the levels of nonunion workers of similar productivities. Although there is some controversy over the methodology of the studies, it is clear that many unions are far less successful than their members would like.

We can explain the failures of some unions and the inability of other unions to be more successful by again noting that unions, like all cartels, must worry about competition from within and without, competition that is difficult to eliminate when it is better to disobey the rules of a cartel than to obey them. For example, a carpenter's union may raise wages from $10 to $20 per hour, but then its members must work less while "scabs" (union members who cheat on a union contract) or nonunion workers work all they want at a $19-per-hour rate.

Another problem that unions must confront, one that we have so far ignored, is that cartels are groups that can have a great deal of difficulty determining what price to charge and what quantity to sell. The price and quantity that maximizes the net gain from trade of a group is generally different than the price and quantity that would maximize the net gain of particular members.

For example, the carpenters' union may maximize its net gain from trade at a $20-per-hour wage, but members with seniority may want the wage to be $40 per hour, realizing that they would still work despite a massive reduction in employment. On the other hand, young carpenters might prefer a $10-per-hour wage if they thought that they would be unemployed at a $20-per-hour wage. These conflicts within a union can undermine the ability of a union to prevent internal and external competition.

Once we recognize that internal politics will play an important role in the behavior of the union, it seems unlikely that the union will ever charge the wage and sell the associated quantity that maximizes the net gain from trade to its members. We can be fairly certain only that the wage will be above the competitive level and that employment will be below that level.

Union problems can be overcome with the help of government. This explains why the unions that have achieved notable successes have generally been the ones that have obtained government protection from competition. For example, the American Medical Association is perhaps the most successful union in the United States. It has been able to restrict the supply of doctors by using government to limit the number of medical schools in the country and then requiring that everyone practicing medicine graduate from one of those schools. Without government restrictions, competition from paramedics, nurses, and pharmacists would greatly reduce demand for and the wages of doctors.

Bilateral Monopoly Exchange

What if a monopolist deals with a monopsonist? Then, unfortunately, we can predict only the price range, not the exact price. The condition is really one of isolated interpersonal exchange.

For example, if the Jackson Restaurant Servers Union negotiated with the Jackson Restaurant Association, the union might seek a $7-per-hour wage and the association might argue for a $4-per-hour wage. If the union was extremely skilled in negotiation and obtained the $7-per-hour wage, monopoly results would be obtained. On the other hand, if the association were more powerful, the wage might be $4 per hour and monopsony results would occur. Finally, if the two groups were balanced in power, the competitive wage of $5.50 per hour might be agreed to and 5.5 servers would be hired. Bilateral monopoly conditions could give rise to competitive results.

Too Many Hamburgers, Insufficient Cancer Operations

Exchanges of resources not only determine resource prices, they also distribute resources. As a result, resource trades affect which products are eventually produced.

Under conditions where products are sold competitively, we can show that competitive resource trades cause the production of goods that are equal in value to the alternatives that could have otherwise been produced. This implies that the most valuable products are produced. For example, in the competitive restaurant servers market, if the marginal server had produced served meals worth $5.50 at a sacrifice of only $5.00 worth of alternative products, more valuable products could have been produced if workers had been shifted from the production of the alternatives and into the production of served meals. On the other hand, if the marginal server had produced served meals worth $5.50 at a sacrifice of alternative products worth $6, more valuable products could have been produced if workers had been shifted from the production of served meals and into the production of the alternatives. Only when the value of the products produced equals the value of the products sacrificed is it impossible to produce more valuable products than the ones being sacrificed.

Equality of the values of all products occurs under competitive product and resource market conditions because competitive resource markets equate the marginal revenue products of resources to their marginal revenue products in alternative employments, and the marginal revenue products of resources, under competitive product market conditions, reflect the values of products to consumers.

For example, in the competitive resource market for restaurant servers, restaurants hired servers until the marginal revenue product of the servers equaled a wage of $5.50 per hour. Similarly, the servers sold their labor until the sacrifice of marginal revenue product in alternative employment equaled the $5.50 wage. These two marginal revenue products indicate that the value of served meals was $5.50 and that the value of the alternative products was also $5.50. The marginal revenue products reveal the values of the products because marginal revenue product equals the marginal product times the marginal revenue and, under competitive product market conditions, marginal revenue equals price. The price, in turn, reflects the value of a product to consumers. For instance, if consumers pay $1 for each additional served meal and an additional server causes 5.5 additional meals to be produced each hour, then the $5.50 marginal revenue product indicates that consumers obtain served meals worth $5.50 per hour.

Compared to competitive resource market conditions, monopsony conditions cause buyers to purchase fewer resources (so the buyers can pay lower prices). As a result, less valuable products are produced elsewhere. For instance, in the restaurant servers market example, once restaurant owners gained monopsony power, they restricted employment to keep the wage rate lower. The wage was only $4 per hour even though the value of the marginal product was $7 per hour. Assuming competitive product markets, some servers were forced to produce alternative products worth only $4 per hour rather than additional meals that would have been worth $7 per hour.

Similarly, under monopoly resource market conditions, sellers restrict sales (to increase resource prices). This also causes less valuable products to be produced elsewhere. In the case of the restaurant servers market, the union of servers kept the wage rate at $7 per hour and employment at 4 servers. Again assuming competitive product markets, the union forced some servers to produce alternative products worth as little as $4 per hour rather than generate served meals in a restaurant that would be worth up to $7 per hour.

In short, restraints of trade in resource markets, whether caused by buyers or sellers, will lower the values of products. Associations of restaurant owners or unions of servers will reduce the production of served meals and force an increase in the production of less valuable alternative products. Likewise, the American Medical Association causes a reduction in the number of cancer operations and an increase in the production of other less valuable alternative products, perhaps Wendy's hamburgers.

Rent, Interest, and Profit

Up to this point, although we have concentrated on labor in our examples, we haven't explicitly distinguished among the various types of resources. Such distinctions were unnecessary because the theory predicts for all resources equally well. We could have just as easily talked about the purchases of additional tables as the employment of more servers.

Nevertheless, some people argue that we must distinguish among the various resources and the earnings generated from their sale. For example, although Karl Marx spent some time on labor markets, the key element of his theory of exploitation focused on the existence of rent, interest, and profit payments to capitalists. Marx argued that labor is the source of all value and that labor should, therefore, eventually receive all output. He then concluded that since rent, interest, and profit don't accrue to workers, exploitation occurs. By using both the theory of this chapter and the theories of capital goods and indirect production of preceding chapters, we can analyze this claim.

Labor and Value

First, let's start with the question of whether labor is responsible for all value. The theory we have just examined denies this. It argues that value doesn't originate with resources, it emanates from the values consumers place on the products of resources. For instance, the value of a radio to a consumer is the same no matter how many hours of labor were used to produce it.

Is labor at least the source of all products if not the source of all value? No. It is true that no products would exist without labor, but it is equally true that no products would exist without land. Every product is a combination of both labor and land. (Capital is also generally involved, but it is a manifestation of labor and land previously produced during indirect production.)

Workers could argue that all land should be owned by them equally. This claim would certainly be more valid if landowners had stolen the land. But most landowners have purchased the land that they own, often from workers who wanted to consume other goods early or who were more optimistic about the yields of other resources.

Interest and Profit as Exploitation

If we assume that labor and land are the sources of all products, does it follow that all payments other than wages and rents represent exploitation? That is, do interest and profits mean that workers are exploited? No. Interest may reveal only that workers were paid early for the products of their labor. If someone hired you for 90 fish to produce 100 fish the following year, you wouldn't be exploited if future goods were 10% less valuable than present goods. The extra 10 fish the buyer of your labor would obtain would make the value of your future product just equal to your present wage.

What about profit? Does profit imply the exploitation of labor? Again, no. As we noted in Chapter 7, labor, land, and capital are capital goods. The workers as well as landowners and capitalists are generally paid the expected values of future marginal revenue products, not the actual values. If you were hired for 90 fish and 90 fish equaled the present value of your expected future marginal revenue product, then you would be paid what you were worth at the time of employment. If your marginal revenue product turned out to be 110 fish rather than the expected 100 fish, a profit would accrue to your employer.

Nevertheless, at the time of employment, you would have been paid what your labor was worth.

By opting to sell your labor, you divested yourself of the possibility that your marginal revenue product might be only 80 fish. At the time, the trade of your labor for guaranteed present fish represented selective risk-bearing. If you subsequently generated a marginal revenue product of only 80 fish, your employer would have incurred a loss.

More generally, once we recognize that production takes time, the values of resources, including labor, no longer equal their marginal revenue products. Instead, they are worth the present value of their expected future marginal revenue products.

So far we have concentrated on the simple sale of resources to producers without saying much about the producers themselves. The producers are usually not individuals but business firms that merge the resources of many individuals. Business firms represent team production. In the next chapter we look closely at business firms, examining what they are, why they exist, and the nature of their production decisions.

MAJOR AND MINOR POINTS

1. The value of a resource is determined by its marginal revenue product, the marginal product times the marginal revenue generated by the units within the marginal product.

2. The marginal product is the change in the total product that occurs with the employment of one more unit of a resource. It is not how much the resource produces, since a resource must always be combined with one or more other resources before any product can be produced.

3. The more of a resource we buy, the lower its marginal revenue product. The marginal revenue product falls because both the marginal product and the marginal revenue generated by the items making up the marginal product decline.

4. The proposition that marginal product will fall as we employ more of a resource is called the law of diminishing returns.

5. Diminishing returns occur because additional units of a resource have less of other resources to work with.

6. The marginal revenue generated by the items comprising the marginal product declines because diminishing valuation forces a price reduction if additional units are to be sold.

7. As we sell more of a resource, its value rises because the marginal revenue product of alternative employment increases.

8. Value differentials result when resource mergers increase production. The differentials cause us to trade resources.

9. Under competitive conditions, equilibrium resource prices are at market-clearing levels determined by supplies and demands.

10. The values of resources determine resource supplies and demands. Since the

values fall as more resources are owned and rise as more are sold, resource demand curves slope downward, whereas resource supply curves slope upward. Furthermore, value differentials make resource supply and demand curves cross.

11. Under competitive conditions, resource trades occur at prices where supply and demand curves cross, because at any other prices, either surpluses or shortages would have caused competition that in turn would have forced prices to change toward the market-clearing levels.

12. A monopsonist is a single buyer. When a monopsonist deals with competitive sellers in a resource market, the price and the quantity of a resource employed will be less than under competitive conditions.

13. When a monopolist trades with competitive buyers in a resource market, the price will be higher and the quantity lower than under competitive conditions.

14. One definition of exploitation is the payment of a price for a resource that is above or below the value of the resource.

15. Exploitation (as defined) doesn't occur in competitive labor markets because wages equal the values of labor to both employers and employees.

16. Exploitation occurs in monopsony resource markets because, to avoid spoiling their markets for resources, employers purchase less, thereby driving the wage down and below the value of the marginal product of labor.

17. When many buyers join together to act as one, they create a monopsonistic cartel.

18. Monopsonistic cartels have generally been destroyed by competition from within and without because it is better for an individual buyer to disobey the rules of a cartel than to obey them. By ignoring the restrictions of a cartel, a buyer doesn't have to limit his or her purchases.

19. Governments are often necessary for the formation of successful monopsonistic cartels because governments can prevent internal and external competition.

20. Many class exploitation theories implicitly assume the presence of a monopsonistic cartel.

21. Exploitation occurs in monopoly labor markets. To avoid spoiling their markets too much, monopolists sell less and drive the wage above the value of labor to the workers.

22. In resource markets, monopoly cartels can lead to the exploitation of buyers. The cartels often take the form of labor unions.

23. Many unions are not successful because they suffer from competition from within and without. They also often have problems determining the monopoly price and quantity because the combination that maximizes the net gain from trade to the group isn't the combination that maximizes the net gain of each the group's members.

24. Many successful unions have received government protection from internal and external competition.

25. When monopolists deal with monopsonists, results can be monopolistic, monopsonistic, or even competitive.

26. Under competitive conditions, resources are allocated so that they produce the most valuable products. Under monopsony or monopoly conditions, some resources are instead allocated so that they produce less valuable other products.

27. The values of resources are determined by marginal revenue products, not by how much labor went into their production. Labor is not the source of all products. Products result from combinations of labor and natural resources.

28. When labor is paid early for products it produces later, it is paid less. But the less it is paid often has a value equal to the more that it produces because of the time-value of goods.

29. When labor is paid early, it is paid the value of its expected marginal revenue product at that time, even if the marginal revenue product is eventually greater or less than was expected.

30. Neither rent, interest, nor profit necessarily represent exploitation (as we have defined it).

QUESTIONS

1. When will the demand for a resource increase?
2. Why will the marginal revenue product of a resource fall as more of the resource is purchased?
3. Why will the marginal revenue product of a resource in alternative employment rise as more of a resource is sold?
4. Why will exchanges involving resources occur?
5. What will be the equilibrium price of a resource in a competitive market? Why?
6. Why will the price and the quantity traded of a resource be lower in a monopsony market than in a competitive market?
7. Why will the price of a resource be higher and the quantity traded lower in a monopoly market than in a competitive market?
8. Why will exploitation of labor not occur in a competitive labor market?
9. Why will exploitation of labor occur in a monopsony labor market?
10. When will a monopsony cartel fail?
11. Why will workers exploit employers in a monopoly labor market?
12. When will a monopoly cartel fail?
13. Why will competitive resource markets distribute resources so that the resources produce the products that consumers value most?
14. Why will monopsony and monopoly resource markets cause an underproduction of some products and an overproduction of other products relative to consumer valuations?
15. Is the value of a product determined by the resources that were used to produce it?
16. What determines the value of a resource once the complication of time is introduced?
17. Discuss the following terms and concepts:

Value of a resource	Exploitation
Marginal revenue product	Monopsony exploitation
Marginal product	Monopoly exploitation
Law of diminishing returns	Cartels

Diminishing valuation	Internal competition
Competitive resource prices	External competition
Resource monopsony	Reaching an agreement
Employer associations	Government intervention
Monopsony resource prices	Class exploitation theories
Resource monopoly	Labor theory of value
Monopoly resource prices	Rent, interest, and profit
Labor unions	

APPLICATIONS

1. Who produces more, a lawyer or a legal secretary?
2. Does a higher value of land result in a higher value of corn, or does a higher value of corn cause a higher value of land?
3. Does the law of diminishing returns say that the employment of additional units of a resource will cause total output to fall?
4. Graph the relationship between the value of a resource and the quantity purchased. Place the value on the vertical axis and quantity of the horizontal.
5. Graph the relationship between the value of a resource and the amount sold. Place the value on the vertical axis and the quantity of the horizontal.
6. If a secretary is worth $10 per hour, what keeps you from hiring him or her for $9 per hour? What keeps him or her from charging $11 per hour?
7. A worker will increase your revenues by $10,000. She asks that she be paid only $5000. Why might you rationally not hire her?
8. Suppose the Jackson Restaurant Association is the only buyer of servers in Jackson. Graph the marginal revenue product, the marginal resource cost, and the supply of labor curves that exist in the market. Then show and explain the monopsony price and quantity.
9. Suppose the Jackson Restaurant Servers Union is the only seller of servers in Jackson. Graph curves representing the marginal revenue product, the supply of labor, and the marginal earnings curves that exist in the labor market. Then show and explain the monopoly wage and quantity sold.
10. Why might it be difficult for American firms to exploit Mexican workers?
11. Why did the Arab oil cartel OPEC reduce its prices in the early 1980s?
12. Why have many nations chosen not to join OPEC?
13. How does Bruce Springsteen keep his wages high?
14. Unions don't exploit employers. They just obtain what workers are worth. Employers wouldn't hire workers unless the workers produced enough to compensate the employers for the wages paid. Comment.
15. Even when a union raises wages, why might you be wise to not join?
16. Unions can raise wages either by negotiating or by restricting the supply of labor. Why does a restriction of supply often look better to the public?
17. A worker's marginal revenue product is 100 apples. The worker was paid only 50 apples. Under what conditions could the worker have been paid the value of his or her labor?

Business Firms

When a hard-driving floor boss shoves a stopwatch in your face and orders you to "speed up," freedom of enterprise seems like an incredible misnomer. And yet, while conditions are usually less harsh, we don't normally work for ourselves. Most of us are "slaves" to business firms.

In this chapter, we explain why business firms exist, the factors that limit their size, the costs they incur, and finally, when and at what levels of output they will produce. To achieve all this, we explain and apply a theory of the business firm.

We are able to construct the theory by recognizing that we can often increase the productivities of resources by engaging in team production. We call the team units **business firms**.

The special topics of this chapter deal with the integration of the home construction industry, the Soviet Union as one large business firm, the alienation of labor, and elite versus mass college educational systems.

A THEORY OF THE BUSINESS FIRM

The Phenomena

When we examine the production of goods in advanced economic systems like those of the United States, Canada, Japan, and the Soviet Union, it is clear that a large proportion of total output is produced by teams of many individuals working together with various resources. The teams are business firms that

a. Bind their members together with complex networks of contracts;
b. Produce particular types of products over an extended period of time;
c. Use managers rather than markets to provide internal coordination and control.

However, although business firms produce many goods, they seldom totally dominate an industry or a product. U.S.X., for example, isn't the only steel producer in the world. In fact, it isn't even completely responsible for producing any of the product that it ships from its factories. The steel industry comprises many steel companies, and various firms outside the industry provide steel producers with coal, educated labor, transportation, and capital equipment.

An Explanation: Producing Pot-Scrubbers

Why do business firms produce most goods and why is the size of the firms limited? To answer these questions, let's examine how we might produce one particular product, an electrically powered pot-scrubber. The scrubber consists of a bent handle with a circular brush on one end, a brush that spins horizontally in a pot or pan. Attached to the other end of the handle is a flexible cable that links the brush to an electric motor bolted beneath the sink. By separating the motor and the brush with a flexible cable, we can overcome the problems of electrocution and excessive weight.

The English Putting-Out System

We could produce the scrubber by subcontracting to hundreds of individuals. Engineers might be hired to design the appliance, a lawyer to obtain a patent, machinists to produce motors and cables, etc. This is essentially the way thread was woven into cloth in England at the dawn of the Industrial Revolution under the "putting-out" system. Suppliers distributed raw cotton thread to various households, where it was woven into cloth. The cloth was then returned to the suppliers.

Subcontracting to individuals suffers from three significant limitations:

1. Since only one worker can be used to perform each job, the size and type of capital and the method of production are severely restricted.
2. Because each producer only produces a small part of the product, many market transactions are required.
3. Since individual producers must research the markets, obtain financing, buy resources, develop technology, and sell their outputs, they can't specialize totally in doing one task.

The Firm and Its Tasks

To overcome these limitations, instead of buying products as inputs into production, we would buy resources and put all production under one roof; we would create a business firm. Our firm could then use capital on a large scale, employ mass-production technology, reduce the number of trades, and increase the specialization of labor. During the Industrial Revolution, these advantages caused the factory system to replace the putting-out system; business firms replaced individual producers.

To achieve the physical production and the sale of the scrubbers, our firm would produce five types of services:

a. Marketing
b. Finance
c. Information
d. Contract negotiation
e. Management

Marketing   First, the firm would conduct research to answer some standard marketing questions: Is there sufficient demand for the scrubbers? Should the firm target commercial or residential consumers? Is a fancy design better than a simple one? How powerful do consumers want their scrubbers? Where are the consumers located? What type of advertising will be most effective in reaching prospective consumers?

By the way, marketing information would be one of the most vital things that our firm would provide workers and other owners of resources. In an economy full of business firms, workers only have to search for jobs; they don't have to develop products or find consumers.

Finance   After it did some preliminary marketing research, our firm would obtain outside financing. Incidentally, outside financing wouldn't be necessary if our firm either (1) used its own money to buy resources, (2) had the owners of resources accept a percentage of future revenues rather than pay, or (3) convinced consumers to buy the scrubbers in advance on a cost-plus basis. All costs and revenues would then accrue to either the owners of the firm, the suppliers of resources, or the consumers of the product, respectively.

Nevertheless, we would probably prefer to shift some costs and risks to outside financial supporters by using debt or equity financing. **Debt financing** consists of borrowing money from creditors, who would be paid fixed amounts of interest plus principle at some future dates. Debt financing would allow us to shift most of the time-value sacrifices associated with production to banks and other creditors, leaving us with most of the future profits or losses. In contrast, **equity financing** consists of obtaining money from investors who are given rights to a certain percentage of future earnings. Investors providing equity financing become part owners of the firm. Equity financing would allow us to reassign more of the profits and losses as well as the time-value sacrifices to partners or shareholders.

Information   Next, the firm would produce a great deal of additional information. The information would be about the willingnesses of financial supporters to invest in the scrubbers, the available methods of technology, and the qualities and prices of various resources.

Contract Negotiation   Closely related to the production of information would be the firm's negotiation and enforcement of various contracts. The firm would have to reach and consummate financial agreements with outside creditors, owners, consumers, workers, and other resource suppliers.

Management: Islands of Coercion   Finally, our firm would produce managerial services to coordinate and control production. This wouldn't have been necessary if the scrubbers had been produced by subcontractors rather than by our firm. Markets would then have coordinated and controlled production. Prices in markets would have told everyone what to do and rewarded them for doing what they had been told. For example, our willingness to pay for electric motors would have informed machinists that their services were wanted. Likewise, the bids that various machinists would have provided us would have told us which machinists were the least costly ones and instructed us to deal with them. These offers and bids would have also motivated the machinists and given us the incentive to hire the least costly ones.

By creating a business firm, we would bypass the markets. Since market prices wouldn't then coordinate and control production, we would hire managers to provide the necessary information and incentives. The managers would tell our machinists what to do and make sure that they worked reasonably hard.

From the perspective of our employees, the firm would be an "island of coercion in a sea of free enterprise." The employees might be free to sell their labor to whatever firm they wished, but while employed by our firm, they would do what our managers told them. Although many workers may prefer to take their orders from the markets, when they work for business firms, they are instead ordered about by managers.

Limits on Size: Subcontracting and Multiple Firms

In an attempt to limit the costs of production, we wouldn't go to the extreme of producing the scrubbers from scratch, starting with raw labor and materials like iron ore and coal. We would instead limit the size of our firm by allowing individuals or other firms to produce some inputs. We might contract the design of our pot-scrubbers to an industrial design firm, the accounting to a CPA firm, and the wholesaling and retailing to a department store.

In addition to using some subcontractors to provide production services, we would buy some capital directly from other firms. It would certainly be less costly to buy steel, educated labor, and trucks than to produce them.

Finally, we might find that we could produce pot-scrubbers at a lower cost by creating more than one firm. After some level of output, a second firm might produce more cheaply than one large firm because, with a smaller management staff, coordination and control would be easier.

The Predictions

The Firm and Its Limited Size

We can use the preceding explanation to predict that we will produce goods by creating business firms, units of team production in which resources are jointly owned. We can also predict that the size of the firms will be limited. Firms will produce only parts of products, and products will be produced by industries comprised of more than one firm.

Marginal and Average Costs

We can also make some predictions about costs. The costs of production are the opportunity costs, the values of the highest valued alternatives sacrificed as resources are employed. As we noted in Chapter 9, production costs include all sacrifices associated with production, whether they require a direct payment of money to suppliers of resources or not. Using our theory, we can predict that as a firm increases output, the marginal and average costs of production will first fall and then rise.

Marginal cost is the change in the total opportunity cost of production that occurs with the production of the next unit of output. As our pot scrubber firm increases its rate of output, marginal cost will initially decrease.

If marginal cost didn't first fall, we wouldn't necessarily bother expanding the size of the firm. We could simply have one firm produce each scrubber. More generally, if marginal costs didn't fall as firms initially expanded production rates, most industries would consist of millions of tiny producers.

Marginal cost will fall because the factors that reduce cost when the firm replaces individual producers will continue as the firm increases its rate of output: The firm will employ more mass-production technology, purchase larger units of capital, make fewer market trades, and further increase the specialization of labor.

However, marginal cost won't continue downward forever. If it did, every industry would have only one firm. That firm could destroy any competitors by charging a lower price to reflect its lower cost.

Marginal cost will eventually rise because high management costs will offset the economies of large-scale production. As our firm's management pyramid expands, internal coordination and control will become very difficult, since information and directives will move only slowly through the firm's bureaucratic maze. These eventual high costs explain why General Motors, New York University, and the U.S. Defense Department decentralize their internal structure into divisions, departments, and project units, creating firms within firms.

Since marginal cost will first fall and then rise with the rate of output, graphing marginal cost relative to quantity generates a U-shaped curve, like the one in Figure 12.1.

Figure 12.1 also contains an average cost curve. **Average cost** is the opportunity cost per unit of output, the total opportunity cost divided by quantity. Average costs can be derived directly from marginal costs. For example, if the marginal costs of the first five pot-scrubbers were $80, $70, $60, $70, and $80, then the average costs would be $80, $75, $70, $70, and $72, respectively.

As the graph in Figure 12.1 illustrates, a U-shaped marginal cost curve creates a U-shaped average cost curve, and the marginal cost curve intersects the average cost curve at the average cost curve's minimum point. This is because marginal cost is what is added to the previous average. As long as marginal cost is less than average cost, average cost falls. When marginal cost equals the average cost, the average cost stays the same. Finally, when marginal cost is above the average cost, the average cost rises.

When to Produce?

Next, we can predict that firms will produce only if, at some levels of production, average revenues will equal or exceed average costs. For example, if the average revenue that our pot-scrubber firm obtains equals or exceeds the average cost at all levels of output between 1000 and 10,000 units, the firm will produce somewhere between 1000 and 10,000 units of output.

The prediction is logically derived from the assumption that as economic individuals, we will choose goods as long as the goods we have to sacri-

Figure 12.1   Marginal and Average Cost Curves

The U-shaped marginal cost curve intersects the U-shaped average cost curve from below at the average cost curve's minimum point.

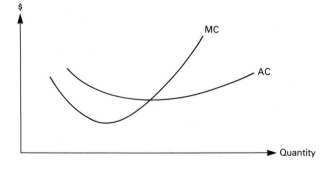

fice are less valuable. In other words, we will try to maximize our net gains, the amounts by which the total values of our gains exceed the total values of our sacrifices. When we own a business firm, the total value of the gains equals the total revenue, the total value of the sacrifices equals the total cost, and the net gain equals the **profit**, the amount by which total revenue exceeds total cost. In short, our assumption that we are economic individuals implies that if we own business firms, we will try to make them earn and maximize profits.

A firm will produce if, at some level of output, average revenue equals or exceeds average cost, because the firm will either break even if average revenue equals average cost or make a profit if average revenue exceeds average cost.

When average revenue equals average cost, the owners of a firm break even, since the the value of the average gain just covers the value of the average sacrifice. For example, if our pot-scrubbers bring in an average revenue of $80 at an average cost of $80, we will break even, making neither a profit nor a loss. This is a point of indifference, but, as we have throughout text, we will for simplicity assume that such options are taken.

Average revenue doesn't have to exceed average cost in order for a firm to break even, since, as we noted earlier, average cost includes all sacrifices. In particular, average cost includes what some economists call **normal profits**, compensations to owners for entrepreneurial abilities (skills and abilities related to the organization and direction of other resources so that production can occur). In a sense, normal profits are wages paid owners for their sacrifices; normal profits don't represent net gains to the owners.

When average revenue exceeds average cost, the owners of a firm make a profit since average revenue more than covers average cost. For instance, if our pot-scrubber firm generates an average revenue of $90 at an average cost of $80, then a profit is earned. If we were to produce and sell 5000 scrubbers, the profit would be $50,000.

We need to know about our average cost and average revenue to decide whether or not to produce, because knowledge of marginal cost and revenue is insufficient. For instance, if we were losing $100,000 by producing 5000 units, it wouldn't matter if marginal revenue were $80 and marginal cost $10. The $70 gain from the production and sale of the 5001st unit would hardly make a dent in our losses.

When a firm earns a profit because average revenue exceeds average cost, the owners of the firm don't necessarily increase their wealth; the owners don't necessarily obtain a capital gain from their ownership of the firm. This is because the capital gain resulting from the profit had already accrued to the owners the moment it was first anticipated. When it is subsequently realized, the owners simply convert their wealth from the ownership value of the firm to realized profits. For the profits to represent an increase in wealth, the profits must be unanticipated.

This explains why the prices of some shares of common stock can fall even when profits are being earned. If the profits imply reductions below what had been previously anticipated, the values of the shares will fall and capital losses will result, reducing the wealth of investors even though profits are being earned.

What Output to Produce?

Next, once firms decide to produce, we can predict that they will select the particular rate of output such that marginal revenue equals marginal cost. We assume not only that firms want profits, but that they want to maximize profits. If marginal revenue exceeded marginal cost, a firm could increase its profit by producing additional units. And if marginal revenue were less than marginal cost, it could increase its profit by producing fewer units.

Firms won't necessarily produce at minimum average cost. Nor will they try to maximize average profit. The only variables with which firms will be concerned once production occurs are marginal revenues and marginal costs. As long as marginal revenues exceed marginal costs, firms will produce and sell larger quantities, and profits will increase.

A Summary of the Theory

Our theory of the firm makes two new assumptions:

a. Teamwork can reduce the costs of production.
b. Teamwork can reduce costs for only limited ranges of production.

By making the two additional assumptions, we can predict that

a. We will create business firms but of limited sizes.
b. Business firms will incur marginal and average costs that first fall and then rise with the rate of output.
c. Business firms will produce if average revenues equal or exceed average costs.
d. Business firms will produce outputs such that marginal revenues will equal marginal costs.

SPECIAL TOPICS

The Integration of Production in Home Construction

We can use our theory to help explain why the home construction industry is highly integrated. Integration sometimes occurs when a product is produced from beginning to end by one firm. In the home-construction industry, this occurs when large construction companies employ excavators, carpenters, plumbers, electricians, masons, drafters, and even salespersons to buy land, build houses, and eventually sell the products. Integration also occurs when an individual firm provides specialized inputs to many producers of final products. In the home-construction industry, this happens when various excavation, carpentry, electrical, masonry, and other firms subcontract their respective services to large firms or general contractors.

Why does integration occur? Because integration can reduce the costs of construction. Integration represents the greater use of team (business firm) production. It allows the use of mass-production technologies, the employment of large units of capital, the avoidance of many transaction costs, and the specialization of labor.

For example, both large construction companies and excavation subcontracting firms can use mass-production technologies and buy large units of capital by excavating many home sites with one large D-6 Caterpillar tractor. Also, they can reduce transaction costs by signing employees to one contract that covers work on many excavation jobs, some not even known at the moment of employment. Moreover, they can specialize particular employees in excavation work.

There is one significant disadvantage to integration, a weakness that explains why one firm doesn't produce all homes—or any homes—completely from beginning to end: Large integrated companies must rely on managers to coordinate and control production. As the integration of production increases, management costs rise geometrically.

This is why general contractors, who hire various subcontractors to build homes, can often compete successfully with large, more integrated construction companies. General contractors can reduce management costs by using market prices rather than managers to coordinate and control production.

The Soviet Union as One Large Business Firm

By recognizing the management problems that limit the size of firms in various industries in the United States, we can explain why the Soviet Union sometimes produces goods at a very high cost.

In one sense, the planned economy of the Soviet Union is one huge business firm. The citizens of the nation are members of a team that continually produces the country's many products. If such a large firm were, in fact, able to produce at a lower cost than the many relatively small independent U.S. producers, then all production in the United States would by now be carried out by one firm. Such a firm could avoid competition with smaller producers by simply keeping its prices lower and in line with its lower costs.

The reason one large firm is less efficient than many smaller firms is that while the costs of coordination and control seem to fall when a firm initially replaces markets with managers, the costs fall only for limited levels of production. At some point as the firm expands, management information and control systems become more costly than those of the markets because humans find it very difficult to provide the geometric increases in information and incentives that are necessary as the firm expands.

For instance, it may be relatively easy for a manager of a small firm to decide who will have access to microcomputers. The manager may know what the various requirements of the employees are and be able to limit access to those who have the most valuable uses. But if the firm contained all the producers in a nation and all its employees wanted to use the machines, the manager couldn't possibly be aware of or evaluate the various reasons for use requests. It might then be easier to revert to market signals, giving the machines only to those willing and able to pay the most.

The Alienation of Labor

With the advance of the Industrial Revolution, it seems that job satisfaction has often been sacrificed for more products. To some extent, workers no longer identify with the products they produce; they are **alienated**. For example, a carpenter who once obtained a great deal of satisfaction by producing a fine piece of furniture may find little joy working for a furniture factory, making a small contribution to the production of thousands of chairs each year.

Following the writings of Karl Marx, Marxists attribute the loss of satisfaction from mass production to the rise of the business firm and, specifically, to the separation of the worker from his or her tools. They argue that since a worker no longer owns the capital used to produce furniture, the worker can no longer identify with the furniture.

Do the Marxists have it right? Perhaps. We can't see alienation, so the answer lies beyond verification. However, we can speculate that alienation emanates from the substitution of team for individual production. The use of teamwork by the firm may be the culprit instead of the way property is owned within the firm. If teamwork is the source of alienation, then even if the workers own the firm and thus the tools, the workers will be alienated.

As an interesting twist, to the extent that Communist countries have increased teamwork by expanding the degree of communal production, they may have increased rather than reduced the alienation of labor.

Elite Versus Mass College Educational Systems

How many people should go to college? Should we limit college to the few as did the elite system of college education that we had in the United States in the nineteenth century, or should we educate many more as we do with our present, mass-orientated educational system?

If we want an educational system that maximizes net gains to students, then we should select one that is neither extremely restrictive nor totally universal. Our goal should be a system that equates the marginal gain from educating students to the marginal cost, obeying a variant of the marginal-revenue-equals-marginal-cost rule that firms follow when they want to maximize their profits.

We shouldn't select a totally elitist system because, although it will yield a higher rate of return per student, it will fail to educate many who would nevertheless gain more value than would be sacrificed. On the other hand, we shouldn't want everyone to go to college either. Then some people who will gain very little or sacrifice an enormous amount will go to school. The value of the marginal gain will often be below the value of the marginal sacrifice, and the net gain from education will fall. The efficient system lies between the two extremes.

Now that we have talked generally about business firms, their costs and their decisions, we will be a bit more specific in the next chapter. We will examine the behaviors of firms that sell their products under competitive circumstances and contrast those behaviors with firms selling under monopoly circumstances.

MAJOR AND MINOR POINTS

1. Business firms consist of teams of individuals, bound together by complex networks of contracts, who produce particular types of products over an extended period of time under dictates and incentives provided by managers.
2. Goods can be produced by a series of individual subcontractors who produce certain portions of goods with the tools they own. This was the essence of the putting-out system that existed in England early in the Industrial Revolution.
3. Individual production restricts the size and type of capital and the method of production, requires many market exchanges, and limits the specialization of labor.
4. Goods can be produced under one roof by business firms, teams of individuals, that essentially purchase resources rather than products. A business firm can use mass-production technology, reduce transaction costs, and increase the specialization of labor.
5. Business firms must produce and integrate services related to marketing, finance, information, contract negotiation, and management.
6. Because firms bypass markets, they must hire managers to coordinate and control production.
7. From the perspective of workers, firms are "islands of coercion in a sea of free enterprise."
8. The size of the firm is often limited because management costs become too great. To limit the size of the firm, piecework, subcontracting, and the purchase of capital from other firms can occur. Also, numerous firms with small management staffs rather than one large company with a large internal bureaucracy can be used to produce products.
9. Marginal cost is the cost of producing one more unit of output.
10. Marginal cost initially decreases with the rate of output because firms can buy larger units of capital, expand the use of mass production technology, reduce the number of transactions, and increase the specialization of labor.
11. Marginal cost eventually increases with the rate of output because management problems increase due to difficulties in transmitting information and directives.
12. Average cost is total cost divided by output. Average cost first falls and then rises because marginal cost initially declines and subsequently increases.

13. A firm will produce if average revenue equals or exceeds average cost. This is because a total revenue either equals or exceeds total cost causing the firm to either break even or earn a profit.

14. Profit is the amount by which total revenue exceeds total cost.

15. Normal profit, a payment for entrepreneurial ability, is not a profit as we define profit since normal profit is a compensation for sacrifices rather than a net gain.

16. Capital gains result when profits are earned only when the profits are unanticipated. Anticipated profits are already reflected in the ownership value of the firm. Their realization is a change in the composition of wealth rather than an increase.

17. Firms produce at the rate of output where marginal revenue equals marginal cost.

18. Integration of production allows a firm to produce a product from beginning to end or to produce a particular input and sell it to many individual producers.

19. Integration of an industry allows the industry to take advantage of team production, but it also increases the costs of coordination and control.

20. The Soviet Union can be viewed as one large business firm. It encounters many problems because management coordination and control become geometrically more difficult as a firm expands. The markets often seem to be more efficient systems of information and control than managers after firms have expanded beyond some size.

21. The alienation of labor may be caused by team production rather than how property is owned. If team production is the source of alienation, the solution is to dissolve business firms and revert to individual production.

22. Both elite and universal systems of higher education fail to maximize the net gain from education to students. The system that maximizes the net gain educates individuals until the value of the marginal gain equals the value of the marginal sacrifice.

QUESTIONS

1. What is a business firm?
2. Why do business firms exist?
3. Why must a business firm provide each of the following functions?
   a. Marketing
   b. Finance
   c. Information
   d. Contract negotiation
   e. Management
4. What happens to the marginal and average cost of production as a business firm increases output?
5. When will a business firm produce and what level of output will it select?
6. Discuss the following terms and concepts:

   Team production   Islands of coercion
   Business firm   Marginal cost

Putting-out system	Average cost
Factory system	$AR \geq AC$
Marketing services	Profit
Finance services	Normal profit
Debt financing	Profit and capital gains
Equity financing	$MR = MC$
Information services	Integration
Contract negotiation services	Managers versus market prices
Management services	The alienation of labor

APPLICATIONS

1. What are the disadvantages of hiring a certified public accounting firm to keep a company's books?

2. When fishermen sign on to a boat for a share of the catch, how does this assign time-value sacrifices and risks?

3. Would you be willing to work for a percentage of the revenues generated by the sales of a firm's pot-scrubbers? Why?

4. To what extent do the earnings of banks, bondholders, partners, and common stockholders represent interest and profits?

5. What advantage does management coordination and control have over market coordination and control?

6. What are the advantages of market coordination and control over management coordination and control from the perspective of a firm? From the perspective of an employee?

7. We are free to leave the jobs we have. Why then do we still feel like slaves to business firms?

8. How does piece-work differ from hourly wages? Why does it require fewer managerial costs?

9. Why are some industries comprised of small firms, whereas others are comprised of large ones?

10. Individual managers at the National Cash Register Corporation decide whether additional units should be produced. But central management must decide whether the firm is to stay in business. Explain.

11. Suppose the profits of General Foods are on the rise. Why can't you be sure that you will obtain capital gains by buying shares of General Foods stock?

12. Why might you produce and sell a marginal pot-scrubber even if it increases the average cost of production? What if it reduces the average rate of return?

13. The managers of firms don't seek maximum profits. Once they obtain enough to get by, they are more concerned with either growth or their own welfare. Evaluate.

14. Do the predictions that a firm will produce if average revenue at least equals average cost and produce the output such that marginal revenue equals marginal cost apply to a socialist firm?

15. If you had to train farmers how to grow potatoes, which farmers would you train if you were concerned with maximum total production?

13

Competitive and Monopoly Firms

Production circumstances are fairly universal: Specialization, indirect production, resource mergers, and team production can often increase output; marginal and average cost curves are U-shaped, with the marginal costs curves intersecting average costs curves at their minimum points. Nevertheless, business firms behave differently. Why? Because exchange conditions vary. Some firms must compete with many other sellers whereas other firms possess significant monopoly power.

In this chapter we explain and predict the prices charged and quantities produced by firms selling under competitive and under monopoly circumstances. To do so, we develop a theory of the competitive industry and a theory of the monopoly firm. Also, after we present and apply each theory, we discuss the sources of monopoly.

The special topics related to competitive industries examine cycles in beef production and the economic effects of taxing landlords more and tenants less. The topics dealing with monopoly firms focus on the licensing of taxicabs and the forms and effects of price discrimination.

A THEORY OF THE COMPETITIVE INDUSTRY

The Phenomena

In a competitive industry, firms sell their products in competitive markets. Perfectly competitive markets contain many traders who each sell or buy so little of the total quantity traded that they can't individually affect the market price by increasing or decreasing their willingnesses to trade.

It is tempting to look only to agriculture for examples of competitive firms, since that industry is as competitive as any in the world. The number of farms is enormous and virtually none of them produces a unique product. But focusing on agriculture implies that highly competitive firms don't exist elsewhere. This simply isn't so. The number of firms producing computers, movies, and cereal may be less and their products may be somewhat special, but the level of competition can nevertheless be sufficient to bring about essentially competitive results. The industries in our economy that we can classify as competitive are more numerous than we might at first suspect.

In our economy, when the demands for industrial as well as agricultural products increase under highly competitive conditions, the prices of products and the quantities sold immediately rise. As time passes, however, the prices tend to come back down while the quantities expand even further.

An Explanation: A Suntan Lotion Industry

To explain this behavior, let's see how a perfectly competitive suntan lotion industry will respond to an increase in the weekly demand for the lotion. Since the response of the industry to the increase in demand depends on how the individual firms respond, let's start by looking at the basic production decisions of those individual firms and work from there.

To understand the reactions of individual firms, we need to know the answers to two questions:

1. When will an individual firm produce?
2. What rate of output will it select?

When Will the Firm Produce?

The competitive firm, like any other firm, will produce if there is some rate of output at which average revenue at least equals average cost. If average revenue exceeds average cost, the firm obtains profits if production occurs.

We can illustrate when a firm in the suntan lotion industry will produce by using the two graphs in Figure 13.1. The graph on the left shows the supply and demand curves in the market. They reveal that supply and demand cause the price to be $5 per 4-ounce bottle.

Figure 13.1 The Competitive Industry and Firm

In the industry on the left, the $5 price is determined by the interation of supply (S) and demand (D). At the $5 price, the individual firm on the right can sell all it wishes, since it is an insignificant seller in the market. As a result, the demand curve the firm confronts is a horizontal line (d) at the $5 price. Since the price equals marginal and average revenue, the average and marginal revenue curves are coincidental with the horizontal demand curve.

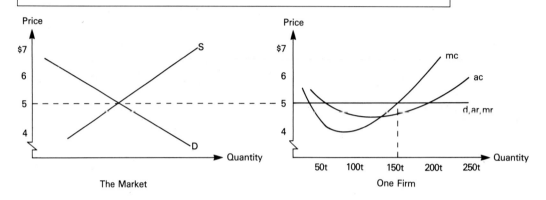

The Market   One Firm

From the perspective of an individual firm, represented by the graph on the right, the $5 price creates a horizontal demand curve (d) at $5. This is because each firm in the industry is an insignificant seller, and as such, it can sell all it wishes at the market price and nothing at a higher price. Also, since every bottle of lotion is sold at the same price, average revenue equals price. The average revenue of each bottle equals the price of $5. As a result, the average revenue curve of the firm (ar) coincides with its demand curve (d).

While the revenue conditions emanate from the market, the cost conditions are determined by the prices of resources and the available technology. From our theory of the firm, we know that the marginal cost curves are U-shaped and give rise to U-shaped average cost curves. U-shaped marginal and average cost curves (mc and ac) are shown by the graph on the right in Figure 13.1, and they reveal the marginal and average costs that one of the firms in the industry incurs at various weekly rates of production.

Since the average revenue curve (ar) lies above the average cost curve (ac) between 50,000 and 200,000 units of output per week, the firm represented on the right will produce. The average revenue of $5 will exceed the average cost at any level of production within that range, and the firm will therefore generate profit for its owners by producing. Of course, outside that range, average cost would exceed average revenue and a loss would be incurred if any one of those particular output rates was produced.

What Output Rate Will the Firm Produce?

Once a firm decides to produce, it will select the profit-maximizing rate of production; it will produce the rate of output at which marginal revenue equals marginal cost. If marginal revenue were greater than marginal cost, profit could be increased with more output; and if marginal revenue were less than marginal cost, profit could be increased with less output.

We can show the profit-maximizing rate of output for the firm represented by the graph on the right in Figure 13.1. Since the firm will charge $5 for every unit it produces, the marginal revenue of each unit will equal the $5 price. That is, the sale of each bottle will cause total revenue to rise by the price of $5, and, therefore, marginal revenue will always be $5. This causes the marginal revenue curve (*mr*) to be a horizontal line that is coincidental with the demand (*d*) and average revenue (*ar*) curves. At the point where the horizontal marginal revenue curve crosses the marginal cost curve, marginal revenue equals marginal cost. Therefore, the firm will produce the associated quantity, 150,000 bottles of suntan lotion, each week.

A Firm's Supply Curve

We can now obtain the supply curve of an individual firm. The production decisions we have just discussed imply that the portion of the marginal cost curve that lies above the average cost curve traces the supply curve of a competitive firm.

For instance, the firm represented by the graph in Figure 13.2 will be willing and able to supply nothing for a price of $4, since average revenue

Figure 13.2 The Supply Curve of the Firm

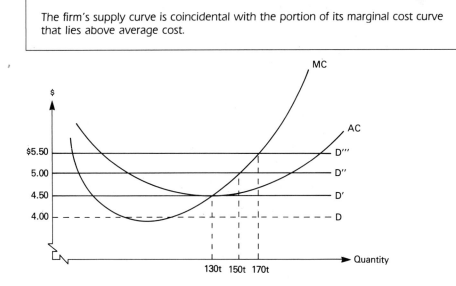

> The firm's supply curve is coincidental with the portion of its marginal cost curve that lies above average cost.

doesn't cover average cost at any rate of output. But for a $4.50 price, the firm will be willing and able to produce and sell 135,000 units. If price then rises to $5, it will produce and sell 150,000. And if the price increases further, it will produce and sell even more. The marginal cost curve will be coincidental with the firm's supply curve as long as the marginal cost curve lies above the average cost curve.

The Industry Supply Curve

To obtain the market supply curve for suntan lotion, we horizontally sum the individual supply curves of the firms. That is, we simply add the quantities that the various firms will supply at each price to obtain the industry quantities supplied. For instance, the preceding firm is willing and able to supply 150,000 bottles per week for a price of $5. If we assume that five other firms in the industry are willing and able to supply a total of 1,850,000 additional bottles per week for that price, then market quantity supplied at $5 will be 2,000,000 bottles per week.

As the price rises the six firms will be willing and able to supply larger quantities. Also, some firms having higher average costs of production than the original six firms in the industry will begin producing at the higher prices once their average costs are covered by average revenues. In fact, the increase in the rate of output caused by more firms entering the industry is often greater than the increase caused by existing firms expanding production. Industry production will increase with price and, therefore, the market supply curve will slope upward, as Figure 13.3 shows.

Short- and Long-Run Supply

The cost curves we have been discussing reveal the average and marginal costs that are incurred after production is ongoing for some time at given levels of output. When production rates are increased or decreased, some time must elapse before firms adjust all of their resources and incur those costs.

Figure 13.3 The Industry Supply Curves

Competitive industry supply curves are the horizontal sums of the supply curves of their individual firms. Since the supply curves of individual firms slope upward and since more firms enter production when higher prices first cover their average costs of production, industry supply curves slope upward.

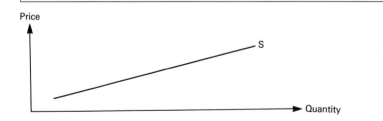

To deal with adjustments of resources over time, we need to define the long and the short run. The **long run** is a period of time in which the quantities of all resources can be adjusted. The **short run** is any shorter period of time. In the short run some resources are fixed (usually large units of capital and land such as the size of a factory or quantity of acreage under cultivation).

When product price increases, supply will be lower in the short run than in the long run. This is because in the short run, rather than obtaining the optimum combination of all resources, firms will usually increase output by adding more variable resources to existing large units of capital and land. In the long run, all resources will be adjusted so that production costs will fall.

For example, if the price of suntan lotion increases, existing firms will initially expand production by adding workers and other variable resources to their fixed factories. This will cause higher unit costs, since the factories will be stretched beyond their optimal rates of output. In the long run, however, existing firms will be able to build more factories efficiently, as will new firms who will enter the industry for the first time. As a result, supply will increase as costs fall.

If industry price decreases, supply will be much lower in the long run than in the short run. This is primarily because in the short-run prices will have to cover only the costs of variable resources, since the costs of fixed resources will be irrelevant. In the short run the cost of factories and other large units of capital represent sunk historical sacrifices that can't be retrieved if production is reduced. Although the costs of variable resources can be saved and production is cut to the extent that prices don't cover those costs, the costs of fixed resources can't be saved (they don't exist). In the long run, however, factories and other fixed resources wear out or can be sold. The firms therefore reduce production much more or leave the industry, rather than replace or avoid selling units of fixed resources.

Since firms supply more in the long than in the short run when price increases, the long-run industry supply curve lies below the short-run curve at prices and quantities higher than those existing. And since firms supply less in the long run than in the short run when price decreases, the long-run industry supply curve is above the short-run supply curve at prices and quantities lower than those existing. In short, the long-run supply curve crosses the short-run supply curve at the existing price and quantity. This is illustrated by Figure 13.4 (in the figure, P and Q represent the existing price and quantity).

Reactions to Increased Demand for Lotion

We can now use the concepts we have discussed and the graph in Figure 13.4 to explain what will happen if the demand for suntan lotion suddenly increases.

If the demand increases to D', as shown in Figure 13.5, then in the short run, price will rise to $8 and firms will increase industry production to 3 million bottles per week. The firms will expand the rate of output because the

Figure 13.4 Short- and Long-Run Supply Curves

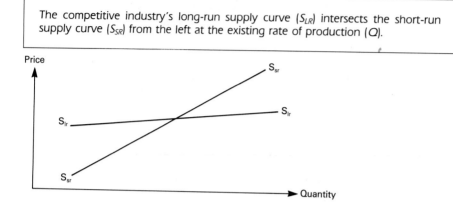

The competitive industry's long-run supply curve (S_{LR}) intersects the short-run supply curve (S_{SR}) from the left at the existing rate of production (Q).

new $8 price will generate higher marginal revenues that will cover higher marginal costs.

Later, in the long run, quantity will rise much more and firms will earn much less, since price won't remain at the same high level. Supply will increase (as shown by the long-run supply curve) as firms build new plants and expand their production facilities. Furthermore, as new firms complete the ac-

Figure 13.5 Increase In Demand

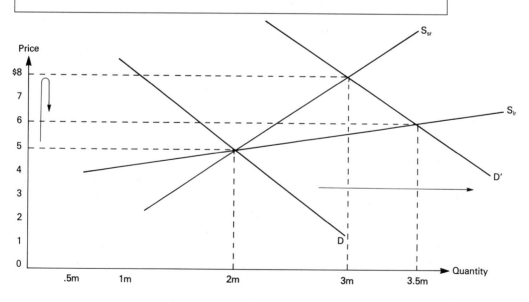

An increase in demand shifts the demand curve to the right, from D to D'. In the short run, price increases from $5 to $8 and quantity increases from 2,000,000 to 3,000,000. In the long run, price decreases back to $6 and quantity increases further to 3,500,000.

quisition and construction of production facilities, they will enter production. The increase in supply will cause the price to decrease to $6 as the quantity increases further to 3.5 million.

Although the price in the long run will fall toward its original level, we can't say whether it will finally settle above, below, or at that level. The final price level depends upon the eventual long-run average costs that the firms in the industry incur. The average costs will be higher than at the original levels of production if the expansion of output exhausts the supply of low-cost resources. On the other hand, the average costs will be lower if resources used in production can be more cheaply produced on a larger scale. If the average costs rise, the long-run price of the product will be higher than it was before the increase in demand, and if the costs decrease, the price will be lower. Otherwise, the long-run price will be at the original level.

The Predictions

Increase in Demand

From the preceding explanation, we can predict that if demand for the product of a competitive industry rises, price and quantity produced by the industry will increase in the short run. In the long run, price will fall back toward the original level and quantity will rise further.

Decrease in Demand

We can also use the explanation and graphical apparatus to predict that if demand for the product of a competitive industry falls, both price and quantity will fall in the short run, but in the long run, price will rise toward the original level and quantity will fall further.

A decrease in demand is shown in Figure 13.6 by the movement of demand to D'. The price will then fall to $2 in the short run. Also, the quantity produced and sold will fall to 1 million. Some firms will cut production, since the price won't cover the marginal costs of some units, and other firms will stop producing, since price will fall below their average costs.

In the long run, the firms in the industry will have to replace old capital equipment if they want to maintain production. For many of them the price won't be high enough to justify doing so. They will then cut production or leave the industry. This will cause supply to fall, as represented by the long-run supply curve. Price will then rise to $4 as the quantity produced and sold will decline further to 500,000.

Higher Costs

Next we can predict that if the costs of production rise, then, in the short run, price will rise as industry quantity falls. In the long run, price will rise more and quantity will fall further.

The higher costs will cause some firms immediately to cut production and others to go out of business. Then, in the long run, firms will further cut

Figure 13.6 Decrease in Demand

A decrease in demand shifts the demand curve to the left, from *D* to *D'*. In the short run, price decreases from $5 to $2 and quantity from 2,000,000 to 1,000,000. In the long run, price increases back to $4 and quantity decreases further to 500,000.

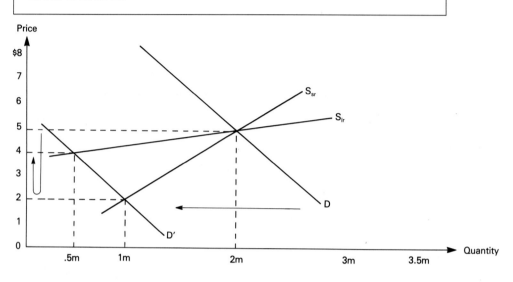

production and more firms will leave the industry. The price will rise as quantity falls further.

The graph in Figure 13.7 illustrates the industry's reaction to higher costs. The higher costs will raise both the short- and long-run curves vertically. In the short run, with the same demand, price will rise to from *P* to *P'* and quantity will fall from *Q* to *Q'*. Then, in the long run, price will rise further to *P''*, while quantity falls more to *Q''*.

Lower Costs

We can also predict what will happen if costs suddenly fall. Lower costs will cause quantity to rise and price to fall in the short run. Then, in the long run, quantity will rise and price will fall further.

Why? Because as soon as costs of some units fall below their prices, firms will produce those units. The greater supply will then reduce price. In time, costs will be even lower as all inputs are adjusted to the new higher rates of output. Supply will then rise even more in the long run and price will continue to fall to a still lower level.

As shown in Figure 13.8, lower costs will push the supply curves vertically downward. In the short run, quantity will rise to *Q'* as price falls to *P'*. In the long run, supply will rise more. Quantity will increase further to *Q''* and price will fall more to *P''*.

Higher costs shift the short- and long-run supply curves, S_{SR} and S_{LR}, upward. In the short run, price rises from P to P' and quantity falls from Q to Q'. In the long run, price rises further to P'' and quantity falls further to Q''.

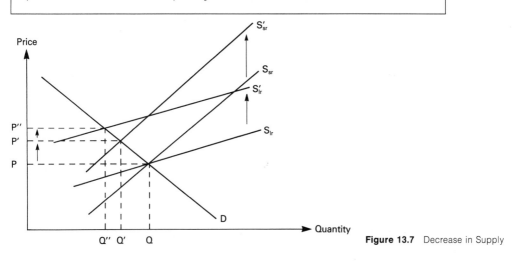

Figure 13.7 Decrease in Supply

Producing the Most Valuable Products

The last prediction deals with how the profit-maximizing decisions of the owners of competitive firms affect the consumers in the economy. We can predict that the products and quantities produced by the firms will be those that consumers value the most. This is because the firms obey the marginal-revenue-equals-marginal-cost rule, and that rule, under competitive conditions, converts to a price-equals-marginal-cost rule. And when price equals marginal cost, a firm produces the products that consumers value most.

Lower costs shift the short- and long-run supply curves downward. In the short run, price decreases from P to P' and quantity increases from Q to Q'. In the long run, price decreases further to P'' and quantity increases further to Q''.

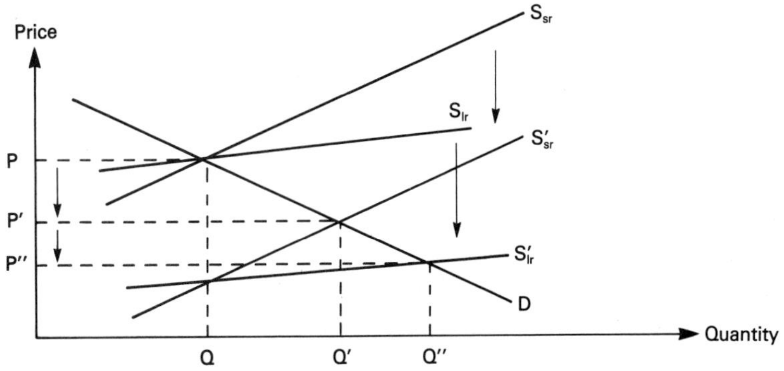

Figure 13.8 Increase in Supply

Why does the price-equals-marginal-cost rule imply that consumers obtain the most valuable products? Because price reveals the value of a product to consumers, whereas marginal cost identifies the values of alternative products to consumers. Price reveals the value of a product, since it is exactly how much consumers are willing and able to pay for the product. Marginal cost identifies the value of alternative products because it reveals what other producers are willing to pay for resources and that, in turn, reflects how much consumers value the products of those producers. If price exceeded marginal cost, an increase in the production of the product and an decrease in the production of other products would give consumers more valuable products. And if price were less than marginal cost, a reduction in production would release resources to produce other products that are more valuable to consumers.

More specifically, when a firm sells suntan lotion for $5 and produces it at a marginal cost of $5, this implies that the consumers are receiving the optimum quantity of the lotion. If price was $5 and marginal cost was only $4, consumers, relative to their values, would be getting too little lotion, since an increase in production would give them additional lotion worth $5 and force them to sacrifice other products worth only $4. Conversely, if price was $5 and marginal cost was $6, consumers would be obtaining too much lotion, since a cut in lotion production would release resources that could then produce $6 worth of other products and cause the sacrifice of only $5 worth of lotion.

A Summary of the Theory

If production occurs in industries selling products in perfectly competitive markets, we can predict that

a. After an increase in demand, both the market price and the quantity sold will rise in the short run and then, in the long run, the price will fall as the quantity rises more.
b. Subsequent to a decrease in demand, price and quantity will fall in the short run and then, in the long run, price will rise as quantity falls further.
c. Following an increase in costs, price will rise and quantity will fall in the short run and then, in the long run, price will rise further as quantity falls more.
d. After a decrease in costs, price will fall and quantity will rise in the short run and then, in the long run, price will fall more as quantity expands further.
e. The products produced will be those that consumers value most.

SPECIAL TOPICS RELATED TO THE COMPETITIVE INDUSTRY

An Increase in Demand for Beef: Over- and Underproduction

Suppose that the demand for beef increases. What does our theory predict will happen? It says that in the short run, the price and quantity will immediately rise. Then in the long run, production will increase and price will fall toward its previous level.

But why will ranchers produce more cattle if they know that price will eventually fall, making it impossible for them to gain as much profit? For the same reason that you will change to a faster lane on the freeway even though you know it will eventually slow down: You can make some progress, and some progress is better than no progress. By increasing their rate of output, the ranchers will increase their profits. True, eventually the price will fall, eliminating the extra profits, but some extra profits are better than no extra profits.

The next questions are a bit more difficult. Won't the high price of beef cause all of the ranchers simultaneously to increase production so much that price will eventually fall far below the previous level? And won't the resulting price decrease then cause all ranchers to cut production so much that the price will again rise to very high levels, calling for another future production increase, price decrease, etc? In short, won't a sudden increase in demand result in cycle of over- and underproduction that in turn causes a cycle of low and high prices?

Not necessarily. Ranchers often monitor the market carefully and are leery of producing if they think that too many others will join them. If over- and underproduction were predictable, farmers would act countercyclically and greatly increase their profit. They would cut production when they anticipated a flood of products on the market and low prices and would increase production during periods of expected low industry output and high prices. This behavior, however, would eliminate the cycles.

Fluctuations, not cycles of over- and underproduction, occur in almost all areas of production. These fluctuations are caused by random, unpredictable changes in output rates and demands. The fluctuations aren't predictable, periodic cycles of expansion and contraction.

Taxing Landlords More, Taxing Tenants Less

Although many people favor letting homeowners deduct interest and other expenses from their taxes, some do not think that landlords should be given the same privileges on their apartment rental properties. What would happen if Congress and the president changed federal tax laws to eliminate the deductions that landlords now receive? Our theory provides the answer.

Since landlords would have to pay higher taxes, the costs of operating apartment houses would rise. To the extent that the short-run marginal and average costs of providing apartments exceeded rents, landlords would stop renting their units and, when possible, sell them as condominiums. In the short run, the supply of apartments would fall, causing rents to rise, but the rents would increase less than the extra taxes landlords would have to pay.

In the long run, as soon as rents failed to cover the costs of maintenance and of using land, many additional units would be demolished and no new apartments would be constructed. This long-run reduction in supply would cause rents to increase further until rents rose to cover all costs, including the new higher taxes.

For example, suppose you own a condominium that you rent to tenants and that your rent revenues are far below the mortgage, tax, maintenance, vacancy, and other costs you incur. Nevertheless, you continue to rent the condo out because the tax deductions and expected appreciation compensate you for the difference between revenues and costs.

If you lost the tax advantages, you might sell the condo, as would many other landlords in the market. The supply would fall and rents would rise. This process would continue until rents rose to cover all costs, including the new higher taxes.

In effect, tenants now receive the tax-breaks on rental units in the form of lower rents. If the tax breaks were eliminated, tenants would have to pay higher rents.

What if, instead of simply eliminating the tax breaks, the government simply transferred the deductions from the landlords to the tenants? A demand increase would then match a supply decrease and

   a. Rents would rise.
   b. The quantities of apartments would stay the same.
   c. Tenants would pay more rent but fewer taxes.
   d. Landlords would pay more taxes but receive higher rents.

However, to the extent that the values of tax deductions depend upon the tax brackets of individuals, tenants in lower brackets than their landlords would be worse off, whereas those in higher brackets would be better off.

A THEORY OF THE MONOPOLY FIRM

Although the theory of the competitive industry may be far more useful than we might at first suspect, we can't use the theory in all cases. If we want to explain and predict additional phenomena, we have to recognize that some products are produced by only one firm. So let's develop a theory of the monopoly firm.

The Phenomena

When we observe monopoly producers, we see that they, like any other monopolists, charge higher prices than comparable competitive sellers. And when conditions change to cause some firms to become the monopolists, prices rise. Moreover, when competition comes into existence, prices fall.

An Explanation: A Producer of Cast Covers

To explain, let's assume that you invent a new product for people who have recently broken their arms or wrists: a washable, fingerless glove that can protect an arm cast from grime. The fabric of the glove is to be covered with the signatures of famous men and women.

After you obtain a patent for this product, you will be a monopoly producer. Under what conditions will you produce? As usual, you will produce if average revenue at least equals average cost. If average revenue exceeds average cost, you will obtain a profit by producing.

As a monopoly producer, you'll be confronted with a downward-sloping demand curve, as shown in Figure 13.9. Assuming that you sell all units at the same price, the average revenue curve will correspond to the demand curve, since price will equal average revenue. Your cost curves will be the same as if you were selling under circumstances of competition. The average and marginal cost curves will be U-shaped and the marginal cost curve will intersect the average cost curve at its lowest point. Since you will produce if average revenue at least equals average cost, you will produce if the demand curve lies above or is tangent to the average cost curve.

Which particular rate of output will you choose? You will select the profit-maximizing rate, the rate at which marginal revenue equals marginal cost. Under monopoly conditions, the marginal revenue curve will lie below the demand curve. Marginal revenue will be less than price because to sell more cast covers, you will have to spoil your market by reducing the price on previous units. To equate marginal revenue with marginal cost, you will charge the price and produce the quantity associated with the intersection of the marginal reve-

Figure 13.9 Price and Quantity of the Monopoly Firm

The monopoly firm produces when the demand curve is above (or tangent to) the average cost curve and produces such that marginal revenue equals marginal cost. Given the conditions on the graph, the monopoly price will be P_m and the quantity, Q_m. The competitive price and quantity would have been P_c and Q_c, respectively.

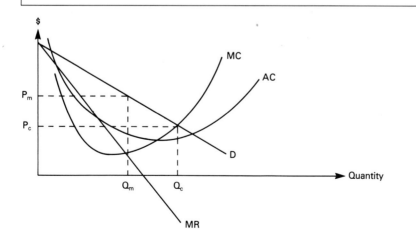

nue and the marginal cost curves. In the situation illustrated in Figure 13.9, you will charge the P_m price and sell the Q_m quantity.   .

The resulting monopoly price is higher than under competitive conditions. Under competitive conditions, no market spoiling would have occurred since your sales would have been an insignificant part of the market. Therefore, marginal revenue and price would have been equal, and this would have caused the marginal revenue curve to be coincidental with the demand curve. Marginal revenue would then have equaled marginal cost at the point where the demand curve crosses the marginal cost curve. In the situation depicted in Figure 13.9, this would have resulted in a lower price, P_c, and a higher quantity, Q_c.

The Predictions

This explanation allows us to make a number of predictions.

Monopoly Firms Charge More

First, we can predict that if a firm is a monopoly seller, it will charge a higher price than a firm selling under competitive conditions. A monopoly firm trying not spoil its market too much will refuse to decrease the price to the competitive level.

Monopoly Firms Produce Less

Next, a monopoly firm will produce and sell less than a competitive industry will. Since a monopoly firm charges a higher price than a competitive industry, it also produces and sells less than would have been produced by that industry.

Underproduction for Consumers

We can also predict that a monopoly firm will produce less than is consistent with the production of the products that consumers value most. That is, consumers would have valued additional units of the monopolist's product more than the other products that are instead produced.

Underproduction relative to consumer valuations occurs because the monopoly firm produces such that price exceeds marginal cost. This means the value of an additional unit of product to consumers, as reflected in the price, is greater than the value to consumers of the alternative products that resources are producing instead, as reflected by marginal cost. A monopoly firm won't produce the additional units because even though consumers may value the units more than alternative products, the market-spoiling effect would cause the firm to obtain less profit. While the prices of additional units would exceed marginal costs, the marginal revenues of those units would lie below marginal costs.

For instance, you might be able to sell one more cast cover for $5 and it might only cost you $3 to produce. But you wouldn't produce it if you had to spoil your market for the first 10,000 covers by reducing their price from $6 to $5 to sell one more. The marginal revenue would be a negative $9995, not to mention the $3 marginal cost.

Although you may maximize your profit by not producing the next unit, you do not produce the most valuable products for consumers. Rather than receiving a product they value at $5 and sacrificing one worth $3, consumers receive the $3 alternative.

Price Discrimination

Next we can predict that if a monopoly firm can charge different prices for different units, avoiding uniform pricing, it will. Since it can then **price discriminate** by pricing initial units higher and subsequent ones lower, it will generate more profit for its owners.

When a monopoly firm price discriminates, it avoids spoiling its market for previous units when it sells additional ones. As a result, the marginal revenues of additional units are higher and tend to be closer to their prices.

Price discrimination does have one surprising effect. It causes monopoly firms to produce the goods that consumers value most (the firms will produce where price equals marginal cost). For example, if your firm doesn't have to reduce price on previous cast covers to sell additional ones, it won't spoil its market when it sells more. Price then equals marginal revenue, and you will produce to the point where price equals marginal cost. Specifically, if a consumer is willing to pay $5 for an additional cover and your production cost is $3, you will produce and sell the item, since your price to other consumers can remain $6. You will continue to produce and sell more until price equals marginal cost.

Of course, while consumers may be pleased that you produced according to their values, they may also feel exploited, since you will charge a higher average price. Although price discriminating monopolists don't reduce the size of the combined gains from trade pie, they do redistribute the pie in their favor even more than monopolists using uniform pricing.

A Summary of the Theory

By assuming that a firm is the only producer and, therefore, the only seller of a product, our theory of the monopoly firm predicts that the firm will

- **a.** Charge a higher price than a competitive firm would have;
- **b.** Sell a lower quantity than a competitive industry would have;
- **c.** Underproduce relative to consumer valuations;
- **d.** Price discriminate whenever possible.

SPECIAL TOPICS RELATED TO MONOPOLY FIRMS

Licensure of the Taxicab Industry

Many municipal governments regulate the taxicab industries in their towns. The regulations vary, but usually they consist of a requirement that all taxicabs have licenses to operate. Then, by limiting the number of licenses, the governments create a monopoly in the taxicab services market.

Since the resulting taxicab markets are monopolistic, we can identify the three effects of monopoly production. First, the fares of taxi services are higher than they would have been under competition. Taxi fares in towns where permits are restricted exceed the fares in towns where they aren't. This is why taxi licenses sell for fairly high prices, sometimes for more than $50,000 each. The high prices of licenses imply that the expected future revenues from providing taxi services are significantly higher than the expected costs. If entry were unrestricted, more cabs would have entered the markets. This would have increased supply and reduced taxi fares.

Second, the quantity of taxi services is less than under competitive conditions. This is obvious, since the number of licenses (and therefore the number of cabs) is restricted.

Finally, the optimal quantities of services in terms of consumer valuations aren't being provided. Since the fares of taxi services are above marginal costs, consumers are revealing that they would value additional taxi services more than the other goods that resources are producing instead.

Of course, the owners of licenses don't necessarily agree that the restrictions cause these three effects, especially higher fares. The owners often contend that taxi fares without regulation would be higher and provide three erroneous arguments to support their contention. First, they claim that without restrictions, so many people would turn their cars into cabs that the industry would be flooded with producers. This would cause vacancy rates to rise and force an increase in taxicab fares.

But this is untrue. Cost doesn't, by itself, determine price. Supply and demand determine price. Surpluses of cabs, if they occurred, would create competition and subsequently force fares to fall, not rise.

A second contention is that fares would rise in the long run because entry into the industry would reduce short-run fares, and that would bankrupt many producers. This eventually would cause supplies to fall and fares to rise above previous levels.

This too is false. Producers base their entry and exit decisions on expectations, not on present prices and costs. Taxi operators wouldn't enter the industry if they expected future fares to be below costs, and they wouldn't leave if they anticipated that fares would soon rise to cover costs.

Also, a large number of cabs wouldn't normally enter an industry at the same moment; entry is usually scattered over time. This means that supplies would rise and fares would decline slowly. As soon as fares fell to a point where they just covered average production costs, new producers would decide against entry. Conversely, if fares fell below costs, everyone wouldn't leave at the same moment. Supplies would fall gradually, causing fares to rise until they just covered average costs.

Finally, the owners often claim that market instability would raise fares. Without restrictions, they contend that constant increases and decreases in supplies would cause fares to fluctuate, and unpredictable fares would cause producers to leave or avoid entering the markets. This would reduce supplies and raise average fares.

However, when prices fluctuate, they move in both directions. Higher prices compensate for lower prices. Producers focus on long-term averages, not short-term relationships. As long as average prices covered average costs, production would continue and supply wouldn't fall.

If owner-operators of taxis wanted to stabilize their take-home earnings, they could borrow money when fares were temporarily low and pay back the debts during better times. Or they could work for a taxicab company at a fixed wage and let the company deal with fare fluctuations.

Price Discrimination

Examples of Price Discrimination

Next we can use our theory to explain why monopoly sellers sometimes charge some buyers lower prices. The sellers do so because they want to increase sales without lowering prices to other buyers willing to pay more. For example, airlines charge lower prices to military personnel, professional basketball teams give discounted tickets to Boy Scouts, and universities grant students partial scholarships. Why? So they can sell more without reducing the prices they charge civilians, the public, and other students, respectively.

Similarly, we can explain why some monopoly sellers charge less for additional units than for initial ones. Again, it is often because they want to sell more without reducing the prices on previous units. For example, if you were selling antigrime cast covers, you might price discriminate by giving quantity discounts. You might charge $8 if someone wants one cast cover and $12 if they buy two. In effect, everyone could then buy one for $8 and a second for only $4.

Examples of quantity discounts include season tickets to football games, admission-plus-ride tickets to a carnival, and monthly-plus-toll telephone bills.

However, sometimes quantity discounts reflect lower production costs. When this is the case, the discounts don't necessarily represent price discrimination.

Finally, we can explain why monopoly sellers sometimes improve a product somewhat and raise the price much more. That way, they can charge wealthy consumers relatively more than poor consumers. Examples of this type of price discrimination include raising the prices of first-class hotel rooms more than the extra costs of those rooms. Similarly, the prices of automobile options are usually far greater than their costs.

Problems With Price Discrimination

Any type of price discrimination increases the profit of sellers. Nevertheless, as we noted in Chapter 5, price discrimination is often difficult to practice. First, the seller must identify who is willing to pay more or less. This isn't always easy. For instance, poor people are often willing to pay more than their wealthy counterparts.

Second, people charged higher prices must be kept from slipping into groups charged lower prices. One of the benefits of selling a Cadillac and buying a Ford may be the thwarting of motel managers who raise room rates whenever they see a luxury car. Third, secondary trades must be impossible. Otherwise consumers who can pay less will buy large quantities and resell to consumers charged more.

Finally, competition must be limited. If other firms sold cast covers, it would be hard to charge some consumers higher prices than others because the consumers charged more would then simply shop elsewhere. This is why price discrimination is a monopoly phenomenon.

The theory of monopoly that we have discussed allows us to explain and predict much of the behavior of monopoly producers. To explain and predict more, we could develop the theories of monopolistic competition and oligopoly, two tools that introduce additional factors and thereby deal with additional phenomena. But for our purposes, the gain in generality would not be worth the sacrifice of simplicity. We have gone far enough.

CAUSES OF MONOPOLY

Although monopolies often result because of the development of new products like our antigrime cast gloves, they are often created and perpetuated by number of other factors. One of the most important is government. Governments often create and support monopolies when they

a. Grant patents and copyrights to producers in order to encourage research, development, and original thought;

b. Protect consumers against low-quality or unsafe products (by eliminating the production of unapproved goods, governments give producers of approved items more price control);

c. Regulate prices (by keeping firms from reducing prices below certain levels, governments protect high-cost producers from low-cost competitors);

d. Restrict international trade (by reducing foreign imports, governments provide domestic producers with greater control over price);

e. Give firms exclusive rights to produce transportation, communication, and various utility services to prevent cost duplication or to reduce costs when demand is very low.

Other causes of monopoly have little to do with government. First, cost factors not only cause governments to support monopolies, they also independently create many single producers of goods. Even without government regulations, very small towns usually have but one electric utility and a single general store.

Another possible nongovernment source of monopoly is advertising. Madison Avenue can sometimes lock consumers into a product for some time period. Also, a high cost of advertising can act as a barrier to the entry of new firms.

However, advertising doesn't always give firms monopoly power. It can often foster competition. With easy access to consumers, new producers or sellers with lower prices can be far more successful. This may explain why some professional organizations consider advertising to be "unethical"; they want to protect established members from competition.

Finally, without government aid, producers sometimes obtain monopoly power by eliminating other producers. They can do so by creating **mergers** (forming one firm out of what was previously two or more firms), by uniting into **cartels** (associations that act as single sellers), or by using **predatory tactics** (strategies that involve below-cost pricing aimed at bankrupting competitors). These methods can be successful, but they often encounter significant problems:

a. A firm creating a monopoly merger may gain very little if it has to pay a great deal to absorb other firms. Also, firms created by mergers often face competition from new firms and firms in other industries. (Many, if not most, mergers are aimed at reducing costs rather than creating monopolies. These mergers tend to be successful.)

b. Cartels tend to encounter competition, both from within and without. A firm can often obtain more profit by cheating on a cartel or staying outside than by being a cartel member and restricting production. Moreover, it is often difficult and costly for cartel members to reach decisions, since every member of a cartel maximizes profit at a different cartel price and quantity.

c. Finally, predatory tactics are very costly. The tactics can also fail if competitors shut down only temporarily or if other competitors subsequently enter the industry. People often confuse pricing practices that reflect low production costs with predatory tactics.

We have now completed our examination of exchange and production decisions from an individual perspective. In the next chapter we will see how these decisions can be coordinated and controlled by economic systems.

MAJOR AND MINOR POINTS

1. Competitive firms sell their products in competitive markets.
2. A competitive firm will produce if average revenue equals or exceeds average cost at some level(s) of output. Since average revenue equals price, it will produce when the demand curve is tangent or above the average cost curve.

3. A competitive firm will produce where marginal revenue equals marginal cost. The equality of marginal revenue and price causes the marginal revenue curve to be coincidental with the demand curve. Therefore, the competitive firm produces the output associated with the intersection of the demand and the marginal cost curves.

4. The supply curve for the individual competitive firm corresponds to the part of the marginal cost curve that lies above the average cost curve.

5. The market supply curve is the horizontal sum of the supply curves of the individual firms.

6. The long-run supply curve represents supply after all adjustments of resources to new levels of production have occurred. The short-run supply curve represents supply when all resource adjustments have not occurred.

7. The long-run supply curve intersects the short-run supply curve from above at the existing rate of production.

8. In a competitive industry, an increase in demand will cause a higher price and quantity in the short run. In the long run, supply will increase as firms expand production facilities and new firms begin production. This will cause price to fall and quantity to increase further.

9. A decrease in demand in a competitive industry will cause price and quantity to fall in the short run. In the long run, supply will fall as firms retire capital facilities and some firms stop producing. This will cause price to rise somewhat and quantity to decline further.

10. Higher costs will cause competitive firms to cut production in the short run. Price will therefore rise. In the long run, the firms will reduce production more and price will increase further.

11. Lower costs will cause competitive firms to increase production in the short run. As a result, prices will fall. In the long run, firms will increase production more and price will fall further.

12. Since marginal revenue equals price, competitive firms produce where consumers obtain the most valuable products: where price equals marginal cost.

13. Over- and underproduction will not be the general responses to demand changes because firms base entry decisions on expectations, not present prices, and because firms usually only gradually increase or decrease production.

14. A monopoly firm produces when average revenue at least equals average cost; it produces when the demand curve is tangent to or above the average cost curve.

15. Like all firms, a monopoly firm produces where marginal revenue equals marginal cost.

16. Monopoly firms charge higher prices than competitive firms and sell lower quantities than competitive industries would have.

17. Since a monopoly firm must spoil its market to sell more units, its marginal revenue is less than price. Therefore, the monopoly firm produces where price exceeds marginal cost, underproducing relative to consumer valuations.

18. Price discrimination, charging high prices for initial units and lower ones for subsequent units, is sometimes practiced by monopoly firms.

19. Price discrimination, by making marginal revenue equal price, causes monopoly firms not to restrict the rate of output. The firms then produce at the point where price equals marginal cost, a rate of output consistent with consumer values.

20. With price discrimination, monopoly firms charge even higher average prices than would have existed under competitive conditions.

21. Price discrimination can involve charging different prices to different people, different prices for different units, or price changes that don't reflect the costs of quality changes.

22. Price discrimination is often difficult to practice because it requires the ability to identify consumer values, the inability of consumers to switch groups, limits on secondary exchanges, and monopoly power.

23. Governments create and support monopolies when they grant patents and copyrights, protect consumers, regulate prices, restrict international trade, and make competition with technological monopolies illegal.

24. Technology can create monopolies when competition causes a duplication of production costs or a loss of economies of large-scale production.

25. Advertising, by locking consumers to products or by acting as a cost barrier to the entry of new firms into an industry, can create some monopoly power. But it can also reduce monopoly power.

26. Firms can reduce competition by merging with competitors, creating cartels, or bankrupting competitors with predatory tactics that involve below-cost pricing.

27. Mergers can be costly or fail because of competition from new producers or firms in other industries.

28. Cartels can fail because of competition from within and without. Also, decisions are often difficult to reach and costly.

29. Predatory tactics are costly and can fail if competitors temporarily shut down or begin production after prices are eventually increased.

QUESTIONS

1. What is a competitive firm and industry?
2. When will a competitive firm produce and what output will it choose? Explain and show graphically.
3. How are the competitive firm and the competitive industry supply curves derived?
4. How does a competitive industry respond to a higher or lower price in the short and the long run?
5. How will an increase or a decrease in demand affect the price and quantity produced by a competitive industry?
6. How will an increase or a decrease in the cost of production affect the price and the quantity produced by a competitive industry?
7. Why will competitive firms produce the products that consumers value most?
8. What is a monopoly firm?
9. When will a monopoly firm produce and what level of output will it select? Explain and show graphically.
10. Why will a monopoly firm underproduce relative to consumer valuations?
11. Why and how will monopoly firms price-discriminate, and what problems will they have to overcome to do so?

12. What are the possible causes of monopoly?
13. Discuss the following terms and concepts:

Competitive firm and industry	Government and monopoly
Competitive price and quantity	Technology and monopoly
Demand and cost changes	Advertising and monopoly
Price equals marginal cost	Mergers
Cycles of production	Cartels
Monopoly producer	Predatory tactics
Monopoly price and quantity	Problems with mergers
Price > marginal cost	Problems with cartels
Price discrimination	Problems with predatory
Forms of price discrimination	tactics
Problems of price discrimination	Below-cost pricing

APPLICATIONS

1. Each of the firms producing suntan lotion in the United States has some control over price. Would a recognition of this control improve our ability to understand their pricing and production decisions, or would it only make the theory more complex?
2. All farmers producing wheat do so at the same cost. In what sense is this true? In what sense is it false?
3. When small farmers argue that they can't stay in business because prices are too low or costs are high, how are consumers valuing the products that the resources of those farmers are producing relative to the products that the resources could have otherwise produced?
4. Do all monopoly firms earn profits?
5. How will an increase in the number of firms producing close substitutes for the product of a monopolist affect the demand for the monopolist's product? When will such monopolistic competition tend to occur?
6. Will monopolists continually raise prices to cause continuous inflation? Will they ever be willing to reduce prices during periods of deflation?
7. Graphically show the effects of price discrimination on total revenue.
8. When government deregulates the trucking industry, low-cost producers initially flood the market and price falls. But eventually, most producers become bankrupt. As a result, only a few monopolistic firms remain and they raise price above the initial level. Evaluate.
9. When a doctor charges needy people lower rates, is he or she helping the poor or soaking the rich?
10. Explain and show graphically the monopoly price and quantity when perfect price discrimination is possible.
11. What arguments might a dentist give for why dentistry should not be deregulated?

14

Capitalism, the Role of Government, and Socialism

In our economy, most products are produced by many different business firms, and the consumers of products are hardly ever the producers. For instance, in the manufacture of novels, some firms generate the paper, others handle the printing, and still others control the distribution. And the people reading the novels are seldom involved in production.

Since production and consumption usually involve many people, then unless we want arbitrary results, we must have **economic systems** to coordinate and control individual decisions. The systems prevent chaos by telling people what to do and giving them the incentives to do it.

Many types of economic systems exist in the world today. In this chapter we will focus on one of them, capitalism; we present and apply a theory of capitalism. However, we also say something about the economic systems of socialism and mercantilism by discussing the role that government plays in our otherwise capitalistic economy.

The special topics related to capitalism deal with capitalist production of education, the hiring of illegal Mexican labor, Ralph Nader and safety, and *Consumer Reports* magazine. The topics dealing with socialism and mercantilism involve government production of computer software, smoking in public places, manners and customs, and Somoza's Nicaragua.

A THEORY OF CAPITALISM

Capitalism is an economic system that contains but one fundamental institution: **private-property rights**. These rights include individual rights to the exclusive use and easy transferability of goods. For example, when you own a Ford, exclusive use rights entitle you to drive it on public roads at various speeds and in particular directions. They also let you decide if someone else can drive. On the other hand, easy transferability rights allow you to sell the car to anyone at any mutually agreeable price.

It becomes obvious that private-property rights are important to the values of goods as soon as the rights become more limited. The value of your Ford would certainly fall if you couldn't drive it over 5 miles per hour, if other people could operate the car without your permission, if you weren't allowed to sell it, or if you couldn't sell it for more than $100.

The Phenomena

Capitalism appears to be the dominant form of economic organization in the private, nongovernment sector of our economy. In that sector, private-property rights are generally well-defined. Individual farmers, manufacturers, and other producers usually have or can buy exclusive use and transferability rights to land, labor, and other resources. After they employ the resources to produce goods, they also normally possess exclusive use and easy transferability rights to the products.

Although producers are free to do as they like, their behavior is nevertheless predictable. For example, when demands for products shift, causing prices to change, producers react by producing less of the products with lower prices and more of the products with higher prices.

An Explanation: Fewer Tomatoes, More Avocados

To explain this behavior, suppose that the products valued most by consumers are initially being produced in a hypothetical capitalist economy, and that suddenly consumers change their values so that they demand fewer tomatoes and more avocados.

Farmers in the economy aren't the consumers and they don't see the changes in demands. But the farmers do see the price of tomatoes fall and that of avocados rise. The new prices tell them that consumers want fewer tomatoes and more avocados.

Moreover, since prices generate revenues for farmers, the new prices also give farmers incentives to shift production. This is important. Farmers react to consumer desires, not because they want to satisfy consumers, but because they simultaneously increase their own wealth.

Farmers gradually respond to the lower price of tomatoes and the higher price of avocados. They reduce the production of tomatoes by using fewer resources to produce tomatoes and increase the production of avocados by using more resources for avocado production.

Farmers don't intially own all the resources that produce their products; they buy some resources from various resource suppliers. How do the resource suppliers know that they should reallocate resources away from the producers of tomatoes and toward the producers of avocados? It is simple: Prices in resource markets give them the information and the incentives.

When the prices of tomatoes fall, farmers growing tomatoes are willing and able to pay less for resources in resource markets. At the same time, since avocado prices rise, avocado farmers offer more for resources. The price offers of the farmers tell the owners of the resources to sell fewer resources to the tomato farmers and more to the avocado farmers. Moreover, since the prices paid for resources generate income for the owners of the resources, the prices provide the owners with incentives as well as instructions.

Resource prices not only signal and reward the owners of resources so that they sell additional resources to avocado farmers, but the prices also signal and reward all producers so that they employ the particular resources that cost consumers the least in terms of the alternative products that could have been produced otherwise. This is accomplished because the resources that cost consumers the least are also the resources that have the lowest prices relative to contributions to production, and producers use the resources with those prices.

For example, suppose that avocado farmers can buy either land that can help produce tomatoes or residential property that can help produce homes. Under these conditions, the values that consumers place on tomatoes are reflected in the prices that tomato farmers are willing to pay for land, whereas the values that consumers place on homes are reflected in the prices that building developers are willing to pay for land.

Now if the value of the homes that would have been sacrificed to grow avocados is greater than the value of the tomatoes that would have been sacrificed, then the price of residential land will lie above the price of tomato-growing land. As a result, avocado farmers will avoid residential land and buy tomato-growing land for production. This in turn causes consumers to do without lower-valued tomatoes rather than higher-valued homes. Scarcity eventually forces consumers to make sacrifices to obtain any products, but the sacrifices are the lowest in value when producers use the resources that have the lowest prices relative to their contributions to production.

The production of fewer tomatoes and more avocados causes the supplies of tomatoes to fall and the supplies of avocados to rise. These supply changes increase the marginal values and prices of tomatoes and reduce the marginal values and prices of avocados. As a result, the values of tomatoes eventually equal the values of the avocados that could have been produced otherwise. At that point, production changes and resource reallocations stop. Products are produced and resources are allocated in line with the new consumer valuations.

The abilities of product and resource prices to coordinate and control production in capitalist systems aren't obvious. For instance, when Soviet citizens visit the United States, they sometimes can't understand why no one tells farmers how much to produce, thinking that without planners giving farmers instructions, massive over- or underproduction must result.

Well, no person tells farmers what to do, but the farmers are directed by market prices. How? Just turn on the radio the next time you drive through Iowa. Whether you like it or not, it won't be long before the commodity market report comes on to give you and local farmers information on the present and future prices of agricultural products. The farmers listen to these broadcasts to get instructions on how to plan future production. They also tune in because the prices represent present and prospective rewards.

The Predictions: The Three Fundamental Questions

From this explanation, we can predict that when consumers shift their demands from some products to others under capitalist conditions, producers will react to the resulting product and resource price changes by producing greater quantities of the goods that consumers demand more and smaller quantities of the goods they demand less. A capitalist system's signals and rewards are prices, rates of exchange that provide producers with the information and the incentives to respond to the values of consumers.

To complete our understanding of capitalism, we can use the explanation to predict how the system answers three basic questions, ones that every economic system must answer:

a. What and how much of each good will be produced?
b. How will the products be produced?
c. To whom will products be distributed?

Our explanation predicts that under capitalism, producers will

a. Produce the goods that consumers value most;
b. Produce goods with the resources that cost consumers the least;
c. Distribute products to the consumers valuing them most.

Of course, producers produce the goods with the highest prices relative to costs, but those goods are also the goods that consumers value most. Producers employ the resources with the lowest prices relative to their contributions to production, but those resources are also the ones that can produce alternative products that are least valuable to consumers. Finally, producers sell their products to consumers paying market prices, but those consumers are the ones who value the products most.

These predictions imply that capitalism is a system of **consumer sovereignty**, a system in which consumers make all of the basic production and distribution decisions. Producers are merely the servants, the agents of consumers.

Although a capitalist system causes the production of goods in line with consumer values, it doesn't necessarily produce the goods that benefit consumers the most. Consumer values differ from benefits. If consumers value heroin, child pornography, gambling services, and prostitution sufficiently, these goods will be produced and distributed to them. And if consumers don't place much value on safety, quality, and information, they won't receive very much.

Also, if business firms are able to control the values of consumers with Madison Avenue advertising techniques, then producing what the consumers value most may be more in line with the best interests of producers rather than consumers. Consumer sovereignty may be but a reflection of producer sovereignty.

Finally, distributing goods to those who value them most is not necessarily the same thing as distributing them to those who will benefit the most. Consumers must have some wealth before they can value anything. If some consumers initially have no goods to trade for food, capitalism will let them starve and instruct producers to distribute the food to others who are willing and able to pay (unless some individuals voluntarily donate food to the very poor).

The theory of capitalism doesn't say that capitalism is a good thing. It says only that if capitalism exists, production and distribution will respond to consumer valuations. It is up to us to decide when these results are good and when they are bad.

A Summary of the Theory

By assuming the presence of private-property rights to products and resources in capitalist systems, we have been able to explain how prices coordinate and control production. We have also been able to predict that producers will

   a. Change production in response to shifts of relative prices;
   b. Produce the goods consumers value most;
   c. Produce goods with the resources that cost consumers the least;
   d. Distribute products to the consumers who value them most.

SPECIAL TOPICS RELATED TO THE THEORY OF CAPITALISM

A GI Bill for Elementary School Students

In the United States, primary education isn't usually produced under capitalist conditions. Private firms don't normally buy resources, produce educational services, and sell the services to consumers. Instead, governments usually tax citizens, buy resources, produce educational services, and provide the services to children free of charge.

What would happen if education were produced under more capitalistic conditions? That is, what would happen if governments still taxed citizens, but instead of spending the money to produce education, the governments gave the dollars to parents, stipulating that the parents had to spend the funds to buy education for their children from profit-seeking private firms?

First, the content and methods of education would be more diverse. Consumers now buy Fords, Toyotas, and Chevys. We can expect that they would buy liberal, conservative, religious, secular, discussion- or lecture-oriented education. They would want some standardization of material so that their children could interact with others in society and would accept some standardization of methods to reduce costs, but content and methods would be less uniform than they are now.

Second, the resources used would be those that parents believed were most valuable relative to their costs. For instance, some parents might want larger classes and more highly paid teachers than are now provided. Others might opt for smaller classes and lower-paid instructors. Also, teaching assistants might be employed more or less often, depending on whether parents thought the benefits were worth the costs.

Finally, the educational products would be sold to those parents valuing them most. No longer would a student living in a particular area of town be kept from attending the school of his or her choice. If a black student in Watts wanted to attend a three-R's school in San Marino, it would probably be possible. After all, it would be costly for a school to reject someone willing and able to pay hard cash (unless the presence of that person would drive away other students).

Although administrators would be making specific decisions about education, market prices would provide signals and rewards. Education would be produced and distributed in line with the values of parents or students rather than administrators, teachers, and PTAs.

Hiring Illegal Mexican Labor

Despite the recent passage of the Immigration Reform Act, some farmers in California, Arizona, New Mexico, and Texas continue to hire illegal Mexican aliens. Why? Is it because they dislike American workers? Perhaps. But there is another possible reason, and our theory of capitalism explains it: Mexican laborers can generally produce at a lower cost than American laborers.

Both Mexican and American workers can produce other products, but the values of the alternative goods differ. The Mexicans can generally produce alternative products that are less valuable to consumers than the alternative products that the Americans can produce. As a result, the employment of the Mexicans on the farms causes consumers to sacrifice less valuable products elsewhere.

Farmers neither know nor often care about consumer sacrifices. Nevertheless, farmers do care about the wages that they have to pay workers. Since the values of alternative products of the Mexicans are lower, the alternative wages of the Mexican workers are lower, and the farmers can, therefore, pay the Mexicans less. By hiring the workers who demand the lowest wages, the farmers coincidentally employ the workers who cause consumers to sacrifice the least-valued alternative products. Workers costing farmers the least also cost consumers the least.

A Mercedes Benz Equipped With Air Bags

Will a capitalist system produce quality and safety as well as quantity? Yes. Producers will produce quality and safety when consumers value it more than quantity. For example, Mercedes Benzes equipped with air bags are being produced in large numbers in West Germany under present capitalistic conditions.

However, when consumers value quantity more than quality and safety, firms respond. They produce goods of lower quality and safety and usually sell those goods at a lower price, thereby allowing consumers to buy more quantity. Some consumers even buy used Corvairs, contrary to the warnings of Ralph Nader's classic book, *Unsafe at Any Speed*. They generally do so not necessarily because they don't want quality or safety, but because they value classical design more.

Automobile companies do not always determine the level of quality and safety for their consumers. They will produce almost anything for which they think consumers are willing and able to pay. In fact, when some automobile companies lobby against government safety regulations, they may be representing only what they think are the wills of their consumers. The companies may fear that consumers won't be willing to pay for the cost of additional safety.

Information and *Consumer Reports*

Capitalism responds to the values of consumers, but before consumers can make informed decisions, they must have information. Will capitalism provide them with that information?

Yes. Simple inspection of capitalistic economies reveals the production of a great deal of information, sometimes by original producers of products and sometimes by firms that specialize in information's generation and dissemination. Private schools, salespersons, advertising, brand names, logos, consumer consultants, *Consumer Reports* magazine, newspapers, and trade journals all serve to give consumers information on how to spend their dollars.

How much information do we buy as consumers? Usually far less then we want. In a world of scarcity, information is costly; to obtain information, we must sacrifice other valuable goods. At some point, the value of additional information is less than the value of other goods, so we stop choosing more information.

This explains why we don't all subscribe to *Consumer Reports*. Although we may value the information the magazine provides, we may value other things more and, therefore, rely on the more limited information that we obtain from other sources. Only those of us who want additional information sufficiently to cover its cost purchase and read *Consumer Reports*.

SOCIALISM AND MERCANTILISM

To obtain capitalist results, we need only have private-property rights to resources and products. But private property rights do not exist naturally. Their establishment and preservation generally require force. Without it, some individuals will steal rather than buy goods and others will try to monopolize markets by eliminating competition.

Achieving Capitalism: Private-Property Rights Protection by Individuals, Voluntary Groups, and Governments

To prevent theft and trade restrictions, we could each strap on six-shooters and try to maintain the exclusive use and free transferability of goods. But this would be a very costly way to protect private-property rights.

As an alternative, some of us might want to join together and form a voluntary association. The association could then collect money and hire a firm to protect our property and keep markets open to all. However, we would then encounter a very basic problem: We wouldn't be able to protect our property rights to the property rights we would create. That is, we wouldn't be able to protect our property rights without also protecting the rights of others. Anyone not joining our group could nevertheless obtain the benefits of living in a capitalist society. As a result, our voluntary group would gradually fall apart as individuals flocked to join the free riders who could obtain the benefits of capitalism without incurring any of the costs.

For example, if some stores in a shopping center formed a group to hire a security service to protect the center, other stores paying nothing would nevertheless be protected from burglars. Once the security was produced, it would accrue to all retailers. Stores would gradually leave the group and join the free riders, and eventually, protection wouldn't be provided even if its value far exceeded its cost.

How could capitalist results then be obtained? Perhaps by using property right arrangements that would expel free riders. For example, if one firm built a shopping center and leased floor space to various retailers, rental fees could include security costs. Stores refusing to pay for the security could then be kept out. However, such private-property right arrangements are often very costly or impossible.

Our only remaining alternative for achieving capitalist results might be government coercion. We could join together, buy police protection, and force everyone to pay taxes to cover the costs.

It may seem contradictory to use government to assure capitalism. Isn't the government interfering with consumer sovereignty when it uses force? Not necessarily. Had exclusive-use rights to the property protection existed, many people would have been willing and able to pay to cover the costs. Therefore, when the government provides the services and requires payment, it may be bringing about what would have happened under capitalism. Rather than interfering with capitalism, government may be bringing about capitalist results.

The protection of private-property rights isn't the only product that governments in many economies produce that may cause rather than change capitalist results. Other examples include

    a. National defense
    b. The judicial system
    c. Basic physics research
    d. A cure for AIDS
    e. Scenic beauty
    f. Peace and quiet
    g. City planning and zoning
    h. Clean air

If private firms produced any of these items, they couldn't force all consumers to pay. People who refused to pay would generally obtain the goods anyway. As a result, the firms wouldn't produce the goods even if they were very valuable to consumers. When governments then produce or bring about the production of these products, they may simply be causing what would have happened under capitalism.

Socialism

Government taxation, production, and distribution creates socialism. **Socialism** is an economic system in which the government forces the communal ownership of property; we are coerced into owning property together rather than owning it privately.

Since we jointly own property, production and distribution decisions are made politically. Coordination and control then come from government administrators rather than from market prices.

Unfortunately, we know very little about group decision making. As a result, we can't predict which goods groups will choose to produce under socialism, nor can we predict how they will produce and distribute the products.

We can, however, describe how decisions are implemented. For instance, the economy of the Soviet Union contains a great deal of socialism. In that economy, the Communist party makes the major production and distribution decisions. The decisions are then carried out by the state planning agency, the Gosplan.

To coordinate and control production and distribution, the Gosplan's administrators essentially establish two lists. One is a short list of available resources. The other is a long prioritized list of desired products. The administrators go down the priority list of products until they run out of resources.

Once the Gosplan's administrators determine which goods will be produced, they provide the managers of various business firms with output quotas and allocate resources to them. By distributing the resources to the firms, the administrators determine how products are to be produced.

Finally, the administrators of Gosplan tell the firms how much to pay employees and how to distribute products. Sometimes the administrators tell firms to sell products in markets to the highest bidders. In those cases, the goods are distributed to those consumers valuing them most. More often, prices are set at very low levels where shortages occur. When this happens, other criteria for distribution are established and goods are allocated to different people, perhaps to those first in line, Communist party members, or friends.

Interfering With Capitalism: Socialism

Governments in capitalistic nations don't limit their activities to areas where capitalism and private-property rights don't exist. They often create socialism where capitalism would have been naturally present. Examples of such government intervention include the post office, municipal utilities, museums, art galleries, theaters, parks, sports arenas, vocational schools, bus systems, and libraries. If individual consumers valued these goods sufficiently, the goods would have been produced—indeed, some have been produced—by private firms responding to private demands. Nevertheless, governments usually have purchased resources, produced and distributed the products, and then forced taxpayers to pay taxes to cover production costs.

Interfering With Capitalism: Mercantilism

In addition to forcing the communal ownership of some property, governments in capitalist economies often interfere with capitalism by keeping some people and firms from producing and selling goods. The remaining producers then obtain monopoly power and profits. In these cases, government intervention within capitalism doesn't constitute socialism, since goods are not communally owned and political decisions do not totally replace prices. Instead, the intervention creates **mercantilism**, an economic system in which the government has given some sellers monopoly power by eliminating their competition. Mercantilism can be thought of as a system of government-created monopoly-capitalism.

Examples of the creation of mercantilism in the U.S. economy include government restrictions on the sale of automobiles, homes, meat products, drugs, medical services, narcotics, gambling services, interstate trucking, postal services, education, alcohol, railroads, and foreign-produced goods.

Mercantilism interferes with consumer sovereignty. If we, as consumers, want to buy cars without seat belts, homes without smoke alarms, low-quality meat, or untested drugs, we can't.

Why do governments create mercantilism? We can only speculate. Some people may want to protect consumers from low-quality products, unsafe goods, and high prices. Other people may only want to become wealthy as the producers of approved products of high quality, safety, and price.

For example, by keeping pharmacists from prescribing drugs, many doctors think that consumers will be protected from the incompetent advice of some pharmacists. Other doctors, however, may want the restrictions because they become wealthier when their competitors are eliminated.

The mixture of capitalism, socialism, and mercantilism makes it difficult for us to explain economic phenomena. Problems such as high-cost medical care and low-quality education no longer obviously emanate from capitalist institutions. But the mixture does give us one dividend: To understand the functioning and the problems of socialism and mercantilism, we don't have to travel abroad. We can simply observe our own socialist and mercantilist institutions.

SPECIAL TOPICS RELATED TO SOCIALISM AND MERCANTILISM

Government Production of Computer Software

Today, many firms produce software programs for the owners of computers who value the programs sufficiently. But what if it were possible to duplicate the programs without cost, to steal them rather than buy them? Then certainly the firms producing and selling the programs would stop production. They couldn't protect their private rights of exclusive use and transferability. Although some people might be honest and pay money to the firms, the number of free riders would probably be sufficient to cut revenues below the costs of production.

How could we then obtain the programs? By government production. The government could either buy the resources and produce the software or subsidize private software firms. Should the government choose to interfere, it wouldn't be interfering with capitalism; it might only be bringing about capitalist results.

How many programs would the government have to produce to bring about capitalist results? The government could neither know nor find out. Without markets revealing the values of the programs to the consumers, it would be impossible to determine the value-maximizing quantity of programs. If government administrators wanted to produce computer programs in line with consumer values, they would have to make educated guesses regarding the optimal quantities.

No Smoking—$50 Fine

Smokers want to consume cigarettes. When governments make smoking illegal in public, aren't they interfering with capitalist results? Aren't they reducing the values of goods to consumers?

Not necessarily. The restrictions do interfere with the rights of smokers to consume their share of clean air. However, the smokers can't use their clean air without also using the clean air that belongs to others. If the value of clean air to nonsmokers is more than the value of smoking, then governments are helping bring about capitalist results when they restrict smoking.

It boils down to how much smokers would be willing and able to pay to smoke and how much nonsmokers would be willing to accept for their clean air. For instance, if smokers value smoking in public at $50 and if the value of the clean air to nonsmokers is $60, then smoking wouldn't have occurred under capitalism. The smokers would not have been willing to buy clean air from nonsmokers for $60. Under capitalism, smoking wouldn't have occurred, so government prohibitions then bring about capitalist results.

Of course, if the clean air is only worth $20 to nonsmokers, then smokers would pay nonsmokers to relinquish their air. Smoking in public would occur under capitalism, and governments are then interfering with capitalist results by prohibiting smoking.

We can't find out what would have happened under capitalism because market prices aren't present to tell us the value of clean air. Nevertheless, some evidence indicates that smokers generally value smoking more than nonsmokers value clean air: Without government restrictions, stores, restaurants, and bars usually don't prohibit smoking. If nonsmokers valued clean air more than smokers value smoking, many of these profit-seeking establishments could have earned greater profits by voluntarily prohibiting smoking. True, they would have lost the patronage of many smokers, but they would have more than offset the lost sales with revenues from nonsmokers. Based on this indirect evidence, government restrictions on smoking often interfere with capitalist results.

Manners and Customs

In addition to government, two other coercive institutions, manners and customs, can bring about capitalist results when private-property rights don't exist, and they can often do it more cheaply. For example, it may be considered very bad manners to steal someone else's property or it may be a custom of a society that people must buy goods from owners before they can use them. Then, to enforce the customs and manners, social ostracism of those violating such rules can be used.

As another example, most of us try to keep our dogs quiet, not so much because there is a law against noise, but because it is bad manners to destroy peace and quiet. If we don't like the manners, we may, nevertheless, obey them if we fear being alienated by our neighbors.

Somoza's Nicaragua: Capitalism or Mercantilism?

To many people, the Sandinista revolution in Nicaragua was a triumph of socialism over capitalism. But did the economy of Nicaragua represent capitalism? Under Nicaragua's Somoza regime, the government granted many individuals in Nicaragua monopoly rights to produce by limiting the private-property rights of potential competitors to use and sell their goods as they pleased. This government intervention increased the wealth of many people, including those in power, but it reduced the wealth of competitors and of consumers. To some extent, the Sandinista revolution was supported by the general public because of problems that were created by mercantilism rather than capitalism.

We have now completed the foundations of our analysis. In the next chapter, we will extend our theory to explain and predict phenomena related to money and banking so that we can subsequently deal with the problems of inflation and unemployment.

MAJOR AND MINOR POINTS

1. Economic systems coordinate and control production and distribution; they tell us what to do and give us the incentives to do it.
2. Capitalism is an economic system characterized by private-property rights.
3. Private-property rights include rights to exclusive use and free transferability.
4. When consumer values change in capitalist systems, higher prices inform and give incentives to producers to increase the production of the goods valued more while lower prices inform and give incentives to producers to reduce the production of goods valued less.
5. The three fundamental questions are
   a. What and how much to produce;
   b. How to produce;
   c. To whom to distribute.
6. Under capitalism, prices inform and motivate producers to produce the goods consumers value most, produce goods at a minimum cost to consumers, and distribute outputs to those consumers valuing the outputs the most.
7. Under capitalism, the content and methods of education would be more in line with consumer valuations.
8. Farmers hire illegal Mexican workers because wages tell the farmers to hire the workers who produce at a minimum cost to consumers and also reward the farmers for doing so.
9. Under capitalism, quality, safety, and information will be produced as long as they are more valuable than other sacrificed goods.

10. If we desire the production of the goods that consumers value most, government must often be used in circumstances where private property rights don't exist.

11. Socialism is an economic system characterized by forced communal ownership of property.

12. Socialism in the U.S. economy sometimes brings about what would have happened under capitalism, but sometimes it represents interference with capitalism.

13. We have no theory to predict which goods will be produced, how they will be produced, and how they will be distributed under socialism.

14. Government sometimes limits private-property rights by restricting the production of some goods. The result is mercantilism, an economic system in which the government has given some sellers monopoly power by eliminating their competition. Mercantilism can be thought of as government-created monopoly-capitalism.

15. If computer software could be costlessly duplicated, government intervention to bring about the production of the software might be consistent with consumer sovereignty.

16. Government may be bringing about capitalist results when it interferes to protect clean air.

17. Manners and customs may be less costly ways of bringing about capitalist results than the use of government.

18. Many problems in South American nations and in the United States result from socialism and mercantilism, not from capitalism.

QUESTIONS

1. What are economic systems and why do they exist?
2. What is capitalism?
3. Which products will be produced under capitalist conditions?
4. How will products be produced under capitalist conditions?
5. To whom will products be distributed under capitalist conditions?
6. Even when consumers value them highly, which products will not be produced in the U.S. economy unless government intervenes?
7. Even when consumers would prefer otherwise, which resources will be used by private firms in the American economy?
8. What is socialism?
9. How are decisions regarding what to produce, how to produce it, and how to distribute the output determined under socialist conditions?
10. What is mercantilism?
11. How do mercantilist results differ from those of capitalism?
12. Discuss the following terms and concepts:

Economic system	What, how, and to whom
Capitalism	Safety, quality, and information

Private-property rights
Exclusive use rights
Free transferability rights
Consumer sovereignty

Government and capitalism
Manners and customs
Socialism
Mercantilism

APPLICATIONS

1. How do wage-price controls limit private-property rights?
2. Suppose consumers value hang gliders more and bicycles less. Explain the effects that this will have on the markets for the two goods.
3. Suppose producers felt that they have a social responsibility to not produce dangerous hang gliders. Why would it nevertheless be difficult for them to ignore consumer desires?
4. Capitalism is a system of freedom. Since people do anything they want, it is extremely inefficient. Government coordination and control is necessary to prevent arbitrary results. Evaluate.
5. Adam Smith, the father of modern economics, once argued that the "invisible hand" of self-interest would motivate producers to respond to the desires of consumers. What makes the self-interest of producers match that of consumers?
6. What prevents producers from selling only to their friends, relatives, whites, and heterosexuals?
7. Parents can't be allowed to make decisions about educational matters because they don't have any information. Evaluate.
8. Under a capitalist educational system, would teachers be paid more or less?
9. Suppose you feel a social responsibility to hire American rather than Mexican labor in your garment factory. How would you and your consumers be affected by your decision?
10. Do you think that the control of food and drugs by the Food and Drug Administration results in the quality and safety that consumers value most?
11. Why is it difficult for socialist administrators to match competitive capitalist results?
12. How can religion bring about capitalist results?
13. Why do people vote in national elections?
14. The resources of North and South America are similar. Are private-property rights to those resources the same? How does this affect the uses to which resources are put?
15. Following is a list of things done by governments in the United States. Which ones may be necessary to bring about consumer-orientated results?

    Governments produce
    a. Court systems
    b. Police protection
    c. Vocational education
    d. Primary and secondary education
    e. Parks

f. City planning and zoning
g. Sports arenas
h. Public tennis courts
i. Public libraries
j. Zoos
k. Museums
l. Fire protection
m. Small boat harbors

Governments place restrictions on
a. Practicing dentistry
b. Gambling
c. Nudity in public
d. Barking and roaming dogs
e. Salmon fishing
f. Consumption of cocaine
g. Product safety
h. Smoking in public places
i. Prostitution

Governments subsidize
a. Fish canneries
b. Agricultural research
c. Agricultural production
d. Low income housing
e. Homes for the aged
f. Small businesses

The Forms, the Supply, and the Value of Money

Money is certainly a perplexing phenomenon. The love of money is said to be the root of all evil, yet churches happily accept monetary contributions. Many Communists think money is partly responsible for exploitation, but every Communist country in the world uses money extensively. And some people claim that paper money is worthless, yet they work hard to earn wages paid in the form of paper money.

We have already resolved some of the paradoxes associated with the use and the value of money in Chapter 3. We resolve others in this chapter by developing a theory of money and banking. The theory specifies that in addition to acting as a medium of exchange, money can reduce transaction costs by providing a store of value, by being a unit of account, and by taking many different forms.

The special topics in this chapter deal with the rock money of Yap, the nature of memory money, the U.S. money supply, the Federal Reserve System, the control which the Federal Reserve System has over the money supply, and what happens during banking holidays.

A THEORY OF MONEY AND BANKING

The Phenomena

When we examine the U.S. economy, it's obvious that money is employed extensively in exchange; very few trades don't directly involve money. It is also noteworthy that many forms of money exist: We buy goods with coins, government notes, and checks. In 1987, of the $753 billion that made up the U.S. money supply (roughly $3000 per person), 27% comprised coins and government notes, and the remainder, 73%, took the form of private debt money (deposits in banks or other financial institutions that could be used in payment for goods. Moreover, although the U.S. money supply has increased during many years of our history, it hasn't expanded to infinity. The money supply remains finite.

An Explanation: The Evolution of a Monetary System

To explain why we create and use money, why we employ many monetary forms, and why the money supply is limited, let's follow the evolution of a hypothetical economy, beginning with a simple barter system and ending with an economy that simultaneously contains many monetary forms. As we follow the evolution, we will gradually approach a level of complexity that approximates that of the U. S. monetary system.

Keep in mind that the evolution is purely imaginary. It is only one of many possible ways that a complex monetary system can come into existence.

Cigarette Money

To begin, suppose you live in a barter economy in which people directly exchange paper for shoes, oranges for apples, books for radios, etc. Unfortunately, to trade under barter circumstances, a double-coincidence-of-wants requirement has to be satisfied. For example, if you want to buy shrimp and are willing to sell your labor, you must find a fisherman who not only wants to sell shrimp but also just happens to want your labor.

You soon discover that it's easier to trade if you use cigarettes as a medium to obtain other goods. To buy shrimp, you sell your labor for cigarettes and use the cigarettes to purchase the shrimp. Although you double the number of exchanges, your total transaction costs fall since many buyers have cigarettes and many sellers want them.

Other people in the economy also find that cigarettes can help reduce transaction costs. In fact, some of the shrimp fishermen willing to accept your cigarettes may be nonsmokers. They may want the cigarettes only as a medium to obtain other goods.

Once cigarettes become generally accepted for their value in trade rather than for their value in consumption, they become money. Money is what money does; the cigarettes become money because they carry out the primary function of money: to act as a medium of exchange.

We discussed the medium of exchange function in Chapter 3. Money can do more, however, to reduce transaction costs. Money can also act as a store of value and a unit of account.

Cigarettes in our hypothetical economy soon become a store of value. Under the previous conditions of barter, you wouldn't have been able to sell your labor at one point in time and buy shrimp later. You would have been forced to trade the labor directly for shrimp and store the shrimp for subsequent consumption. As a result, you would have had to incur some storage costs. But once money is present, you can choose another alternative: You can exchange your labor for cigarettes and store the cigarettes until you want to buy the shrimp. To the extent that the cigarettes are less costly to store, your transaction costs fall.

Cigarettes also soon perform the monetary function of being a unit of account. In a barter economy, the number of prices of each item equal the number of other goods. In a money-using economy, however, each good usually has only one price—its money price. All prices and accounts dealing with income, wealth, and debts in our imaginary economy are soon expressed in terms of cigarettes.

We have explained why people in the economy use money. We can also reveal why, up to this point, the supply of money is limited: Cigarettes are generally produced with resources and resources are limited in supply. Unless more resources are either discovered or shifted away from the production of other goods, the money supply will remain constant.

Gold

After some time, people discover that gold reduces transaction costs more than cigarettes. Gold is more generally acceptable, its value fluctuates less, and it stores more easily. Since people would have to be irrational not to reduce transaction costs when given the opportunity, gold replaces cigarettes as the basic monetary form of the economy.

To be specific, let's assume that the money supply in the economy becomes $10 million in gold, as shown in Table 15.1. (Of course, no dollars yet exist in our economy, only ounces of gold. Nevertheless, we can greatly simplify our discussion if we assume that units of gold are measured in dollars, a change that will occur anyway after dollars are later introduced.)

The supply of gold is limited. Only when new gold is discovered and mined does the supply increase.

TABLE 15.1   *The Money Supply*

MONEY SUPPLY	
Gold	$10,000,000

Private Notes

While gold is a superior monetary form to cigarettes, privately created debt money is even better. It comes into existence in our imaginary economy after you go to a general store and discover that you've forgotten your gold at home, but you still want to buy various commodities. Since the merchant trusts you, he accepts your IOU, a note for $100 in gold, as temporary payment.

Later that day, a wholesaler delivers produce to the store. The merchant doesn't have enough gold to buy the supplies, so he uses your note to pay the wholesaler. The wholesaler accepts the note you wrote because she knows and also trusts you. Later, she passes the note to a farmer when she buys his products.

The note circulates in the same way as gold. In fact, when you later stop someone with the note and offer to give them gold, they reject your offer. Not only do they consider the note "as good as gold," but better. They realize that the note is easier to transfer and store. Your note becomes privately created debt money.

You issue more notes as merchants request payment in notes rather than gold. Some people even bring gold to you to trade for notes.

Eventually, you wind up issuing $1 million of your notes. To back them up, you take $1 million in gold out of the economy's money supply and place it in your vault to act as a reserve. (Note that the gold in reserve is not part of the money supply, since it doesn't circulate as a medium of exchange.)

Your actions have changed the composition of the money supply but not its level, as shown in Table 15.2. Since the notes are backed by 100% gold reserves, the factors that constrain the supply of gold also limit the supply of your notes.

Many Monetary Forms

Although your notes have replaced $1 million of the gold in the economy, $9 million in gold continues to circulate. The money supply comprises more than one monetary form. This is because the relative efficiency of a monetary form depends on the particular function performed or the trade being made. Your notes reduce transaction costs the most when they act as a local medium of exchange, but gold is still superior as a medium to buy foreign goods, and people keep it for such trades.

TABLE 15.2 *The Money Supply*

	MONEY SUPPLY	RESERVES	
Gold	$9,000,000		
Your notes	1,000,000	$1,000,000	Gold

Fractional Reserves

Before long, you realize that most of your gold reserves are unnecessary. People prefer your notes to gold and ask for gold only when they leave town. Moreover, when some people leave town, others arrive and deposit gold with you. You have to maintain reserves to meet only temporary differences between outflows and inflows.

You find from experience that it's enough to keep $1 of gold in reserve for every $10 in notes outstanding, maintaining a 10% reserve. (The percentage was chosen only to make computations easier. Actual percentages would depend on particular conditions.) You have $1 million in gold reserves so you create another $9 million in notes. As Table 15.3 reveals, the money supply grows by $9 million.

The process of expanding the money supply greatly increases your wealth. Not only do you purchase consumption commodities with the new money, but you also buy bonds as you lend some of the money out to earn future interest. Since you could get fabulously rich, you would like to create massive quantities of money. But although only fractional gold reserves are necessary, the fractional requirements must nevertheless be met. The gold supply continues to constrain the money supply, although the limit on the money supply is higher.

High-Powered Money

Once gold can act to support newly created notes only fractionally , it becomes high-powered money. **High-powered money** is a monetary form of which an increase in supply can cause a more than proportionate increase in the supply of money. For example, a $1 increase in the supply of gold can cause a $10 increase in the money supply. One dollar of gold can support $10 of your notes.

The high-powered nature of money becomes evident in our imaginary economy after a prospector discovers $3 million in gold. The prospector gives $1 million to you in exchange for $1 million of your notes. Your reserves rise by $1 million in gold as do your outstanding notes. But since $1 million in gold can support $10 million in notes, you issue $9 million more of the notes. The $3 million gold discovery causes a $12 increase in the money supply, as shown in Table 15.4.

TABLE 15.3 The Money Supply

MONEY SUPPLY		RESERVES	
Gold	$ 9,000,000		
Your notes	10,000,000	Gold	$1,000,000

TABLE 15.4 The Money Supply

MONEY SUPPLY		RESERVES	
Gold	$11,000,000		
Your notes	20,000,000	Gold	$2,000,000

Bank Notes and Demand Deposits

You lend most of your notes to debtors at the going interest rate and become fairly wealthy. Next, to get even richer, you join with your friends to form the Honesty Bank. You and your friends start the bank by giving it $2 million worth of property (a building, computers, furniture, and so forth) in exchange for its common stock. This is shown in Table 15.5.

Next, the bank hires workers and opens its doors to the public. Depositors subsequently come into the bank wanting to trade their gold for the bank's notes. The bank issues $4 million of its notes and takes in $4 million in gold. The gold is then placed in reserve to back the notes, as Table 15.6 reveals.

The composition of the economy's money supply changes as the bank pulls $4 million in gold out of the money supply to act as a reserve and replaces it with $4 million of Honesty Bank notes. This is shown in Table 15.7.

Unfortunately, the bank notes can easily be stolen. As a result, people eventually ask your bank to keep their money in demand deposits, checking accounts. They then write checks instructing the bank to transfer the money to other people.

People convert the $4 million in bank notes to demand deposits, as shown in Table 15.8.

This changes the composition of the economy's money supply, as shown in Table 15.9.

Bank Money Creation

You and your friends didn't form the Honesty Bank to provide services to the public. You built the bank to get rich and you become wealthy by earning interest. The managers of your bank soon discover that 10% reserves are enough to back outstanding demand deposits. The $4 million in reserves can support $40 million in deposits, not just $4 million. The bank can and does create additional money: It grants borrowers $36 million in demand deposits in exchange for their promises to repay the money with interest as shown in Table 15.10.

TABLE 15.5 The Honesty Bank

THE HONESTY BANK		
ASSETS		LIABILITIES
Property	$2,000,000	Common stock $2,000,000

TABLE 15.6 The Honesty Bank

THE HONESTY BANK			
ASSETS		LIABILITIES	
Property	$2,000,000	Common stock	$2,000,000
Reserves	4,000,000	Honesty notes	4,000,000

TABLE 15.7 The Money Supply

MONEY SUPPLY		RESERVES	
Gold	$ 7,000,000		
Your notes	20,000,000	Gold	$2,000,000
Honesty Bank notes	4,000,000	Gold	4,000,000

TABLE 15.8 The Honesty Bank

THE HONESTY BANK			
ASSETS		LIABILITIES	
Property	$2,000,000	Common stock	$2,000,000
Reserves	4,000,000	Demand deposits	4,000,000

TABLE 15.9 The Money Supply

MONEY SUPPLY		RESERVES	
Gold	$ 7,000,000		
Your notes	20,000,000	Gold	$2,000,000
Honesty demand deposits	4,000,000	Gold	4,000,000

TABLE 15.10 The Honesty Bank

THE HONESTY BANK			
ASSETS		LIABILITIES	
Property	$2,000,000	Common stock	$2,000,000
Reserves	4,000,000	Demand deposits	40,000,000
Loans	36,000,000		

TABLE 15.11   *The Money Supply*

MONEY SUPPLY		RESERVES	
Gold	$7,000,000		
Your notes	20,000,000	Gold	$2,000,000
Honesty demand deposits	40,000,000	Gold	4,000,000

As a result, the money supply in the economy increases by $36 million as shown in Table 15.11.

A Monopoly Bank's Ability to Create Money

With reserves of $4 million and demand deposits of $4 million, your bank has been able to increase the money supply by a maximum of $36 million. A convenient way of determining how much a bank like yours can increase the money supply is to multiply its **excess reserves** (total reserves minus desired or required reserves) by the **reciprocal of the reserve ratio** (one divided by the reserve ratio. For example, only $400,000 in reserves were necessary to support $4 million in demand deposits. Since the bank had $4 million in reserves, excess reserves were $3,600,000. The reciprocal of the reserve ratio of .10 is 10 (that is, 1/.10). Therefore, the bank was able to create an additional $36 million, since $3,600,000 times 10 is $36 million.

Your bank has been able to create 10 times its excess reserves because it's the only bank in town—it's a monopoly bank. When borrowers write checks telling your bank to give $36 million to other people, this doesn't drain reserves. Since everyone has an account with your bank, demand deposits just move from one account to another as the $36 million in checks clear. The $4 million in reserves remain intact, supporting $40 million in demand deposits.

A Banking System's Ability to Create Money

Earning income by creating money and charging interest is very attractive to other people in the economy. Other new banks are begun. The construction of many new banks tends to reduce the interest rate that your bank can charge on loans. It also reduces the quantity of money that your bank can create. New loans now often drain reserves because the checks of borrowers are often deposited in other banks, and those banks then ask for your reserves.

If you assume that all new loans will now cause a drain on reserves as new demand deposits are placed in other banks, your individual bank can create only an amount of money equal to its excess reserves (since it can afford to loose only those reserves).

But the banking system's ability to create money is the same as it was for your monopoly bank, an amount of money equal to the reciprocal of the reserve ratio times the excess reserves. This is because the reserves don't leave the banking system. Four million dollars in bank reserves can still support $40 million in demand deposits, so the system creates $36 million in new demand deposits.

A multibank system operates the same way as a monopoly bank with many branches. While reserves may leave one bank and flow to another, they don't leave the system, and therefore the system doesn't lose reserves. With only a fractional reserve requirement, a multibank system can create money equal to a multiple of its excess reserves, a multiple equal to the reciprocal of its reserve ratio.

At this point, two things are worth pointing out. First, government doesn't need to create money for money to exist. We have examined the use of cigarettes, gold, private debts, and bank debts as money and haven't mentioned government. Second, the money supply will not grow to infinity without government controls. Private money has been created and its supply will remain constant unless new gold discoveries are made.

Nevertheless, government money does exist in real economies, and it's time to introduce it into our imaginary system.

Government Money

The last step in our imaginary monetary evolution is the introduction of government money. Politicians decide that the government should have the power to create money for the following reasons:

1. The creation of government money provides the economy with a more general medium of exchange and thereby reduces transaction costs.
2. The addition of government money to the money supply can facilitate the greater number of exchanges that occur during periods of economic growth.
3. Issues of government money can offset massive decreases in the money supply that occur during banking panics. The decreases in money supply occur because people shift from demand deposits to gold, causing banks to reduce their loans of demand deposits. Just as the money supply can grow rapidly when people deposit gold or other high-powered money with their banks, so the money supply can fall rapidly when people withdraw gold or other high-powered money.
4. By creating money, the government can buy more goods without either directly taxing or borrowing from the public.
5. The injection of government money into the economy may act as a stimulus to the economy, temporarily increasing national production and reducing unemployment.

The government in our economy begins by creating coins. Vending machines don't accept chunks of gold, notes, or demand deposits. Although private individuals could mint and sell coins, the government in our imaginary economy decides to monopolize this activity. Its treasury uses $1 million in gold to mint $2 million dollars in gold coins.

It doesn't include more gold in the coins for two reasons. First, why waste gold on coins? The coins will have a $2 million exchange value whether they contain $2 million or 20¢ in gold. The treasury uses $1 million in gold only to maintain the durability of the coins.

Second, if the coins contained $2 million in gold, an increase in the price of gold would raise the commodity value of the coins above their exchange value. The coins would then be melted down for their metallic content.

Once the coins are created, they become high-powered money. Of the $2 million that are minted and spent by the government, $1 million are eventually pulled out of circulation when people deposit them in the banks. The banks respond by creating $10 million in new demand deposits. As indicated in Table 15.12, the money supply in the economy grows not by just $1 million, but by $10 million. (The $2 million in coins increased the money supply initially by only $1 million because their production absorbed $1 million in gold.)

Next, the government creates some government debt money. The politicians could have the treasury simply create the new money by printing and spending treasury notes, but they decide against this alternative. They don't want to allow the agency in charge of government financing, the treasury, to have the power to run the presses.

So they opt for another alternative. They form a government bank. The bank is then instructed to buy treasury bonds with new money. It purchases $10 million in treasury bonds with $5 million in government bank notes plus $5 million in government bank demand deposits. The money supply immediately grows by $10 million.

The newly created money is high-powered; it can be used by private banks as a reserve. The $5 million in government bank demand deposits all flow into reserves and support the creation of $50 million in private bank demand deposits. The eventual effect of the initial $10 million increase in government bank money is a $55 million increase in the supply of money, as shown in Table 15.13.

As long as the money supply either comprised gold or needed to be backed totally or fractionally by gold reserves, the supply was constrained by the supply of gold. However, after the government issues government bank debt money, the only restrictions on the size of the money supply are those that the government imposes on itself.

In our hypothetical economy, the government has chosen to let the

TABLE 15.12   *The Money Supply*

	MONEY SUPPLY		RESERVES
Gold	$ 6,000,000		
Your notes	20,000,000	Gold	2,000,000
Bank demand deposits	50,000,000	Gold	4,000,000
		Coins	1,000,000
Coins	1,000,000		

TABLE 15.13 The Money Supply

MONEY SUPPLY		RESERVES	
Gold	$ 5,000,000		
Your notes	20,000,000	Gold	$2,000,000
Bank demand deposits	100,000,000	Gold	4,000,000
		Coins	1,000,000
		Government bank demand deposits	5,000,000
Coins	1,000,000		
Government bank notes	5,000,000		

government bank issue notes and demand deposits without any reserve backing. The government bank can therefore issue as much money as the government wants it to. The money supply is limited only by political constraints. However, those constraints are significant in the hypothetical economy, so the money supply remains limited.

The Predictions

This explanation allows us to make some general predictions about the forms, the supply, and the value of money.

The Use of Many Monetary Forms

First, we can predict that if many monetary forms can reduce transaction costs, then the ones that will be used will be those that reduce the costs the most. For example, in our hypothetical economy, gold replaced cigarette money and private notes replaced some gold, reducing transaction costs in each case.

Furthermore, we can predict that if the efficiency of monetary forms differs depending on the monetary function performed or the exchange being made, then a variety of monetary forms will be simultaneously employed.

In the U.S. economy, since 27% of the money supply comprises government coins and notes and 73% is private bank money, it appears that government currency is most efficient for only 27% of our monetary uses, whereas the remaining 73% call for demand deposit money.

However, the ratios do change. Around the holiday season, we write fewer checks and use more government currency because government currency is less of a hassle when we make many exchanges in rapid succession. After the holiday season, we generally deposit some proportion of our government currency in demand deposits and revert to writing more checks. Each of us keeps the combination of coins, government notes, and demand deposits that minimizes our transaction costs.

Limits on the Money Supply

Next, we can predict that if the money supply comprises commodity money or if the money supply must be backed to some extent by a commodity, then the money supply will expand only if the supply of the particular commodity increases. However, if the government can issue money, then monetary constraints become political in nature.

For example, as long as the money supply in the hypothetical economy comprised gold or had to be backed by gold, the money supply was constrained by the supply of gold. But after the government bank was able to issue notes and demand deposits, only political constraints remained.

One of the political constraints that sometimes limits the supply of government money is a reserve requirement imposed by law on the government bank or treasury. If, for example, the politicians in our imaginary economy had decided to require the government bank to keep 10% gold reserves to support outstanding government bank notes and demand deposits, then even with government money, the supply of gold would have put a lid on the supply of money.

This is one of the effects of an international gold standard. The United States was on such a standard between 1879 and 1934 (with the exception of war years). The standard required nations to define their money relative to gold and stand ready to sell gold in exchange for their currencies. Their gold reserves then limited how much money their treasuries and government banks could create.

Of course, a government reserve requirement is self-imposed. To limit the supply of government money, other political constraints are still necessary, since politicians who impose reserve requirements can also lift them.

The Value of Money

We also can predict that an increase in the supply of money will reduce the value of money, and a decrease in the supply of money will increase the value of money.

The value of money is derived from what it will buy. For example, if $10,000 in gold can buy a new car, then the gold is worth at least as much as the new car. If a slip of paper is acceptable in trade for a house, then that slip is at least as valuable as the house. However, what money will buy is in turn determined by how much money exists relative to the other goods it can purchase. As a result, an increase in the supply of money will reduce the value of money value, and a decrease in the supply of money will increase the value of money.

The relationship between the supply of money and the value of money explains why commodity monies or commodity-backed monies are sometimes desirable. It isn't so that if all else fails, someone holding money can obtain the consumption value of the commodity. When only fractional commodity reserves are present, only some people can succeed in doing this anyway. Rather, the role of the commodity is to limit the supply of money and thereby assure a stable value of money in trade. When commodity or commodity-backed monies are used, the value of money will generally fall only if the supplies of the base commodities expand.

A Redistribution of Wealth

Finally, we can make a prediction about the distribution of nonmoney goods. By definition, *nonmoney* goods are all the goods in the economy other than money. They include physical consumption commodities, resources, and financial assets.

We can predict that the people or institutions creating new money will obtain more nonmoney goods at everyone else's expense. For example, when you doubled the money supply in the hypothetical economy by issuing your notes, the supply of nonmoney goods didn't change. As a result, you reduced the value of money by half. However, since you had much more money and everyone else had the same amount, you were able to buy more while everyone else bought less. Although quantity of nonmoney goods in the economy didn't change, you redistributed nonmoney goods in your favor. Similarly, when the prospector, the banks, and the government in the hypothetical economy increased the money supply, they gained relative to everyone else.

To the extent that the government is owned by the public, government money creation may represent only a change in the form of the nonmoney goods of many individuals rather than a decline. For example, if the government creates new money and buys a bridge, the value of money falls. Your money may suddenly buy one less winter coat than before. Since you are a citizen, however, you are a part owner of the new bridge. The value of nonmoney goods you own may remain the same; the form of the nonmoney goods may simply change from the coat to part of the bridge, from private to public goods.

By the way, in reality, new money is seldom created as rapidly as it was in the hypothetical economy. Therefore, actual redistribution of nonmoney goods caused by the creation of new money is far less significant than it was in that economy.

A Summary of the Theory

We have now developed a theory of money and banking. We have specified that

a. Money can reduce transaction costs by acting as a medium of exchange, a store of value, and a unit of account.
b. Depending on the functions served and the trades being made, monetary forms differ in their abilities to reduce transaction costs.
c. All individuals and institutions will not be able to create money.

Given these specifications, we can predict that

a. We will employ the most efficient form of money.
b. We will use a variety of monetary forms.

c. The supply of money will increase when either resources produce more commodity money, or when political constraints allow an increase in government money.

d. The value of money will fall if the supply of money increases and vice versa.

e. Nonmoney goods will be redistributed toward the people or institutions creating new money.

SPECIAL TOPICS

Yap's Rock Money

On the South Pacific island of Yap, the natives have created a Mecca for economic anthropologists by using a unique monetary form: circular stones. This form makes it very clear that the value of money emanates from its exchange value rather than its commodity value and that backing is only important because it fixes the supply of money.

The stones were moved to various islands many years ago. Their size, often more than 10 feet in circumference, and their location—many of them lie under water—keeps them from being moved. Rather than physically trading the stones, the natives simply exchange ownership rights to them. The ownership rights aren't even written down. Everyone simply knows who owns each stone.

The stones have no value in consumption. Nevertheless, they serve as a surprisingly efficient medium of exchange, store of value, and unit of account.

Many islanders think that the value of the stones is determined by how difficult it was to transport them to the islands, but this belief misses the obvious. Their value is determined by the value of what they will buy. If a stone can be traded for a boat, it is worth at least as much as the boat.

While the stones aren't backed by a commodity value, they are backed to the extent that their supply can't be easily or suddenly increased. Everyone knows that the stone supply is relatively fixed and, therefore, that the value of stones in trade will not suddenly fall.

Gold has served as a successful form of money throughout the ages largely because it has been "backed" by the belief that its supply wouldn't suddenly increase to reduce its value. Had the alchemists of the Middle Ages succeeded in creating gold, they would have extinguished the value of gold as a monetary form, unless they somehow managed to regulate the gold supply.

Memory Money

Are the stones on Yap actually money or are they a monetary form, a physical representation of money? Perhaps the reason money is so difficult to understand lies in the answer to this question. Although the terms *money* and *monetary form* are used synonymously, strictly speaking, money is a claim to an economy's wealth, whereas a monetary form is a manifestation of that claim.

To explain, let's invent money that has no manifest form. Suppose that we were all perfectly intelligent and honest so that we would always know how much money we had and would refuse to create new money, either by mistake or on purpose. Under these conditions, once the initial distribution of money and its quantity were determined, money would simply exist in our memory as a transferable claim against the economy's products, resources, and financial assets.

We would then use that claim in trade by verbally exchanging it for other goods. For example, to pay your wages, your employer might simply tell you that he or she is giving you rights to $10,000. You could then verbally transfer the $10,000 to a computer firm in exchange for a new computer. The firm could subsequently pay its workers by transferring some of the money to them, again verbally. Since no one would miscalculate or cheat, the memory money would stay fixed in supply and would float around the economy much the same way as coins, government notes, and demand deposits.

This thought experiment reveals that the only reason we have to resort to either commodity or written monetary forms is that we lack some intelligence and are sometimes dishonest. Gold, demand deposits, government currency, and other monetary forms provide us with efficient accounting systems and also assure the value of money by keeping people from creating illegal claims for goods, thereby reducing the values of legitimate claims.

The U.S. Money Supply

The money supply in the United States comprises neither rocks nor memory money. It is made up of a variety of other monetary forms created by various private and public financial institutions. The money was created by

- **a.** The United States Treasury;
- **b.** Private commercial banks and other lending institutions that exist under state or local charters;
- **c.** Private commercial banks that are members of the Federal Reserve System;
- **d.** Central Federal Reserve banks.

The Federal Reserve System

The **Federal Reserve System** (the Fed) is the heart of the monetary system in the United States. It was created by an act of Congress in 1913 after public unrest over a series of banking panics. The panics eventually left many banks insolvent, destroyed the assets of thousands of depositors, reduced the national money supply, and caused recessionary decreases in employment and production.

The Fed was also created because many politicians wanted to make the money supply in the United States more **elastic**, capable of increasing with the growth of national production and subsequent trade. For almost a century before the creation of the Fed, the money supply had remained relatively constant and people thought that this had put a damper on economic growth.

Although they wanted to control money and banking, politicians were leary of creating one very powerful national bank. They therefore opted for a decentralized Federal Reserve System, a multibanking system that could nevertheless control the U.S. money supply and regulate most banks.

The Federal Reserve System that was created comprises three parts:

a. Private commercial banks and other lending institutions that are members of the system;
b. Federal Reserve banks;
c. The board of governors.

The private commercial banks and other institutions that comprise the first part of the Fed are the institutions at which most of us have our checking accounts. All national banks are members of the Fed, as are many banks and lending institutions that exist under state and local charters.

The Federal Reserve banks that make up the second part of the Fed are the central banks of the system. The United States is divided into 12 Federal Reserve districts, each under the control of a central Federal Reserve bank. The 12 Federal Reserve banks are "owned" by member banks in their districts. This ownership occurs because the member banks are required to buy shares in their district Federal Reserve bank when they join the Fed.

The central Federal Reserve banks are often called bankers' banks because they do for commercial banks what the commercial banks do for us: They hold the demand deposits of the banks, make loans to the banks, and clear interbank checks. The Fed banks also hold the demand deposits of the U.S. Treasury.

The central Federal Reserve banks are owned by their district member banks, but they are controlled by public officials that make up the third part of the system: the board of governors. The board consists of seven members appointed to 14-year terms by the president of the United States, with the advice and consent of the Senate. One term expires every other year.

Although the board is largely independent of the executive branch and Congress, it can be subjected to some political influences. Presidential appointments affect the board and politicians can threaten to regulate the board's behavior, since the Fed exists under an act of Congress, a law that can be modified. Unlike the Supreme Court, the board is not a constitutionally separate entity.

The Fed's Control of the U.S. Money Supply

The primary function of the board of governors of the Federal Reserve System is to regulate the U.S. money supply in order to promote prosperity without inflation. The board regulates the money supply by exerting total control over the banks within the system and, since 1981, partial control over all other depository institutions (nonmember commercial banks, savings banks, saving and loan associations, and credit unions).

To regulate the money supply, the board of governors can use three tools. The most commonly employed tool involves open market operations. These operations call for the sale or purchase of federal government bonds, usually by the New York Federal Reserve Bank in the New York bond market.

Purchases and sales of government bonds can change the supply of money by directly changing the supply of high-powered government money. For instance, to increase the supply of money, the board can instruct the Federal Reserve banks to buy government bonds. In exchange for the bonds, the Fed banks will issue Federal Reserve demand deposits or Federal Reserve notes (government paper currency). That is, the banks buy the bonds with newly created Federal Reserve bank debt money.

Since the new money is high-powered, some of it will eventually wind up in the reserves of various depository institutions. This will increase excess reserves. The banks will respond by increasing demand or other checkable deposits as they make new loans. The money supply will rise by more than the initial increase in government bank debt money.

When the board wants to reduce the supply of money, it tells the Fed banks to sell bonds. The bond sales absorb high-powered money from the economy and subsequently cause a reduction in the economy's money supply.

Another method of monetary control, used only indirectly since 1980 in the United States (but commonly employed in Europe), is to change the required reserve ratio. Most depository institutions are required to keep a ratio of required reserves to their deposits. By lowering the required reserve ratio, the ability of depository institutions to create money is greatly increased, since formerly required reserves become excess reserves. The money supply can then rise. On the other hand, if the board raises the required reserve ratio, some excess reserves become required reserves and the money supply can fall.

Finally, the board can change the discount rate, the interest rate that the Federal Reserve banks charge for loans. Most depository institutions borrow money so they can build reserves. When the board lowers the rate, the banks borrow more, increase their reserves, and then create more demand deposits. Conversely, when the board raises the rate, the banks borrow less, their reserves fall, and they create less money.

In summary, the board can control the supply of high-powered money as well as the supply of checkable deposits by using open market operations, changes in the required reserve ratio, and changes in the discount rate. Therefore, the board can control the U.S. money supply.

Banking Holidays: Illiquidity versus Bankruptcy

Since most of our money has been created by banks and other depository institutions, it isn't surprising that many of us panic when we hear of a "run on a bank." While the demand deposits of most institutions are insured up to $100,000 by the Federal Deposit Insurance Corporation (FDIC), some financial

TABLE 15.14 Your Bank

YOUR BANK			
ASSETS		LIABILITIES	
Property	$5,000,000	Common stock	$5,000,000
Currency reserves	1,000,000	Demand deposits	41,000,000
Loans	40,000,000		

institutions aren't members of FDIC. And even when deposits are covered, it may be some time before claims can be processed.

A run doesn't necessarily mean that the affected depository institution is bankrupt; it may simply be illiquid, its assets be in nonmonetary forms. As a final special topic, let's look at the distinction between a bank that is illiquid and one that is bankrupt. In the process, we will also shed more light on how banks in our economy operate.

Suppose you are a major stockholder and the president of the totally unregulated bank represented in Table 15.14.

Your position is fairly strong until depositors suddenly decide to trade $1 million in their demand deposits for reserves. You instruct your tellers to distribute the money and your circumstances become uncomfortable. As indicated in Table 15.15, you no longer have currency to give other depositors.

The next day your worst fears are realized. Depositors come in and want to withdraw another $1 million. At this point, you are illiquid. You simply don't have money to cover your demand deposit liabilities. However, you aren't bankrupt. Your assets still cover liabilities—the assets simply aren't in a liquid, monetary form.

To deal with this problem, you declare a "bank holiday" and close the bank's doors. During the holiday, you do a number of things to become liquid. You sell some of your loan assets to other banks for currency. You borrow money from other banks. You allow loans to be repaid, converted into currency. You even call in some loans; you ask your debtors to pay back what they owe. Finally, you ask the government to audit your bank to show everyone that you aren't bankrupt. It is likely that the only reason everyone wants to exchange their demand deposits for currency is that they fear your bank is bankrupt rather than illiquid. If this is the case, an audit will probably stop the run on your bank.

TABLE 15.15 Your Bank

YOUR BANK			
ASSETS		LIABILITIES	
Property	$5,000,000	Common stock	$5,000,000
Cash reserves	0	Demand deposits	40,000,000
Loans	40,000,000		

TABLE 15.16 Your Bank

	YOUR BANK		
ASSETS		LIABILITIES	
Property	$5,000,000	Common stock	0
Cash reserves	1,000,000	Demand deposits	$41,000,000
Loans	30,000,000		

Every depository institution is illiquid in the sense that it keeps earning assets rather than barren cash. In a sense, one of the objectives of depository institutions is to stay as illiquid as possible.

Bankruptcy occurs when a bank loses assets in excess of those contributed by owners. For instance, if your bank, as shown in Table 15.14, had made $10 million in loans to developing nations and those nations refused to repay them, your bank would suffer losses of $10 million in assets. The owners, as shown in Table 15.16, would immediately lose their equity. Nevertheless, the remaining assets of $36 million couldn't cover the $41 million in demand deposits. Your bank would be bankrupt and would be dissolved. The $36 million in assets would then be divided proportionately among the depositors.

The rationality of a banking panic is now easy to understand. When a bank is bankrupt but doesn't immediately close, the first depositors asking for $1 million lose nothing, whereas the others will have to divide the smaller remains. People who take part in a run on a bank are sometimes able to avoid losing wealth.

We have now completed our examination of money and banking. In the next chapter, we will discuss inflation, a phenomenon that is directly related to money's presence and use.

MAJOR AND MINOR POINTS

1. Money can reduce transaction costs by acting as a medium of exchange to eliminate the double-coincidence-of-wants requirement of barter.
2. Money can also reduce transaction costs by acting as a store of value and a unit of account.
3. Commodity money can reduce transaction costs.
4. Privately created debt money, the IOUs of individuals, replaces commodity money when it reduces transaction costs more.
5. We simultaneously employ a number of different monetary forms because the ability of the forms to reduce transaction costs varies depending on the particular monetary function being performed and the trade being made.
6. Since people generally prefer debt money to the type of money held in reserves, only fractional reserves are usually necessary.
7. When fractional reserves are sufficient to support debt money, monetary forms

that can act as reserves become high-powered money: An increase in their supply can cause a more than proportional increase in the supply of money.

8. Banks can increase the money supply by issuing bank notes and demand deposits, money that is backed only by fractional reserves.

9. A monopoly bank and a multibanking system can create an amount of money equal to the reciprocal of the reserve ratio times the excess reserves.

10. An individual bank in a multibanking system can create an amount of money equal only to its excess reserves. This is because the clearing of checks written by borrowers drains reserves.

11. A multibanking system can create the same amount of money that a monopoly bank can because, although reserves may leave individual banks, they don't leave the system.

12. Governments create money for a number of reasons:

   a. The creation of government money provides the economy with a more general medium of exchange and thereby reduces transaction costs.

   b. The addition of government money to the money supply can facilitate the greater number of exchanges that occur during periods of economic growth.

   c. Issues of government money can offset decreases in the money supply during banking panics.

   d. By creating money, the government may be able to buy more goods without either directly taxing or borrowing from the public.

   e. The issue of government money may act as a stimulus to the economy, temporarily increasing national production and reducing unemployment.

13. Coins don't contain a metallic value equal to their exchange value. This saves metal and keeps coins from being melted down whenever the prices of metals rise.

14. Government money can be issued by a treasury or by a government bank that buys government bonds with government bank notes or demand deposits.

15. Government banks don't generally need reserves to support their money creation.

16. Government money is high-powered money.

17. When commodity money is present or when private debt money must be backed totally or partially by some commodity reserve, the supply of money will increase only when the supply of the commodity expands.

18. Political constraints usually limit the supply of government money.

19. The value of money is determined by what it will buy. An increase in the supply of money relative to other goods will reduce the value of money and vice versa.

20. Commodity reserves secure the value of money by restricting its supply, not by providing an indirect consumption value.

21. The people or institutions creating new money will gain wealth at the expense of everyone else.

22. When government gains wealth by creating new money, many citizens only transform their wealth from private to public goods. This is because citizens own the government.

23. Money is fundamentally a claim that a person has to the other goods in the

economy. In a perfectly intelligent and honest society, that claim could remain in the minds of the people, making physical monetary forms unnecessary.

24. Money in the United States has been created by the Treasury, private commercial banks, various private depository institutions and the Federal Reserve banks.

25. Most money in the U.S. has emanated from the commercial banks, other lending institutions, and central banks making up the Federal Reserve System, the "Fed."

26. The Fed comprises member commercial banks, Federal Reserve banks, and the board of governors.

27. The board of governors of the Fed can increase the supply of money by
    a. Instructing the Federal Reserve banks to purchase government bonds with new money;
    b. Reducing the required reserves that depository institutions must maintain;
    c. Lowering the interest rate that the Federal Reserve banks charge depository institutions for loans.

28. A reverse of the preceding policies will reduce the supply of money.

29. An illiquid bank has insufficient reserves to meet demands for money. A bankrupt bank has insufficient assets relative to its liabilities.

QUESTIONS

1. Why will people create and use money?
2. Why will one form of commodity money sometimes replace another form of commodity money?
3. Why do people simultaneously hold a number of different monetary forms?
4. Why has paper money generally replaced commodity money?
5. Why can paper money have only fractional reserve backing?
6. When will an increase in the supply of some monetary forms cause a more than proportional increase in the supply of money?
7. Why has bank money in the form of notes and demand deposits been created?
8. Why can a monopoly bank or a multibanking system create an amount of money equal to the reserve ratio times the excess reserves?
9. Why can an individual bank in a multibanking system create an amount of money equal to only the excess reserves of the bank?
10. Why have governments chosen to create money?
11. Why is the value of the metal in coins usually far less than the exchange value of the coins?
12. When will banks become illiquid?
13. When will banks become bankrupt?
14. Why is the supply of money usually limited?
15. When will the creation of money redistribute wealth?

16. Why will the value of money fall when the money supply is increased?
17. Of what is the U.S. money supply comprised and what makes the U.S. money supply grow?
18. Discuss the following terms and concepts:

The functions of money	Limits on government money
Commodity money	Value of money
Private debt money	Yap money
Fractional reserves	Memory money
High-powered money	Federal Reserve System
Wealth redistribution	Federal Reserve banks
The creation of a bank	Board of governors
Bank money creation	Open-market operations
Demand deposits	Required reserve ratio
Monopoly bank	Discount rate
Individual bank	Illiquid bank
Multibank system	Bankrupt bank
Government money creation	

APPLICATIONS

1. What are some of the characteristics of a commodity that might help it qualify as a monetary form?
2. In the hypothetical economy, what major factor determined how many reserves were necessary to back outstanding notes?
3. In the hypothetical economy, what limited the money supply once you were able to issue notes?
4. What two factors determine the extent to which a monetary form is high-powered?
5. Why do banks want to make as many loans as possible?
6. In early American history, "wildcat banks" were located where the wildcats lived. Why?
7. Do banks generally increase the money supply when they grant new loans?
8. How much money can the monopoly Honesty Bank in Table 15.17 create if the reserve ratio is 10%? 20%?

TABLE 15.17   *The Honesty Bank*

THE HONESTY BANK			
ASSETS		LIABILITIES	
Reserves	$2,000,000	Demand deposits	$2,000,000

9. Suppose the Honesty Bank in Table 15.17 is an individual bank in a multibank system. How much money can it create if the desired reserve ratio is 10%? 20%?

10. Suppose the Honesty Bank in Table 15.17 is a member of a multibank system. How much money can the multibank system create if the desired reserve ratio is 10%? 20%? Why?

11. Why do governments sometimes avoid forcing their government banks to hold reserves?

12. The U.S. money supply should be backed by gold to secure its value. Evaluate.

13. When the Spanish galleons arrived laden with gold found in the New World, did the wealth of Europe increase or was it redistributed?

14. In what sense are depositors of a bank investing in business firms?

15. If banks were totally unregulated, some of them would pay depositors high interest rates and then make loans to risky firms to earn high interest rates. The firms would periodically go bankrupt and some of the banks would fold. How could depositors avoid losses?

16

Inflation

Directly related to the use of money is one of the most feared of economic phenomena: inflation. The moment prices start upward, stories circulate about the runaway hyperinflation that struck Germany after World War I. At its peak, workers were paid literally with bushels of almost worthless marks. Eventually, the German economy fell into a depression, an economic catastrophe that resulted in the unemployment of millions of men and women.

In this chapter, we discuss a theory of inflation and then cover some related, special topics. The theory not only let's us predict when inflation will occur, it also allows us to understand the effects of inflation and devise some possible solutions.

The special topics related to inflation deal with monopoly firms and unions, alchemists and counterfeiters, hidden taxes, the post-Civil War Greenback Movement and the German hyperinflation of the 1920s. The topics also examine the Fed's control of inflation, wars without wage-price controls, the consumer price index (CPI), and the relationship between limited information and the rate of inflation.

A THEORY OF INFLATION

The Phenomena

Inflation is a general increase in prices. This doesn't mean that all prices are going up or that rising prices are moving up at the same rate. Inflation implies only that the average of all prices (weighted by the number of goods traded at each price) is rising. In short, the average price level is increasing.

Before World War II, the price level in the United States fluctuated. Inflation was the norm in wartime. It has occurred during every war since the War of 1812. In peacetime, however, **deflation**, a decrease in the level of prices, was more common. The price level was actually lower in 1900 than in 1800, and during the Great Depression of the 1930s, the price level fell by about one-third.

Since World War II, things have changed a bit. Inflation has become both a wartime and a peacetime phenomenon; from 1941 to the present, the price level has continually increased. At first, the rates of peacetime inflation were relatively low, between 1% and 5% per year between World War II and the mid 1960s. Then during the late 1960s, through the 1970s and into the early 1980s, the rates rose significantly, reaching 13% in 1980. Since 1982, however, inflation has subsided to rates below 5%.

While U.S. inflations have created a great deal of concern, they have nevertheless been minimal compared to some inflations in other nations, as Table 16.1 reveals.

An Explanation

The Circular-Flow Diagram

To explain the nature of inflation, let's take a look at the circular-flow diagram shown in Figure 16.1. It illustrates the economic activity that occurs within an economy comprising households and business firms trading three goods—money, resources, and products—in resource and product markets.

TABLE 16.1   Historical Inflation Rates in Various Nations

INFLATIONS	RATES
U.S (1960s)	4%
U.S. (1970s)	7%
U.S. (1979–1982)	11%
Italy (1970s)	25%
Brazil (1970s)	45%
Israel (1980s)	125%
Germany (1922)	5,470%
Poland (1923)	250,000%
Germany (1923)	130,000,000,000,000%

Figure 16.1 The Circular-Flow Diagram

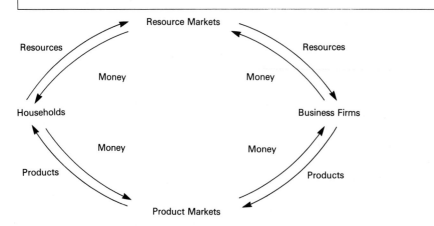

Firms use money to buy resources from households. Households then use the money to buy products from firms. Money circulates from firms to households and back to the firms. Households sell resources to firms. The firms use the resources to produce products and sell the products to the firms. Real goods circulate from the households to the firms and back to the households.

Resource Markets

Resources

Money   Money

Resources

Households   Business Firms

Money   Money

Products   Products

Product Markets

At the left part of the diagram are the households. They sell their resources for money in the resource markets at the top and use the money to buy products in the product markets at the bottom. The business firms on the right use money to buy resources in the resource markets, combine the resources into products, and sell the products for money to households in the product markets. Nonmoney goods in the form first of resources and then of products flow from households to firms and back to households in a clockwise fashion. Money flows from firms to households and back to firms in a counterclockwise fashion.

In each round of exchange, new resources are sold to the firms, who then convert them into products that are subsequently purchased and consumed by households. But the money is generally old. It just continues to circulate from firms to households and back to firms.

How would an increase in the supply of money affect the economy represented by the diagram? It would depend on whether the money was spent or held. In the unlikely event that households and business firms simply held on to all of the new money, nothing would happen. On the other hand, if the households and firms began to use some of the new money to buy products or resources and thereby increased the monetary flow of the economy, demands for resources and products would rise. If the supplies of resources and products remained the same, prices would increase and inflation would occur until prices reached equilibrium at new market-clearing levels.

Inflation could occur even if the supply of money remained the same. If households and business firms had been holding some money out of circulation and then suddenly started spending it, demands would increase relative to supplies and inflation would follow.

Finally, inflation could occur under conditions where both the supply of money and the holding of money remained constant. If the supplies of resources and products suddenly fell, then with the same demands, prices would rise.

In short, inflation could be caused by an increase in the money supply, an increase in the rate of money spending, or a decrease in the supplies of resources and products.

Aggregate Demand, Aggregate Supply, and the Equation of Exchange

We can also explain inflation by using the concepts of aggregate demand and aggregate supply and the equation of exchange. Let's start by defining aggregate demand and aggregate supply.

Aggregate demand is the total money demand for all of the goods for sale in the economy. In a monetary economy, aggregate demand equals the money supply (M) times the **velocity of money** (V). The velocity of money is the number of times money is spent on goods in a given time period. Aggregate demand equals (MV).

The money supply is a determinant of aggregate demand because in a monetary economy we must express our demands for goods as willingnesses and abilities to spend money. If we don't have money in a monetary economy, we can't demand any goods. Velocity is a determinant of aggregate demand, since $1 dollar can cause many dollars of aggregate demand if it is spent many times on goods. As the circular-flow diagram illustrates, money serves as a medium of exchange, moving from buyers to sellers, who then spend it again as buyers.

If the money supply is $200 billion and the velocity is 3, aggregate demand equals $600 billion. And if the money supply expands to $250 billion and the velocity increases to 4, aggregate demand will rise to $1 trillion.

Aggregate supply is the total money value of all of the goods for sale in the economy. It is the product of the average price of each item for sale (P) and the total number of products, resources, and other nonmoney goods being sold (Q). In short, aggregate supply equals (PQ). For example, if the average price of each item for sale is $2 and the quantity of items is 500 billion, then aggregate supply will equal $1 trillion.

Now, if goods are sold in competitive markets, prices will adjust to equate quantities demanded to quantities supplied. The average price level will therefore equate aggregate demand to aggregate supply. That is: $MV = PQ$. This is the **equation of exchange**. By solving for P, we can obtain a form of the equation that can help us explain inflation: $P = (MV)/Q$.

The new form of the equation states that the average price level (P) is determined by aggregate demand (MV) divided by the quantity of nonmoney goods for sale (Q). For example, if aggregate demand is $300 billion and 10 billion items are for sale, then the average price level is $30. This in turn implies that an increase in aggregate demand relative to the supply of nonmoney goods will cause inflation. For example, if aggregate demand rises to $600 billion and 10 billion items are still for sale, then the price level will rise to $60. Similarly, the price level will double to $60 if the supply of nonmoney goods falls to 5 billion while aggregate demand remains at $300 billion.

Changes in Relative Prices

When inflations occur, prices don't all rise relative to what they would have otherwise been. To explain why, we need to recognize that buyers and sellers differ in their anticipations of inflation. If some buyers and sellers correctly anticipate inflation, they will raise their prices at rates equal to or greater than the rate of inflation. But if other buyers and sellers fail to anticipate inflation, they will raise their prices more slowly.

Particular prices will lag behind inflation only temporarily. For example, as soon as the sellers of labor expect higher prices, they demand higher wages, and producers pay the higher wages if they anticipate higher product prices. Likewise, creditors ask for more interest if they think that inflation will erode the purchasing power of future money and debtors offer more interest if they also believe that the value of the money they must repay will fall. Finally, if people think that inflation will reduce the value of money, they will try to hold nonmoney assets.

To see why wages eventually rise at the same rates as inflation, suppose that they initially don't. For example, assume that before inflation, an accounting firm charges $10,000 for an audit and then distributes $8000 to its employees and $2000 to the owners of the firm.

Now suppose that 100% inflation suddenly occurs, allowing the price of an audit to rise to $20,000. If the firm still pays its workers only $8000, the owners are much better off relative to the employees. Both have to pay twice as much to buy products in the economy, but the workers have the same income, whereas the owners have far more than double the amount.

Hiring workers to provide audits is now a very profitable business, not only for the accounting firm but for other firms as well. As a result, existing firms try to expand their operations and new firms enter the industry. This greatly increases competition for the existing employees and wage rates rise. The rates continue to rise until doing audits is as good a deal as it was before—until wages absorb $16,000 of a $20,000 audit.

The reason for these results is that the accounting firm wasn't paying workers $8000 before the inflation because its owners were being nice. The firm paid $8000 because competition required it. And after 100% inflation, competition will require it to pay $16,000.

Similarly, interest rates may lag inflation when inflation suddenly occurs. However, once inflation is recognized and anticipated, supplies and demands for money available for lending will shift to increase the rates.

For instance, suppose money interest rates are 5% in an economy where inflation is nonexistent and none is anticipated. This implies that creditors are willing to give up command over present commodities only if they are compensated with 5% more future commodities the following year.

Now suppose that 100% inflation, a doubling of prices, is suddenly anticipated. Creditors will realize that the 5% extra money they receive won't allow them to buy more future goods. They will therefore be unwilling to lend very much money at 5%. Borrowers, on the other hand, will realize that they won't have to sacrifice more future goods to obtain present ones and they will be willing to borrow more at 5%. As a result, the supply of money available for lending will decrease while the demand increases, creating a shortage. Competition among the borrowers will then drive up the interest rate to 110% (not 105% because with all prices doubled, 10% more money is necessary to buy 5% more nonmoney goods). Only if the interest rate is 110% will borrowers be compensating creditors with 5% extra future commodities for sacrificing present commodities.

The Predictions

With our explanation, we can predict when inflation will occur, the effects of inflation, and how government can eliminate inflation.

Money-Caused Inflations

The most important prediction of inflation focuses on the money supply. We can predict that if the money supply increases, then inflation will follow (as long as either the velocity of money doesn't fall or the supplies of resources and products don't rise significantly). In more simple but less general terms, if V and Q remain constant, an increase in M will raise P:

$$\uparrow P = \frac{\uparrow M \overline{V}}{\overline{Q}}$$

Inflations caused by increases in the money supply have been by far the most significant historically. All **sustained inflations**, those lasting more than 4 years, have been associated with sustained and large increases in the money supply. Also, all sustained and large increases in the money supply have been associated with sustained inflation. Therefore, sustained and large increases in the money supply have been the causes of sustained inflation.

The prediction is so powerful that some conservatives have defined inflation as an increase in the money supply. However, if we were to define inflation this way, we would not be able to explain many short-term, **transitory inflations**, ones lasting less than 4 years. Some transitory inflations have been caused by factors other than increases in the supply of money.

Velocity Inflations

A second prediction of the theory is that if the velocity of money increases, inflation will follow (if significant decreases in the money supply or increases in the supplies of nonmoney goods don't occur at the same time). Put more simply though less generally, with a constant M and Q, an increase in V will raise P:

$$\uparrow P = \frac{\overline{M} \uparrow V}{\overline{Q}}$$

Velocity increases have caused only transitory inflation because rapid increases in velocity have occurred only temporarily. Velocity is generally determined by variables that usually change only gradually, factors such as how often workers are paid, the use of credit cards, and the efficiency of banking institutions.

Supply Decreases and Inflation

A third prediction of the theory is that if the supplies of nonmoney goods available for sale fall, then inflation will occur (assuming that the supply or the velocity of money doesn't fall significantly). Again, more simply though less generally, if MV is constant, a decrease in Q will raise P:

$$\uparrow P = \frac{\overline{MV}}{\downarrow Q}$$

Decreases in supplies have been caused by reduced resource supplies, war, famine, plague, and natural disaster. For example, after the bubonic plague swept across Europe in the Middle Ages, the population fell by about one-third and, with it, agricultural output. But although the quantity of nonmoney goods decreased, aggregate demand remained the same (money was simply concentrated in fewer hands). As a result, prices increased rapidly.

Inflations caused by decreases in the supplies of nonmoney goods have been only transitory because the supplies of those goods have historically increased. With few exceptions, we have increased rather than decreased our production and consumption of products.

When an increase in the supply of money or its velocity raises the level of prices, the result is called **demand-pull inflation**. Demand increases essentially "pull" prices upward. On the other hand, when the supplies of nonmoney goods fall, the resulting inflation is called **cost-push inflation**. The term cost-push originates from the belief that when supplies fall, they "push" prices upward.

A Redistribution of Nonmoney Goods

The next two predictions identify the effects of inflation. We noted in the preceding chapter that increases in the supply of money will redistribute nonmoney goods in favor of those creating the new money. We can also predict that subsequent inflation will redistribute nonmoney goods further if some sellers fail to anticipate the extent of inflation. Those sellers will raise prices slower than the rate of inflation and lose nonmoney goods relative to other sellers. Nonmoney goods will usually shift from people on fixed incomes, creditors, and the holders of money to people on flexible incomes, debtors, and the holders of nonmoney assets.

The redistribution effect is minimal once an inflation is ongoing and people anticipate most of it. Only sudden, unanticipated inflations will have radical effects on the distribution of nonmoney goods in an economy.

No Change in the Total Supply of Nonmoney Goods

Next we can predict that although inflation may redistribute wealth, it will have no real effect on the total quantity of nonmoney goods. For the most part, inflation will change only the "vocabulary of trade." For example, maybe instead of buying goods for cents, we will have to use dollars, but the same physical goods will be traded and produced in the economy. In terms of the equation of exchange, if MV increases or if Q falls, the result will be a rise only in P, but the rise in P will not cause a subsequent change in Q.

This means that inflation will not generally increase the supply of products or resources in the economy. And why should it? If inflation increased the supplies of these goods, we would have a solution to scarcity: Government could raise supply of money to infinity to cause infinite inflation and thereby an infinite increase in production.

Low to moderate inflation also doesn't tend to reduce the supplies of products and resources. For instance, prosperity could continue forever at an inflation rate of 100% per year. Under these conditions, product and resource prices would simply rise together. Consumers would pay 100% more for products each year, but they would earn 100% or more in wages, rents, interest, and profits. Producers would pay 100% more to the suppliers of resources, but the prices of products would also rise 100%.

The only way that inflation can cause a massive reduction in the supply of resources and products is for the rate to be so high that people revert to barter, refusing to accept money as a medium of exchange. Production will then radically fall because of the transaction costs that barter requires. For inflation to destroy a monetary form, however, it seems that the rate must be far above 1000% per year.

Nevertheless, although inflation won't cause changes in the supplies of products and resources, the sudden increases in aggregate demands that cause some inflations can sometimes cause temporary increases in production.

This is because producers sometimes react to increases in demands by temporarily increasing production as well as prices. They can increase production by employing formerly unemployed resources. (We discuss these temporary increases in production in the next chapter. They are important. We have ignored them only to keep our discussion of inflation as simple as possible.)

Controlling Inflation

The final prediction identifies a possible solution to inflation. We can predict that if the government has control over the supply of money, it can stop inflation by reducing the money supply. Obviously, a reduction in the money supply can stop the growth of the money supply. It can also offset an increase in the velocity of money or a reduction in the supply of nonmoney goods.

A Summary of the Theory

We have constructed our theory of inflation by assuming that

a. Aggregate demand equals the supply of money (M) times the velocity of money (V), while aggregate supply equals the average price level (P) times the quantity of nonmoney items available for sale (Q).
b. The average price level will rise if the level of aggregate demand increases relative to the supply of nonmoney items.
c. Some buyers and sellers will fail to anticipate the extent of inflation.

These assumptions imply that

a. If the supply of money increases, then demand-pull inflation will occur.
b. If the velocity of money increases, then demand-pull inflation will follow.
c. If the supply of nonmoney items decreases, cost-push inflation will occur.
d. If inflation occurs, the distribution of nonmoney goods in the economy will change relative to noninflationary conditions.
e. If inflation occurs, the total supply of nonmoney goods in the economy will remain the same.
f. If the government reduces the supply of money sufficiently, it can eliminate inflation.

SPECIAL TOPICS

Monopoly Firms, Labor Unions, and Inflation

Do monopoly firms and labor unions cause sustained inflation? According to the evidence, no. In the past, sustained inflations have been caused by sustained, large increases in the money supply.

We may mistakenly suspect monopoly firms and labor unions if we notice that they increase prices and wages during inflationary times. However, the firms and unions have been with us for a long time, during periods of price stability and deflation as well as inflation. If they were the causes of inflation, inflation would be a perpetual phenomenon.

Our theory of monopoly, contained in Chapter 5, sheds some light on monopoly pricing. We saw that while monopolists do charge higher prices than competitive sellers, they don't raise prices constantly. The creations of monopolies cause only once-and-for-all price increases to the profit-maximizing levels, but subsequently, monopoly prices rise for only the same reasons that competitive prices rise: because of increases in demands or costs.

For example, in the 1970s, the Organization of Petroleum Exporting Countries (OPEC) caused worldwide inflation by reducing the supply of oil and raising the price to a profit-maximizing level. Once the price was at that level, however, OPEC wouldn't have raised it further had it not been for the increases in demand that subsequently occurred. Those increases were caused by money supply increases in the United States and elsewhere. By raising money supplies, monetary authorities converted what began as a transitory cost-push inflation into a sustained demand-pull inflation.

Alchemists and Counterfeiters

Since monetary increases rather than monopoly firms or labor unions cause sustained inflations, we can get a pretty good idea of what would have happened if the alchemists of the Middle Ages had succeeded in transforming base metals into gold. The result would have been massive worldwide inflation.

The alchemists would have become wealthy, but their gains would have resulted in losses to others. After all, world production and resources wouldn't have expanded simply because more gold became available.

Historically, very much the same results occurred when the Spanish sailed into Europe with South American gold. Prices rose over 100% as more gold chased the same products and resources. Since the Spanish had a much larger share of the greater supply of gold, their command over the available products and resources increased while that of other Europeans declined.

Alchemists were little more than counterfeiters. Had they succeeded, they would have become wealthy by obtaining a larger share of a more debased money supply. The only reason they weren't treated like counterfeiters is because many people mistakenly believed that gold would have kept its value as a commodity and that an increase in its supply would therefore have benefited the alchemists but not harmed others.

The success of the alchemists would probably have been very temporary. As noted in the preceding chapter, unless the alchemists were able to control their money creation, they would have expanded the supply of gold and created such inflation that gold would have become unacceptable as a medium of exchange. At that point, silver might have replaced gold as the monetary form, and the alchemists would have faced a new challenge.

The Hidden Tax

Our government has outdone the alchemists. It has been able to create billions of new dollars out of thin air (in reality, vegetable fibers).

If our government wanted to, it could make all its purchases with newly printed money. As an interesting thought experiment, what would happen if it decided to do this? That is, rather than taxing or borrowing from the public, what if the U.S. Treasury simply borrowed new money from the Federal Reserve system and then spent it?

If this occurred, individuals would be able to keep their tax dollars, but the resulting higher prices would force everyone to buy less. This would release goods for the government's consumption. Instead of being taxed explicitly, the public would be taxed implicitly with inflation.

Using new money to finance all government spending would have some clear advantages. It would reduce the costs of tax collection and create a tax that couldn't be easily avoided. These two advantages alone could justify the creation of new money to finance some government spending in certain lesser-developed nations. New money might also have the advantage of temporarily fostering prosperity. In the short term, some producers would increase production and employment as well as prices.

Some disadvantages, however, might also follow. Inflation might be a political liability, one that would eventually have to be dealt with. And the inflation would be massive. In the United States, the federal government's spending is now about double the money supply. As a result, new government money alone would increase the money supply by 200% each year. Additionally, since government money is high-powered, bank demand deposits would expand, since much of the government money would flow into the reserves of private banks. Moreover, the massive increase in the money supply would have a more than proportional affect on aggregate demand, since it would be multiplied by the velocity of money. The new dollars would be spent many times during the year on products, resources, and financial assets. To make things even worse, the velocity of money would rise because of the resulting inflation. In the end, the huge increase in aggregate demand might create inflation that would make the German hyperinflation of the 1920s look mild by comparison.

Another disadvantage might be that the incidence of an inflation tax couldn't be controlled. Everyone would effectively pay taxes in a fixed proportion to their purchases. Of course, some politicians would consider such "flat taxation" an advantage.

Finally, another effect that can be viewed as either a disadvantage or an advantage is that an inflation tax would tend to increase government spending. Voters penalize politicians when they raise taxes, increase public borrowing, or run the presses. Running the presses, however, is the least costly of the three financing methods, since voters don't generally associate the resulting inflation with government financing. The inflation tax is hidden. As a result, the political cost of increasing government spending is reduced when the inflation tax is employed.

The Greenback Movement

Although inflation is seldom a desirable phenomenon, sometimes politicians and voters try to force the government to create it. To some extent, the creation of inflation was the motivation behind the Greenback Movement of the 1870s.

During most of the 1800s, the U.S. money supply was relatively fixed while the supply of products and resources was expanding at a rate of about 3% per year. The result was general deflation. With a constant M and V, an increase in Q resulted in a drop in P:

$$\downarrow P = \frac{\overline{MV}}{\uparrow Q}$$

During the Civil War, however, the government issued greenbacks, government notes with green backsides, to pay for its military expenditures. The notes required no reserve backing, so their supply was limited only by political constraints. As the distribution of the notes increased, so did the money supply, and wartime inflation followed. After the Civil War, the issues of greenbacks were stopped and the Treasury even reduced their supply, buying some of them with gold-backed currency. As a result, deflation returned.

The deflation adversely affected farmers. The prices of agricultural products fell. To the extent that the prices of labor and some other resources were also lower, the farmers didn't mind. But all prices didn't fall. Most farmers were debtors who had purchased land and other resources with money they borrowed at fixed interest rates. This created a problem: At the same time that product prices were falling, loan payments stayed the same. The farmers felt the banks were profiting at their expense. They therefore sought government aid in the form of inflationary or at least antideflationary issues of greenbacks.

Were the farmers interpreting events correctly? Not completely. During the 1800s, deflation was an ongoing peacetime phenomenon. To the extent that the post-Civil War deflation was anticipated, the prices farmers had paid for land and the interest rates they were paying on loans had been reduced to reflect the lower anticipated future food prices and the higher anticipated value of future dollars. In effect, farmers had been compensated for deflation in advance.

If farmers had succeeded in forcing a massive increase in the supply of money, inflation would have occurred and they would have profited from higher land prices and would have gained at the expense of their creditors. But all these benefits would have been temporary, since the anticipation of future inflation would have subsequently increased the prices of land and the interest rates on new loans.

In short, only unanticipated deflation and inflation will redistribute nonmoney goods.

The German Hyperinflation of the 1920s

Moderate inflations have usually only redistributed nonmoney goods with little loss of economic efficiency, but on occasion, hyperinflations have caused economies to collapse. This occurred in the 1920s in Germany. The Allies confronted the Weimar government with a 132-billion gold mark reparations bill for damages created by World War I. Rather than raising taxes to enormous levels, the German government simply ran the presses. As a result, citizens and foreign nations were taxed with inflation.

During 1922, the average price level rose 5470% and in 1923 it increased by 1300 billion percent. At those rates, some workers were paid many times daily and given time off to go shopping; restaurants changed menu prices while people were still eating lunch; housewives used money to start fires; and children used bundles of paper money as building blocks (paper money's value in use rose above its value in exchange).

One of the effects of the inflation was to reduce the value of the reparation payments. Foreign nations purchased fewer German commodities and Germans were able to buy more than otherwise.

Another effect was eventually to bring the German economy to a halt. The inflation rate became so high that the system reverted to barter as people refused marks in trade. The recession that occurred helped bring Adolf Hitler to power and was partly responsible for World War II.

The Fed's Control of Inflation

Inflations are seldom desirable, even when they don't approach the levels of the German inflation of the 1920s. Although the U.S. Treasury doesn't have the power to change the money supply and control inflation, the board of governors of the Federal Reserve system does. To stop inflation, the board can reduce the supply of money by

a. Having the Federal Reserve Banks sell government bonds on the open bond market;

b. Increasing the required reserve ratio that commercial banks and other depository institutions must fulfill;

c. Raising the discount rate charged to depository institutions on loans from the Fed banks.

Any combination of these policies will either directly reduce the supply of government money or reduce the quantity of money that depository institutions create.

To stem the growth of prices, a reduction in the money supply is seldom necessary. Usually the supply of goods is growing at about 3% per year, so the elimination of inflation requires a reduction of the growth of the money supply only to about 3%.

Since the Fed has control over the money supply, it can not only eliminate inflation, but it, rather than the president or Congress, is also primarily responsible for inflation. The blame does not, however, totally lie with the Fed. The president and Congress can exert pressure on the Fed to raise the money supply. The president can change the political complexion of the board when new appointments are made; and the president and Congress can threaten to pass legislation that will force the board to create less money.

A War Without Wage-Price Controls

Is it ever possible to increase the money supply substantially without causing inflation? Only by using wage-price controls. The U.S. government usually has imposed such controls during wartime, but some controls have been enacted during peacetime, most recently in the early 1970s by the Nixon administration.

The problems with wage-price controls are that they create all the economic effects we discussed in Chapter 6. That is, they

     a. Eliminate inventories for inspection and immediate purchase;
     b. Prevent changes in relative prices;
     c. Cause in-kind shifts of wealth from sellers to buyers;
     d. Create shortages of resources and products;
     e. Force nonprice criteria for distribution;
     f. Cause nonprice competition;
     g. Increase transaction costs;
     h. Create black markets and kickbacks;
     i. Reduce product quality and work effort;
     j. Cause product quality and work effort to fall over time.

Furthermore, since wage-price controls interfere with relative wages and prices, they eliminate the economy's systems of coordination and control. As time passes, the signals provided by fixed prices and wages become arbitrary and erroneous and must be replaced by government regulations. If maintained, government control of prices eventually requires government control of production and distribution.

We have relied on prices to coordinate production and distribution during peacetime. Could we have done so during times of war? That is, could we have conducted the two world wars without wage-price controls and a War Production Control Board?

Yes. The government could have increased taxes and purchased any goods it wanted. Demands would have shifted from private consumption and capital goods and toward war materials. Relative prices would then have informed and rewarded producers for quickly reallocating resources toward the war effort. In fact, after the wars were concluded, wage-price controls were generally lifted and prices were relied on to tell producers to produce fewer war goods and more private-consumption and capital goods.

Why is it that we seem to believe in the efficiency of prices and wages in peacetime but not during periods of war? Perhaps because when demands for goods rise, prices must temporarily increase to stimulate production, and when the government is the buyer, it doesn't want to pay higher prices. Also, producers who quickly produce products wanted by the government become wealthier. We may not want people to profiteer from a war.

If prices and wages had been used to coordinate and control production during World War I and World War II, some benefits would have been derived. First, some producers, anticipating a war, would have gambled and would have begun the production of war materials in advance. Therefore, our nation might have been more prepared when conflict eventually broke out. Some of the preparation was eliminated because producers expected that future prices wouldn't be allowed to rise.

Next, the costs of the war would have been more obvious, since market prices would have reflected all the sacrifices incurred. For example, when troops were drafted, low wages wrongly implied low costs. Had the labor services of troops been purchased in labor markets, high wages would have reflected actual high costs.

Furthermore, the costs of the wars might have been borne more equitably. Since troops would have been paid more and people back home would have been taxed more, soldiers would have been relatively better compensated for their obviously greater sacrifices.

Finally, with markets, there would have been no shortages, less non-price discrimination and competition, lower transaction costs, no black markets or kickbacks, improved product quality, and greater work efforts.

The Consumer Price Index (CPI)

Whether the government wants to stop inflation by reducing the money supply or by implementing wage-price controls, it first needs to know that inflation is occurring. Since relative prices are constantly moving, measuring inflation can be a difficult task.

In the United States, the best-known measure of inflation is the **consumer price index (CPI)**. It is computed monthly by the Bureau of Labor Statistics of the U.S. Department of Labor. The CPI attempts to measure the rate of inflation by measuring the total cost of a representative market basket of some 400 goods. The goods in the basket are based on the responses of households to a survey that was first conducted during 1971 and 1972 and has been periodically updated since.

To some degree, the CPI is an inaccurate measure of inflation. It ignores many consumption goods and all resources. Also, it doesn't reflect the prices of new products such as personal computers and video recorders. Moreover, by assuming that we buy the same quantities of all goods from year to year, the CPI overestimates inflation. We in fact generally buy fewer of the goods with higher prices and more of the ones with lower prices.

Because of these reasons, the CPI doesn't perfectly reflect and tends to exaggerate the rate of inflation. Nevertheless, since prices do tend to rise together during inflationary periods and our purchases change slowly, the index is a reasonably useful indicator. In fact, other measures of inflation, such as the wholesale price index (WPI), which keeps track of the prices of about 2200 commodities sold in wholesale markets, have risen at about the same rates as the CPI.

Inflation in a World of Limited Information

Before we end our discussion of inflation, it is worth adding a final complication to our theory. Although prices are generally determined by demands and supplies, when demands or supplies suddenly change, prices in most markets temporarily remain the same. This is because most markets contain buyers and sellers who have limited market information. We will refer to such buyers and sellers as **price searchers**, since they are forced to find market-clearing equilibrium prices.

Price searcher is a term that is sometimes used to refer to monopolists, since market power gives monopolists the option of selling greater quantities at lower prices and limited information then forces them to search for the optimum price-quantity combinations. We will, however, use the term more generally to identify any seller or buyer who must search for the optimal price.

To understand price-searching behavior, suppose you were a landlord and demand increased following an increase in the money supply. Would you raise your rents immediately? Probably not. You wouldn't see demand rise. If you watched prevailing rents, they wouldn't tell you anything, since they'd also be initially stuck at the old levels. Only after some time passed would you charge more, perhaps after you noticed that your apartments were renting very quickly or that the prevailing rents were increasing.

By complicating our theory of inflation with price searching, the theory's long-run predictions don't change. That is, aggregate demand and the supply of nonmoney goods still determine the average price level, and inflation will follow an increase in aggregate demand relative to the supply of nonmoney goods. The theory becomes more general only because it can deal with short- as well as long-run results. The change is that inflation will lag behind increases in aggregate demand relative to the supplies of nonmoney goods.

Inflation is a feared phenomenon. Nevertheless, in the next chapter, we deal with what many people consider to be a worse problem: unemployment.

MAJOR AND MINOR POINTS

1. Inflation is a general increase in prices.
2. The circular-flow diagram shows how money and nonmoney goods flow in the economy between household and business firms. Using the diagram, we can explain how inflation can be caused by more money, more money spending, or lower product and resource supplies.
3. Aggregate demand is the total money demand for the nonmoney goods for sale in the economy. It is equal to the money supply (M) times the velocity of money (V); aggregate demand equals (MV).
4. Aggregate supply is the money value of all of the goods for sale in the economy. It is equal to the average price level (P) times the quantity of nonmoney goods (Q); aggregate supply equals (PQ).
5. The average price level equates aggregate demand to aggregate supply.
6. The equation of exchange, $MV = PQ$, can aid our understanding of inflation. Solving for P, it converts to $P = (MV)/Q$.
7. Inflation will occur if aggregate demand increases relative to the supply of nonmoney goods.
8. Some prices will rise at below-inflationary rates to the extent that inflation is unanticipated.
9. An increase in the supply of money will cause demand-pull inflation:

$$\uparrow P = \frac{\uparrow M \overline{V}}{\overline{Q}}$$

10. Sustained inflations have been caused by too much money chasing too few goods.
11. An increase in the velocity of money will also cause demand-pull inflation:

$$\uparrow P = \frac{\overline{M} \uparrow V}{\overline{Q}}$$

12. A decrease in the supply of nonmoney goods will cause cost-push inflation:

$$\uparrow P = \frac{\overline{MV}}{\downarrow \overline{Q}}$$

13. Decreases in the supplies of nonmoney goods have been caused by reductions in the supplies of resources, by war, famine, plague, and natural disaster.
14. Transitory inflations were caused by too much money, increases in the velocity of money, and decreases in the supplies of nonmoney goods:

$$\uparrow P = \frac{\uparrow M \uparrow V}{\downarrow Q}$$

15. To the extent that inflations are unanticipated, they will redistribute wealth in the economy, usually toward people with flexible incomes, debtors, and individuals holding very little money.

16. Low to moderate inflation will neither increase nor reduce total wealth.

17. If a government can control the supply of money, it can eliminate inflation by reducing the supply of money.

18. Monopoly firms and unions don't generally cause inflation.

19. Resource monopolists, by reducing resource supplies, may cause transitory cost-push inflation.

20. Had alchemists succeeded in changing base metals into gold, they would have temporarily redistributed wealth toward themselves and caused inflation. Eventually, however, gold would have stopped being a medium of exchange.

21. The government can finance all of its spending by creating new money. This would probably
    a. Reduce tax collection costs;
    b. Temporarily increase production and employment;
    c. Eventually cause inflation (a "hidden tax");
    d. Change the tax burden;
    e. Leave long-run production and employment unaffected.

22. Only unanticipated inflation shifts wealth.

23. Had the Greenback Movement succeeded in causing inflation, farmers would have obtained higher product prices and could have temporarily gained wealth. But in the long run they would have gained little since they would have had to pay higher prices for land and higher interest rates for loans.

24. The Federal Reserve system can control the money supply in the United States. As a result, it can stop inflation by reducing the money supply. It also follows that the Fed is responsible for inflation.

25. The use of wage-price controls to eliminate inflation eventually also eliminates capitalism.

26. Though imperfect, the consumer price index (CPI) is useful and is the most commonly employed measure of inflation.

27. Once we have only limited information and become price searchers, sudden increases in aggregate demand relative to the supplies of nonmoney goods may cause inflation only after some time has passed.

QUESTIONS

1. What is inflation?
2. When will inflation occur? (This question should be answered with the aid of both the circular flow diagram and the equation of exchange.)
3. When will inflation not cause recession?
4. When will inflation cause recession?
5. When will inflation not change the distribution of wealth?
6. When will inflation change the distribution of wealth?

7. How can inflation be either eliminated or its rate reduced?
8. Discuss the following terms and concepts:

Inflation
Circular-flow diagram
Aggregate demand
The velocity of money
Aggregate supply
The equation of exchange
Sustained inflation
Transitory inflation
Demand-pull inflation

Cost-push inflation
Wealth redistribution
Cure for inflation
Hidden tax
Greenback Movement
Fed and inflation
Wage-price controls
Consumer price index (CPI)
Price searchers

APPLICATIONS

1. How do people survive in countries where inflationary rates exceed 100%?
2. In Canada, many mortgages have adjustable interest rates. That is, the rates change as the economy's prevailing rates of interest change. As a creditor, why might you be willing to accept a lower mortgage rate if the debtor agrees to the adjustable-rate feature?
3. Can a nation have continuous 500% yearly inflation and not suffer a recession?
4. Does greed cause inflation?
5. Will increases in government spending, decreases in taxes, and decreases in the value of the dollar in terms of foreign currencies cause sustained inflation?
6. What are the economic effects of successful counterfeiting?
7. Who is responsible for inflation, the president, Congress, or the board of governors of the Federal Reserve system?
8. What are the economic effects of deflation?
9. Suppose the required reserve ratio is 10%. How much money can the Veracity Bank in Table 16.2 create if it is a member of a multibank system? How much money can the system create? If the Veracity Bank buys $50,000 in government bonds from the Fed, how much money can the bank subsequently create? The multibank system?
10. How much money can the Veracity Bank in Table 16.2 create if the required reserve ratio rises to 20%? How much money can the multibank system create if the ratio rises to 20%?
11. How much money can the Veracity Bank in Table 16.2 create if it borrows $100,000 from a Federal Reserve bank? How much money can the multibank system create? If the discount rate increases and the bank borrows

TABLE 16.2

VERACITY BANK			
ASSETS		LIABILITIES	
Reserves	$300,000	Demand deposits	$300,000

only $50,000, how will this affect the bank's money creation? How will the multibank system's ability to create money be affected by the higher discount rate?

12. Why are members of the Federal Reserve system's board of governors appointed to 14-year terms?

13. How can your personal rate of inflation be greater than the rate indicated by the rise of the CPI?

14. Use the equation of exchange to explain how price searching can cause an inequality between aggregate demand and aggregate supply.

17

===

Unemployment

The People's Republic of China is the most populous nation in the world and yet her labor supply is insufficient. The central planners of the Chinese economy find that their list of desired products far exceeds the productive abilities of China's labor and other resources. For the same reason, the Soviet Union claims that her labor force leaves 20 million jobs unfilled.

In the U.S. economy, we certainly suffer from the same labor scarcities. Each of us wants more housing, food, and recreation, products that can be produced by labor, but labor is limited in supply and we must do without.

Under these conditions, unemployment is truly a paradox. Rather than too few jobs, shouldn't there be too many? In this chapter, we resolve this paradox by constructing a theory that explains and predicts classical, frictional, and cyclical unemployment. We explain that although we have many things to do, unemployment is still possible if wages are fixed or if market information is limited.

The special topics related to unemployment deal with equal pay for the handicapped, a government employment agency, the ability of farmers to avoid a recession, full employment in a world of unlimited information, and relative versus absolute levels of aggregate demand and money supply. The topics also discuss whether technology, immigration, or excessive production can cause unemployment; the meaning and measurement of the gross national product (GNP); and algebraic and graphical views of the multiplier.

A THEORY OF UNEMPLOYMENT

The Phenomena

Unemployment is fairly difficult to define. Obviously, one requirement of being unemployed is not working. But that's not all. We must also be willing and able to work at wages that we think are equal to or less than our productivities. For example, if we are looking for work and believe we can produce $20,000 worth of products, then we are unemployed only if we are willing and able to work for $20,000 or less.

We are not unemployed if we demand wages that we know exceed our productivities. We then simply value leisure more than the products of our labor. That is, if we know that we can produce only $20,000 worth of goods and if we nevertheless demand $100,000, then we are choosing leisure over work.

Unemployment has been a common phenomenon in the U.S. economy. During this century, the unemployment rate of the U.S. **labor force** (the people working plus those looking for work) has ranged from a low of 1.2% in 1944 to a high of 24.9% in 1933. There have also been three periods of significant unemployment:

a. The Great Depression years (1930 to 1939), with an average unemployment rate of 18.3%;
b. The sluggish 1950s (1954 to 1960), with a 5.2% average unemployment rate;
c. The stagnant 1970s (1975 to 1984), with an average unemployment rate of 7.6%.

In these times of high unemployment, three types of unemployment have simultaneously occurred: classical, frictional, and cyclical.

An Explanation: Three Types of Unemployment

Classical Unemployment

Classical unemployment, first identified by the classical economists of the sixteenth and seventeenth centuries, is unemployment that occurs when wages are set above market-clearing levels by third parties. It generally follows the passage of minimum-wage laws and the negotiation of union contracts.

To explain how the laws and contracts cause classical unemployment, suppose that you can produce $4000 worth of goods per year, that you are willing to work for a $4000 yearly salary, and that a firm is willing to hire you at that salary. Under these conditions, you will nevertheless be unemployed if the government decrees a $5000 minimum annual salary or if your union negotiates a $5000 per year salary and fringe benefit package. Only those workers whose productivities at least equal $5000 per year will work.

To some extent, minimum-wage laws and union contracts cause unemployment because while the laws and contracts raise wages, they can't usually force firms to hire workers at those wages. Nor can the laws and contracts increase worker productivities. If they could, Bangladesh would be able to eliminate a great deal of poverty either by declaring a $50 minimum hourly wage or by forcing all workers into a union that negotiates a $50 hourly wage.

Frictional (and Structural) Unemployment

Frictional unemployment is unemployment that occurs when workers move from one job to another or when workers initially enter or return to the labor market. It is primarily caused by shifts in the composition of aggregate demand under conditions where market information is significantly limited. Limited information forces producers and workers to become **price searchers**, individuals who must produce information about prices or goods. After demands for products have moved because of a shift in the composition of aggregate demand, many price-searching producers and workers must search for other products to produce or other jobs to hold.

For example, suppose consumers shift their demands from automobiles to computers in an economy containing price-searching producers and workers. Individual automobile companies then cut production, laying off employees.

If wages could instead be cut, the firms could reduce prices and profitably maintain sales. But workers rationally refuse wage reductions. They assume, in this case correctly, that jobs at the same wages exist elsewhere. The workers make the assumption because consumers are constantly changing their demands for products, which causes employment opportunities to constantly shift from firm to firm, from industry to industry. Also, the general wage level remains the same; this means that other firms are paying the same wages and are even hiring new workers at those wages.

After the workers are laid off, they must obtain new jobs. Where are the new jobs? Although we know the jobs have been created in the computer industry, the workers don't. The workers have to search for the jobs and while they do so, they are frictionally unemployed.

Wages in the computer industry don't rise. The computer firms discover the shortage of labor only after some time has passed and by then the influx of former autoworkers has eliminated it. Computer prices also don't change. Increases in production meet the greater demands before the computer firms start to raise prices.

In both the short and the long term, relative prices and wages in both the automobile and the computer industries remain unchanged. Production and employment, however, shift to reflect the new consumer values. Unfortunately, to achieve these long-run results, frictional unemployment is necessary.

How much frictional unemployment occurs after a shift in demand from one product to another? It depends on how long workers take to find new jobs. The longer they search, the greater the level of frictional unemployment.

One important factor that can cause job searches to increase is the extent to which workers can transfer their job skills from one firm or industry to another. If job skills are nontransferable, then workers will have to accept lower wages to compensate for their lower productivities and the costs of retraining. Job searches will then increase, since in addition to finding new jobs, workers will have to discover that they must accept lower wages.

Frictional unemployment aggravated by the nontransferability of job skills is called **structural unemployment**. Although structural unemployment often results when demands shift from one industry to another, structural unemployment can also be caused by changes in technology. Generally, it can occur any time workers try to obtain jobs that require different job skills than those that the workers possess.

Structurally unemployed workers remain unemployed only if they truly fail to recognize that they can't demand the same wages as more skilled workers. If they know they are less skilled relative to the demands of the market and they still demand the same wages as before, then they are choosing leisure over work and are not unemployed. Otherwise, all workers not wanting jobs could claim that they are unemployed because they lack the necessary skills to be doctors.

Cyclical Unemployment

Finally, **cyclical unemployment** results after a reduction in aggregate demand in a capitalistic, money-using economy containing price-searching producers and workers. It is called cyclical unemployment because it is associated with fluctuations in national output and, specifically, with decreases in national output, or **recessions**.

The reductions in aggregate demand that give rise to cyclical unemployment have come from a variety of sources, but most have involved reductions in **investment** (the total demand for capital by business firms). While **consumption** (the total demand for consumption commodities by households) has remained a fairly stable proportion of total household income, investment has varied a great deal, largely because it is determined by profit expectations, a variable that can suddenly change.

Although the term cyclical unemployment is commonly employed by economists, and we will, therefore, employ it here, the term is a misnomer because cyclical unemployment implies internal causation—that a period of prosperity gives rise to forces that cause a subsequent recession and that a recession creates forces that cause subsequent prosperity. The theory we will examine denies that such internal causation exists. There is no natural reason why the level of employment should fall.

Also, cyclical unemployment implies that recessions occur periodically when they don't. To be periodic, recessions would have to occur at regular intervals, say every 4 or 5 years. Instead, recessions tend to be relatively random occurrences.

Although not periodic, recessions have been fairly common events in our economy. They have occurred once or twice a decade since independence in 1776. Just since 1929, the U.S. economy has endured eight recessions of varying intensities.

Incidentally, decreases in national production haven't always been called recessions. They were once referred to as panics or depressions, but those terms brought to mind terrible images of stock market crashes, bank failures, soup kitchens, and dust bowls.

Cyclical unemployment is surely the most severe problem that capitalist economies face. It has probably brought about more misery and fear and won more converts to socialist ideology than any other single capitalist phenomenon. It is also one of the most difficult of phenomena to explain because real factors don't cause a recession. During the Great Depression, for example, people's desires for products, their willingnesses to sacrifice leisure, and their abilities to produce were basically the same as in the prosperous 1920s.

The Initial Stage of Recession   To explain cyclical unemployment, suppose that investment falls as business firms in the economy suddenly decide to buy half as many capital goods as before. As a result, aggregate demand decreases.

Price-searching firms producing capital react to decreases in demands for their products by reducing output. They could profitably reduce prices if workers would accept wage cuts, but the workers won't. They won't because they assume, this time wrongly, that they can find jobs with other firms at roughly the same wage rates.

What if the workers read the *Wall Street Journal* and, therefore, knew that aggregate demand is decreasing? This wouldn't help, because relative demands change constantly, even during periods of declining aggregate demand. The workers wouldn't be able to tell if the decreases in demands for their particular products weren't being accentuated by relative shifts in demands to other products, shifts that call for reallocations of labor.

For example, during the recession of the early 1980s, demands for the products of "smokestack" industries fell radically. It was clear that aggregate demand was declining during that period, but many people speculated that the particular demand decreases for the products of the heavy industries represented shifts of demand to other industries, perhaps electronics. To the extent that those beliefs were correct, the workers maximized their long-term income when they refused pay cuts, quit their jobs, and looked elsewhere.

After demands fall following the decrease in aggregate demand, firms lay off employees, who then search for jobs with other firms. However, the other firms are not hiring; demands for their products have remained the same. As a result, a pool of unemployed workers is created—people looking for work at wages where jobs don't exist. A recession begins.

The Multiplier Stage   Things get worse before they get better. As Figure 17.1 illustrates, the recession moves from the initial stage and into the multiplier stage.

Why? Because while workers search for jobs, they gradually run out of money and other liquid assets. As a result, they cut their purchases of con-

Figure 17.1 Three Stages of Recession

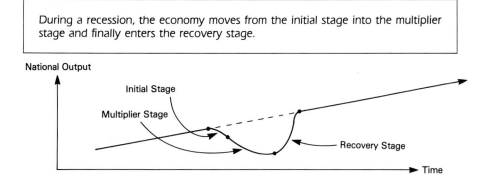

During a recession, the economy moves from the initial stage into the multiplier stage and finally enters the recovery stage.

sumption goods. This causes aggregate demand to fall further, causing firms to cut production and employment more, creating even more unemployment. The recession deepens.

The newly unemployed workers also search for jobs at the wrong wage rates and run out of liquid assets. They too eventually reduce their consumption, and aggregate demand falls again. More workers are laid off, and so on. This multiplier process continues until the recession bottoms out.

We show later mathematically that the multiplier process eventually becomes insignificant. For now, an intuitive example will suffice. Suppose that a small town has five large companies, firms that sell their products throughout the U.S. economy. It also has various small businesses that service the employees of the five firms. If one of the large firms suddenly moves its location to another town, then the employees of that firm immediately lose their jobs.

A multiplier process then begins, since the laid-off workers were buying goods from the small business in town. Demands for the products of grocery stores, gas stations, restaurants, and barber shops fall. The small businesses subsequently lay off some of their employees. Those employees, in turn, cut their demands for the products of small businesses, and additional layoffs will occur. This process will continue forever but eventually will become insignificant. Although many more workers will lose their jobs than were employed by the exiting large firm, the employment rate will not fall to zero because the remaining four large companies will continue to employ workers and the spending of those workers will support a large number of small businesses.

Employers can't individually stop the multiplier stage of the recession by keeping employees. For instance, if Firestone didn't lay off anyone during a recession, demand for Firestone tires would still fall because other firms would release workers. Firestone employees purchase an insignificant number of Firestone tires.

The multiplier stage of the recession is disastrous. The cuts in consumption spending that emanate from the increasingly larger group of unemployed workers cause aggregate demand to fall and create more subsequent unemployment than was created by the initial decrease in aggregate demand. During the multiplier stage of a recession, the economy spirals much farther below full employment than it did when the recession began.

The Recovery   There is hope. Unemployed workers eventually begin to accept lower-paying jobs and wages begin to fall. Product prices then fall, increasing quantities demanded. Firms respond by raising production and employment. Furthermore, the multiplier process that made the recession worsen operates in reverse to aid the recovery. As unemployed workers find jobs and begin to earn income, they increase their demands for consumption goods. Aggregate demand increases, reinforcing the effects of lower prices and wages. In time, cyclical unemployment disappears.

The Predictions

From these explanations of classical, frictional, and cyclical unemployment, we can make some simple predictions.

Unemployment

First, if governments and unions raise wages above the productivities of some workers, classical unemployment will result. Next, if the composition of aggregate demand changes, frictional unemployment will follow. Finally, if aggregate demand suddenly falls, cyclical unemployment will occur.

Reducing Classical Unemployment

We can also make three predictions that identify possible solutions to unemployment. First, since the causes of classical unemployment are often government minimum-wage laws and labor unions, then if minimum-wage laws and labor unions are eliminated, classical unemployment will fall.

Just how many more workers will find jobs is questionable. It depends on how many workers have productivities that are below the previous high wages. The employment rate of certain of workers with particularly low levels of education and jobs skills will be especially increased: minorities, immigrants, teenagers, and workers entering the labor market for the first time. In the past, these groups have compensated for their lower average productivities by accepting lower wages. After the elimination of minimum-wage laws and labor unions, they will be able to do so again.

Reducing Frictional Unemployment

Next, if government forces consumers to buy the same products each year and keeps workers from changing jobs until they have another job lined up, frictional unemployment will be reduced.

However, the social cost will be enormous. Although resources might be constantly employed, the values of products to consumers will quickly fall relative to the values of the alternative products that consumers would have preferred. Had such restrictions been imposed in the 1800s, we would still have an agricultural economy whose small industrial sector would be producing carriages and buggy whips.

In a sense, the term unemployment is a misnomer when applied to frictionally unemployed workers. We aren't idle when we're looking for a better job; instead, we're producing information that we value more than other products. The information derives its value from the higher wages that we eventually earn, and those wages, in turn, emanate from the higher values of the products that we end up producing.

For example, if you turned down a job for $10,000 to search for one week, total production would certainly fall during the week that you weren't working. But if the week of searching yielded a $20,000 job, the higher wages would compensate you for the loss of one week's production. Also, the higher wages would reveal that consumers would obtain goods that they valued more. An economy with frictional unemployment may produce fewer products, but the earnings of workers and the values of products to consumers are greater.

Reducing Cyclical Unemployment

Finally, if government increases aggregate demand after aggregate demand has suddenly fallen, cyclical unemployment will decline. Rather than waiting for the painful decline of prices and wages, the government can quickly increase aggregate demand by using government fiscal and monetary policies. We will discuss these policies in Chapter 19.

The elimination of cyclical unemployment is important because, unlike frictional unemployment, cyclical unemployment is a complete social waste. It represents market searches for jobs at wages where no jobs exist. A recession is a high price to pay only to reduce prices and wages and obtain no real beneficial effects; it can be a sacrifice of substance only to obtain form.

Although a recession represents a loss of products and value, individual managers and workers behave very rationally throughout the recessionary process. As price searchers seeking to maximize their profits and earnings, managers and workers must assume that when demands for their particular products and resources fall, the declines represent changes in the composition of aggregate demand rather than the much less common decreases in its level. This assumption causes them to initially reduce production and employment, not prices and wages.

A Summary of the Theory

We have assumed that

a. Firms will refuse to pay workers more than the value of what the workers contribute to production.

b. Price-searching producers and workers respond to decreases in demands for particular products by cutting production and employment first, and, when necessary, prices and wages only later.

    c. Workers have limited information and must produce information about jobs and wages if they desire more.

As a result, we have been able to predict that

    a. If minimum-wage laws or labor unions raise wages, classical unemployment will occur.

    b. If the composition of aggregate demand changes, frictional unemployment will follow.

    c. If the level of aggregate demand declines, cyclical unemployment will result.

    e. If minimum-wage laws or unions are eliminated, classical unemployment will decline.

    f. If consumers are forced to buy the same products year after year or workers are kept from changing jobs until they find new ones, frictional unemployment will fall.

    g. If aggregate demand is increased, recessionary unemployment will be reduced.

SPECIAL TOPICS

Equal Pay For the Handicapped

In recent years, many people have become more concerned with the plight of the handicapped. In addition to sponsoring legislation providing special parking places, elevators, and automatic doors, some people have argued that handicapped workers should be paid the same wages as their nonhandicapped counterparts.

If the advocates of the handicapped succeeded in passing legislation requiring employers to pay the same wages to both handicapped and nonhandicapped employees, what would happen? Some handicapped workers, those already earning the going wage, wouldn't be affected. But those who have productivities below the going wage would be worse off, since most of them would become unemployed. Although employers would have to pay prevailing wages if they hired those workers, they would simply avoid hiring them. Paying workers more than their contributions to production would cause employers to lose profits.

The same principles apply to any group of workers. If whites, blacks, men, women, residents, or aliens had to be paid the same wages, some would be unaffected, and others, those with productivities below the going wages, would become classically unemployed.

A Federal Government Employment Agency

Although classical unemployment is significant, it is far less extensive than frictional unemployment. To reduce frictional unemployment, the federal government could establish a government employment agency. By producing job and wage information, the agency would reduce the frictional unemployment rate.

Information about jobs is already produced by private employment agencies, personnel departments, newspapers, trade journals, college placement departments, and unemployed workers. These institutions and individuals don't produce more of this information only because the value of additional information is less than its cost of production. Therefore, the extra information produced by a government employment agency would be worth less than the cost of running the agency. Although the agency would increase production by reducing unemployment, the value of total production would fall.

We live in a world of scarcity where we want many goods as well as information. We choose to produce information only to the extent that its value is greater than the values of the alternative products that we must sacrifice. When government forces us to produce more information, then the value of the information is less than its cost.

This doesn't mean that we wouldn't value the information more than the alternatives sacrificed after the government produced it. The values we place on information are often based on incorrect predictions about the future. If government administrators can anticipate the benefits of more information better than individual citizens, then the production of more information by the government may improve our well-being.

One more point. If property rights to information are poorly defined so that information becomes a public good, then information will be underproduced relative to its value. Under such conditions, government production (or subsidy) of information is necessary if the optimal quantity of information is to be produced.

Can Farmers Avoid Cyclical Unemployment?

Are farmers, as many people believe, able to avoid the effects of a recession? Not usually. To explain, suppose the federal government suddenly reduced the supply of money by half and that, as a result, aggregate demand fell by half. If the decrease in aggregate demand then caused demands for farm commodities to fall, farm prices would immediately decline. This is because farmers sell their products in competitive markets in which auctioneers instantly reduce prices when demands decrease. Unlike other producers in the economy, farmers are not price searchers who lack price information.

If the prices of the resources used by farmers also fell, then there wouldn't be much of a problem. Lower costs would compensate for lower revenues. But most of the resources purchased by farmers are sold by price searchers. Price-searching resource owners would assume that demands had shifted to other products and would, therefore, refuse to accept lower prices for their resources. Since farmers then would have to pay the same prices for resources but would earn less for their products, they would cut production. Cyclical unemployment would then occur in the agricultural sector of the economy.

Of course, some farmers own all the resources used in production. Subsistence farmers producing independently of markets can easily ride out a recession. Such farmers are, however, rare.

Full Employment in a World of Unlimited Information

The reason farmers would cut production during a recession is that while farm prices would fall, the other prices in the economy wouldn't. The other prices would stay constant or fall slowly because other products and resources are sold by price searchers. This implies that recessionary unemployment wouldn't occur if all products and resources were all sold in competitive markets in which auctioneers reduced prices after a decrease in aggregate demand.

Producers would then be willing and able to produce as much as before the decrease in aggregate demand because lower product prices would immediately be offset by lower resource prices. Furthermore, producers would see all product prices falling and wouldn't be tempted to shift resources toward the production of other goods. Likewise, workers would accept lower wages because lower product prices would allow them to buy the same products as before. And the drop in the general wage rate would tell workers that all other workers were earning less and, therefore, they wouldn't have an incentive to quit and search for other jobs. With a decrease in aggregate demand, only prices and wages would fall, not production and employment.

The complication that our theory of recessionary unemployment introduces is the presence of limited information and, therefore, price searching. Under competitive market conditions in which auctioneers set prices, price information would be almost unlimited and recessions wouldn't occur.

Relative Versus Absolute Levels of Aggregate Demand and Money Supply

Although price searching is a precondition for cyclical unemployment, the cause is a sudden decrease in aggregate demand. But this doesn't mean that recessionary unemployment emanates from a low absolute level of aggregate demand. The absolute level of aggregate demand is irrelevant. What matters is the relationship between aggregate demand and the price-wage level. Ten dollars of aggregate demand could buy all the products and generate enough revenue to buy all the resources in the U.S. economy if prices and wages were low enough.

Similarly, since aggregate demand is largely determined by the supply of money, we may be tempted to argue mistakenly that recessions are caused by an insufficient amount of money. During the Great Depression, people regularly complained about the lack of money in the economy. Nevertheless, any amount of money can be consistent with full employment if prices and wages are low enough.

For that matter, any quantity of money will cause unemployment if prices and wages are sufficiently high. Imagine, for example, that the federal government suddenly forced all prices and wages to double. Workers wouldn't mind, since their higher wages would allow them to buy the higher-priced products. Firms would be indifferent, since higher resource prices would be offset by higher product prices. Nevertheless, huge surpluses would occur. Twice as much money would be necessary to facilitate the same transactions if prices and wages doubled. The product and labor surpluses would appear to reflect a lack of money, but they would be equally attributable to high prices and wages.

As we have seen, cyclical unemployment is caused by a sudden decline of aggregate demand in an economy where price searchers fail to reduce prices and wages instantly. But no matter what the absolute level of aggregate demand or money supply, full employment can eventually be brought about by lower prices and wages.

In fact, if price searchers have enough time, recessions need not follow decreases in aggregate demand. For example, during the nineteenth century, aggregate demand generally decreased relative to the supply of non-money goods. However, since price searchers had sufficient time to find profit- and income-maximizing prices and wages, price and wage decreases generally prevented unemployment (some recessions occurred, but economic expansion was the norm for most of the century).

Knowing that price searchers may eventually eliminate cyclical unemployment by cutting prices and wages may be of little consolation. As the late economist John Maynard Keynes once said, "In the long run, we are all dead." Government may want to speed things up by increasing aggregate demand with some of the fiscal and monetary policies we will discuss in Chapter 19.

Technology, Immigration, and Overproduction

Cyclical unemployment is caused by sudden reductions in aggregate demand. It is not caused by advances in technology, immigration, or excessive production.

Advances in technology can cause only temporary frictional unemployment, since they do cause some workers to be laid off. While some jobs may be lost, other jobs will be created. For example, in the Soviet Union, when advances in technology reduce the amount of labor that is necessary for the production of various products, workers are then shifted to the production of other products that couldn't have been produced previously. Likewise, subsistence farmers who find easier ways to grow vegetables don't become unemployed; they just produce larger quantities of other goods.

Of course, workers may have temporarily lower productivities in their new jobs. For instance, if steel workers are laid off because of a new milling process, their best alternative jobs may be in other industries where the pay is much lower. It may take some time to find out that the lower-paying jobs are the best available. As a result, frictional unemployment in the form of structural unemployment may increase. Once the alternatives become clear, however, workers will cease being unemployed, since they will either take the existing, lower-paying jobs or drop out of the work force by selecting leisure over work.

Technological changes haven't caused extended job searches in the past. The periods of greatest technological change have also been periods of relative prosperity and full employment. It is during recessions that unemployment has grown, and that is when technological change has been the slowest.

Immigration also hasn't caused cyclical unemployment. The increases in the labor supply have usually caused only increases in production. With more labor, more jobs were filled and production expanded.

Finally, general overproduction hasn't caused cyclical unemployment because general overproduction has never occurred. Even today, while we are certainly better off materially than at any point in history, we still want larger homes, second cars, more services, and better food. This means that we have more jobs than we have workers to fill them. Recession is the paradox, not full employment.

The U.S. Gross National Product

How do we know if we are in a recession? We can't claim there is a recession simply because we see some firms around us cutting production. Individual firms reduce production and employment even during periods of prosperity. To identify a recession, we need a measure of national production.

The most important measure of national production is the **gross national product,** the **GNP.** Computed quarterly by the U.S. Department of Commerce, the GNP reveals the monetary value of all the products produced and exchanged in the economy in a given period of time.

Statisticians determine the GNP by using a number of different approaches. One approach, the **expenditures approach**, requires the addition of the expenditures of consumers, business firms, and governments on final products. Since almost all products produced are sold, the sum of all expenditures will approximate the value of total production.

Table 17.1 shows how the expenditures approach yields a GNP of $4235 billion for the United States in 1986.

Another approach to calculating the GNP, the **incomes approach**, involves adding all the incomes of individuals in the economy. This method yields the value of all products because revenues resulting from the sales of products are distributed as either wages, interest, rents, or profits. For example, when a computer is produced and sold for $5000, the suppliers of the resources purchased to produce the computer and the producer of the product earn a total of $5000. National income must equal national output.

The circular-flow diagram of the economy that we discussed in the preceding chapter shows the equivalence of the incomes and the expenditure approaches to computing the GNP. In the diagram, the money spent for re-

TABLE 17.1 Expenditures Approach to Computing the U.S. GNP

THE U.S. GROSS NATIONAL PRODUCT, 1986

EXPENDITURES		BILLIONS OF DOLLARS
Personal consumption		$2800
Durable goods	402	
Nondurable goods	939	
Services	1458	
Gross private domestic investment		671
Fixed investment	655	
Change in business inventories	16	
Net Exports		−106
Exports	376	
Imports	482	
Government purchases		870
Gross national product		$4235

Source: U.S. Department of Commerce

sources by firms is earned by households, which then turn around and spend it on final products. As long as households don't hold more money, they will spend what they earn and earnings will equal expenditures.

Table 17.2 shows the computation of the U.S. GNP for 1986 using the incomes approach. Of course, items 4 and 5 are not incomes. However, they indirectly represent money that was earned but not paid to households.

With this understanding of the GNP, we can provide a more specific definition of a recession. A **recession** is defined as a decrease in the GNP that lasts for at least two calendar quarters.

TABLE 17.2 The Incomes Approach to Computing the U.S. GNP

THE U.S. GROSS NATIONAL PRODUCT, 1986

	BILLIONS OF DOLLARS
Wages and other employee supplements	$2505
Proprietors' income	290
Rental income of persons	17
Corporate profits	284
Net interest	326
Indirect business taxes, adjustments, and statistical discrepancy	356
Depreciation	457
The gross national product	$4235

The GNP, an Imperfect Measure

Since the GNP measures national production, we can employ it to measure material well-being and economic growth. When the GNP rises, we can usually say that material well-being has improved and that economic growth has occurred.

However, we need to recognize that despite its usefulness, the GNP is an imperfect measure. We can identify six reasons why:

1. The GNP changes when prices as well as physical outputs change. If we want a measure of physical output, we must adjust for inflation or deflation to obtain the "real," or constant dollar, GNP.

2. Since the GNP ignores population, a high GNP doesn't mean a high GNP per person. If we divide the GNP by the population, we can obtain the GNP per capita, a measure that may reflect material well-being more precisely.

3. The GNP fails to record many social costs and benefits that emanate from market production. Production often causes the sacrifice or the creation of clean air, clean water, scenic beauty, etc., goods that often fail to be reflected in prices or outputs.

4. The GNP doesn't reflect changes in the quality or the variety of products. Advances in technology may result in superior goods and greater choices, but if prices stay the same, the GNP remains the same.

5. The GNP ignores leisure. In the past, material well-being improved more than the GNP to the extent that the work week declined.

6. Finally, the GNP fails to measure products that aren't sold in markets. Goods produced and consumed within households and by do-it-yourselfers, as well as the products produced in the illegal underground economy, are excluded from the GNP because of difficulties in determining their market values.

Despite these imperfections, we continue to use the GNP both because the inaccuracies are usually insignificant in the short run and because the measure is more objective than others that are available.

The Multiplier

If we make some simplifying assumptions, we can determine the value of the **multiplier**, the factor by which we must multiply an initial change in aggregate demand to determine the total change in aggregate demand that will eventually occur. By knowing the eventual change in aggregate demand, we will be able to predict the change in national output and income that will result.

Suppose that aggregate demand consists only of two components: demand for consumption commodities by households, called consumption (C), and demand for capital by business firms, called investment (I). Suppose further that the level of national output and income is represented by the variable (Y)— we can represent output and income with one variable since, as we have seen in computing the GNP, national output always equals national income. Furthermore, assume that current national output and income (Y) is determined by aggregate demand ($C + I$). In short

$$Y = C + I \tag{1}$$

Next, assume that some consumption (a) occurs autonomously (independently) of the level of current national income. For example, even if current national income were zero, households might consume $100 billion worth of consumption goods by spending past savings. Autonomous consumption (a) would then be $100 billion.

Assume also that some additional consumption is determined by current national income (Y). More specifically, suppose the additional consumption is a fixed proportion (b) of national income (Y). That is, consumption determined by income equals bY. For instance, if (b) equals ¾ and households earn $100 billion, consumption caused by income will be $75 billion.

Total consumption will equal autonomous consumption plus consumption determined by current income:

$$C = a + bY \tag{2}$$

Finally, let's assume that investment (I) is a given.

The two equations are linear, independent equations in two variables, Y and C. We can therefore obtain solutions for Y and C. Let's solve for Y.

Substituting the second equation's value of C into the first equation, we obtain

$$Y = a + bY + I$$

Subtracting bY from both sides gives us

$$Y - bY = a + I$$

Factoring Y out of the left side results in

$$Y(1 - b) = a + I$$

And finally, multiplying both sides by $1/(1 - b)$ yields the solution value for Y:

$$Y = \left[\frac{1}{1 - b} \right] [a + I]$$

From this final equation, we can see that any change in autonomous consumption (a) or investment (I) will change current national income Y by $1/(1 - b)$ times the change in (a) or (I). Therefore, the multiplier equals $[1/(1 - b)]$.

This doesn't mean much until we plug in some values. If autonomous consumption is $50 billion, if investment is $100 billion, and if consumers spend $\frac{3}{4}$ of all additional current income, then the level of output will be $600 billion.

$$Y = \left(\frac{1}{1 - \frac{3}{4}}\right) (\$50 \text{ billion} + \$100 \text{ billion})$$
$$Y = (4)(\$150 \text{ billion})$$
$$Y = \$600 \text{ billion}$$

Now, if investment subsequently falls by $25 billion, initially reducing aggregate demand by $25 billion, output and income will fall by $100 billion rather than just $25 billion, to $500 billion. The multiplier, $1/(1 - b)$, equals 4; any exogenous (independent) change in consumption or investment will be multiplied by 4.

To explain this, look at the original equations. When I falls in the first equation, it reduces Y. The drop in Y causes a further reduction in C in the second equation. The reduction in C then cuts Y in the first equation to again reduce C in the second equation, and on to infinity. Nevertheless, even though the multiplier goes on forever, it approaches a limit. Eventually, Y drops by 4 times the initial decrease in I; Y doesn't drop to 0.

A Graphical View of the Multiplier

We can illustrate the results we obtained from the preceding equations with the graph in Figure 17.2.

Figure 17.2   National Income and Aggregate Demand

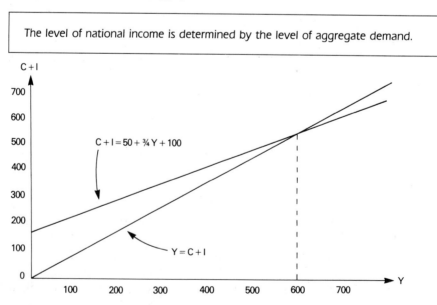

The first equation, $Y = C + I$, is represented by the 45° line. The second equation is represented by the other line, except that I has been added to both sides, yielding the equation $C + I = a + bY + I$. That way, the equation can be plotted on a graph that has $C + I$ on the vertical axis.

To obtain the various points on the line, convert the second equation by replacing a, b, and I with $50 billion, $\frac{3}{4}$, and $100 billion, respectively. This yields $C + I = \$50$ billion $+ \frac{3}{4}Y + \$100$ billion. Then plug in various values of Y and solve for $C + I$. For example, if $Y = 0$, $C + I = \$150$ billion; if $Y = \$100$ billion, $C + I = \$225$ billion; and if $Y = \$200$, $C + I = \$300$ billion. Finally, the solution for the two equations is $600, as shown by the intersection of the two curves.

We can now show the multiplier effect. As Figure 17.3 illustrates, if business firms become pessimistic about earnings from capital investments and this causes them to reduce investment by $25 billion, the second equation changes and the second curve falls by $25 billion. The intersection of the two curves then reveals a $100 billion decrease in Y. A $25 billion initial decrease in aggregate demand causes an eventual $100 billion drop in aggregate demand and current output and income because as output and income decrease in response to the initial reduction in aggregate demand, additional decreases in aggregate demand follow.

Our explanation of multiplier-related unemployment, as well as the unemployment that initially occurs when a recession begins, has been rather simple. In the next chapter, we will complicate the explanation so that we can also identify the interactions that occur between the money, bond, labor, capital, and financial markets during the recessionary process.

Figure 17.3 A Graphical View of the Multiplier

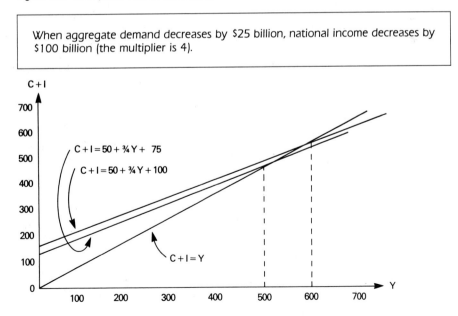

When aggregate demand decreases by $25 billion, national income decreases by $100 billion (the multiplier is 4).

MAJOR AND MINOR POINTS

1. It is a paradox that unemployment exists in a world of scarce products. There should be too many jobs, not too few.

2. We are unemployed when we are willing to work at a wage that we think reflects our productivity, but we don't work.

3. We aren't unemployed when we choose leisure over work. And we choose leisure over work when we refuse to work for wages that we know reflect our productivities.

4. We can predict that unemployment will occur if minimum-wage laws pass, if unions increase wages, if the composition of aggregate demand changes, or if the level of aggregate demand declines.

5. Classical unemployment occurs when third parties fix wages above our productivities.

6. Price searchers are individuals who have limited information about prices, qualities, demands, and supplies. To obtain more information, price searchers must produce or purchase it.

7. Frictional unemployment is caused by a change in the composition of aggregate demand in an economy containing price-searching firms and workers. When demands fall, firms and workers don't change prices and wages but do reduce production and employment. Workers must then search for new jobs and are frictionally unemployed during the searches.

8. Cyclical unemployment occurs during recessions, periods of reduced national output.

9. The term cyclical unemployment is a misnomer to the extent that recessions are neither periodic nor caused by previous periods of high employment.

10. Cyclical unemployment is caused by a sudden decrease of aggregate demand in a money-using, capitalistic economy that contains price searchers.

11. Decreases in aggregate demand have generally been caused by decreases in investment rather than consumption. However, decreases in consumption caused by the multiplier process have made recessions much more severe.

12. Cyclical unemployment occurs during a recession because firms and workers reduce production and employment rather than prices and wages after a decrease of aggregate demand. The workers then search for new jobs at wages where jobs don't exist.

13. What information the markets do give workers during a recession is wrong. General wage rates stay constant. This wrongly tells workers experiencing demand decreases that demands for products and labor exist elsewhere.

14. If the composition of aggregate demand stayed the same while aggregate demand fell, it would be easier for producers and workers to react to a lower level of aggregate demand by reducing prices and wages. But the composition of aggregate demand changes constantly, even when aggregate demand is falling.

15. After recessions begin, the multiplier process causes them to get worse. Once unemployed workers exhaust their savings, they reduce consumption and therefore aggregate demand. The decrease in demand causes more workers to be laid off. Those workers then also eventually cut consumption and aggregate demand falls even further. More employees lose their jobs, and so on.

16. Recoveries from recessions occur because workers eventually begin to accept lower wages. Product prices then decline, increasing quantities demanded. The greater quantities demanded cause increases in production and employment, eliminating recessionary unemployment.

17. Recoveries from recessions are aided by the multiplier process. As workers find jobs and earn income, they increase their consumption and aggregate demand rises.

18. Classical unemployment can be reduced by eliminating minimum-wage laws and unions that have increased wages.

19. Frictional unemployment can be reduced if workers are given more job information.

20. Frictional unemployment can be efficient both for individuals and consumers. The discoveries of better jobs mean higher wages for workers and more valuable products to consumers.

21. Cyclical unemployment can be reduced if the government increases aggregate demand by using fiscal and monetary policies.

22. Cyclical unemployment is a total loss. It changes only the levels of prices. Nevertheless, during the recessionary process, all firms and workers behave rationally, seeking to maximize profits and incomes.

23. Unless carefully written, equal-pay laws can create classical unemployment if they force private firms to pay wages in excess of the productivities of some workers.

24. Most farmers don't initially own many of the resources they use. As a result, like the rest of the economy, the agricultural sector is hit hard by recessions.

25. Since competitive markets generate unlimited market information, instantaneous price and wage reductions will prevent cyclical unemployment.

26. Cyclical unemployment is not caused by a low absolute level of aggregate demand or by a small amount of money. Any level of aggregate demand or any amount of money can bring about full employment if prices and money wages are low enough. And any level of aggregate demand or money supply can cause unemployment if prices and money wages are sufficiently high.

27. Recessions can be avoided if aggregate demand decreases slowly enough to allow price searchers time to find market-clearing equilibrium prices and wages.

28. Advances in technology, immigration, and general overproduction don't cause cyclical unemployment.

29. The gross national product (GNP) is a money measure of national production.

30. The GNP can be computed by adding either the products sold or the incomes earned in the economy.

31. Recessions are two-quarter decreases in the GNP.

32. The GNP is an imperfect measure. It
    a. Includes price changes
    b. Ignores population
    c. Fails to include social costs and benefits
    d. Imperfectly reflects the changing quality or variety of products produced over time
    e. Ignores leisure
    f. Ignores products that aren't sold in legal markets.

33. If $Y = C + I$, and $C = a + bY$, then $Y = [1/1(1 - b)][a + I]$. The multiplier is finite and equal to $1/(1 - b)$.

QUESTIONS

1. What is unemployment?
2. When will classical unemployment occur?
3. When will frictional unemployment occur?
4. When will a recession and its associated cyclical unemployment occur?
5. Why will a recession get worse before it gets better?
6. When will recovery from a recession occur?
7. How can classical unemployment be reduced?
8. When will the level of frictional unemployment fall?
9. How can a recession, along with its associated cyclical unemployment, be avoided?
10. Discuss the following terms and concepts:

The paradox of unemployment	Recovery from recession
Unemployment	Equal pay laws
Classical unemployment	Public employment agency
Frictional unemployment	Farmers and unemployment
Structural unemployment	Limited information
Cyclical unemployment	Relative aggregate demand
Recession	Relative money supply
Cyclical unemployment misnomer	Technology
	Immigration
Unemployment's preconditions	Overproduction
Initial stage	Gross national product
Multiplier stage	Problems with the GNP
Finite multiplier	$Y = C + I, C = a + bY$

APPLICATIONS

1. Is unemployment generally caused by too few jobs? Why?
2. Are people unemployed if they can't find a job that pays enough to live on?
3. During the early 1970s, demands for engineers decreased drastically causing many to be laid off. Did they become unemployed?
4. Would frictional unemployment occur under conditions of unlimited information?
5. Many economists argue that the rate of frictional unemployment in the economy has increased from about 2% to about 4% in recent years. As causes, they cite the entry of women and teenagers into the labor force, the increase in unemployment and welfare benefits, and a higher level of income. Explain how these three factors might increase frictional unemployment.

6. Besides shifts in demands, how can frictional unemployment be caused by searches for better jobs, increases in population, and changes in technology?

7. Structural unemployment occurs when the average length of frictional unemployment is increased by different skill requirements of jobs. Explain how this might happen after demands shift from autos to computers.

8. A decrease in the money supply can cause a reduction in aggregate demand by reducing M and therefore MV. How might a reduction in spending on capital by business firms (a reduction in investment) reduce V and therefore MV to cause a recession?

9. Some economists have argued that monopoly firms and unions cause recessions by refusing to lower prices and wages following a decrease in aggregate demand. How do monopoly firms and unions respond when demands for their goods fall?

10. If firms owned all the resources used in production, why would they still cut employment and production rather than prices and wages after a decrease in demand?

11. Our emphasis has been on labor unemployment. Are other resources unemployed during recessions. Why?

12. During the early 1980s, a reporter for the *New York Times* argued that lower prices and wages signaled the beginning of a recession. Did they?

13. In what sense are we employed when we are frictionally unemployed?

14. Why might you be happy if I found a job paying $50,000 per year instead of one paying only $30,000 per year?

15. If people knew the nature of demand decreases during a recession, they could stop the recessions. In what sense is this true? In what sense is it false?

16. For simplicity, the chapter discussed sudden decreases in aggregate demands as the causes of recessions. More generally, recessions are caused by sudden reductions in the growth of aggregate demand relative to the growth of the price-wage level. Suppose the money supply, aggregate demand, and the price-wage level are growing at 10% per year. How can a recession be caused by a sudden reduction in the growth of the money supply to only 5% per year?

18

The Recessionary Process

Under pure capitalism, the systems of coordination and control are markets and the specific signals and rewards are prices. But when market information is limited, things change. Prices still provide signals and rewards in the long run, but in the short run, instructions and incentives are provided primarily by shortages and surpluses.

Shortages and surpluses provide efficient signals and rewards when the composition of aggregate demand changes. If aggregate demand suddenly falls, however, three fundamental failures can occur, causing a recession. Up to now, we have neglected to explain the exact nature of these information and control failures and the role of money in allowing them to occur. In this chapter, we eliminate these theoretical deficiencies.

To explain the failures, we begin with a discussion of aggregation. Then we aggregate all items exchanged in the economy into five sets of goods and assume that households and business firms trade the goods in four markets. Next, we explain Say's principle and its claim that all shortages must be matched by surpluses. Finally, we use that claim to examine the recessionary process.

AGGREGATION, SAY'S PRINCIPLE, AND SAY'S LAW

The Concept of Aggregation

To explain the functioning of a complex economy, we must reduce the number of goods and markets to manageable levels. We can achieve this by **aggregation**, a process of combining goods or markets into single units. Aggregation allows us to reveal essential forces and eliminate unnecessary details.

As a rule, if we want to achieve more fundamental but more limited objectives, we aggregate more; but if we want to understand specifics, we aggregate less. For example, if we only want to understand the effect of an increase in the money supply on the prices of nonmoney goods, then we may want to deal with money and nonmoney goods. However, if we are also interested in understanding how an increase in the money supply will affect interest rates, product prices, and resource prices, then we may want to divide nonmoney goods into financial assets, products, and resources. By aggregating goods in the economy into four rather than two categories, we will make things more complex, but we will also reveal more specifics about prices. We will sacrifice simplicity but gain generality.

Five Goods and Four Markets

Our goal in this chapter is to explain the recessionary process more clearly. To achieve this goal, we aggregate the many goods in the economy into five groups—consumption commodities, capital, labor, bonds, and money—and assume that the five groups are exchanged in four markets.

Consumption Commodities and Their Market

Let's start by looking at **consumption commodities**. These are products that are produced by business firms and sold to households in the consumption commodities market. Households buy the commodities to satisfy immediate wants, whereas firms produce them to obtain profits.

In the consumption commodities market, demand, called **consumption**, comes from price-searching households and is determined mainly by household incomes. However, the relationship between consumption and incomes is generally delayed. When incomes fall, for example, households reduce consumption—but only after some time has passed. In the interim, households continue buying consumption commodities with the money they have or can obtain by selling off their **liquid assets**, items that can be easily converted into money.

The supply of consumption commodities emanates from price-searching firms. The firms set prices and production according to supply and demand in the long run but adjust production to changes in demand in the short run.

Capital and Its Market

Capital comprises the resources that are produced by business firms and sold to other business firms in the capital market.

Demand for capital, called **investment**, originates with price-searching firms. The demand is inversely related to the rate of interest and directly related to future expected demands for products. For example, if the interest rate rises or if future expected product demands fall, investment will decline.

The supply of capital also comes from price-searching firms. They set prices and production according to supply and demand in the long run but adjust production to changes in demand in the short run.

Labor and Its Market

Labor is the basic human resource and is sold by households to business firms. It is exchanged in the labor market where its price is the wage rate.

Demand for labor comes from price-searching firms who set wages and employment according to supply and demand in the long run and adjust employment to changes in product demand in the short run. The supply of labor is provided by price-searching households, which sell their labor at market-clearing equilibrium wages in the long run but adjust supply to demand in the short run.

Bonds and Their Market

Bonds are financial assets sold by firms to households. They are traded in a competitive bond market.

Demand for bonds comes from price-taking households wishing to lend money so that they can earn interest. The supply of bonds emanates from price-taking firms that want to borrow money so they can buy capital.

The bonds in the economy have their interest yields printed on them in terms of dollars. As a result, when the price of bonds falls, the effective interest yield rises, and vice versa. For example, if a bond promises to yield $100 interest per year, forever, and sells for $1000, then its effective yield is 10% per year. If the price of the bond then falls to $500, the price decrease raises the interest yield to 20%. On the other hand, if the price increases to $2000, the interest yield falls to 5%.

Money and Its Many Markets

Finally, **money** is the economy's medium of exchange. Because money is the medium of exchange, there is no money market as such. Households and firms buy money when they sell goods in the other four markets and sell money when they buy goods in those markets.

Since households and firms exchange money for other goods in the other four markets, we can express the price of money in terms of any of the four other goods. When the prices of the other goods fall, the price of money in terms of those goods rises. For example, if the price of a book falls from $2 to $1, then the price of $1 rises from one-half of a book to one book.

Demand for money originates with households and firms who want money for its value as a medium of exchange and a store of value. The demand is inversely related to the interest rate. When the interest rate rises, the cost of holding money rises. Therefore, households and firms try to hold less money.

The supply of money is generated by the economy's banking system, which is under government control. The system changes the money supply whenever the government wants it to.

Say's Principle and Say's Law

Since our trades always involve two goods, we must supply one good when we demand another. This proposition is **Say's principle**. The principle recognizes, for example, that to demand one Pepsi when the price of a Pepsi is $1, we must also supply $1 when the price of a dollar is one Pepsi.

This implies that when a surplus of Pepsis is present, a shortage of money must also exist. For example, if a Pepsi machine wants to sell one Pepsi more than we want to buy at a price of $1, it also wants to buy $1 more than we want to sell when the price of a dollar is one Pepsi.

More generally, Say's principle implies that a surplus of one good must always be matched by a shortage of one or more other goods. This implication is the basic conceptual tool that we will use to trace a recession through the economy's various markets.

In an economy where no money or financial assets exist—in a pure barter system—we could use a more strict proposition called Say's law. **Say's law** states that the act of supplying any nonmoney good implies the act of demanding another nonmoney good.

Say's law holds in barter systems but not in monetary economies. In monetary economies it is possible to supply a nonmoney good and demand money in trade. Since we are primarily concerned with monetary economies, we will employ the more general Say's principle.

THE RECESSIONARY PROCESS

Barter and Full Employment

Before we use the concepts we have developed to analyze the recessionary process, let's first employ them to explain why a recession is unlikely in a barter economy that contains neither money nor bonds.

Suppose all markets in such an economy are clearing when a surplus of labor, unemployment, suddenly occurs. According to Say's principle, a surplus of labor has to be matched by a shortage elsewhere. In the barter economy, the shortage must be of consumption commodities or capital, since no other goods exist. By attempting to sell their labor, workers create a shortage of consumption commodities or capital.

This situation is represented in the Table 18.1. In the table, the markets for consumption commodities, capital, labor, bonds, and money are represented by the letters C, I, L, B, and M, respectively. Also, surpluses and shortages are identified by SU and SH, respectively. When unemployment occurs in the barter economy, the economy moves from the full employment situation of row 1 to the unemployment situation of row 2.

Prolonged unemployment in this circumstance is unlikely because the product shortages balance the labor surplus. Workers are asking for jobs and firms will hire them since demand for the consumption commodities and capital that the workers will produce exceeds the supply.

The Beginning of a Recession

In a more complex economy containing bonds and money, consumption commodity and capital shortages don't have to match a labor surplus. Indeed they won't following a reduction in aggregate demand. Let's see why.

To start a recession, let's begin by assuming that the supply of money in an economy falls. By assuming the money supply falls, we will be able to explain recessions caused by both decreases in the money supply and decreases in investment.

Specifically, suppose government suddenly reduces the money supply in a monetary economy containing not only consumption commodities, capital, and labor but also bonds and money. Under such conditions, a shortage of money immediately occurs. To make the same purchases at the same prices and wages, households and business firms want as much money as before.

Say's principle tells us that the shortage of money must be matched by a surplus elsewhere, but where? In the bond market. To obtain more money, households try to reduce their holdings of their most liquid assets, bonds, either by attempting to sell the bonds they already have or by reducing their demands for new ones. At the same time, business firms try to build up their money holdings by attempting to increase their bond sales. Bond demand falls and the supply increases to cause a surplus (row 3 of Table 18.2).

Since bonds are exchanged by price takers in highly competitive markets, the price of bonds immediately falls, raising the interest rate. Although the new bond price clears the bond market, it also affects demand for both money and capital. To some extent, the demand for money falls. The higher interest

TABLE 18.1   *The Economy*

	C	I	L	B	M
1. Full employment	—	—	—		
2. Unemployment	SH	SH	SU		

TABLE 18.2 The Economy

	C	I	L	B	M
1. Full employment	—	—	—		
2. Unemployment	SH	SH	SU		
3. Less money	—	—	—	SU	SH

rate induces households to sacrifice some of their new desire for cash so they can earn more interest. As a result, the shortage of money shrinks, to SH' (row 4 in Table 18.3—the prime identifies a different, and in this case smaller, shortage).

But the higher interest rate also creates a problem in the capital market. The higher interest rate reduces the desire for capital causing investment to decline. With the decline in investment, a surplus of capital occurs (row 4).

To eliminate the surplus of capital, price-searching producers in the capital industries cut production. This eliminates the surplus of capital but creates a surplus of labor (unemployment) in the labor market. A recession begins (row 5 in Table 18.4).

A recession follows a decline in aggregate demand because a labor surplus isn't accompanied by product shortages. Such shortage signals must exist if producers are to raise production and employment, but, instead, a surplus of labor is matched by a shortage of money.

As we have seen, in a barter economy unemployed workers would not just ask for jobs. Their requests for jobs would take the form of offers to buy products. If you, for example, wanted to work in a shoe factory, your request for wages would be in the form of a demand for shoes, since you would be paid with shoes. As long as you demanded fewer shoes than you would contribute to a firm's output, your demand for wages would be a sufficient signal and reward for the firm to hire you and eliminate your unemployment.

Nevertheless, after a fall in aggregate demand in a monetary economy, workers accompany their job requests only with demands for money. Unfortunately, shortages of money mean nothing to firms, since firms don't produce money.

If money were cheese, demands for money could provide enough instructions and incentives to prevent unemployment. Firms would hire work-

TABLE 18.3 The Economy

	C	I	L	B	M
1. Full employment	—	—	—		
2. Unemployment	SH	SH	SU		
3. Less money	—	—	—	SU	SH
4. Higher i rates	—	SU	—	—	SH'

TABLE 18.4   *The Economy*

	C	I	L	B	M
1. Full employment	—	—	—		
2. Unemployment	SH	SH	SU		
3. Less money	—	—	—	SU	SH
4. Higher *i*, lower *I*	—	SU	—	—	SH′
5. A recession begins	—	—	SU	—	SH′

ers to produce cheese. Nevertheless, money isn't cheese. Demands for money are different from demands for products.

This absence of product shortages to match a labor surplus is the first of three coordination and control failures that occur during a recession. The other two appear later in the recessionary process.

Recessionary Expectations

Once cyclical unemployment begins, the recession is aggravated by a further decline in investment, even before the multiplier process takes hold. This is because the reductions in production and employment that have occurred create recessionary expectations. When firms anticipate difficulties in selling future products, they cut their investment.

The reduction in investment creates another surplus of capital. This time the surplus is matched by a shortage of bonds. Firms want to borrow less money to buy capital, so they reduce the bond supply, creating the bond shortage (row 6 in Table 18.5).

The shortage of bonds instantly raises the price of bonds, lowering the interest rate, until the bond market clears. The lower interest rate then increases the quantity of capital demanded, reducing the capital surplus. It also raises the demand for liquidity, increasing the shortage in the money "market" (row 7 in Table 18.6).

In terms of unemployment, the first effect is fortunate; a greater

TABLE 18.5   *The Economy*

	C	I	L	B	M
1. Full employment	—	—	—		
2. Unemployment	SH	SH	SU		
3. Less money	—	—	—	SU	SH
4. Higher *i*, lower *I*	—	SU	—	—	SH′
5. Recession begins	—	—	SU	—	SH′
6. Expected recession	—	SU	—	SH	SH′

TABLE 18.6   *The Economy*

	C	I	L	B	M
1. Full employment	—	—	—		
2. Unemployment	SH	SH	SU		
3. Less money	—	—	—	SU	SH
4. Higher *i*, lower *I*	—	SU	—	—	SH'
5. Recession begins	—	—	SU	—	SH'
6. Expected recession	—	SU	SU	SH	SH'
7. Lower *i*	—	SU'	SU	—	SH"
8. Greater unemployment	—	—	SU'	—	SH"

quantity of investment means less unemployment. If this were the only effect, the interest rate would decline sufficiently to eliminate the surplus of capital. Nevertheless, the second effect keeps this from happening. Some of the demand that would have been for capital is instead diverted to the money market because more liquidity is desired. Rather than demanding more products, households and firms demand more money.

The interest rate decline is unable to clear the capital market and a surplus remains in that market, matched by a shortage of money. To eliminate the surplus of capital, price-searching firms cut production and employment, shifting the surplus to the labor market. Unemployment worsens (row 8 in Table 18.6).

The interest rate, if it could have fallen far enough, would have eliminated the surplus of capital by raising investment. Demand for money, however, kept the rate from falling, in effect, by diverting money—funds that would have been supplied in the bond market for investment—to the money market to satisfy greater demands for money holding. This inability of the interest rate to fall sufficiently is the second coordination and control failure that occurs during a recession.

The Multiplier Process

As the recession continues, things get worse. The unemployed workers eventually run out of liquid assets. As a result, they reduce their demands for consumption commodities, creating a surplus. The surplus is matched by a greater shortage of money. The households want more money so they can spend it on products (row 9 in Table 18.7).

Firms react to the reduction in consumption by reducing production and employment, shifting the surplus to the labor market (row 10 in Table 18.7). Unemployment grows.

The newly unemployed workers also eventually exhaust their liquid assets and reduce consumption. Firms again react by cutting output and laying

TABLE 18.7 *The Economy*

	C	*I*	*L*	*B*	*M*
1. Full employment	—	—	—		
2. Unemployment	SH	SH	SU		
3. Less money	—	—	—	SU	SH
4. Higher *i*, lower *I*	—	SU	—	—	SH'
5. Recession begins	—	—	SU	—	SH'
6. Expected recession	—	SU	SU	SH	SH'
7. Lower *i*	—	SU'	SU	—	SH''
8. Greater unemployment	—	—	SU'	—	SH''
9. Multiplier begins	SU	—	SU'	—	SH'''
10. More unemployment	—	—	SU''	—	SH'''
11. Multiplier expands	—	—	SU^n	—	SH^n

off more workers. This continues until the recession reaches bottom at a point where the multiplier process plays itself out (row 11 of Table 18.7).

During the multiplier process, household demand for money really represents a demand for products. Households ask for money only because it is the medium of exchange. But firms won't read the demand for money the same way they read a direct demand for products; the demand for money is not an effective signal and reward for firms. For one thing, demand for money is often simply a demand to hold, not a demand eventually to spend. For another, eventual spending usually accrues to other producers.

Even if firms want to hire the workers, the money is often unavailable. Firms say to workers, "You must buy our products before we hire you, since we need money to pay your wages." Simultaneously, the workers say to firms, "You must hire us before we buy your products, since we need money to buy your products." Nevertheless, given the level of prices and wages, there isn't enough money for all transactions to occur.

The inability of a demand for money to be an effective demand for products is the third coordination and control failure that occurs during a recessionary process.

Recovery

In time, recovery begins. Price-searching workers, discovering that no jobs exist at previous wages, start to accept lower wages. Lower wages are better than no wages. Firms in the economy respond by raising production and employment, and reducing product prices. Once workers earn more, they resume their consumption expenditures. This causes the multiplier process to act in reverse. Also, recessionary expectations are eliminated. This causes investment to increase to further increase aggregate demand. Full employment resumes (row 12 in Table 18.8).

TABLE 18.8   The Economy

	C	I	L	B	M
1. Full employment	—	—	—		
2. Unemployment	SH	SH	SU		
3. Less money	—	—	—	SU	SH
4. Higher i, lower I	—	SU	—	—	SH'
5. Recession begins	—	—	SU	—	SH'
6. Expected recession	—	SU	SU	SH	SH'
7. Lower i	—	SU'	SU	—	SH''
8. Greater unemployment	—	—	SU'	—	SH''
9. Multiplier begins	SU	—	SU'	—	SH'''
10. More unemployment	—	—	SU''	—	SH'''
11. Multiplier expands	—	—	SU^n	—	SH^n
12. Recovery	—	—	—	—	—

MONEY AND THREE MARKET FAILURES

In Chapter 17, we noted that recessions are associated with money-using, capitalistic economies. They occur when price searchers respond to sudden decreases in aggregate demand by reducing production and employment rather than prices and wages. From our discussion in this chapter, we can also say that they are caused by a series of breakdowns in the economy's systems of coordination and control, failures that result largely from the role that money can play both as a medium of exchange and as a store of value.

We can easily see money's role in each of the failures. In the first failure, product shortages don't match the labor surplus only because people can demand money rather than products. When the second failure occurs, the interest rate fails to decline enough to increase investment and eliminate the surplus of capital only because some of the demand that could have gone to investment is diverted to the money "market." The lower interest rate increases the liquidity demand for money, something that wouldn't be possible but for the presence of money. Finally, if money didn't exist, then during the multiplier process, households would be forced to demand consumption commodities directly. If they did, the demand for products would be effective in stimulating production and employment.

Our explanation of recession makes it clear that a recession is a system failure rather than the fault of workers or business firms. A recession is an automatic response to a sudden decline in aggregate demand in a price-searching, money-using, capitalistic economy.

Even if the economy eventually adjusts its wages and prices to the new level of aggregate demand to eliminate the recession, the accompanying unemployment makes it a very costly adjustment. It is often much easier to simply avoid the adjustment by increasing aggregate demand with the government fiscal and monetary policies that we will discuss in the next chapter.

MAJOR AND MINOR POINTS

1. Under conditions of unlimited information, prices provide all signals and rewards under capitalism. But when information becomes more limited, whereas prices still provide signals and rewards in the long run, in the short, price searchers respond to surpluses and shortages.

2. Surplus and shortage signals fail to prevent recessions when aggregate demand falls.

3. Aggregation is a process of combining goods or markets into single units.

4. To understand the recessionary process, we can aggregate all goods into five groups:
   a. Consumption commodities
   b. Capital
   c. Labor
   d. Bonds
   e. Money.

5. Consumption commodities, capital, and labor are traded in markets dominated by price searchers. Bonds are traded by price takers. There is no money market as such; money is traded in the other four markets.

6. Higher bond prices are associated with lower interest rates and vice versa.

7. Higher interest rates shift demand from money to bonds. Conversely, lower interest rates shift demand from bonds to money.

8. Say's principle states that supplying one good means demanding another. It implies that a surplus of one good must be matched by a shortage of other goods.

9. Say's law is a special case of Say's principle. It claims that the act of supplying one nonmoney good implies the act of demanding another nonmoney good. Say's law holds only in a barter economy where neither money nor financial assets exist. Once money is present, people can supply a nonmoney good and demand money in trade.

10. Unemployment is unlikely in a barter economy because workers would demand products in trade for their labor. Product shortages would match labor surpluses (row 2 in Table 18.9).

11. A reduction in the money supply causes a shortage of money. The shortage is matched by a bond surplus as households demand fewer bonds so they can build up their money holdings (row 3). The price of bonds falls as the interest rate rises, eliminating the bond surplus. But the higher interest rate, although it reduces the shortage of money, also causes a surplus of capital, since a higher interest rate reduces investment (row 4). Price-searching firms cut production and employment in the capital industries, shifting the surplus to the labor market (row 5). Cyclical unemployment begins.

12. With reductions in production and employment, recessionary expectations occur. Investment then falls to create a surplus of capital. The surplus is matched by a shortage of bonds as firms borrow less since they want to buy less capital (row 6). The bond shortage raises the bond price; it lowers the interest rate. The lower interest rate increases investment but also raises demand for money. Some of the surplus of capital remains and is matched by a shortage of money

TABLE 18.9 The Economy

	C	I	L	B	M
1. Full employment	—	—	—		
2. Barter unemployment	SH	SH	SU		
3. Less money	—	—	—	SU	SH
4. Higher interest	—	SU	—	—	SH$'$
5. A recession begins	—	—	SU	—	SH$'$
6. Expected recession	—	SU	SU	SH	SH$'$
7. Lower interest	—	SU$'$	SU	—	SH$''$
8. More unemployment	—	—	SU$'$	—	SH$''$
9. Multiplier begins	SU	—	SU$'$	—	SH$'''$
10. More unemployment	—	—	SU$''$	—	SH$'''$
11. Multiplier expands	—	—	SU^n	—	SH^n
12. Recovery	—	—	—	—	—

(row 7). Firms reduce production and employment, shifting the surplus from the capital market to the labor market, increasing cyclical unemployment (row 8).

13. Unemployed workers eventually run out of savings and reduce their demands for consumption commodities. A surplus of consumption commodities occurs and is matched by a shortage of money. The money shortage represents a desire not for money but for products that can later be purchased with money (row 9). The multiplier continues until it plays itself out (row 11). Nevertheless, firms cut the production of consumption commodities, shift the surplus to the labor market, and cause unemployment to grow (row 10).

14. Eventual recovery occurs as price-searching workers accept lower wages. Greater production reduces prices. With greater earnings and the elimination of recessionary expectations, demands for consumption commodities and capital increase (row 12).

15. During the recessionary process, three money-associated coordination and control failures occur:

    a. Product shortages don't match labor surpluses. People demand money instead of products.

    b. Interest rates don't fall far enough to raise investment to eliminate all surpluses of capital. As interest rates fall, people demand money as well as capital.

    c. Workers demand money to buy commodities, but the money demands are ineffective in signaling and rewarding production increases.

QUESTIONS

1. Why will unemployment be quickly eliminated in a strictly barter economy?
2. What might cause a decrease in aggregate demand?
3. Why will a sudden decrease in the supply of money start a recession?
4. How can a decrease in production and employment reduce investment?

5. How can consumption fall to make a recession worsen?
6. When will recovery from a recession occur?
7. What is money's role in the recessionary process?
8. Discuss the following terms and concepts:

Aggregation	Say's law
Consumption commodities market	Barter and unemployment
	Beginning of a recession
Capital market	Failure 1: money holding
Labor market	Recessionary expectations
Bond market	Failure 2: high interest rate
Price of bonds and interest	Multiplier process
Money and its "market"	Failure 3: money to spend
Say's principle	Recovery

APPLICATIONS

1. Why don't we aggregate money and all other items into two goods when we want to explain a recession?
2. Suppose you purchase a government bond yielding 10% interest on its face value. If the economy's interest rate suddenly rises so that new bonds yield 20%, how can you nevertheless sell your bond?
3. When the U. S. Treasury sells bonds, it keeps payments on the bonds the same. The bonds are simply auctioned off to the highest bidders. When the bonds are sold at higher prices, what does this tell you about the economy's interest rate?
4. If there is no money market, how can you buy money?
5. Why will people hold more money when the interest rate falls and less when it rises?
6. Explain the relationship between MV and money holding.
7. How could you reduce the velocity of the money you own?
8. The price of money is the interest rate. Is this true?
9. Are bonds the only things people will sell to obtain money?
10. Does Say's principle imply that the act of demanding a consumption commodity or a unit of capital requires the simultaneous act of supplying some other physical good?
11. Say's principle will hold as long as we neither steal goods nor give them away. Explain.
12. How does the shortage of money that occurs during the multiplier process differ from the shortage of money that occurs during the beginning of a recession?
13. Are we as individuals to blame for a recession?
14. Are recessions a result of monopolistic behavior?

19

Fiscal and Monetary Policies

Cyclical unemployment occurs after price searchers respond to a sudden decrease in aggregate demand by reducing production and employment rather than prices and wages. It is a problem that lies beyond our individual control. The federal government, however, may be able to solve it. Although the government can't do much to push prices and wages downward, it can adjust aggregate demand upward.

To increase aggregate demand, the government can use antirecessionary fiscal or monetary policies. **Fiscal policies** change the levels of government spending and taxation whereas **monetary policies** change the money supply.

In this chapter, we first explain antirecessionary fiscal policies, their economic effects, and some problems associated with their use. Then we look at antirecessionary monetary policies, their effects, and problems.

But that's not all. Fiscal policies may be able to directly increase aggregate supply by increasing the production of goods. They can do this by causing an expansion of the labor force and an increase in investment. In the chapter's last section, we examine these and other supply-side effects of fiscal policies. They were the focus of the theories guiding the fiscal policies of the Reagan presidency.

ANTIRECESSIONARY FISCAL POLICIES

Antirecessionary fiscal policies attempt to increase the level of aggregate demand by increasing government spending or by reducing taxes. To explain how the policies work, we need to begin by restricting our definition of **aggregate demand** (AD) to the total demand for just the products produced in the economy. Aggregate demand comprises three elements:

  a. Consumption (C)—demand for consumption commodities by households;
  b. Investment (I)—demand for capital by business firms;
  c. Government spending (G)—demand for public goods by government.

That is, $AD = C + I + G$.

To increase aggregate demand, antirecessionary fiscal policies try to increase one or more of the components. When government spending is increased, the policies raise the demand directly by increasing G. When taxes are cut, the policies raise aggregate demand indirectly by stimulating private spending, $C + I$.

There is more to antirecessionary fiscal policies than increasing government spending or cutting taxes. The policies also require that the Treasury obtain funds by using one of three financing methods:

  a. Taxation;
  b. Borrowing previously created money by selling bonds to the public;
  c. Borrowing newly created money by selling bonds to the Federal Reserve banks.

These financing methods can indirectly reduce some of the components of aggregate demand. As a result, before we can determine the expansionary effects that a fiscal policy will have on aggregate demand, we need to know how the policy is financed.

Five Antirecessionary Fiscal Policies

The many antirecessionary fiscal policies that can be employed are combinations of but five basic policies. Let's examine each of the five policies and see how they can increase aggregate demand.

$\uparrow G + \uparrow T$.   The first policy is a balanced budget increase in government spending and taxes. The increase in government spending directly stimulates aggregate demand, whereas the higher taxes indirectly depress aggregate demand by reducing private consumption and investment. Private spending falls because consumers and firms usually pay taxes with money they would have otherwise spent on consumption commodities and capital, respectively.

The policy increases aggregate demand to the extent that government spending rises more than private spending falls.

For example, suppose the government increases G by $100 billion and obtains the money by raising taxes by $100 billion. If the tax increase then causes private spending (C + I) to fall by, say, $90 billion, the policy raises aggregate demand a net of $10 billion. The policy raises aggregate demand $10 billion because the taxes absorb $10 billion that wouldn't have otherwise been spent and give it to the government to spend. The other 90 billion tax dollars that the government spends would have otherwise been $90 billion of C + I.

↑ G + ↑ Bp. The second spending policy raises government spending, keeps taxes the same, and calls on the Treasury to sell bonds to the public to finance the resulting deficit. The policy avoids the negative effects that taxes have on private consumption and investment. However, the Treasury's borrowing has its own negative effects on private spending. To sell its bonds, the Treasury offers higher interest rates so that it can borrow money that would have otherwise been borrowed by business firms. Firms are "crowded out" of the bond market and forced to reduce their demands for capital. Investment, I, falls. Also, the higher interest rate motivates households to save more, reducing consumption, C.

The policy increases aggregate demand only to the extent that the government borrows money that would have been held rather than invested or consumed. If it borrows money that households or firms would have eventually spent, reductions in C + I offset the increase in G.

↑ G + ↑ Bf. The third spending policy increases government spending, keeps taxes constant, and has the Treasury finance the resulting deficit by selling bonds to the Federal Reserve banks in exchange for newly created money. The Treasury's sale of bonds on the open bond market corresponds with the Fed's purchases of bonds in that market. Since the policy calls on the Treasury to obtain new money, private consumption and investment remain the same. This policy is by far the most antirecessionary of all fiscal policies.

The preceding three policies each increase government spending. If politicians prefer to keep government spending constant, they can use one of the following two fiscal policies that involve tax cuts. However, dollar for dollar, tax cuts are less effective in stimulating aggregate demand than increases in government spending. The reason is simple: Although the government spends every dollar it receives, households and business firms often hold some of the money they indirectly obtain from tax cuts.

↓ T + ↑ Bp. The fourth policy reduces taxes, maintains the same level of government spending, and requires the Treasury to finance the resulting deficit by selling bonds to the public. Aggregate demand rises when tax cuts raise consumption and investment more than the bond sales reduce consumption and investment.

$\downarrow T + \uparrow Bf$.   Finally, the fifth policy cuts taxes, keeps government spending constant, and finances the resulting deficit with new money. Instead of borrowing old money from the public, the Treasury borrows new money from the Fed banks. Since borrowing new money doesn't reduce private spending, the policy strongly stimulates aggregate demand.

In addition to the financing method used, the antirecessionary effects of a fiscal policy depend on the particular goods that the government buys. For maximum effect, the government needs to buy goods the public wouldn't have otherwise bought. If instead the government buys goods like food or hydroelectric projects, private consumption and investment will fall, partly offsetting the stimulus provided by the increase in government spending.

Furthermore, when taxes or bond sales to the public are involved, the expansionary effects depend on which particular individuals are affected by the taxes or bond sales. For maximum effect, the government needs to obtain money that wouldn't have been spent or give money to individuals who are most likely to spend it. For example, since the rich spend a smaller proportion of their income than the poor, taxing or borrowing from the rich will reduce private spending less, while granting the poor tax breaks will increase private spending more.

As noted previously, the antirecessionary fiscal policies that are actually employed in the real world are any one of the many possible combinations of the preceding five policies. We can, however, summarize with a simple prescription for fighting a recession: raise government spending, cut taxes, and fund the resulting deficits by borrowing old or, preferably, new money.

Automatic Stabilizers

Although very strong antirecessionary fiscal policies require new legislation, some fiscal policies occur automatically. For example, if the economy declines, existing laws raise government spending on unemployment and welfare benefits. At the same time, tax revenues decline. The resulting deficits can then be financed by borrowing from the public or the Fed.

By understanding these automatic adjustments, we can explain why presidential candidates spend so much time debating the size of future government deficits. The deficits will depend upon future economic activity since many spending and tax laws don't specify dollar amounts. During the 1984 presidential campaign, Ronald Reagan predicted smaller deficits than Walter Mondale by assuming a more prosperous economic future.

The Side Effects of Fiscal Policies

Although antirecessionary fiscal policies can eliminate recessions, the policies can have other economic effects that may prevent their use. They can create inflation, increase the national debt, and misallocate resources and wealth.

Inflationary Effects

Before we explain how fiscal policies can cause inflation, let's complicate our theory by recognizing that price searchers will initially respond to sudden changes in demands by changing prices and wages as well as employment and production. For example, a price-searching firm will increase its price as well as its production when demand for its product suddenly rises. And when the demand suddenly falls, it will reduce its price as well as its production.

The assumption that price searchers change prices and wages as well as production and employment gives rise to a short-term trade-off between inflation and unemployment. Less unemployment is accompanied by more inflation; less inflation is accompanied by more unemployment.

The trade-off doesn't exist in the long term. When aggregate demand decreases or increases, price searchers eventually change only prices and wages. Employment and production move to the level where cyclical unemployment doesn't exist.

We can explain all this better and also deal with how antirecessionary fiscal policies can cause inflation by using a graphical analysis. Suppose that the total unemployment rate in the economy is 10% (a combination of 2% classical, 3% frictional, and 5% cyclical unemployment) and that inflation doesn't exist. This circumstance is identified by point *A* in Figure 19.1.

Figure 19.1   Inflation and Unemployment

Fiscal and monetary policies can only temporarily reduce the level of unemployment below the classical plus frictional level (shown by the vertical dashed line). In the long run, unemployment will be on that line. The level of inflation, a particular point, will be determined by the extent to which aggregate demand grows relative to the supply of nonmoney goods.

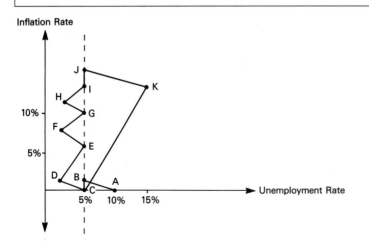

Under these recessionary conditions, an antirecessionary fiscal policy can be relatively noninflationary. Price searchers will initially respond to an increase in aggregate demand by increasing prices and wages only slightly and production and employment significantly. If the increase in demand is just sufficient to reduce unemployment to the 5% classical plus frictional unemployment level, inflation may be very low, perhaps only 1%. This is shown in Figure 19.1 by movement from *A* to *B*.

The curve made by the movement from *A* to *B* is a **Phillips curve**, a curve that illustrates the relationship between inflation and unemployment. The assumption that price searchers initially (in the short term) respond to changes in demands by changing prices and wages as well as production and employment implies that the short-term Phillips curve slopes downward, reflecting a trade-off between inflation and unemployment.

The economy won't stay at point *B*. Since the increases in demands will be matched by increases in supplies, prices will eventually stop increasing and the inflation will cease. The economy will move to a situation represented by point *C* where unemployment is 5% and inflation is nonexistent. After enough time has passed for all adjustments to take place (in the long term), expansionary fiscal policies need not be inflationary.

What if the government mistakenly thinks that the classical plus frictional unemployment level is only 3% rather than 5% and responds by increasing aggregate demand even more? Then price searchers will again respond initially by increasing prices, wages, employment, and production. The greater demands will be met by higher prices and wages and expanding supplies. Inflation will rise while unemployment drops below the 5% classical plus frictional unemployment level. It can drop below that level because labor and other resources normally used to search for better jobs will be used to produce products. To some degree, the greater outputs will keep prices from rising as much as they otherwise would have. The economy will move from a point represented in Figure 19.1 by *C* to *D*.

In the long term, prices and wages will increase much more and production and employment will decline. Labor surpluses below the 5% classical plus frictional unemployment level are inefficient. Workers will eventually discover that when they search longer for jobs, employers reward them with higher wages. Job searches will gradually increase, wages will rise, and output will fall. The reductions in employment and production will push unemployment up to 5%, and the reduction in product supply relative to demand will create, say, 6% inflation. This is represented in Figure 19.1 by a movement from *D* to *E*.

These new levels of unemployment and inflation could continue if the government kept increasing aggregate demand at the same rate, feeding the 6% price increases. However, if government still thinks that 5% unemployment is recessionary, it may raise aggregate demand still more. The greater increase in aggregate demand will then again cause temporary increases in prices, wages, employment, and production; inflation will rise and unemployment will fall. This is shown in Figure 19.1 by the movement from point *E* to *F*. In the long term, however, unemployment will return to 5% and inflation will increase to perhaps 10%, as reflected by point G.

Government may again increase the growth of aggregate demand and perhaps unemployment will fall once more. But eventually, price searchers will develop expectations of even greater inflation. As a result, they will increase the growth of prices and wages immediately. Such a change is represented on the graph by a movement from I to J. It seems that the ability of fiscal policies to drive unemployment temporarily below classical plus frictional levels depends on the degree to which price searchers can be continually fooled.

In time, the government may decide to eliminate the inflation. To do so, it will have to cut aggregate demand. It can reduce aggregate demand by cutting its spending, raising taxes, and reducing the money supply, reversing the antirecessionary fiscal policies we discussed earlier. Unfortunately, price searchers will respond initially by cutting production and employment as well as the growth of prices and wages. A recession will be one of the costs of reducing inflation. The economy might move from a position represented in Figure 19.1 by J to one represented by K. Then, in the long term, after a recession, the economy can return to full employment and zero inflation, as represented by point C.

This analysis implies that although the Phillips curve may initially sloped downward—reflecting a trade-off between unemployment and inflation—the Phillips curve is eventually vertical. If enough time passes, there is no cyclical unemployment. The unemployment rate stays at the classical plus frictional level. And the inflation rate is determined by the growth of the supply of money relative to the supply of nonmoney goods. In the long term, inflation is unrelated to the level of unemployment.

The National Debt

In addition to possibly causing inflation, antirecessionary fiscal policies usually increase the size of the **national debt**, the dollar value of all outstanding federal government bonds. The national debt rises whenever deficits require the Treasury to borrow more money from the public or the Federal Reserve system.

In 1986, the U.S. national debt was $2125 billion, about $9000 per person and 50% of the GNP. Although the size of the U.S. national debt as a percentage of the GNP has risen a great deal in the last 5 years, still, compared to earlier periods and to the debts of other nations, it remains fairly small. For example, at the end of World War II, the U.S. national debt was more than the GNP. Also, England's national debt in 1818, just before her greatest century of economic progress, is estimated to have been twice as large as her GNP.

The effects related to the national debt are complex. To simplify our analysis, let's begin by assuming that national output stays the same. We will later relax this assumption. It is a very restrictive assumption since the usual reason for increasing the national debt is to raise production.

If the government consumes more and if the Treasury doesn't borrow from foreigners (foreigners own about one-fourth of the U.S national debt), then the public must immediately consume and invest less. This is obvious when taxes are increased, since households and firms must give up money that they would have otherwise spent.

It is less obvious but equally true when the government chooses to borrow from private creditors, thereby increasing the national debt. The burden of reduced consumption and investment is then simply concentrated on the government's creditors rather than being borne by the public at large. The creditors reduce consumption and investment so the government can consume more and other citizens can consume and invest the same amount. Of course, the creditors expect to be compensated by the other citizens in the form of future interest plus principle. In the future, the creditors will be able to consume and invest more while other citizens consume less.

Rather than raising taxes or selling bonds to private creditors, the government can finance its spending by selling bonds to the Fed; this is called *monetizing the debt*. Nevertheless, private consumption and investment must immediately fall if government spending rises while national production stays the same. The reduction in private spending is caused by the inflation tax. The public will be able to keep its money and spend the same amount; it will simply buy fewer goods because of inflation. The government will then be able to buy more goods.

The national debt, or any government financing method, doesn't determine when particular individuals must reduce consumption and investment. If the government chooses to increase the national debt by borrowing from private creditors, individuals can nevertheless cut their personal consumption or investment whenever they wish. If they want to delay personal spending reductions, they can simply do nothing and be forced to cut back later when taxes or inflation increase as the Treasury pays interest or principle on the national debt. If individuals instead want to reduce their spending immediately, they can join the government's creditors by purchasing government bonds. In the future, they will be able to maintain consumption and investment by using the interest and principle from their bonds to pay higher taxes or prices.

If the government uses the inflation tax, individuals can also cut spending whenever they want. If individuals want to cut back immediately, no action is necessary. Higher inflation will force them to buy fewer goods. If they prefer to maintain present consumption and investment and reduce spending in the future, they can borrow from private creditors to pay the higher prices.

Finally, taxes don't force individuals to reduce consumption and investment at any point in time. If individuals want to reduce spending immediately, they can do so and pay the taxes. If they want to cut spending later, they can borrow from private creditors, raising the national private debt, and cut spending in the future to pay their creditors.

The way the government finances its spending doesn't necessarily matter to individuals. What matters is that government spending sooner or later forces individuals to consume less.

All that we have said is predicated on the assumption that national output stays the same. If national output increases, then it is possible for government to buy more without the public buying less. Formerly unemployed resources can essentially produce the public goods.

Misallocations of Resources and Wealth

In addition to possibly causing inflation and increasing the national debt, fiscal policies can misallocate resources and wealth. Misallocations of resources will occur when the public goods that are purchased as part of a fiscal policy are less valuable than the private goods that could have been produced instead. For example, when government constructs a highway as part of a fiscal policy aimed at increasing aggregate demand, it isn't because the public necessarily wants the highway rather than more private housing. The highway is built to reduce unemployment. If, however, additional housing would have been possible and more preferable, then the reallocation of resources toward the highway and away from housing will be a misallocation.

Reallocations of wealth will occur if government subsidies or tax cuts are unevenly distributed among households and firms in the economy. If the reallocations are undesirable, they become misallocations.

Problems With Fiscal Policies

It appears that the negative side effects of fiscal policies can be significant. Nevertheless, even if government is willing to take the risk of high costs, it must still overcome some problems before the policies can be implemented.

Political Problems

The first problem is political. An increase in government spending or a tax cut requires the Congress to pass and the president to sign various specific laws. Therefore, not only do the president and Congress have to agree to use an antirecessionary fiscal policy, but they must also agree on the particular expenditures that the federal government will make and the exact taxes that will be cut and by how much. These agreements can be difficult to achieve.

Moreover, the most effective antirecessionary fiscal policies require that government deficits be funded by the Fed. In these instances, the Fed's board of governors must also be willing to create new money to stimulate aggregate demand. But the board's cooperation is uncertain. More than once, the expansionary effects of the deficit spending policies of presidents and Congress have been minimized by the board's unwillingness to increase the supply of money.

Time Lags

Political problems accentuate another problem: time lags. First, it takes time for the president and Congress to agree and pass legislation changing spending and taxing. It generally takes many months for a budget to be passed by Congress and signed into law by the president.

A second lag occurs because the federal government and taxpayers don't spend money immediately. Five years may pass before a $1 billion dam is built. Also, households may take six months to spend a tax cut.

Finally, once the money is spent, it won't have an immediate effect on production and employment. Price searchers can't adjust production and employment instantly and it takes time for the multiplier process to work its way through the economy.

Prediction Difficulties

Time lags would not be a problem if the government could predict future economic activity. With accurate predictions, the government could simply begin sooner. However, the government's abilities to predict are not that good. When recessionary predictions are wrong, antirecessionary fiscal policies will become very inflationary policies.

Political, time-lag, and prediction problems prevent the use of fiscal policies as devices to fine-tune the economy. The problems relegate the effective use of fiscal policies to significant and certain recessionary conditions.

EXPANSIONARY MONETARY POLICIES

The costs and problems associated with fiscal policies explain why many economists and politicians prefer monetary policies. Although increases in the money supply can be inflationary, they don't increase the national debt nor do they extensively reallocate resources and wealth. Furthermore, there are fewer political bottlenecks; the Fed's board is relatively independent of the president and Congress.

However, monetary policies also suffer from time lag and prediction problems. It can take months before an increase in the money supply causes its ultimate increase in production and employment. Furthermore, abilities to predict are still limited.

Although monetary policies seem to have lower costs and lack some of the problems of fiscal policies, two possibilities can make them ineffective in raising aggregate demand. The first is called the *reserves trap*. When the board tries to increase the money supply, it usually increases the excess reserves of commercial banks and other depository institutions. The intent is that these institutions then make new loans and create new money. But especially during recessionary periods, depository institutions may be content to hold greater reserves to avoid granting loans to firms that may become bankrupt. If the depository institutions simply hold greater reserves, the money supply may grow very little.

The Fed can usually solve the reserves-trap problem. It can simply create even greater reserves.

The second problem is the *liquidity trap*. People hold money for its liquidity, the attribute that it can be easily exchanged for other goods. Perfect liquidity is why money functions as a medium of exchange. There is a cost, however: the sacrifice of interest that could have been earned had bonds or other financial instruments been held instead. If the interest rate falls, the cost of liquidity declines and people will hold more money.

Now when the Fed increases the money supply, the rate of interest in the economy usually falls. As a result, more money is held. Unfortunately, if the interest rate falls far enough, almost all of the new money may be held—trapped—and not spent. Aggregate demand will remain almost the same as the greater M is offset by a lower V. Under these conditions, monetary policies may be abandoned and fiscal policies employed instead. If the public won't spend new money, then the money may simply be given to the government, which can spend it.

SUPPLY-SIDE FISCAL POLICIES

Up to now, our concern has been with the effects that fiscal policies have on aggregate demand. However, changes in government spending and taxes also can have **supply-side** effects, effects on the supply of products in the nation, because they can directly cause changes in employment, production, and economic growth.

Taxes, Employment, Production, and Growth

Taxes directly affect employment and production because workers are motivated by take-home pay, not gross earnings. For example, when lower taxes increase take-home pay, individuals usually choose to work more. As they do, employment rises and with it, production.

The increases in work take various forms. Workers

   a. Shift from part-time to full-time jobs
   b. Stop being housepersons and find paying jobs
   c. Take shorter and less frequent vacations
   d. Opt for later retirement
   e. Increase their work weeks
   f. Reduce the time they spend between jobs.

Tax cuts also increase the value of the products produced in the economy. The ranks of accountants, lawyers, investment advisors, and tax consultants shrink as people reduce their efforts to avoid taxes. These professionals can then be employed to produce more socially valuable consumption goods or capital rather than act to redistribute existing income. Also, households and business firms base their spending and investment decisions on the fundamental values of alternatives rather than on eventual taxes.

Moreover, tax cuts can increase economic growth. If taxes on interest earnings are reduced, households will consume less and save more, making more money available for investment. Also, if business earnings are taxed less, business firms will increase investment. With less consumption, more savings, and greater investment, resources will be shifted away from the production of present consumption items and toward capital formation. As a result, productive capacity will increase; economic growth will occur.

Tax Rates and Tax Revenues

Since lower taxes increase employment, production, and economic growth, a decrease in tax rates will not cause a proportional decrease in tax revenues. For instance, a 10% reduction in tax rates may reduce tax revenues only 5% if employment and production rise 5%. In fact, at very high rates of taxation, a decrease in tax rates can increase tax revenues. For example, if tax rates are cut from 90% to 80%, and employment and production rise by 20%, tax revenues will increase.

We can use the **Laffer curve** to understand these effects. It is a curve that illustrates the relationship between **marginal tax rates** (the rates on additional income) and tax revenues. As shown in Figure 19.2, when marginal tax rates initially increase, tax revenues rise. Although workers may reduce employment somewhat when tax rates initially rise, they don't cut back enough to offset the positive effects of the higher tax rates. However, tax rates eventually reach such high levels that workers cut employment so much that the positive effects of the higher tax rates are negated. In the extreme case where taxes are 100%, no work occurs and no revenues are collected.

Figure 19.2 The Laffer Curve

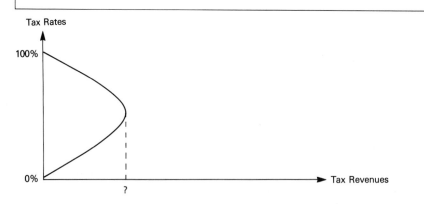

Tax revenues rise when tax rates are initially increased. At sufficiently high tax rates, however, further increases cause tax revenues to fall, until at the 100% tax rate, no revenues are obtained.

Although the Laffer curve eventually bends backward, we can't predict at which rate. Most advocates of supply-side economics argue that the rate is fairly low. They therefore feel that reducing most tax rates will significantly raise revenues. Their critics believe that the rate at which the tax revenues will fall is relatively high and therefore a lowering most tax rates will usually reduce revenues. At this point in time, the evidence is inconclusive.

Deficit Financing

When lower tax rates increase tax revenues, the lower rates will increase employment, production, saving, and economic growth. But when lower tax rates cause tax revenues to fall, the expansionary supply-side effects will be greatly reduced if government spending is maintained at previous levels. This is because the government will have to finance the resulting deficits, and that financing will reduce the rewards for work and investment to offset the effects of the lower tax rates.

For example, if the Treasury borrows new money from the Fed banks to finance the deficits, then the money supply will rise and the public will be taxed with inflation. The tax cut may increase take-home pay, but inflation will eat up the value of the extra dollars. Net real rewards for work and investment will fall and households and firms will respond the same way they would have responded to higher taxes: They will cut employment, consumption, saving, and investment.

If, on the other hand, the Treasury borrows old money from private creditors, the public at large can temporarily maintain consumption. But future consumption will have to be reduced when either taxes rise or inflation occurs so that interest or principle can be paid on the national debt. Also, present investment will fall because interest rates will increase. The Treasury will borrow money that business firms would have otherwise borrowed and spent on capital. Economic growth will then decline.

Reducing Government Spending

Of course, government spending can be reduced if tax revenues fall. Under these conditions, supply-side expansionary effects can be obtained. With lower tax payments and less government spending, the direct rewards to individuals for work and investment will rise and with those increases, so will employment, saving, investment, and economic growth.

The fact that individuals can obtain more private goods with the same amount of work and investment doesn't mean that they obtain goods of greater value. Government goods may be more valuable to them than the private goods they receive instead. It's just that as individuals, they can obtain the government goods whether or not they work and invest. Therefore, individuals will not consider government goods as direct rewards for their personal work and investment.

Demand- and Supply-Side Economics

The supply-side policies we have been discussing aren't intentionally antirecessionary fiscal policies. Rather than pulling workers out of the ranks of the unemployed, supply-side policies are aimed at causing more people to opt for work rather than leisure. Also, the policies are directed at changing the mix of products in favor of capital and away from consumption commodities, to increase economic growth. Supply-side policies may be able to achieve these goals during periods of relative prosperity as well as during recessions.

Nevertheless, supply-side policies can become antirecessionary fiscal policies that increase aggregate demand. This will occur to the extent that reductions in tax rates fail to increase tax revenues. If government spending remains the same, deficits will result and to finance the deficits, the Treasury will have to borrow either old or new money. The tax reductions financed by old or new money will then increase aggregate demand. Many economists argue that the supply-side policies of the Reagan presidency stimulated the economy, not primarily by raising the returns to work, saving, and investing, but by increasing aggregate demand.

We have now completed our discussion of fiscal and monetary policies. In the next chapter, we deal with international trade, examining exchange and production from a worldwide perspective.

MAJOR AND MINOR POINTS

1. Government can avoid or eliminate a recession by increasing aggregate demand.
2. Aggregate demand is basically comprised of consumption, investment, and government spending.
3. Fiscal policies that involve changes in government spending and financing, and monetary policies that raise the money supply, may increase aggregate demand.
4. Increases in government spending can raise aggregate demand, but only to the extent that Treasury financing doesn't reduce consumption and investment.
5. Both taxes and more borrowing in bond markets can reduce private spending significantly. Only when the Treasury sells bonds to the Fed in exchange for new money is private spending unaffected.
6. Tax cuts can increase consumption and investment. But when resulting deficits are financed by borrowing from the public, some of the increase can be offset by lower investment. Financing with new money is much more expansionary.
7. When recessions occur, government spending rises and taxes decline automatically to stimulate aggregate demand.
8. Fiscal policies can cause inflation, but when cyclical unemployment exists, inflation will be low since greater supplies will generally meet greater demands.
9. Governments can cause unemployment to fall temporarily below frictional unemployment levels. But in the long term, inflation will be the only result.

10. We can illustrate the relationship between inflation and unemployment with a Phillips curve. Our theory implies that while the short-term Phillips curve may slope downward, reflecting a trade-off between inflation and unemployment, the long-term Phillips curve is vertical. In the long term, unemployment is at the classical plus frictional unemployment level, while inflation is largely determined by the growth of the money supply relative to the supply of products.

11. Deficit spending policies stimulate aggregate demand. They also raise the national debt.

12. When national output is constant, the national debt doesn't allow the nation to increase government spending without cutting present private consumption and investment.

13. We can cut our individual consumption and investment in the present or in the future, no matter how the government finances its spending.

14. If government spending increases national output, neither consumption nor investment need to decline. Essentially, public goods can be produced with formerly unemployed resources.

15. Fiscal policies can misallocate resources and wealth by causing an undesirable increase in the production of public goods relative to private goods, and a shift in wealth among the citizens.

16. Fiscal policies can encounter political problems because they require agreements among the president, Congress, and the Fed.

17. Also, time-lag problems can occur because it takes time to pass laws, spend money, and increase production and employment.

18. Finally, prediction difficulties can make antirecessionary fiscal policies inflationary.

19. Monetary policies don't have some of the costs and problems of fiscal policies.

20. But monetary policies can suffer from a reserves trap if banks keep greater reserves and don't increase the money supply.

21. Monetary policies can also suffer from a liquidity trap if lower interest rates induce the public to hold new money rather than spend it to increase aggregate demand.

22. When monetary policies fail because the public won't spend new money, fiscal policies can be used. The new money can be given to the government and spent on public goods.

23. Tax reductions can increase employment, production, and economic growth by raising the rewards to work, saving, and investment.

24. The Laffer curve is a backward-bending curve that shows tax revenues initially rising with higher marginal tax rates. However, at sufficiently high rates, the curve bends backwards as tax revenues fall.

25. If tax rates are reduced and tax revenues fall, and if government spending is maintained, deficit financing will result. The deficit financing can largely offset the positive effects of the tax reductions on employment, production, and economic growth. If deficits are financed with new money, an inflation tax will reduce the gains to work and investment. If deficits are financed by borrowing old money, higher interest rates will reduce investment immediately and higher future taxes will reduce consumption and investment in the future.

26. A reduction in government spending and taxes will increase the direct gains to individuals from work and investment. This is because government goods are not directly linked to work and investment while private goods are.

27. Supply-side economic policies are primarily concerned with increasing the size of the labor force and raising the amount of saving and investment, not with cyclical unemployment. However, when the policies involve cutting taxes and the financing of the resulting deficits by borrowing new or old money, the policies may also increase aggregate demand to create either a recovery from a recession or inflation.

QUESTIONS

1. What are fiscal and monetary policies and how can they be used to reduce cyclical unemployment?
2. When will an increase in government spending, financed by an increase in taxes, increase aggregate demand?
3. When will an increase in government spending, financed by bond sales to the public, increase aggregate demand?
4. When will an increase in government spending, financed by bond sales to the Federal Reserve banks, increase aggregate demand?
5. When will a decrease in taxes (with constant government spending), financed by bond sales to the public, increase aggregate demand?
6. When will a decrease in taxes (with constant government spending), financed by bond sales to the Federal Reserve banks, increase aggregate demand?
7. How can a recession automatically increase aggregate demand via fiscal policy?
8. When will an antirecessionary fiscal policy cause inflation?
9. When will antirecessionary fiscal policy increase the national debt?
10. Will deficit financing allow a nation to avoid immediate reductions in private consumption and investment?
11. Will deficit financing force particular households to change their consumption and investment decisions relative to other financing methods?
12. How can antirecessionary fiscal policies misallocate resources and wealth?
13. When will antirecessionary fiscal policies be ineffective in fine tuning the economy?
14. When will monetary policies be effective in eliminating recessions?
15. When will monetary policies be ineffective in eliminating recessions?
16. How can taxes reduce employment, production, and economic growth?
17. How can tax cuts increase employment, production, and economic growth?
18. How can decreases in tax rates cause increases in tax revenues?
19. When will supply-side tax cuts increase aggregate demand to increase production and employment?

20. Discuss the following terms and concepts:

Fiscal policies	National debt
Monetary policies	Resource and wealth misallocation
Deficit spending	Agreement problem
$\quad G + T$	Time-lag problem
$\quad G + Bp$	Prediction problem
$\quad G + Bf$	Reserves trap
$\quad T + Bp$	Liquidity trap
$\quad T + Bf$	Supply-side economics
Automatic stabilizers	Tax rate versus tax revenue
Inflation and unemployment	Laffer curve
Phillips curve—short term	Supply- and demand-side
Phillips curve—long term	

APPLICATIONS

1. Foreigners buy consumption and capital goods in the United States. How does this affect aggregate demand?

2. When fiscal policies raise aggregate demand, how is MV affected?

3. Antirecessionary fiscal policies don't work. They were tried during the Great Depression and failed. A war was necessary to pull the economy out of that catastrophe. Evaluate.

4. Was the Great Depression caused by overproduction? Explain.

5. What would the government have to do to keep the level of unemployment in the economy below the level the classical plus frictional unemployment?

6. How can antirecessionary fiscal policies indirectly cause recessions?

7. In equilibrium, the rents of apartments are at levels where 6% vacancies exist. The vacant apartments provide prospective tenants with apartments they can inspect and immediately occupy. But landlords are price searchers and when demands increase, landlords don't raise rents immediately. Vacancy rates fall instead, below the normal 6% level. If government believed that the normal apartment vacancy rate is only 2%, how could it reduce the vacancy rate to 2% and keep it there? Could it do so perpetually?

8. Higher taxes won't raise the national public debt but they may increase the national private debt. Explain.

9. Suppose you presently owe $75,000 on your house and your share of the national debt is $25,000. Had the government raised your taxes in the past, why might it essentially not have affected your total debt or total debt payments?

10. If the government decided to raise taxes by $25,000 to pay off the national debt, how would you react?

11. Who might want the Treasury to borrow from the public or tax them with inflation rather than raise income taxes?

12. Why might political conservatives see deficit spending as a road to socialism?

13. Because of inabilities to predict, fiscal and monetary policies have done more to cause inflation and recession then to solve it. Is this possible?

14. If people negate the antirecessionary effects of new money by not spending it, who will spend it?

15. Supply-side theories are narrow in their perspectives. While they recognize that people may work less because of higher taxes, they don't recognize that people will work more when the taxes are spent to buy them public goods. Is this true?

International Trade and Finance

Foreign currency markets, exchange controls, balance of payments deficits, international gold movements, tariffs—these are just some of the terms associated with international trade, terms that give us the impression that it is teeming with unique phenomena and controlled by complex forces unrelated to domestic exchange. Nevertheless, as we study a theory of international trade in this chapter, we will find that for the most part, international trade is but a complicated special case of interpersonal exchange.

We first develop the theory by recognizing that whereas individuals may live in separate countries and use different national currencies, they nevertheless often value mutually desired goods differently. Then we discuss the theory's explanation and predictions.

After we have examined the theory, we consider five special topics. The topics deal with the impossibility of a balance of payments deficit; your personal Caribbean nation; and tariffs, quotas, and exchange controls. They also discuss the United States Consitition, the British Empire, the European Common Market, and fixed exchange rates.

A THEORY OF INTERNATIONAL TRADE

The Phenomena

International trade is simply trade that moves goods across national boundaries. In the United States, the trade is a significant and rising proportion of total exchange, now accounting for roughly 10% of the goods produced and consumed in the nation. This means that about 10% of the goods we consume were produced by foreigners, and also that foreigners buy approximately 10% of our GNP. For many other nations, international trade is even more extensive, as Table 20.1 shows.

An Explanation: Trading Your Labor for Parisian Cuisine

Value Differentials

To explain the nature of international trade, we must first recognize that international trades are usually between individuals, not governments. Although we may say that the United States buys goods from France, in actuality, citizens in the United States generally purchase goods from their counterparts in France.

Like domestic trades, international trades occur because of value differentials. If you and I value mutually desired goods differently, we will trade. If we live in different countries, the trade will simply be international rather than domestic.

Although both international and domestic trade are caused by value differentials, international trade is more complex because countries employ different monetary forms. For example, if you wanted to trade your labor for some food sold by a New York restaurant, you could sell your labor for dollars and then use the dollars to buy the food. However, if you wanted to visit France and dine in a Parisian restaurant, you couldn't pay with dollars. Dollars buy U.S. goods, not French goods. What would you do? You certainly wouldn't try to find a Parisian restaurant that would give you a job. Instead, you would sell your labor for dollars in the United States, then trade the dollars for French francs (perhaps by dealing with a foreign currency broker), and finally use the francs to buy the Parisian cuisine.

The reason for going from labor, to dollars, to francs, and finally to Parisian cuisine is simple. The number of exchanges would rise, but total transaction costs would still be much lower than the costs of finding a Parisian restaurant that just happened to want either your labor or your dollars.

TABLE 20.1   Exports by Various Nations

COUNTRY	1980 EXPORTS (PERCENTAGE OF GNP)	TOTAL VOLUME (BILLIONS)
The Netherlands	44	$ 74
Canada	25	64
West Germany	24	193
United Kingdom	22	115
Italy	20	78
Japan	12	129

International Currency Markets

The broker from whom you might buy the francs would probably buy them in an **international currency market**, a competitive market in which dollars and other national currencies are traded. Francs can be purchased in that market from other brokers representing French citizens who want to trade francs for dollars so they can subsequently purchase U.S. products, resources, or financial assets. You would generally be able to buy Parisian cuisine only if a French citizen was willing to trade his or her claim against that cuisine for U.S. products, resources, or financial assets. Generally, international currency exchanges are manifestations of international trades of nonmoney goods.

In the international currency market, the dollar price of a franc, the dollar's **foreign exchange rate** (or just the exchange rate), is determined by the supply and demand for francs. That supply and demand is determined primarily by the desires of U.S. and French citizens for each other's products, resources, and financial assets.

In the market, the demand and supply curves have their usual slopes, as shown in Figure 20.1.

The demand curve slopes downward because at a lower dollar price of a franc, U.S. citizens sacrifice fewer U.S. goods to buy the same quantities of French goods. As a result, they want to buy more of the French goods and are therefore willing to buy more francs. For example, if the dollar price of a franc

Figure 20.1   The Dollar Price of a Franc

The exchange rate of dollars and francs is determined by the interaction of supply and demand in the currency market. The supply curve slopes upward and the demand curve downward. The equilibrium exchange rate is the rate associated with the crossing of the curves.

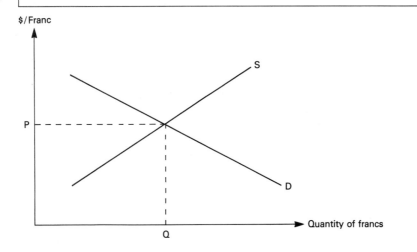

fell by half, you would have to sacrifice half as much labor to buy the same Parisian cuisine. You would then demand more Parisian cuisine and therefore demand a larger quantity of francs.

On the other hand, the supply curve of francs slopes upward. As the dollar price of the franc falls, the French must sacrifice more French goods to buy the same quantities of U.S. goods. They therefore reduce the quantities of the U.S. goods that they demand, and this reduces their desire for dollars. They respond by supplying a smaller quantity of francs. For example, if the dollar price of a franc fell by half (if the franc price of a dollar doubled), a French citizen visiting New York would have to sacrifice twice as many French products to buy a meal in a New York restaurant. Therefore, the French citizen would want to dine less often in the New York restaurant and would respond by wanting to exchange fewer francs for dollars.

Since the demand and supply curves have the normal slopes and since the market is competitive, the exchange rate is at the equilibrium level where the market clears. At above or below market-clearing exchange rates, surpluses or shortages would have existed. They would have created competition among sellers or buyers and caused the exchange rates to change. As the rates changed, quantities demanded and supplied would have changed, eventually eliminating the shortages or surpluses.

For example, if the dollar price of the franc had been above market clearing, a surplus of francs would have occurred. All French citizens willing and able to sell their francs for dollars wouldn't have been able to do so. Competition among them would have ensued causing some of them to accept few dollars for francs. As the dollar price of the franc fell, U.S. citizens would have increased the quantities of francs demanded and French citizens would have reduced their quantities supplied. The exchange rate would have continued to fall until the surplus was eliminated and the market cleared.

Conversely, if the dollar price of the franc had been below market clearing, there would have been a shortage of francs. Competition for francs among U.S. citizens wanting to buy French products, resources, or financial assets would have forced the exchange rate upward. As the rate increased, quantities demanded by U.S. citizens would have fallen and quantities supplied by French citizens would have risen. The exchange rate would have continued to increase until the shortage was eliminated and the market cleared.

Trade only occurs at the market-clearing equilibrium exchange rate, the rate where everyone willing and able to buy or sell at that rate can do so. This means that your broker would be able to buy all the francs you want at the market rate; there would be no shortage of francs.

The Predictions

Based on this explanation, we can make a number of predictions regarding international trade.

International Trades and Currency Exchanges

The first prediction is simple: If individuals live in different countries, own different currencies, and value products, resources, and financial assets differently, then international trades of both national currencies and nonmoney goods will occur. The currency exchanges that occur will reduce the transaction costs of the exchanges of the products, resources, and financial assets.

Comparative Advantages, Resource Specialization, and International Trade

Next, if resources have comparative advantages in production, international specialization will occur and international trade will increase. Specialization will increase production and value differentials.

We discussed specialization and trade caused by comparative advantages when we examined specialization in Chapter 10. It would be redundant to cover all of the same ground here. However, we can highlight the reasoning and the conclusions by expanding the example of trade between the Old South and England during the 1800s.

In the example, we assumed that both the Old South and England were able to produce cotton and garments, but the resources of the Old South had a comparative advantage in producing cotton relative to the resources of England.

Suppose the Old South had to sacrifice 3 bales of cotton to produce one garment. On the other hand, suppose England had to sacrifice only 1 bale of cotton to produce one garment.

Since the Old South had to sacrifice 3 bales of cotton to produce one garment, Southerners would have been willing to pay up to 3 bales of cotton to buy one garment from the English. Since England had to sacrifice one garment to produce 1 bale of cotton, the English would have been pleased to sell a garment in trade for more than 1 bale of cotton. Under these hypothetical conditions, a value differential caused by the presence of different resources and their comparative advantages would have caused trade at a price between 1 and 3 bales of cotton for one garment.

The comparative advantages of different resources gave rise to value differentials, thereby causing international trade between the Old South and England. Of course, since England used pounds while the United States employed dollars, the trades of products were accompanied by exchanges of pounds and dollars.

A Balance of Payments

A third prediction is that if international trade occurs, then the monetary value of every import of a foreign good will be matched by the monetary value of the export of a domestic good. For example, if we want to buy $5 billion worth of French goods, we must sell the French $5 billion worth of U.S. goods.

The types of goods can be different. For example, we may want to import $5 billion worth of merchandise while the French may opt to buy $4 billion worth of merchandise plus $1 billion dollars worth of U.S. Treasury bonds. In that case, our merchandise imports will exceed our merchandise exports, but we will be able to pay for the extra imports because we export U.S. financial assets.

One of the goods the French may want is U.S. dollars. Although they usually use dollars as a medium to obtain other U.S. goods, they will sometimes also temporarily hold dollars as a safe, liquid store of international purchasing power. To the extent that dollars are so used, the United States benefits by being able to import more nonmoney goods than it exports, making up the difference by exporting dollars.

Equilibrium Exchange Rates

A fourth prediction is that if people buy and sell foreign currencies in competitive markets, then neither shortages nor surpluses of foreign exchange will occur. Foreign exchange rates will be in equilibrium at levels where the markets for foreign exchange clear, where the quantities of foreign exchange demanded exactly equal the quantities supplied.

Changes in Exchange Rates

Finally, if supplies or demands for foreign goods change under competitive conditions, foreign exchange rates will also change. For example, suppose that U.S. citizens suddenly demand more French products, resources, and financial assets. Since these French goods can be purchased only with francs, the demand for francs rises. As a result, the dollar price of francs also rises, as shown graphically in Figure 20.2

At the old dollar price of a franc, a shortage of francs would have existed. That shortage would have created competition among the U.S. citizens wanting francs, competition that would have forced the price upward.

As the price of the franc increased, quantity demanded of francs would have fallen. U.S. nationals, realizing that they would have had to sacrifice more U.S. goods to obtain the same French goods, would have reduced their demand for French goods and thus reduced the quantity of francs they would have demanded. Simultaneously, the quantity of francs supplied would have increased. French nationals would have been able to obtain more U.S. nonmoney goods at the sacrifice of the same French nonmoney goods and would have wanted more of the U.S. goods. This would have caused them to want to sell more francs to obtain dollars.

The lower quantity of francs demanded and the higher quantity supplied would have reduced the shortage. Competition would have continued until the dollar price of the franc rose to the equilibrium market-clearing level where quantity demanded equaled quantity supplied.

Figure 20.2 An Increase in Demand for Francs

An increase in demand for francs shifts the demand curve to the right, from *D* to *D'*. The dollar price of the franc rises from *P* to *P'*.

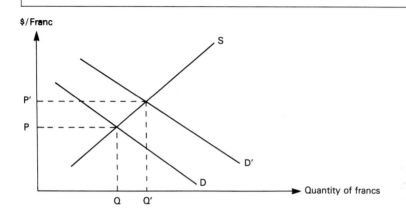

Similarly, any other factors that can cause a change in the demand or the supply of francs will cause a change in the exchange rate.

A Summary of the Theory

We have assumed that

a. Individuals living in different nations value mutually desired goods differently.
b. Nations use different currencies.
c. Resources are unevenly distributed among nations.
d. Foreign currencies are traded in competitive markets.

This has allowed us to predict that

a. International trade involving both nonmoney goods and national currencies will occur.
b. Specialization of resources according to comparative advantages will occur and cause international trade to increase.
c. The monetary value of purchases by foreigners will equal the monetary value of sales to foreigners.
d. Exchange rates among foreign currencies will be in equilibrium at market-clearing levels.
e. Exchange rates will change when either supplies or demands for foreign products, resources, or financial assets change.

SPECIAL TOPICS

The Impossibility of a U.S. Balance of Payments Deficit

Since our theory predicts that the money value of foreign goods purchased by a nation will always equal the money value of goods sold by the nation, it implies that the dollar value of the goods purchased by the United States (its citizens, firms, and governments) will equal the dollar value of the goods sold by the United States to foreign countries. And this means that the United States will not incur a deficit of its balance of payments.

To see why, let's examine the balance of payments account for the United States in 1986, as shown in Table 20.2.

The numbers reveal that whereas various accounts can have deficits, they are matched by surpluses in other accounts. For example, in 1986, the United States had a deficit in the current account. The sum of merchandise imports and exports, investment income and payments, net military expenditures, travel, and other services caused a net outflow of $141.4 billion. However, the current account deficit was offset by surpluses in the capital account and the statistical discrepancy. Investments in the United States by foreigners exceeded investments abroad by U.S. citizens by $117.4 billion, and the statistical discrepancy accounted for $24 billion, for a net inflow of $141.4 billion.

So what is all the talk about a balance of payments deficit? Usually, when people are talking about such a deficit, they are referring to a deficit somewhere *in* the balance of payments rather than *of* the balance of payments as a whole. For example, a merchandise trade deficit of $144.3 billion and a current

TABLE 20.2   The U.S. Balance of Payments, 1986 (in billions of dollars)

Merchandise		−144.3
Exports	224.4	
Imports	−368.7	
Investment income		20.8
Receipts	88.2	
Payments	−67.4	
Net military transactions		−3.7
Net travel		−9.9
Other services		11.4
Balance of goods and services		−125.7
Remittances, pensions, and gifts		−15.7
Balance on current account		−141.4
International capital flows		
U.S. investments abroad	−96.0	
Foreign investment in United States	213.4	
Balance on capital account		117.4
Statistical discrepancy		24.0
Balance of the current account, capital account, and statistical discrepancy ...		$0.0

Source: The Economic Report of the President (Washington D.C.: U.S. Government Printing Office, 1988), pp. 364, 365.

account deficit of $141.4 billion were present in the 1986 balance of payments. Nevertheless, as a whole, the 1986 accounts balanced.

We should not necessarily be concerned when we run a deficit in the current account. To an extent, the United States was built by such deficits. In early American history, the United States regularly ran current account deficits that were financed by capital account surpluses. The capital account surpluses were caused by massive investments by foreigners in U.S. industries. Without those investments, economic expansion would have been much more difficult.

Of course, foreigners didn't invest in our industries because they wanted to help Americans. The investments were motivated by strict self-interest. In later years, foreign investors were usually repaid with interest. Nevertheless, the investments also caused economic growth that gave benefits to U.S. workers and business firms.

To a large degree, recent deficits in the balance of payments were financed by foreign purchases of federal government bonds rather than investment in U.S. corporations. But these purchases, nevertheless, indirectly helped U.S. economic growth. Had foreigners not purchased the bonds, the bonds would have been sold in bond markets in competition with business firms seeking to finance investment spending and this would have forced the firms to reduce their investment. The purchases of bonds by foreigners released funds for domestic investment.

Your Personal Caribbean Nation

To get a better perspective on the balance of payments and the effects of a current account deficit, suppose that you are the only one living on an island in the Caribbean and that your island is a nation. There isn't much on the island so each year you go to Miami to work for 6 months. While there, you sell $50,000 worth of your labor and spend $20,000 of it. You bring the remaining $30,000 back to the island and spend it during the rest of the year by purchasing consumption products imported from the United States.

Under these conditions, the current account in your balance of payments would be balanced. Merchandise imports (−$30,000) and travel purchases abroad (−$20,000) would be balanced by labor service exports (+$50,000).

Now suppose that after you come back from Miami, you change your behavior and decide to spend all of the remaining $30,000 to develop a fishing industry on the island. You combine the $30,000 with another $170,000 that you borrow from a friend living in New York and buy a $200,000 fishing boat from a New Orleans boat builder.

Your dollar outflows will now rise to $220,000, $200,000 for the boat plus $20,000 for foreign travel. All this will be offset partly by foreign labor service sales of $50,000. Your current account will show a deficit of $170,000. But you will still have a balance of payments, since your capital account will show a surplus of $170,000. You will have exported a financial asset worth $170,000, the note that you gave your New York friend for the loan.

Is the balance of payments deficit in the current account a problem? Not if the fishing boat is a sound investment. The only reason you would buy the boat is if you expected to be able to catch enough fish to both pay off the New York investor and return your $30,000 downpayment. If you catch and export enough fish, you will be able to cover the price of the boat and interest and you may even have some money left over. Should this occur, you will eventually have a surplus in your current account that will be created by your fish exports.

The example isn't too unrealistic. Relative to the rest of the economy, each of us is a nation. Whenever we borrow money, we run a deficit in our current account, spending more dollars than we earn. We may, however, rationally want to do so, either because we want to invest in various capital projects or because we prefer present to future consumption. In any case, we don't normally view such borrowing as inconsistent with our personal welfare. There is no reason to view national current account deficits any differently.

Furthermore, since the national balance of payments is primarily a sum of many individual foreign transactions, a deficit in the nation's current account doesn't mean that we individually have deficits on our own accounts. Transactions with foreigners are the responsibilities of particular individuals and therefore affect only those individuals.

For example, if I borrow $200,000 from a German national to run a small business, then the principal and interest on the loan are my responsibility, not yours. If I subsequently go bankrupt and can't repay the loan, the German loses. You bear no responsibility for my loan. For that matter, why should you care if I borrow the money from a German or a U.S. citizen? In either case, you will be unaffected.

Tariffs, Regulatory Controls, Quotas, and Exchange Controls

Since international trade is generally interpersonal trade beyond national boundaries, it has the same effects as interpersonal trade. International trade

a. Distributes goods to those who value them more;
b. Increases the values of goods;
c. Moves trading parties to more preferred positions;
d. Allows greater resource specialization and, therefore, greater production by both trading partners.

Although the effects of international trade may be the same as those of interpersonal trade, international trade is usually subjected to many more restrictions. Whether the restrictions take the form of (1) **tariffs** (taxes on imports), (2) regulatory controls (rules restricting the sales of foreign goods, (3) **quotas** (restrictions on the quantities of imports), or (4) **exchange controls** (limits on how much foreign exchange citizens are allowed to buy), the effects of the restrictions are the same:

a. Goods are distributed to people who value them less.
b. The values of goods are lower.
c. Potential trading partners remain in less preferred positions.
d. Resource despecialization occurs, causing a reduction in production by potential trading partners.

At first glance, these effects certainly appear to be adverse. Why, then, are international trade restrictions so common? This is a political question, but let's see if we can provide a few answers.

The most basic reason is that although free trade moves the people involved to more preferred positions, other people may be made worse off. If those individuals have the political muscle, then they may be able to get the government to limit the exchanges.

For example, suppose I'm willing to pay you $5 to mow my lawn, but José, a Mexican working in the United States, is willing and able to do the job for $1. If José and I negotiate and settle on a $1 wage rate, you will certainly be unhappy. You might then call your congressperson to lobby for the passage of a law restricting work in the United States by foreign nationals.

Another related reason for international trade restrictions is that people mistakenly believe that international trade causes unemployment. This is erroneous because although international trade eliminates some jobs, domestic workers simply take other jobs. For example, although it is true that you wouldn't be able to sell your gardening services to me for $5, you wouldn't necessarily become unemployed. You might simply take some $4 alternative job.

What about the possibility that a massive increase in demand for foreign products will reduce aggregate demand for U.S. products? First, this won't usually happen. Although demands for particular U.S. products might fall, aggregate demand will usually stay the same. This is because demands for foreign goods require that U.S. citizens buy foreign currencies. To buy foreign currencies, however, they must find sellers wanting dollars. But sellers will usually want dollars so they can buy U.S. products. As a result, increases in demands for foreign products by U.S. citizens will normally imply increases in demands for U.S. products by foreigners. Imports might rise but, usually, so will exports. The net result will normally be a shift in the composition of aggregate demand, not a reduction in its level. Second, when aggregate demand does fall because U.S. citizens buy foreign products while foreigners buy financial assets, unemployment can be prevented by expansionary fiscal and monetary policies or price-wage reductions.

Other restrictions on international trade occur because people mistakenly believe that **infant industries**, ones that are growing, need to be protected from low-cost foreign competition. In time, the argument goes, everyone will benefit when large-scale domestic production eventually cuts costs and prices.

The weakness of this argument is that if the eventual gains are expected to cover the early investment sacrifices, then the firms should be willing to initially produce at high costs and low prices, since they will be compensated by future gains. Only when future gains don't cover costs will government protection be necessary.

Finally, one of the most powerful arguments against international trade is that it creates dependence on other nations. If those nations suddenly become enemies, they may cut exports and the shock of readjustment may prove the margin of defeat.

There is some truth to this argument. However, it calls for only selective trade restrictions, not general ones. Most items are of little value for either military defense or offense.

The U.S. Constitution, the British Empire, and the European Common Market

To avoid restrictions on international trade and thereby to achieve the beneficial effects of that trade, various political options exist. The most obvious is to convert international trades into domestic trades by eliminating international and interregional boundaries. The drafters of the U.S. Constitution achieved this result by forming one nation under a strong federal government to replace the Confederation of American States.

Under the Confederation, individual states retained the right to control interstate commerce, and control it they did. Every state passed legislation restricting trade with its neighbors, and the volume of interstate trade declined rapidly. In contrast, the Constitution gave the federal government the sole right to regulate interstate commerce. With an elimination of state restrictions, trade flourished, and with it, production.

Another example is the British Empire. By forming an empire, Great Britain eliminated potential barriers to free trade. Both England and her colonies prospered from mutually beneficial exchange as well as the specialization in production that trade allowed. To a large extent, the gains to Britain from her empire came from a mutually beneficial expansion of wealth.

Incidentally, one side-effect of the elimination of national boundaries is a total lack of concern about account deficits. For example, no one knows if Nevada's current account of trade with New Mexico is balanced, in deficit, or in surplus, and no one really cares. Each individual in each state is responsible for his or her personal transactions with other individuals.

Other attempts to secure the benefits of unrestricted international trade are the Common Market, the British Commonwealth, and various mutual trade agreements between nations.

Political arrangements that eliminate national boundaries or other restrictions to international trade seldom go unopposed. Individuals who have to compete with other sellers will argue strongly for restrictions. In the process, they won't always address the problem of competition head on. For example, they might argue that the control of interstate commerce is a state's rights issue having little to do with economics. Is it? The British Empire is the ultimate form of imperialism. Without markets for her products, where would England be?

Where would the colonies be without markets for their resources? The European Common Market will destroy French industry. Which French industries will it eliminate?

Fixed Exchange Rates

To stimulate international trade, not only have governments sometimes tried to eliminate international trade restrictions, they have also intervened in foreign currency markets to stabilize foreign exchange rates. Until 1971, the United States and other nations regularly attempted to fix exchange rates between international currencies by intervening in international currency markets.

The rates are determined by supplies and demands and therefore would have changed whenever supplies and demands changed. To keep the rates from changing, the governments simply attempted to offset shifts in public demands and supplies with their own purchases or sales of foreign currencies.

For example, if demand for marks fell because of reduced demand for German products by U.S. citizens, then the U.S. government entered the foreign exchange market and purchased marks. The government's increase in demand offset the private decrease to fix the dollar price of the mark. Conversely, if the demand for the marks rose because of an increase in the public's desire for German bonds, the U.S. government sold some of the marks it had purchased in the past, again stabilizing mark demand and the exchange rate.

Exchange rate stabilization policies were (and still are) based on the belief that fluctuating rates discourage international trade. However, such fluctuations don't necessarily discourage trade. It is correct that fluctuating exchange rates can inflict losses on people who have contracts written in terms of foreign currencies. For example, if you sign a contract that requires you to pay a seller Swedish kronor next year, you will incur a loss if the dollar price of the krona rises before you have had a chance to buy them. Nevertheless, fluctuating exchange rates also yield profits, and the profits tend to equal the losses.

Moreover, foreign currency futures markets exist. Individuals can avoid the risks of losses caused by exchange rate fluctuations by buying or selling foreign currencies in advance at known prices (We discussed these trades in Chapter 7).

Many economists recognize these possibilities but nevertheless think that they are insufficient to keep exchange rate fluctuations from discouraging trade. As a result, they believe that exchange rate stability would greatly increase the amount of foreign trade and recommend that the United States and other nations should again try to stabilize the prices of foreign exchange.

Our body of theory is now complete. We have come a long way in our analysis of distribution and production, starting with our reactions to changes in the prices and the costs of goods, and ending with international trade phenomena. I sincerely hope that you have learned a great deal and that you have found the process both interesting and enjoyable.

MAJOR AND MINOR POINTS

1. International trades are generally interpersonal trades that cross national boundaries. They usually involve individuals, not nations.

2. International trades occur because of value differentials.

3. Because nations use different currencies, international exchanges of products, resources, and financial assets are generally accompanied by national currency exchanges.

4. National currencies are traded in competitive international currency markets. Their prices are called foreign exchange rates.

5. Foreign exchange rates are in equilibrium at market-clearing levels determined by supply and demand.

6. The supply of and the demand for a national currency are determined by the supplies and demands for the nation's products, resources, and financial assets.

7. Comparative advantages will cause resource specialization, greater production, and an increase in the extent of international trade.

8. The monetary value of the purchases of foreign goods will always equal the monetary value of the sales of foreign goods (remember that goods include money, products, resources, and financial assets).

9. Foreign exchange rates will change when changes occur in the supplies and demands for the products, resources, and financial assets of various nations.

10. The balance of payments will always balance, although particular account deficits may have to be matched by other account surpluses.

11. Although the U.S. balance of payments will always be balanced, a deficit in the merchandise account or in the current account can exist.

12. Individuals can be thought of as nations who trade with the outside world. Although the money going out will match the money coming in, their spending need not match their income. They can borrow or lend.

13. Restrictions on international trade will redistribute goods to people valuing them less, reduce the values of goods, move parties to less preferred positions, and reduce total production.

14. Restrictions on international trade may benefit people initially uninvolved with the trades, individuals who subsequently don't have to compete with foreigners. They may also foster a stronger national defense. But the restrictions don't generally cause greater employment nor are they prerequisites to the growth of efficient infant industries.

15. The U.S. Constitution, the British Empire, and the European Common Market each reduced trade barriers and thereby increased production and trade.

16. To fix foreign exchange rates, governments sometimes buy and sell foreign currencies. The sales and purchases are aimed at stabilizing supplies and demands.

17. Foreign exchange rate fluctuations don't necessarily discourage international trade. Profits generally match losses and futures markets allow advance purchases of foreign currencies at known rates.

QUESTIONS

1. What is international trade, and why does it occur?
2. Why do international exchanges of national currencies accompany international exchanges of nonmoney goods?
3. What determines the demands, the supplies, and the exchange rates of foreign currencies when the currencies are traded in competitive markets?
4. How does specialization affect international trade?
5. What are the effects of barriers to international trade?
6. Why is the balance of payments always balanced?
7. Why do governments sometimes act to stabilize foreign exchange rates?
8. How can governments stabilize foreign exchange rates?
9. Discuss the following terms and concepts:

International trade	Regulatory controls
Foreign currency exchanges	Quotas
Foreign exchange rate	Exchange controls
Equilibrium exchange rate	Infant industries
Changes in exchange rates	The U.S. Constitution
Comparative advantages	British Empire
Balance of payments	European Common Market
Balance of payments deficit	Fixed exchange rates
Tariffs	

APPLICATIONS

1. What would be the advantage of having only one world currency?
2. Value differentials may be the basic cause of trade, but production keeps trade going. Explain.
3. What would cause the value of the dollar to rise relative to foreign currencies?
4. How does a federal budget deficit affect our balance of payments and the value of the dollar?
5. Why should we worry if foreign currencies rise in value relative to the dollar?
6. How might you be affected if I can buy products or borrow money from foreigners?
7. Does a trade deficit that is balanced by foreign purchases of U.S. Treasury bonds have a different economic effect from a deficit balanced by foreign purchases of bonds sold by U.S. corporations?
8. What evidence can you cite to show that international trade doesn't cause unemployment?
9. How do Japanese regulations that restrict imports from the United States affect the yen price of the dollar?
10. Who opposed the U.S. Constitution, the creation of the British Empire, and formation of the European Common Market?

11. If you are going to France next year, how can you protect yourself against a sudden increase in the price of francs?

12. What limits the ability of United States and of foreign banks when they seek to keep the dollar from dropping relative to foreign currencies?

13. How could you become wealthy if you knew the value of the dollar was about to fall relative to the Austrian shilling?

14. If Japan sells the United States goods below cost, is this a problem for the United States or is it a problem for Japan?

Glossary

accuracy   a measure of how successfully a theory allows someone to predict phenomena

aggregate demand   the combined demand for all nonmoney goods in the economy (MV); the combined demand for all products in the economy (C+I+G)

aggregate supply   the combined supply of all nonmoney goods in the economy (PQ); the combined supply of all products in the economy (Y)

aggregation   the combining of initially separate and somehow similar goods, demands, or markets into single groups

alchemists   individuals who tried to convert base metals into gold

alienation of labor   the inability of workers to identify with final products

automatic stabilizers   changes in government spending and taxing that occur automatically when national output and income changes

average cost   the total cost of production divided by quantity

balance of payments deficit   when the sum of all of the accounts in the balance of payments is negative

balance of trade deficit   the imports of foreign real goods exceed the exports of foreign real goods

bank   a financial institution that holds deposits, grants loans, and creates money

bank holiday   a bank closure for purposes of refinancing or dissolution

bankrupt bank   a bank that has more liabilities than assets

barter   a system in which nonmoney goods are exchanged directly for other nonmoney goods

bilateral monopoly   a single buyer dealing with a single seller; a monopsonist dealing with a monopolist

black market   an illegal market

Board of Governors of the Federal Reserve System a group of seven individuals who control the Federal Reserve System and thus the U.S. money supply

bond a financial asset entitling its owner to principle plus interest from a debtor

business firm a unit of team production in which labor is merged with other units of labor, along with other resources, to form products

capital a produced resource used to produce other goods, examples include machinery, office buildings, and trucks

capital gain an unexpected increase in the prices or quantities of the capital goods that an individual owns

capital good any good, real or not, that is expected to yield a stream of future goods; examples include financial assets, resources, and capital consumption commodities

capital loss an unexpected decrease in the prices or the quantities of the capital goods that an individual owns

capital value the present value of a good

capitalism an economic system in which private property rights exist to all goods

cartel a group of buyers or sellers acting as one to set price or quantity

classical unemployment unemployment that occurs when third parties set prices above the productivities of some workers or resources

clearing price a market-clearing price, the price at which the quantity demand equals the quantity supplied; the price at which neither shortages nor surpluses exist

coercion the threat of or use of force by a person or persons to obtain goods from some other person or persons

combined net gains from trade to society the total of the net gains from trade to buyers and sellers

commodity futures markets markets in which the rights to future commodities are traded

commodity money money that has a physical form, often a use value as well as an exchange value

common stock financial assets representing the ownership rights to a corporation

comparative advantage a resource has a comparative advantage in production relative to another resource when it can produce a product at a lower physical sacrifice of some other product than the other resource

competitive firm a business firm in a competitive industry

competitive industry an industry containing a very large number of firms

competitive market a trade condition in which many buyers and sellers exist, each having a very small effect on the market price (see **perfectly competitive market**)

complement a good whose demand is directly related to the demand of some other good; ham is a complement of eggs

conservationists individuals who hold goods for the future; individuals who want more goods to be held for the future

consumer price index (CPI) a measure of the level of the prices of consumer goods in an economy

consumer sovereignty rule by the consumers; consumers decide what will be produced, how goods will be produced, and to whom products will be distributed

consumption demand for consumer goods

continuous inflation an on-going increase in the level of prices within an economy

co-operatives groups of buyers or sellers who produce transaction services to by-pass middlemen

cost-push inflation   inflation caused by a reduction in the supply of nonmoney goods

cyclical unemployment   unemployment that follows a sudden decrease in aggregate demand; unemployment that is associated with recession

debt financing   money obtained by promising creditors principle plus interest

deficit spending   the financing of government spending with the sale of bonds rather than taxes

deflation   a decrease in the level of prices in an economy

demand   the amounts of a good that people are willing and able to buy at various prices in a given time period

demand deposits   positive checking account balances

demand-pull inflation   inflation caused by an increase in aggregate demand relative to aggregate supply; inflation caused by an increase in MV

depression   a severe recession

determinants of demand   factors that cause individuals to be willing and able to buy various quantities of goods at various prices in a given time period

determinants of supply   factors that cause individuals to be willing and able to sell various quantities of goods at various prices in a given time period

devaluation of the dollar   a reduction of the price of the dollar in terms of one or more foreign currencies

diminishing valuation attribute   each person values an additional unit of a desired good less than the previous unit

direct production   the combining of land and labor into final products

discount rate   the rate the Federal Reserve banks charge financial institutions for loans; the interest rate used to discount future values to obtain their present values

distribution   the act of moving a good to a person

double-coincidence-of-wants   the simultaneous desire of two individuals for each other's goods

equation of exchange   an equation stating that aggregate demand equals aggregate supply; $MV = PQ$

equity financing   money obtained by promising suppliers of money some percentage of future earnings

economic growth   an expansion of production possibilities caused by a greater supply of resources

economic individual   a person with the attributes of scarcity, multiplicity of wants, diminishing valuation, substitutability, and rationality; the universal human constant of economic theory as identified by the law of demand

economic system   a set of institutions that coordinate and control production

economically efficient   production or distribution in such a way that more of a valuable good can't be chosen without the sacrifice of other more valuable goods

economics   a scientific study dealing with phenomena related to scarcity

elastic demand   demand such that a change in price causes a more than proportional change in quantity demanded

elastic money supply   a money supply that grows to facilitate greater exchange and production

elasticity of demand   the relative (%) sensitivity of quantity demanded to price changes

entrepreneurial ability   the skills and abilities employed to combine other resources into products

equilibrium price a rate of exchange that has no tendency to change; a price that represents a balance of forces; in a competitive market, the market-clearing price

European Common Market a group of European nations that have agreed to reduce trade barriers among themselves to allow more free trade; often referred to as the European Economic Community

exchange controls government regulations limiting the prices or quantities of foreign currencies

explanation a component of a theory that links the prediction to other phenomena via fundamental forces

exploitation the payment of a price for a resource that is greater than or less than the value of the resource

excess reserves reserves that are unnecessary for providing support to outstanding notes or demand deposits

factors of production resources taking the form of either land, labor, or capital

Federal Reserve Bank one of twelve central banks in the Federal Reserve System

Federal Reserve System the major banking system of the United States

firm a business firm; a unit of team production

fiscal policy a policy involving changes in government spending or financing aimed at changing aggregate demand

fixed exchange rates foreign currency prices that are held constant by government actions

fluctuating exchange rates foreign currency prices that are free to change in response to changes in supplies or demands

foreign exchange rate the price of one national currency in terms of another national currency

foreign exchange market a market in which foreign currencies are traded

frictional unemployment unemployment that occurs when workers or other resource owners search for employment, often because the composition of aggregate demand has changed

generality a measure of how many sets of phenomena a theory can deal with

good any desired entity, anything anyone wants; examples include money, consumption commodities, resources, financial assets, love, and air.

government money money that has been issued by the government

Greenback Movement a political attempt by farmers to have government print more money to cause inflation or at least to stop deflation

Gross National Product (GNP) a money measure of national output during one year

hidden tax the inflation that follows the government's creation of money to finance government spending

high-powered money a monetary form that can act as a reserve in a fractional reserve monetary system

hyper-inflation an inflationary rate beyond 100 percent per year

illiquid bank a bank that can't meet sudden demands for cash but may have assets equal to liabilities

inelastic demand demand such that a change in price causes a less than proportional change in quantity demanded

income the stream of future money or nonmoney goods generated by a capital good

indirect production roundabout production; the production first of capital and then the use of capital with other resources to produce products

inflation   an increase in the level of prices in a nation

infant industry   an industry that is in the early stages of formation

in-kind   in the form of a commodity or linked to a commodity; not monetary but physical

interest   the extra amount a borrower must repay on a loan

interest rate   the extra amount a borrower must repay on a loan as a percentage of principle for a given period of time

international trade   exchange occurring between individuals or governments in different nations

investment   demand for capital

kick-back   a payment or compensation made to a buyer or seller for agreeing to trade

labor force   people either working or looking for work at wages that they think are less than or equal to their productivities

Laffer curve   a backward-bending curve showing the relationship between tax revenues and tax rates

land   a resource (factor of production) consisting of all natural resources; the land and everything under, over, or next to it

law   a theory that has been very heavily supported by the evidence; a theory that has withstood the test of time

law of demand   a theory that explains and predicts individual reactions to changes in the prices and the costs of goods

law of diminishing returns   the proposition that the marginal product of a resource will fall as more of the resource is added to a fixed set of other resources

law of increasing cost   the proposition that the cost of producing additional units of a product will rise as more of the product is produced

liquid assets   assets that can be quickly exchanged for other assets with a minimal loss of wealth; assets that can be quickly exchanged for money with a minimal loss of wealth

loan   the exchange of present and future goods in which a debtor buys present goods from a creditor in exchange for future goods

long run   a period of time sufficiently long for all resources to be adjusted efficiently

macroeconomics   a subset of economics that studies the behavior of aggregates such as national output and the level of prices

marginal cost   the change in total cost that occurs when one more unit of a good is produced or sold; the value of the highest valued alternatives sacrificed when one more unit of a good is chosen

marginal product   the change in total product caused by the employment of one more unit of some resource

marginal revenue   the change in total revenue when one more unit of some good is sold

marginal revenue product   the marginal product times the marginal revenue of the units within the marginal product

marginal tax rates   the rates paid on additional dollars of income

market-clearing price   a price at which quantity demanded equals quantity supplied

market   an institution that brings buyers and sellers together for trade

market spoiling   the losing of money by lowering the price on some units to sell more units

medium of exchange   a function of money as an intermediate good that is obtained so some other good can be purchased subsequently

mercantilism   an economic system of government-created monopoly-power

merger   the combination of two or more business firms

monetary policy   a policy that changes the money supply, usually to change aggregate demand

money   anything that carries out the functions of money; anything that acts as a medium of exchange, a store of value, and a unit of account

money interest rate   the interest rate for borrowing money; a rate that reflects the real interest rate plus expected inflation

monopoly   a single seller of some good

monopoly bank   a single bank

monopoly cartel   a group of sellers acting as one seller

monopoly demand   the demand for a good sold by a monopolist; monopoly demand curves slope downward

monopoly firm   a firm that is the only producer and seller of a product

monopoly profit   the extent by which total revenue exceeds total cost because of monopoly power alone; also called monopoly rent

monopoly rent   the extent to which monopoly power allows total revenue to exceed total cost; monopoly profit

monopsony   a single buyer of a good

monopsony cartel   a group of buyers acting as one buyer of a good

micro-economics   a subset of economics that studies the behavior of individual units such as the household or the business firm

middlemen   individuals who buy goods from some people and sell the goods to other people

model   a specific formulation of a theory that sacrifices generality and simplicity to gain accuracy

multibanking system   a banking system comprised of many individual banks

multiplicity of wants attribute   each person wants more than one type of scarce good

multiplier   the multiple by which output and income changes after an initial change in aggregate demand

multiplier process   the decreases in output and income that follow decreases in consumption caused by unemployment

national debt   the nominal value of all outstanding federal government bonds

need   a category of goods, some of which is necessary for human survival

net gain from trade   the difference between the total value of the sacrifices and the gains to either buyers or sellers because of trade

nonmoney goods   goods other than money; examples include financial assets, products, nonmaterial goods, resources, and used goods

nonprice competition   attempts to fulfill criteria other than price

nonprice discrimination   choosing among buyers or sellers by using a criterion other than price

normal good   a good for which demand increases when income rises

open-market operations   the purchase or sale of government bonds by Federal Reserve banks on the open bond market

opportunity cost   the value of the highest valued alternative sacrificed when a decision is made

paper capital gains   capital gains that have not been converted into money via the sale of capital goods

paper capital losses capital losses that have not been converted into money losses via the sale of capital goods

paradox of unemployment in a world of scarce products, resources should be scarce

perfectly competitive market a trade situation in which buyers and sellers are insignificant; they cannot affect the market price by buying or selling different quantities

persuasion the act of using language to motivate people to change their opinions or to act in some manner

phenomenon any observable thing or event

Phillips curve a curve showing the relationship between inflation and unemployment

predatory tactics actions aimed at eliminating competitors by temporarily reducing prices below cost

predictions the component of a theory that specifically forecasts some phenomenon or set of phenomena

present value the value of a future good in the present

price a rate of exchange; what must be directly sacrificed in trade to obtain one unit of some good

price discrimination charging different prices for different units

price/earnings ratio the present price of a share of common stock divided by the present yearly earnings of the share

price searcher a seller or buyer who has limited market information and must therefore find the optimal price to charge or pay

price searching the act of trying to find the optimal price, usually by slowly changing a price and observing the responses of buyers or sellers

price setting the fixing of the price by a seller, usually a monopolist

price setter usually a monopoly seller who sets the price, generally above the competitive level

price taking the act of accepting the price as given by the market; selling or buying at the market price

private property rights individual rights to exclusive use and transferability

production the combining of goods (resources) to form other goods

production possibilities schedule a schedule showing various maximum possible production combinations

production possibilities frontier a graphical depiction of the upper limits of production that are possible with given resources at some moment in time

profit the difference between total revenue and total cost; the difference between the total value of gains and the total value of sacrifices

quantity demanded the amount of a good people are willing and able to buy at some specific price in a given time period

quantity supplied the amount of a good people are willing and able to sell at some specific price in a given time period

quotas regulations limiting the quantities of foreign imports

rationality attribute each person is decisive and consistent in values and behavior

real referring to the nonmoney or the physical aspect

real interest rate an interest rate adjusted for inflation and therefore reflecting only the values of present nonmoney goods in terms of future nonmoney goods

recession a decrease in national production that lasts two or more consecutive quarters; a decrease in national output caused by a high level of cyclical unemployment

reciprocal of the reserve ratio 1 divided by the reserve ratio

required reserve ratio   the ratio of reserves that financial institutions in the Federal Reserve system must maintain to support outstanding demand deposits

resources   the goods that are combined to form other goods during production

run on a bank   a sudden demand for cash by many demand depositors who fear that a bank has liabilities that exceed its assets

saving   the nonspending of income; money saved can be held or loaned to someone else who spends it

Say's Law   the proposition that the supply of any real good implies a demand for another real good

Say's Principle   the proposition that the supply on any good, real or not, implies a demand for another good, real or not

scarcity   a condition in which the desire for goods is greater than the quantities of goods that are available

scarcity attribute   for each person, some good is scarce

science   a study that tries to provide verifiable predictions of phenomena

scope   the range of phenomena with which a study is concerned

shares of common stock   proportional rights to the common stock of a corporation

shortage   a situation in which the quantity of a good demanded exceeds the quantity supplied at the existing price

short run   a period of time in which some resources are fixed in supply

simplicity   a measure of how few phenomena or forces a theory identifies in its explanation and prediction

specialization   the concentration of a resource on the production of one or a few products

speculators   individuals who buy goods only so they can later sell them

store of value   the use of money to bridge sales and purchases

substitute   a good that can be purchased to satisfy the same basic desire that some other good satisfies; Fords are substitutes for Chevrolets

substitutability attribute   each person is willing and able to substitute some of any desired good for enough of any other desired good

substitutable resource   a resource that can be shifted from the production of one product and into the production of another

supply   the amounts of a good that people are willing and able to sell at various prices in a given time period

supply-side economics   tax reduction policies aimed at increasing saving, investing, and the size of the labor force to cause economic growth and greater tax revenues

surplus   a situation in which the quantity of a good supplied exceeds the quantity demanded at the existing price

sustained inflation   inflation lasting more than four years

tariff   a tax on imports

technology   knowledge of how to combine resources to produce goods

testability   a measure of how well a theory allows itself to be verified, either directly or indirectly, by observable evidence

theory   a simplification of reality; a conceptual tool used to explain and predict phenomena

three fundamental questions   what to produce, which resources to employ, and to whom to distribute the output

time-value   the value of a good reflecting the time in which it is available

total cost   the total value of the highest valued alternatives sacrificed when a given quantity of goods is produced or sold; the average cost times the quantity of goods sold

total revenue   the total amount of money obtained when goods are sold; when the same price is charged for all units, total revenue equals price times quantity

trade   the exchange of some goods for others

transitory inflation   inflation lasting less than four years

unemployment   not using a resource; a worker is unemployed when the worker is willing and able to work at a wage equal to or less than his or her contribution to production but doesn't work

underemployment   physical inefficiency; using resources, but not in a manner that yields the maximum possible output or value

uniform pricing   charging one price for all units sold

unit elastic   demand is unit elastic when a change in price causes an equal proportional change in quantity demanded

unit of account   a function of money as a measure of value

value   the amount of any good that a person is willing and able to sacrifice to obtain one more unit of some other good; a marginal personal rate of substitutability

value differential   a circumstance in which one person values a good differently from another person; a circumstance that gives rise to trade

value of a capital good   the present value of the expected future income of the capital good

value of a resource   the marginal revenue product of the resource; the present value of the expected future marginal revenue product of a resource

velocity of money   the number of times money is spent on nonmoney goods in a given time period; the number of times money is spent on products in a given time period

verifiable   capable of being supported directly or indirectly by observable evidence

wage-price controls   government limitations on wage and price increases

wealth   the market value of capital goods

worth   the value of a good (see **value**)

Answers to Application Questions

To help you find particular answers, questions are first identified by chapter numbers and then by question numbers.

CHAPTER 1

1-1. **Which of the following might science try to explain and predict?**
   a. Happiness
   b. Stock market prices
   c. The disadvantages of more government
   d. Satisfaction
   e. The exploitation of labor
   f. Just prices
   g. Psychosis

   The only correct choice is (b), stock market prices. They are the only things that we can observe. Happiness, disadvantages, satisfaction, exploitation, justice, and psychosis may exist, but we can't see or measure them.

1-2. **Someone predicts that criminals who have found Jesus will commit fewer crimes. Is this a scientific prediction?**

   No. Although we can measure crimes, we can't see if criminals have found Jesus; we can't see inside their minds.

1-3. **Sociology isn't a science because sociologists haven't learned much about group behavior. Comment.**

   This is not true. Sociologists may have been less successful in providing verifiable predictions of phenomena than many natural and physical scientists, but we do not determine whether or not a study is a science by its successes or failures. Physics was a science long before Newton; it was a science on the first day that some prehistoric man or woman tried to provide a verifiable prediction of some observable physical phenomenon.

1-4. Can you use economics to prove that it is better to go to college than to begin work after high school?

No. Economics can only show what the effects of a college education might be or try to predict who will go to college. Economics is concerned with what is, not what should be.

1-5. Why might it be more difficult to predict objectively the effects of minimum-wage laws than the effects of the moon on the tides of the earth?

If you are a worker or businessperson, minimum wages may have a more direct effect on your wealth. Also, you may be able to influence politicians to pass or oppose minimum-wage legislation.

On the other hand, the effects of the moon on the tides don't directly affect your wealth, and there isn't much you could do about the effects if they did.

1-6. Distinguish between theory and reality.

A theory is a simplification of reality, a tool we construct to deal with real phenomena. It is useful precisely because it is unreal; it includes only some aspects of the real world, not all of them.

1-7. We learn to predict phenomena in much the same way that we learn to see and listen. Explain.

We predict by distinguishing what is common about events from what is unique, abstracting, and simplifying. For example, we can learn to predict that the cars we are following will slow down by focusing on the taillights and ignoring other factors.

1-8. Examinations in economics courses predict student knowledge imperfectly. Should they be given?

They may be more general predictors of student knowledge than any available alternatives.

1-9. Do you think Newton's laws of physics yield perfect predictions?

The laws don't yield perfect predictions. Einstein's theory of relativity is more accurate. But even the theory of relativity fails to predict some phenomena.

1-10. Which theory is more general, one that implies that Hitler caused World War II or one that claims a megalomaniac was responsible?

The theory focusing on megalomaniacs is more general (although not easily testable); the theory can be used to predict many wars, not just World War II.

1-11. Why might a theory that predicts the effects of higher prices on consumer purchases be more useful than a theory that predicts the effects that higher oil prices have on oil consumption?

The theory dealing with higher prices is more general. We can use it to predict the effects of many price increases, not just those related to oil.

1-12. Can a theory that assumes the existence of perfect competition be useful even when some monopoly sellers are present?

Yes. If the effects of monopoly are insignificant, we may not gain accuracy by recognizing monopoly power. Monopoly may be only an unnecessary complication. The purpose of theories is to explain and predict phenomena as simply as possible, not to describe the real world.

Even if we gained accuracy and generality by recognizing monopoly power, the gains may not be worth the sacrifice of simplicity. We are usually willing to trade off accuracy and generality if we can obtain enough simplicity.

1-13. Some students argue that the theories presented in this text are useless because the theories are unreal. Do you think those students predict and explain economic phenomena with theories that are duplicates of reality?

No. All theories are unreal simplifications of the real world, tools rather than reality. The question is not whether theories are real, but whether they work better than any alternatives.

1-14. In what two basic ways can you go on a diet?

You can either change yourself (by refusing to eat apple pie), or you can change your circumstances (by getting the apple pie out of the house).

1-15. Freudian psychoanalysts try to deal directly with the minds of the insane when they want to cure psychotics. How else can psychologists change the behavior of the mentally ill?

Behavioral psychologists try to change the circumstances that the patients confront. After all, some circumstances would drive us all crazy.

CHAPTER 2

2-1. Distinguish among the price, the cost, and the value of this book.

The price of the book was how much money you paid to purchase it, the rate of exchange. The cost of the book was the value of the highest valued alternative you sacrificed to obtain it. And the value of the book was the highest amount you were willing and able to pay.

The cost was probably greater than the price. The cost included the price and the value of all of the other sacrifices you made to get the book. You probably had to travel to the book store, find the text, stand in line, and write out a check, all in addition to buying the book.

The value was also probably greater than the price. You might have been willing and able to pay twice as much as you had to pay.

2-2. Resolve this paradox: The value of water is high, whereas that of diamonds is low, and yet water has a low price while diamonds have a high price.

The value of water isn't high, it's low; the value of diamonds isn't low, it's high. Value doesn't refer to all units; it deals with just the marginal ones. When we own a great deal of water, its value can be low; and when we possess only a few diamonds, they may be worth a great deal. How much would you be willing and able to pay for one more gallon of water? How much would you be willing and able to pay for one more diamond? The prices of these goods correctly reflect their values.

2-3. Are there any times when the values of goods rise with consumption?

It seems that some goods such as classical music and tennis lessons become more valuable as we purchase more units, perhaps because we develop a greater appreciation for them. Nevertheless, even the values of these goods eventually fall. If they didn't, we wouldn't buy anything else once we bought the first units.

2-4. Does substitutability imply that we will sacrifice all of our clean air for jobs?

No, substitutability implies only that we will sacrifice *some* clean air for *some* jobs if we want both clean air and jobs. The law of demand does not assume that categories of goods are substitutable, only that individual units within categories are substitutable.

2-5. Are economic individuals selfish in the sense that they want only commodities that directly benefit themselves?

No. Some people place very high values on the welfare of other people. In fact, almost all of us are willing to sacrifice to help other people, sometimes family and friends, sometimes strangers. The law of demand claims only that we are willing to substitute between our own well-being and the well-being of others at some rate when we want both goods.

2-6.   Are patients in a hospital for the mentally ill rational?

Sometimes. Some people have been committed because they make arbitrary choices and are thus irrational according to our definition. But other people have been committed because they couldn't survive with the particular values that they have, even though they are rational to the extent that they are decisive and consistent in their values and behavior. (These patients are predictable and controllable.)

2-7.   Do we have the same specific values? Do we have the same value structure?

We generally have very different specific values, but our values are structured in the same way. The five attributes identified by the law of demand refer only to the structure of our values. For example, you may value Cokes while I value Pepsis, but both of us want more of each drink than we have, desire other goods as well as the sodas, etc.

2-8.   In 1986, the United States attacked Libya in retaliation for various terrorist attacks on U.S. citizens. Does the law of demand predict Libya's response?

No. The United States and Libya are nations governed by group decisions. Although groups often choose less when the cost of a good rises, the law doesn't specifically deal with groups.

2-9.   Explain how we react to costs by using an example involving studying economics and watching TV.

If watching TV is the highest-valued alternative sacrificed when studying economics, then the value of the TV sacrificed is the cost of studying. We will study economics to the point where the value of studying equals its cost (the value of the sacrificed TV). This is because if the value of studying exceeded the cost, we would study more and watch less, and if the value of studying were less than the cost, we would study less and watch more.

If the value of watching TV suddenly rose, increasing the cost of studying economics, we would study less and watch more. As we did so, diminishing valuation would increase the value of studying and reduce the value of TV until the value of studying again equaled its cost, the value of sacrificed TV. We would then select the associated combination of the two goods.

2-10.   Is the quality of food more important than the quantity?

No. The law of demand argues that nothing is more important than anything else; we have no priorities. We want both quality and quantity and are willing to sacrifice some of each to obtain some of the other.

The trade-off is much more visible in developing nations. For example, people in Biafra often die of food poisoning. Nevertheless, if the quality of food were improved, quantity would fall and many would starve. However morbid the choice, many Biafrans select a quality-quantity combination that minimizes the probability of their death.

2-11.   Can we expect American workers to work as many hours as their grandparents?

No. As the productivities of American workers have risen, they have sacrificed some wage increases to obtain a shorter and less intensive work week.

2-12.   Although we may talk idealistically about honesty, we act practically and tell lies. Explain.

We want honesty and other goods, and we are willing and able to substitute among all goods at some rates. We don't live in the Garden of Eden where we can have everything we want. The law of demand implies that we are practical rather than idealistic.

2-13. **How might you be entrapped to commit a crime?**

Loosely speaking, entrapment occurs when criminals are tricked into a crime that is invented by the police. The idea for the crime doesn't come from the mind of the criminal.

The law of demand implies that all of us can be entrapped, although not necessarily by the same offers. For example, if I offered you $10,000, would you be willing to drive through a red light? Before you say no, think of the times you have driven above the speed limit just to be somewhere a few minutes earlier.

2-14. **Does the law of demand explain and predict instinctive behavior?**

Yes. We don't have to be conscious of what we do, nor do we have to know why we do it, in order to purchase less when prices rise and more when they fall.

2-15. **Since basketball players want to win as well as to obtain personal glory, when is a team going to display more teamwork, when the score is 98-12 or 98-96? Why?**

More teamwork will be chosen when the score is close because the cost of personal glory (in terms of possibly losing the game) will be higher.

2-16. **Why is it more likely that you will finish a job than that you will start it?**

Once a job has begun, the cost of completion is lower. Fewer costs remain after some costs have been incurred. At a lower cost, you will choose more.

CHAPTER 3

3-1. **Before the Mediterranean and the Baltic could trade, the Baltic had to have more food than it could consume. Is this true?**

No. The Baltic still doesn't have more food than people can consume. Nevertheless, people in the Baltic do place a lower value on additional food than people in the Mediterranean. For trade, zero values aren't necessary, just different values on mutually desired goods.

3-2. **It was necessary for us to satisfy our desire for food before the Industrial Revolution could begin. Is this true?**

No. We still haven't satisfied our desire for food. Most of us want more food; we simply value it less than other goods. The Industrial Revolution required a supply of food just great enough to reduce the value of food below that of easily produced manufacturing items.

3-3. **I buy a lamp that I later discover doesn't work. Has trade increased the values of goods?**

Yes. If I hadn't valued the lamp as much or more than the money, I wouldn't have purchased it. The value of the lamp subsequently declined, but at the time of trade, the value equaled or exceeded the price.

It is possible for the value of the lamp to change because the value of the lamp isn't in the lamp. It is something attributed to the lamp and that attribution can change.

3-4. **Suppose your 5-year-old daughter wanted to purchase a stick of chewing gum for $10, a stick she valued at more than $10. Would you allow the trade to occur? Why?**

Probably not. High values are not always good values. We often interfere with the trades of children when we feel their values aren't closely related to the benefits, the satisfaction, or the welfare they will receive.

3-5. **Trade is necessarily an exploitative phenomenon. People get rich by selling us goods with low values and buying from us goods with high values. Is this true?**

No. If this were true, we wouldn't continue to buy the same categories of goods from the same parties. Of course, sometimes the values of goods decline after we buy, and we may think that we gave up goods that were more valuable than the ones we received, but at the time of the exchanges, the values of goods purchased exceeded the values of those sold.

3-6. Both trade and coercion can be used to redistribute goods. Distinguish between the effects of each.

We can use trade or coercion to obtain goods from other people. From our own perspectives, the two methods may be very similar. In each case, we may have to surrender some goods we value to obtain other goods we value more.

However, from the perspective of the people from whom we obtain goods, the methods are very different. Trade provides them with goods they value more and moves them to more preferred positions. They, as well as we, can benefit. On the other hand, coercion makes other people worse off. They must choose between the lesser of two worse positions.

Also, in contrast to trade, coercion not only redistributes goods, it also often destroys some goods.

3-7. Is war irrational?

No. War represents a rational use of coercion to redistribute goods. Wars may look irrational because they destroy total wealth, but the parties engaged in the wars may think that their wealth will be greater than otherwise, and they sometimes are correct.

3-8. When politicians trade votes on various pieces of legislation, the practice is known as logrolling. Why does logrolling occur?

Like all free trades, logrolling occurs because value differentials exist. Politicians are able to sell their votes on some bills in exchange for votes on other bills.

For example, a Georgia senator may be willing to vote for a bill supporting a federal subsidy on Kansas wheat if a Kansas senator is willing to vote for a subsidy on Georgia peanuts.

3-9. Politicians aren't allowed to take explicit bribes. What type of implicit bribes might they accept?

By regularly voting for defense appropriation bills, a congressperson may eventually be able get a job with a defense contractor such as TRW. TRW might make this a likely possibility by regularly hiring former congresspersons who voted "correctly." Nothing needs to be said or written down.

3-10. Farmers receive only about one-fourth of the final retail price of peaches. Why don't they usually set up fruit stands so they can obtain more revenue?

Farmers can't grow peaches at the same time that they operate fruit stands. The peaches not grown might be worth more than the gains from higher prices.

3-11. In the United States, the number of farmers, manufacturers, and builders is small compared to the number of wholesalers, retailers, and shippers. In many industries, people growing, producing, and building goods receive less total income than middlemen. What's going on?

Although mass production technologies greatly increase production, they also tend to concentrate production among business firms and in geographic areas. This concentration then requires extensive transaction services before final distribution to consumers is possible. Nevertheless, the gains from mass production more than compensate for the losses resulting from higher transaction costs. Growers, producers, and builders, as well as middlemen, move to more preferred positions.

3-12. If you want to buy a used car, why might you be willing to pay more to a used-car dealer than to a private party?

A used-car dealer can reduce transaction costs in the same way that a market can: The dealer can make it possible for you to inspect as many cars in one day as you might inspect in one week by driving around to the homes of private parties.

3-13. Because of the German hyperinflation of the 1920s, many Germans refused to accept money in payment for goods. What effect did this have on exchange?

The transaction costs of trade greatly increased, since people had to spend a great deal of time shopping to fulfill the double-coincidence-of-wants requirement of barter. While producing transaction services, they weren't able to simultaneously produce other products.

3-14. Why do some wholesalers want Chicago's commodity market to be eliminated?

Some wholesalers want the market to be eliminated because without the market, they will be able to pay isolated farmers less for their products. The presence of a market makes wholesalers compete with other wholesalers.

CHAPTER 4

4-1. Why do economists often call buyers and sellers in competitive markets "price takers?"

Competitive buyers and sellers are price takers because they "take" the price from the market. They can't set the prices, they can't affect the prices by buying or selling different quantities, and they can't negotiate. Buyers and sellers only make a decision on how much they want to trade. Competition keeps them from trading at anything but the market price.

4-2. Did a shortage of food exist during the 1985 Ethiopian famine?

Generally, no. There was a scarcity of food; there wasn't enough food for everyone who wanted it. But a shortage wasn't present; everyone willing and able to pay the price for food was generally able to buy.

Had Ethiopians had more income, they would have been willing and able to purchase more food. The quantity supplied would have risen (primarily as a result of imports from other nations) and starvation would have been prevented.

4-3. Which of the following will fail to cause an increase in demand for dental services?
   a. Less fluoride in water
   b. Greater consumption of candy
   c. A lower price of dental services
   d. An increase in the price of toothpaste

The answer is (c), a lower price of dental services. A lower price will only increase the quantity of dental services demanded. The other factors are likely to increase demand rather than quantity demanded; at the same prices, larger amounts will probably be demanded.

4-4. Following are the supply and demand schedules representing supply and demand for lobsters in a Denver fish market. Derive the supply and demand curves from the schedules.

PRICE	QUANTITY DEMANDED	QUANTITY SUPPLIED
$25	2,000	8,000
20	4,000	7,000
15	6,000	6,000
10	8,000	5,000
5	10,000	4,000

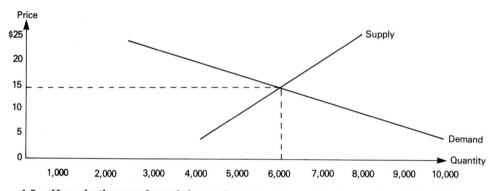

4-5. **How do the supply and demand curves associated with the Denver fish market illustrate the law of demand?**

The curves illustrate the law with their slopes. The law of demand predicts that demand curves will slope downward because people are willing and able to buy more at lower prices. The law also predicts that supply curves will slope upward because people are willing and able to sell more at higher prices.

As mentioned in the body of the chapter, the reason we have to say only that the demand curve slopes downward, rather than downward and to the right, is that whenever curves are discussed, we always assume that we are looking from the origin (the point representing the 0-0 combination where the two axes meet). Looking from that point, the demand curve slopes downward and the supply curve slopes upward.

4-6. **What will be the equilibrium price of the lobsters in the Denver fish market? Show graphically.**

The equilibrium price will be at the market-clearing level where quantity demanded equals quantity supplied; specifically, it will be $15. Graphically, $15 is the price associated with the intersection of the supply and demand curves.

4-7. **The market price of my house is $100,000. Why wouldn't I sell for less? Why wouldn't you buy for more?**

I wouldn't sell for less because I could sell to other buyers for $100,000. You wouldn't pay more because you could buy from other sellers. Competition among buyers keeps them from buying for less than the market price while competition among sellers prevents them from charging more than the market price.

Notice that buyers in a market compete with buyers while sellers compete with sellers. Buyers don't compete with sellers.

4-8. **What would happen to the price of lobsters in the Denver fish market if demand increased by 3000 at each price? Explain and show graphically.**

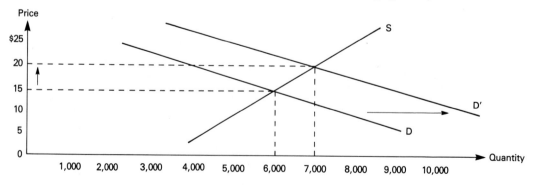

The demand curve would shift parallel to the right by 3000 units, causing the price to rise from $15 to $20.

4-9. **Explain and show graphically how an elimination of Medicare would affect the price of medical services.**

The price would fall. Without the government subsidy, the demand for the services would decline; at the same prices, older patients would be willing and able to buy less. To prevent a surplus, price would fall increasing quantity demanded and reducing quantity supplied until equilibrium was established at the new clearing level.

Graphically, demand would fall from *D* to *D'* as shown below. To prevent a surplus, the price would decline from *P* to *P'*, thereby increasing quantity demanded and decreasing quantity supplied, both to *Q'*.

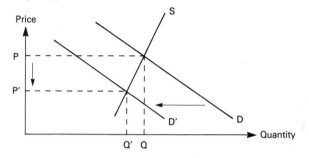

4-10. **Do patients pay for the increased prices of medical malpractice insurance?**

The patients pay only when the supply of doctors falls. If doctors are already earning more than is necessary to keep them working, and if earnings remain high enough to motivate people to become doctors, then the supply of doctors won't fall and the price will remain the same.

Supply changes and therefore price changes are most likely to occur when some doctors (obstetricians and neurosurgeons) shift to other areas of medicine because of differences in malpractice insurance. In such cases, prices will change to reflect the differences in malpractice insurance rates.

4-11. **If the wages of carpenters declined, how would the rental rates of apartments be affected?**

The wages of carpenters affect the cost of constructing new apartments and are therefore an eventual determinant of apartment supply. A fall in wages would eventually increase the supply of apartments, as shown by the shift from *S* to *S'*. To prevent a surplus, competition among landlords would force the rent down from *R* to *R'* and the number of apartments rented would rise from *Q* to *Q'*.

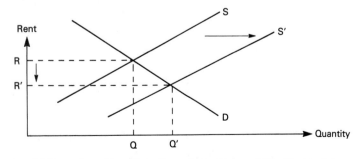

4-12. **How would the price of beef be affected if a disease killed half of the cattle in the United States? Explain and show graphically.**

If half the cattle in the United States were to die, the supply would fall and price would rise.

Graphically, the supply curve would shift to the left, from S to S'. The price would rise from P to P' to prevent a shortage.

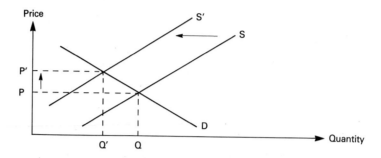

4-13.   **Some years ago in California, voters passed Proposition 13. Among other things, the proposition reduced the taxes landlords had to pay. Many people predicted that rents would fall as a result. Rents not only failed to fall, but in some cases, they rose. What happened?**

The rents failed to decline because taxes on apartments didn't immediately affect supply or demand. In fact, rents, which had been rising, continued to rise because demand had increased as the population of California continued to expand.

Things eventually changed. Taxes eventually become a strong determinant of apartment supply. With lower taxes and the same rents, new apartments were constructed. The increase in supply gradually reduced rents, at least below what they would have otherwise been.

If we ignore incidental changes in supply or demand, we can illustrate the price and quantity effects of the tax decrease with the graph below. The tax break eventually increased supply, shifting the supply curve to the right, from S to S'. As a result, rent decreased to R', preventing the surplus.

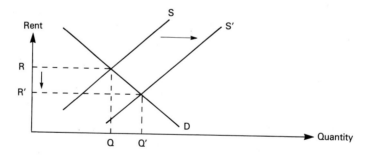

4-14.   **Wilson is the only seller of Wilson tennis balls. How is the price of Wilson tennis balls determined?**

If Wilson must worry that producers of other tennis balls will obtain greater sales should Wilson raise its price, then the market is tennis balls rather than specifically Wilson tennis balls. Supply and demand will then determine the price of Wilson tennis balls, not the Wilson corporation.

4-15.   **Both building subcontractors and small town golf clubs can charge higher prices and still sell some quantities. Would we better understand their prices and price changes if we included this in our analysis?**

The complications may add very little to our understanding of where prices are and when they will change. The gain in generality may not be worth the sacrifice of simplicity.

CHAPTER 5

5-1. There are no pure monopolists. All monopolists must compete with the sellers of other goods. Explain.

The law of demand—and, specifically, the attribute of subsitutability—implies that consumers are willing and able to sacrifice some of any desired good for enough of any other desired good. Substitutes are everywhere and therefore competition is everywhere. A monopolist, like any other seller confronts a downward-sloping demand curve. The only difference between a monopolist and a seller in a perfectly competitive market is that the substitutes for the good sold by the monopolist aren't perfect. Therefore, the monopolist can raise price and not have sales fall to zero.

5-2. If monopoly demand curves were vertical, what prices would monopolists charge?

If demand curves were vertical, monopolists would charge virtually infinite prices.

5-3. If price discrimination were possible, what would be the relationship between marginal revenue and price?

With perfect price discrimination, marginal revenue would equal price; total revenue would always rise by the price of the next unit. For example, if the first unit could be sold for $10, then total revenue would rise from 0 to $10 and marginal revenue would be $10. If the price then had to be reduced to $9 to sell the second unit, total revenue would rise to $19 and the unit's sale and marginal revenue would thus be $9. The first unit's price would be unaffected by the sale of the second since uniform pricing would be unnecessary.

5-4. The Roxie Theater is sold out of tickets to a special movie about Africa. Should the owners be happy or sad?

The owners should probably be sad. It is likely that a higher price would have brought in more revenue than would have been lost because of some empty seats. For instance, if the owners had increased the price by 20%, total revenues would have increased even if as many as 10% of the seats became vacant.

5-5. If Louisiana fishermen were granted monopoly power, their wealth would be greater and so would the wealth of Louisiana. Is this true?

Generally, yes. Most of the fish are sold outside of Louisiana and therefore an increase in the net gain from trade to the fishermen would imply more wealth for Louisiana (we can assume that an increase in net gain from trade implies an increase in wealth). Of course, the increase in net gain to fishermen would come at the expense of consumers outside of Louisiana.

If the fish were sold in Louisiana, the answer would be no. Fishermen would gain at the expense of Louisiana consumers. Also, the combined net gains from trade would fall since fewer fish would be caught and sold. The wealth of Louisiana would not only fail to rise, it would fall.

5-6. What is good for General Motors is good for America. Would this apply to the granting of monopoly power to General Motors?

We can't say what is good or bad using economics alone. We can say only that although General Motors might increase its net gain from trade, the net gain from trade of consumers would fall and the combined net gains of General Motors plus the consumers would fall.

5-7. Does Liz need to know economics to restrict her sale of home-cooked meals?

No. Liz needs to behave only according to what maximizes her net gain from trade. In fact, she may truly believe that she wants no more home-cooked meals when she restricts supply. Economics wouldn't be much of a science if everyone had to know its theories before they could behave according to them.

5-8. Distinguish between total value and marginal value.

The total value of a good is the sum of the marginal values of individual units. The marginal value is just the value of the next unit. When we talk of value, we are referring to the marginal unit, not to the total.

5-9. During a drought, the price of food rises. Does this mean that the total value of food rises?

No. During a drought, the marginal value of food increases and this causes the price to rise. The total value, the sum of the values of all of the marginal units, is lower since less food is available.

5-10. A crop failure reduces the California grape harvest and farmers make more money. How is this possible?

Farmers make more money because the price of all grapes is based on the price of the marginal unit sold. When the harvest fails, the value of the marginal unit increases and this raises the price of the marginal unit. When the price of the marginal unit go up, so does the price of all other units. This price effect, if it is sufficient, can offset the effect of a lower quantity sold. For example, a 60% price increase can offset a 50% drop in sales.

5-11. When questioned about his monopoly power, a monopolist argues the he charges only what his goods are worth—no more, no less. Evaluate.

It is true that the consumer pays what the good is worth, but the only reason the good is worth so much is that the monopolist has restricted the supply of the good.

5-12. How did nature allow Elvis Presley to obtain monopoly power?

Elvis was granted a monopoly on his services. Other musicians could not have entered the market just because they were willing and able to sell.

5-13. Distinguish between the elasticity of demand for gasoline and the elasticity of demand for gasoline sold by a particular gasoline station.

Demand for gasoline is relatively less elastic than demand for the gasoline sold by a particular station. This is because the substitutes for gasoline are worse than the substitutes for gasoline sold by a particular station. If the price of gasoline rises, consumers must buy other goods; if the price of gasoline at a particular station rises, consumers can simply buy gasoline from other stations.

5-14. If demand curves of monopolists remained inelastic as the monopolists increased price, how would the monopolists behave?

They would raise prices to infinity. Higher prices might reduce sales, but the revenues lost from lower sales would be more than offset by the revenues gained from the higher prices. Also, since fewer units would be sold, costs would decline at the same time that revenues would rise.

The reason monopolists stop raising prices and charge finite prices is that they eventually encounter the elastic portions of their demand curves. When they do, they keep raising prices only as long as lower costs offset lost revenues.

CHAPTER 6

6-1. Distinguish among price takers, price setters, and price searchers.

Price takers are competitive buyers and sellers who take prices from markets. Price setters are monopoly sellers who set prices at higher than competitive levels. Price searchers are buyers and sellers who have limited market information about the prices and qualities of goods. Price searchers must search for optimal prices.

Almost all buyers and sellers are both price setters and price searchers; they are monopolists who have limited market information. However, we don't want to introduce monopoly power and limited information unless we can gain enough accuracy or generality to justify the sacrifice of simplicity. Our recognition of price setting in Chapter 5 and then price searching in this chapter has been justified only because it was necessary for the explanation and prediction of certain additional phenomena.

6-2. The Soviet Union's economy is much more efficient because wasteful inventories are not present on store shelves. Comment.

Not necessarily. The Soviet Union does save a great deal by not maintaining inventories, but consumers are then forced to plan ahead, wait, or obtain information without being able to inspect goods cheaply beforehand. Judging from the general failure of stores in the United States to survive when they don't have inventories (even if their prices are lower), the additional costs that consumers in the Soviet Union incur because of the lack of inventories exceed the costs that would have been incurred had inventories been maintained.

6-3. Even when the Bureau of Indian Affairs gives Native Americans goods having high market values, why are the Native Americans sometimes ungrateful?

The values of the in-kind gifts to recipients are determined by what the recipients would have paid for them, not by the market values.

6-4. Rent controls make it possible for the poor to obtain apartments. Is this true?

Not necessarily. The poor sometimes obtain fewer apartments subsequent to the imposition of rent controls. Although the poor may be willing and able to pay lower rents, so are the rich. The presence of shortages force landlords to use nonprice criteria for discrimination. If criteria such as number of children, race, or the prospect of paying rent on time are employed, the poor may be discriminated against.

6-5. Would price controls on kidney-dialysis machines make it possible for everyone to buy them? Who would benefit from the controls?

No. The number of machines would stay the same. In time, the number might even fall.

Different people would probably obtain the machines. The people who would benefit would be those who could meet the new nonprice criteria of discrimination. Sometimes the wealthy would benefit from the controls.

6-6. If racial discrimination in the selling of homes exists, how might you get rich?

If you are not a member of the race being discriminated against, then you can buy homes and resell them at a higher price to members of that race.

6-7. When socialism replaces capitalism, cooperation will replace competition. Discuss.

Scarcity causes competition, not capitalism. Socialism may eliminate market competition, but it then forces other types of competition since there still aren't enough goods for everyone who wants them.

Cooperation has little to do with competition. Cooperation occurs when people get together to achieve a goal that they couldn't or didn't want to achieve independently. Socialism creates a great deal of cooperation. But capitalism allows cooperation as well. The family unit is a cooperative, and so is a corporation. These are simply voluntary cooperatives rather than coercive ones.

6-8. Does the law of the jungle determine who receives goods in competitive markets?

No. The law of the jungle is physical force. In markets, you can obtain goods only by voluntarily sacrificing other goods, not through force. Some people buying large amounts of goods in markets would do poorly in the jungle, while some buying very small quantities would do better.

6-9. Why are black markets and kickbacks so difficult to eliminate?

Because the parties involved all move to more preferred positions when free (though illegal) trade occurs.

6-10. Secondary exchanges make it difficult to keep goods away from people of a particular sex, race, or creed. Explain.

Secondary trades can redistribute goods to those valuing them most, regardless of sex, race, or creed.

6-11. If price controls were imposed on automobiles, what would happen to their durability?

Durability would fall. Shortages of cars would cause sellers to be less concerned about quality. If some consumers didn't want less quality, other consumers easily could be found.

6-12. Why do we wait for dentists, whereas grocery clerks wait for us?

Because inventories of dentists would be very costly, whereas inventories of clerks are usually inexpensive. We aren't usually willing and able to pay dentists enough to wait for us, but we are normally willing and able to pay grocery clerks to wait.

6-13. At J.C. Penney's, why do some customers pay higher store prices while others pay lower catalogue prices?

Because the costs of planning ahead or waiting are low for some customers and high for others. When the costs of planning ahead or waiting exceed the costs of inventories, customers shop in the store. Otherwise, customers buy from the catalogue.

6-14. Congressional seats are sold at the below market price of zero. What are the economic effects of these below-clearing prices?

All 10 effects of nonclearing market prices occur:
1. There is a shortage of seats and a surplus of candidates available for inspection and immediate purchase.
2. The price of the seats is constant and doesn't change.
3. Candidates are wealthier and the public is poorer since candidates don't have to pay for their seats.
4. Many candidates who would like to buy the seats can't do so and are frustrated.
5. Nonprice discrimination occurs as candidates are selected according to criteria other than willingness and ability to pay for the seats.
6. Nonprice competition results as candidates compete to fulfill the various nonprice criteria for discrimination.
7. Transaction costs rise as candidates must spend time and money to win elections rather than spend money to directly buy the seats.
8. Black markets sometimes occur when candidates bribe voters.
9. Shortages increase as more candidates want to be politicians.
10. The quality of the seats falls as the public thinks it can treat politicians poorly since there is a surplus of them and a shortage of seats.

6-15. **What are the ten effects of distributing desirable men and women in Newport Beach at zero prices?**

1. Inventories for inspection and immediate purchase tend not to exist. To buy the men or women, consumers often have to inspect the desirable people while the individuals are still owned by others. Also, the consumers can only buy when the desirable men and women just happen to be available.
2. The price is zero and doesn't change.
3. Wealth is shifted to the buyers, since they can obtain the desirable men and women at zero prices.
4. Shortages of the desirable men and women exist, and therefore some buyers are unable to buy. They are frustrated and gain nothing from the zero prices.
5. Nonprice discrimination is used to distribute the desirable men and women. The individuals are sometimes distributed to those with the most personality, good looks, or education rather than those willing and able to pay the most.
6. The nonprice discrimination causes nonprice competition. When the desirable men and women want partners with pleasing personalities, good looks, or education, consumers will compete with each other by trying to be nice, well-groomed, and educated.
7. Transaction costs increase since buyers must spend time, effort, and money trying to be nice, good-looking, and knowledgeable.
8. Some black markets crop up. Male and female prostitutes sometimes decide they care more about money than about personality, good looks, or education.
9. Shortages increase as more buyers come to the beach to find the desirable men and women sold at zero prices.
10. Quality falls. Desirable men and women, faced with a mass of buyers, tend to be less concerned with the product they provide. If some buyers are turned off by the lower quality, other buyers can easily be found to take their place.

    Of course, many of the desirable men and women are competing for others like themselves who are also in short supply. This tends to limit the erosion of quality.

CHAPTER 7

7-1. **Distinguish among money, capital, and capital goods.**

Money is a medium of exchange. It can reduce transaction costs and give an individual the ability to buy resources, but money doesn't directly produce anything. Capital is a produced resource that can be used to produce other goods. Capital goods are items that yield income. The set of capital goods includes units of capital as special cases.

7-2. **What determines the value of an apple tree?**

The value of an apple tree is determined by the value of the expected future apples that it will yield. If the tree is expected to yield 1000 future apples and if the present value of those future apples is $1000, then the tree is worth $1000.

7-3. **Would capital gains and capital losses occur in a world of unlimited information? Would there still be exchange and production?**

Capital gains and capital losses wouldn't occur in a world of unlimited information. Everyone would know the future and the prices of capital goods would equal the actual present values of the future goods that the capital goods would yield. There would be no surprises.

    Exchange and production would still occur. People would simply know the value of what they would obtain via trade and production. If those values were worth the sacrifices, people would exchange and produce goods.

7-4. **If you hear that the earnings of National Steel are going to rise next quarter, why can't you buy the stock now and make a capital gain?**

Because if you have heard the news, so have other investors. When the information first became available, the investors who owned the stock reduced their supplies, other investors increased their demands, and the price of the shares rose. As a result, the price has already risen to reflect the higher expected earnings.

7-5. **If you strike oil on your land, when will you obtain the capital gain, immediately, after the oil is sold, or when you sell the land?**

The value of the land will immediately increase causing the price to unexpectedly rise giving you a capital gain. Your wealth will rise since the value of the capital goods you own will increase. By selling the oil or land later, you will simply convert your greater wealth from oil or land to cash.

7-6. **Why do stockbrokers, bookies, security analysts, corporation presidents, and horse trainers get up in the morning and go to work?**

Because on the average they can't predict the future better than the markets.

7-7. **What two conditions have to be fulfilled before you can knowingly buy some land and make a capital gain?**

The sellers must not know the value of the land and other knowledgeable buyers can't be present. If the sellers knew that the land was worth more, they would sell it to their friends or family, not you. And if other buyers were present, the buyers would compete with you to obtain the implicit capital gain. As a result, they would bid up the price until the price reflected the present information and no capital gain could be anticipated.

7-8. **There are no known bad or good deals in the *Wall Street Journal*. Is this true?**

True, although some people may know when the prices of capital are incorrect predictors of future values, but we haven't been able to identify them in advance. The bad news is that it's impossible to make money by simply being intelligent, hard-working, or knowledgeable. But the good news is that it also seems impossible to lose money by simply being unintelligent, lazy, or ignorant. In competitive capital markets, experts seem to have no advantage, and people choosing stocks arbitrarily seem to be at no disadvantage.

7-9. **What is the easiest way to determine the value of the future earnings of Mobil Oil Company stock?**

Look at the market price of Mobil Oil Company shares. You don't have to hire an expert to protect yourself if you want to buy shares of common stock since market prices already reflect expert evaluations of public information. The only time it seems to pay to consult experts is when well-organized markets don't exist.

7-10. **The Alaska Native Land Claims Settlement Act forces Alaska natives to hold wealth in the form of shares in native regional corporations. In what sense do the corporations represent socialism?**

Since stockholders are forced to hold their wealth in the form of the native regional firms, they can't selectively bear risks. They will make the capital gains and losses associated with the shares even if they are pessimistic about the values of corporate holdings and are more optimistic about the values of other capital goods.

7-11. **Explain all the economic effects of commodity trades in oil futures.**

We can make the following predictions:
a. Speculators will buy future oil as long as they think that the value of future oil will exceed its present value plus the conservation costs.
b. Speculators will obtain capital gains and losses when new information becomes available indicating either higher or lower future values of oil.

c. Speculators will not obtain capital gains unless they have very special abilities, knowledge, or methods of predicting the future.

d. Speculators will be the ones who selectively bear the risks of losses that may result from low values of future oil.

e. Speculators will shift oil into the future, acting as conservationists of oil.

f. Speculators will force present oil prices upward but will reduce future oil prices.

g. Speculators will incur the costs of conservation.

7-12.   Conservationists just talk; speculators put their money where their mouths are. Evaluate.

People who claim that insufficient conservation is occurring in our economy are often called conservationists. If these individuals were correct, they could become wealthy by buying present goods and shifting them into the future, or by buying future goods at present expected prices. Speculators are conservationists who are doing just that. But speculators, while they are concerned with the future, must also be concerned with the present. If they shift too much or too little into the future, they lose money.

7-13.   In what sense are labor markets futures markets?

When workers sell their labor, they are essentially selling the products of their labor in advance. If the products are eventually worth less than was expected as reflected in the wages that were paid workers, the employers incur capital losses; if the products are worth more, the employers make capital gains.

7-14.   Since people only live 80 years or so, future generations can't depend on speculators to conserve goods for them. Is this true? Explain.

No. Intermediate speculators will buy the goods and bet that the future prices will cover present prices plus conservation costs. The goods will go from one person to another until the highest bidder is a present consumer rather than a speculator representing a future consumer.

7-15.   Since land will be here in the future with or without speculators, land speculation results in a wasteful withdrawal of present land. Is this true? Explain.

No. Income property management firms will see to it that present land is used as long as the future value of the land isn't significantly reduced by the intermediate use. This is why some gasoline stations operate in downtown Los Angeles, why mobile homes are parked on million-dollar property, and why cattle ranches exist on land that will produce oil in the future.

CHAPTER 8

8-1.   All of us value future goods less than present goods by the degree reflected in the rate of interest. In what sense is this true?

The interest rate reflects the price of present goods in terms of future goods. Although we may initially value present goods in terms of future goods differently, after we have made all possible trades, we will generally value the goods the same way.

For example, if the going interest rate is 10% and you value present goods 15% more than future goods, then you will borrow until the value of present goods falls and the value of future goods rises to the point where present goods are just 10% more valuable than future goods. Conversely, if you value present goods 5% more than future goods, you will lend until the values of present goods rise to be 10% more than the values of future goods. In an economy where the commodity or the money interest rate is 10%, everyone eventually values present commodities or money 10% more than future commodities or money.

8-2. What would happen to the rate of interest if a nuclear war was suddenly expected in the near future? Why?

The interest rate would rise. Present goods would become far more valuable in terms of future goods. As a result, to buy present goods from creditors, many more future goods would have to be promised.

8-3. Are present goods more valuable than future goods in socialist as well as capitalist economies?

Yes. The values of goods over time seem to have little to do with whether property is owned individually or communally. In socialist economies, people usually prefer present goods to future goods. As a result, to buy present goods, debtors usually have to pay creditors a premium in terms of future goods. However, for ideological reasons, the repayments of extra future goods in socialist economic systems may not be called interest.

8-4. Are capital gains and interest rates phenomena that arise from production?

Our theory denies this since we have been able to explain and predict both capital gains and interest without mentioning production. As we will see later, capital gains and interest are related to production, but since capital gains and losses also occur in productionless economies, they can't fundamentally emanate from production. Capital gains and interest are caused by uncertainty and time-value rather than production.

8-5. All other things the same, why might college students be less likely to borrow money?

All other things the same, the fact that the students are choosing to forgo present consumption to obtain higher future earnings while their noncollege counterparts aren't implies that the students value future goods more relative to present goods.

8-6. Are interest rates monetary phenomena?

Fundamentally, no. Interest rates exist in barter economies where money isn't present. However, interest rates are affected by monetary factors in monetary economies. When inflation rises, money interest rates increase so that lenders are compensated for the relatively lower value of future money as well as the relatively lower value of future commodities.

8-7. If the interest rate is 10%, what is the present value of a car that will yield $1000 per year in transportation services for 5 years?

The present value is $3789 (the sum of $909, $826, $751, $683, and $620).

8-8. You expect to earn $40,000 per year, forever. If the interest rate is 10%, how much is your labor worth now? What if the interest rate rises or falls while your expected income remains the same?

The present value of a $40,000-per-year perpetuity at 10% is $400,000. If the interest rate rises, your labor will be worth less since a higher interest rate means that future money is worth less relative to present money than was the case previously. For example, if the interest rate rises to 20%, the present value of your future earnings will fall to $200,000. Conversely, if the interest rate falls, future money is worth more relative to present money, and your future earnings are worth more. For instance, if the interest rate falls to 5%, the value of your future earnings will rise to $800,000.

8-9. If the interest rate is 10%, how much is a share of common stock that will perpetually yield $40 per year in dividends worth now? What if the interest rate rises or falls and the yield remains the same?

At 10%, the share is worth $400. If the interest rate rises, the price of the share will fall. But if the rate decreases, the price will rise. All this occurs because the interest rate is used to discount the future earnings of shares of stock. When the rate falls, the earnings are worth more and a lower discount is appropriate. The opposite occurs when the rate rises.

8-10. **Relative to the price you paid for shares of Chrysler Corporation stock, your yearly rate of return is 2%. Have you increased your wealth by buying the stock?**

You have not increased your wealth if the interest rate is 10% and the rate of return is expected to remain 2% forever. A 2% return doesn't compensate you for the goods you sacrificed when you purchased the shares. You may have 2% per year more money in the future, but you have the money later and it is worth 10% per year less. In fact, assuming the market has already anticipated the low future earnings, the price has already fallen, creating a capital loss, to make the future anticipated rate of return to new buyers 10%.

8-11. **Suppose a criminal can obtain $10,000 by committing a robbery and the cost of being caught is $15,000. How can a rational criminal still commit the crime?**

The cost is incurred in the future while the benefits are obtained in the present. If the costs are far enough in the future, discounting can bring their value down below $10,000.

The costs also have to be discounted by the probability of their being incurred (the probability of being caught, convicted, and sentenced). If the probability is 50%, then that discounting alone can bring the cost down to $7500.

8-12. **How will higher anticipated inflation affect the price of a home mortgage? A hotel? A common stock? Why?**

Higher anticipated inflation will raise the interest rate. This will reduce the value of a mortgage that is paying the old lower rate. The price of the mortgage will fall to make its effective rate the same as the going rate of interest.

Higher anticipated inflation rate won't lower the values of hotels and common stocks because the higher interest discount rate will be offset by the greater future earnings generated by the inflation. That is, greater inflation will raise future room rates and product prices as well as present interest rates. This is why common stocks and real estate are often good hedges against inflation.

8-13. **If you were asked to determine the value of a small business so that a divorced woman could get her half of community property, how would you go about it?**

You would forecast the future revenues and costs of the firm and then discount by the appropriate interest rate to obtain the present value, the capital value, of the firm.

8-14. **The U.S. Army Corps of Engineers builds capital projects. Why do you think the corps has historically used a low interest rate to determine the feasibility of these projects?**

Perhaps because its managers have wanted to build the projects. By using low rates for discounting, the projects become more feasible. Since the costs of the projects are early and their revenues late, higher discount rates would have made capital projects less economical.

8-15. **Suppose you could drop a well for a total present cost of $3000. If you also had the option of hooking up to the public water utility for $30 per month, forever, which would you choose?**

It would depend on the interest rate. At 10%, the $3000 cost would be lower than the $3600 present value of future utility payments, so you would drop the well. However, at 20%, the present value of the utility payments would be only $1800. You would then hook up to the utility.

CHAPTER 9

9-1. Do the physical characteristics of goods have to change before production can occur?

No. For example, if you combine your labor with a truck and some furniture and move the furniture to another location, production will have occurred even though the physical characteristics of the furniture will not have changed.

9-2. Undiscovered natural gas is land. Is discovered natural gas land? Is exploration a productive process? Explain.

Discovered natural gas is capital, a combination of undiscovered natural gas and the resources used to discover the natural gas. Exploration is clearly a productive process even if it doesn't change the physical characteristics of goods.

9-3. There are really only two basic resources, labor and land. Capital is but a manifestation of a way of combining labor and land to produce products. Is this true?

Yes. In the next chapter, we will see that we can look at capital from two different perspectives. One is as a produced resource used in subsequent production. Another is as an intermediate manifestation of some final products, a part of a particular production process that combines land and labor into products.

9-4. Money is capital. In what sense is this true? In what sense is it false?

Money is capital to the extent that money is a produced resource that can reduce transaction costs. Money is not capital in the sense that an increase in the supply of money will not reduce transaction costs further. Also, money cannot be used as an input to produce other products.

9-5. Since we can't see if we are producing the most valuable goods, how do we know that we do so?

The only observable evidence that we produce the most valuable goods is indirect. It comes from how we react to changes in costs. For example, if Eric is producing wood and vegetables so that the value of wood is equal to its cost (the value of sacrificed vegetables), then he should produce more wood if we give him 100 pounds of vegetables. With more vegetables, the marginal value of the vegetables will fall, reducing the cost of wood below its value.

9-6. When the government helps small farmers by subsidizing food prices, what are the economic effects of this aid?

The farmers are wealthier and taxpayers are poorer. The farmers produce more and other producers produce less.

9-7. How does an increase in production by one of Eric's neighbors affect Eric? How does an increase in production by Japan affect the United States?

As long as Eric has the same resources as before, his neighbor's production shouldn't have any affect on Eric. This also applies to the United States and Japan. Of course, some individuals in the United States and Japan may be worse off if they encounter more competition when they sell their products.

9-8. Why does it often cost more to do a job within a more limited time period?

It costs more when time is more limited because resources must be used when the values of their alternative products are higher than if the resources had been used later.

9-9. How could someone have spent $2000 to repair a Toyota Landcruiser worth only $1500?

For example, if your car is worth $1500 and the anticipated cost of repair is $900, you will tell the mechanic to go ahead and fix it. Then, if, after the $900 has been spent, it becomes evident that an additional $1100 is necessary, you will tell the mechanic to continue. Spending $1100 to obtain a car worth $1500 is rational. The $900 already spent is irrelevant since it can't be retrieved.

9-10.   Why do new oil taxes affect prospective wells more than old wells?

New taxes affect prospective wells more than old ones because prospective wells have all their cost before them. The addition of the taxes to other costs can make them uneconomical. In contrast, old wells cost so little to operate that even if relatively high taxes are levied, the total costs are likely to be less than the revenues.

9-11.   Do generals continue battles so that the dead will not have died in vain?

No. The dead are gone. Generals continue battles because the additional benefits are more valuable than the additional costs. From a different perspective, if historical costs counted, battles would never be stopped until all soldiers were dead.

9-12.   Why might you liquidate your small business even though it gives you an accounting profit of $10,000 per year?

You would liquidate it if you could make $10,001 per year working elsewhere and the business paid you no salary. Also, you might liquidate if some of the firm's resources were undervalued on the books, perhaps because they were purchased many years earlier.

9-13.   Can the government produce goods at a lower cost than a private firm?

Generally, no. The government can produce at a lower cost than a private firm only if it uses less costly resources than a private firm. The government may charge users less or pay resource owners less for resources, but the cost of production is nevertheless the value of the highest-valued alternatives sacrificed.

9-14.   The benefits of a revolution in Poland would be far greater than the costs, and yet, the majority allows itself to be controlled by a few Communists. This shows that people are irrational. Explain how it is possible for the majority to be rational under such circumstances.

Groups of people don't make decisions; individuals do. As long as individuals think that their personal costs of rebelling against the government are greater than their personal gains, they won't rebel. One guard can control hundreds of prisoners, one dictator can rule over millions of people, and a small political party can dominate a country by dealing with individuals rather than groups.

9-15.   Why are government employees often unwilling to do things that benefit other people more than they cost those people?

Government employees behave this way because, like everyone else, they are generally concerned only with their individual benefits and costs, not with the benefits and costs that accrue to others. Of course, by bribing or screaming at them, you may be able to increase their benefits or costs and motivate them to behave differently.

9-16.   How can the Soviet Union motivate managers to focus on group costs of production?

The same way owners of corporations in the United States do: make the individual welfare of the managers correspond with the reduction of group costs of production by paying the managers more when group costs are low. However, Marxist ideology generally prohibits extensive monetary rewards. The only alternatives are other rewards such as prestige, promotions, and Stars of Lenin.

CHAPTER 10

10-1. Given the conditions shown in the following table, which nation's resources have a comparative advantage in the production of guns? Butter? What will be the gains from specialization according to comparative advantages?

	GUNS		BUTTER	
United States	30	$(\frac{2}{3})$	40	$(\frac{1}{3})$
Australia	15	$(\frac{2}{3})$	30	$(\frac{1}{3})$

The United States has the comparative advantage in guns. Although she can produce both more guns and butter than Australia, her resources have the greatest advantage in guns. To produce 30 units of guns, the United States has to sacrifice 80 units of butter compared to the 120 units that Australia would have to sacrifice.

Australia has the comparative advantage in butter. Although she has a disadvantage in both guns and butter, the disadvantage is smallest in butter. To produce 30 units of butter, Australia sacrifices 7.5 units of guns as compared to the 11.5 units of guns that the United States would have to sacrifice.

The gain from specialization would be 20 units of butter. Australia would then produce 90 units of butter while the United States would produce 45 units of guns.

10-2. What does the law of increasing costs do to the shape of the production possibilities frontier?

The law of increasing costs makes the production possibilities frontier concave (to the origin). For example, the frontier below shows the production possibilities that result when the resources of the United States and Australia in Question 10-1 are used to produce guns and butter. To produce the first 45 units of guns, only 120 units of butter are sacrificed because the United States produces the guns. But, to produce just 22.5 more units of guns, 90 units of butter are sacrificed, since Australia's resources have to be shifted into gun production.

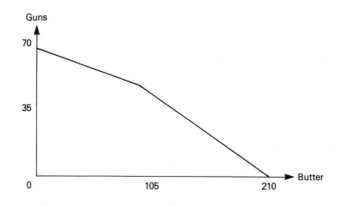

10-3. Opposites attract. In what sense are marriages between opposites more productive?

Marriages between opposites can be more productive because lower-cost resources can be more extensively employed.

For instance, if my wife is a good cook and a poor mechanic while I'm a poor cook and a good mechanic, then with specialization, we will eat good food as well as drive cars that run well. But if we are both good cooks and bad mechanics, we will still eat good food, but we will drive poorly tuned cars.

10-4. **Restrictions on foreign trade are necessary to stimulate industrial development and protect small developing firms from foreign competition. Evaluate.**

No. If comparative advantages exist, industrialization will occur without foreign trade restrictions or subsidies.

10-5. **To the extent that West Virginia specializes in the production and sale of natural resources (coal), does the rest of the world represent an imperialist power exploiting the state for its resources?**

No. The people of both West Virginia and the rest of the world move to more preferred positions by specializing according to comparative advantages.

As another example, many people argue that England exploited the colonies within the English empire. This may be partly correct. However, England also benefited from her colonies in another way. By having trading partners, she was able to increase specialization and expand her production possibilities. The colonies also obtained England as a trading partner and were therefore able to specialize and expand their production possibilities.

10-6. **When will farmers quit producing corn and get jobs with IBM?**

Farmers will quit producing corn when they develop comparative advantages in working for IBM. They will go to work for IBM as soon as they can produce so much by working for IBM that their pay more than compensates them for the wages and working conditions that they would sacrifice by not working on the farm. In short, if they can produce a great deal at IBM, it will become too costly to continue farming.

10-7. **Why does the United States both produce and import steel?**

The United States both produces and imports steel largely because of the law of increasing costs. Demand for steel exceeds the capabilities of the lowest cost resources in the United States. Once resources with comparative advantages in steel are exhausted, it becomes cheaper to import additional steel than to produce it.

10-8. **Is alienation caused by the separation of a worker from his or her tools, or by the insignificant nature of the contribution the worker makes to a final product?**

We can't see alienation so we don't know.

10-9. **Economics reveals that people should specialize. Does it?**

No. Economics doesn't say what should be, only what is. It simply identifies the effects of specialization: greater production possibilities, more repetitive work, greater interdependence, and more trade.

10-10. **Economics shows that trade barriers shouldn't be erected. Does it?**

No. Economics just identifies the effects of trade barriers.

10-11. **What argument could oil producers in Michigan make for restricting Oklahoma oil imports?**

By restricting Oklahoma oil imports, more jobs would be created in the Michigan oil industry, the industry would pay more taxes, and the oil industry's stockholders would earn more dividends.

10-12. **If you were not allowed to buy anything, how would your output be affected?**

If you were prevented from trading with others, you would despecialize and your production possibilities would fall toward or below subsistence. If you couldn't buy products, you wouldn't sell your labor and would instead use the labor to produce for yourself.

10-13. Does foreign trade create jobs? Does it destroy them?

Foreign trade shifts some jobs away from firms producing for domestic consumption and toward firms producing for export.

10-14. What is the relationship between the real interest rate and the level of investment? Why?

At higher real interest rates, future commodities are less valuable. This means that capital goods are less valuable. And this causes a reduction in the purchase of capital—a decline in investment. From a different perspective, the real interest rate on borrowed money rises and this increases the cost of borrowing money for investment. As a result, investment declines.

10-15. Suppose the anticipated value of your total future sacrifices from going to college was $150,000 and the anticipated value of your total future gains was $200,000. Under what conditions would avoiding college nevertheless by rational?

It would be rational to avoid college if the present value of the anticipated value of the total future sacrifices exceeded the present value of the anticipated value of the total future gains.

10-16. If the early industrialists had not been willing to accept many of the risks associated with building factories, would the factories have been built?

Possibly not. Judging from the problems many of them had when they tried to convince other investors to accept much smaller risks, the general opinion was that the factories would not be worth the costs.

CHAPTER 11

11-1. Who produces more, a lawyer or a legal secretary?

There is no way to know. Since a lawyer does different things than a legal secretary, a physical comparison of marginal products is impossible. Also, if the lawyer and the legal secretary cooperate to produce a legal brief, it is impossible to measure the direct contributions of each since the brief wouldn't have been produced if either one of them had not been involved in production.

Fortunately, it is not necessary for a firm to know the extra proportional contributions of resources when resources are hired. All that is necessary is some idea of marginal product and that product is usually, though roughly, measurable. For example, when a law firm is deciding whether or not to hire another lawyer or legal secretary, the question that it needs to answer is how much more will the law firm produce if one more unit of either resource is hired; that is, what will be the marginal product of each resource? The value of that product to the firm, the marginal revenue product, can then be compared to the marginal resource cost to arrive at a hiring decision.

11-2. Does a higher value of land result in a higher value of corn, or does a higher value of corn cause a higher value of land?

Land that doesn't produce anything of value is worthless. The value of corn determines the value of the land, not vice versa (assuming that corn is the highest-valued product that the land can produce).

More generally, the values of resources are determined by their marginal revenue products, not the other way around.

11-3. Does the law of diminishing returns say that the employment of additional units of a resource will cause total output to fall?

No. The law says only that as additional units of a resource are hired, their contributions will eventually be less than the contributions of previous units. For example, by adding an additional fisherman to a fishing boat, 100 more fish may be caught, but the 100 unit marginal product may still be less than the marginal product of the previous fisherman, in which case, diminishing returns occur.

11-4. Graph the relationship between the value of a resource and the quantity purchased. Place the value on the vertical axis and quantity on the horizontal.

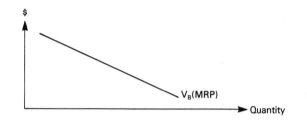

The curve slopes downward because as more of a resource is purchased, its marginal revenue product falls. The marginal revenue product declines because both the marginal product and the marginal revenue of the units within the marginal product decline.

11-5. Graph the relationship between the value of a resource and the amount sold. Place the value on the vertical axis and the quantity on the horizontal.

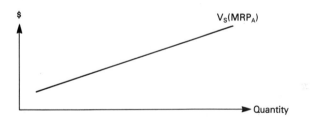

The curve slopes upward because as more of a resource is sold, its value to the seller increases because the marginal revenue product of alternative employment rises.

11-6. If a secretary is worth $10 per hour, what keeps you from hiring him or her for $9 per hour? What keeps him or her from charging $11 per hour?

Competition from other employers keeps you from paying less than $10. Competition from other secretaries keeps him or her from charging more than $10.

11-7. A worker will increase your revenues by $10,000. She asks only that she be paid $5000. Why might you rationally not hire her?

If you are a monopsonist, her employment might cause you to have to raise the pay of other workers so much that in total, she might cost you more than $10,000.

11-8. Suppose the Jackson Restaurant Association is the only buyer of servers in Jackson. Graph the marginal revenue product, the marginal resource cost, and the supply of labor curves that exist in the labor market. Then show and explain the monopsony price and quantity.

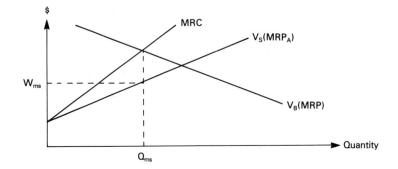

The monopsony wage is *Wms* and the quantity employed is *Qms,* the wage and quantity that correspond to the equality of the marginal revenue product and the resource cost of the servers.

11-9. **Suppose the Jackson Restaurant Servers Union is the only seller of servers in Jackson. Graph the marginal revenue product, the supply of labor, and the marginal earnings curves that exist in the labor market. Then show and explain the monopoly price and quantity.**

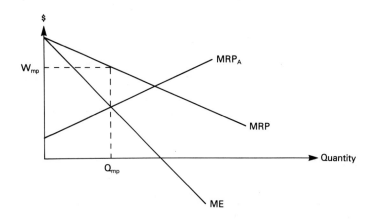

The monopoly wage is *Wmp* and the quantity employed is *Qmp,* the wage and quantity that correspond to the equality of marginal earnings and the marginal revenue product of alternative employment of the servers.

11-10. **Why might it be difficult for American firms to exploit Mexican workers?**

It might be difficult because other firms, both foreign and domestic, want to do the same thing.

11-11. **Why did the Arab oil cartel OPEC reduce its prices in the early 1980s?**

Because of competition from within and without the cartel. Many OPEC members cheated on the cartel's production quotas and prices and non-OPEC nations such as Mexico and England increased production and sales.

11-12. **Why have many nations chosen not to join OPEC?**

By not joining OPEC, some producing nations can act independently and sell all the oil they want at slightly below the cartel's prices.

11-13. **How does Bruce Springsteen keep his wages high?**

He refuses to produce unless he is paid a certain wage. In effect, he reduces the supply of his services to a level where he is able to obtain a high monopoly wage.

11-14. **Unions don't exploit employers. They just obtain what workers are worth. Employers wouldn't hire workers unless the workers produced more than they were paid. Comment.**

Workers are worth what they are paid only because more workers can't be hired. By restricting supply, unions artificially raise the marginal revenue product of labor.

11-15. **Even when a union raises wages, why might you be wise not to join?**

By being outside the union, you would be free of union constraints. As a result, you could work all you wished at slightly less than the union wage.

11-16. **Unions can raise wages either by negotiating or by restricting the supply of labor. Why does a restriction of supply often look better to the public?**

A restriction of supply is less visible and can often be justified in the name of better quality or safety.

11-17. **A worker's marginal product is 100 apples. The worker has been paid only 50 apples. Under what conditions could the worker have been paid the value of his or her labor?**

First, if future goods are worth far less than present goods, the present 50 apples the worker was paid might have been worth as much as the future 100 apples that were later produced. The extra 50 apples may have represented an interest payment compensating the buyers for time-value sacrifices.

Second, the 100 apples may have been unexpected at the time of the trade. If everyone thought that the worker would produce only 50 future apples, then the payment could have reflected what the worker was worth at the time he or she was paid.

CHAPTER 12

12-1. **What are the disadvantages of hiring a certified public accounting firm to keep a company's books?**

The firm can only do a limited amount of work; it can't take advantage of specialization to as great an extent; and some transaction costs are associated with finding the firm and in negotiating a contract.

12-2. **When fishermen sign on to a boat for a share of the catch, how does this assign time-value sacrifices and risks?**

When they sign on for a percentage of the catch, then they accept both most of the time-value sacrifices and the capital gains and losses related to their future labor services. They will be paid only after fish are sold and will make capital gains if the catch is unexpectedly large and losses if it is unexpectedly small.

12-3. **Would you be willing to work for a percentage of the revenues generated by the sales of a firm's pot-scrubbers? Why?**

Most workers wouldn't. The chance that you would just happen to value one particular capital good more than any others or want to accept its particular level of expected value fluctuation is remote.

12-4. **To what extent do the earnings of banks, bondholders, partners, and common stockholders represent interest and profits?**

All the groups make time-value sacrifices, since all sacrifice the purchases of present goods when they buy either debt or equity assets. They also all accept risks, although the degree to which they accept risks varies. Banks and bondholders accept fewer risks of capital losses since they have first claims on earnings, but they also obtain few capital gains relative to partners and common stockholders, since payments to banks and bondholders are limited.

12-5. **What advantage does management coordination and control have over market coordination and control?**

By reducing the number of transactions, management coordination and control can reduce transaction costs.

12-6. **What advantages does market coordination and control have over management coordination and control from the perspective of a firm? From the perspective of an employee?**

From the perspective of a firm, market coordination and control reduces management costs. From the perspective of an employee, markets may be easier to obey than managers.

12-7. **We are free to leave the jobs we have. Why then do we still feel like slaves to business firms?**

We may feel like slaves because as long as we work for one particular firm, we must do what its managers tell us. Furthermore, having limited information, we may not know of alternative jobs. Also, switching jobs may be a difficult process. Finally, we may be paid so much to do a job that we may not feel free to leave.

12-8. **How does piecework differ from hourly wages? Why does it require fewer managerial costs?**

Piecework is a form of the putting-out system. People sell their product rather than their labor. As a result, they respond more to market prices than to the dictates of managers. Since workers are driven by pay, fewer managers are necessary.

Piecework has received some bad press, perhaps because many managers have used it as a way of raising production without raising wages. However, all subcontractors and most salespersons are essentially on piecework contracts and many of them prefer it to working for a boss.

12-9. **Why are some industries comprised of many small firms, whereas others are comprised of a few large ones?**

In some industries, firms must be very large before they can take advantage of most of the economies of large scale production. In other industries, the economies are exhausted while firms are still small.

12-10. **Individual managers at the National Cash Register Corporation decide whether additional units should be produced. But central management must decide whether the firm is to stay in business. Explain.**

Individual managers need to know only whether the marginal revenue of a given decision will cover its marginal cost. If it does, the profit of the firm increases. Individuals don't need to know anything about average revenue and cost.

Central management, however, must make the overall decision about whether the firm is to stay in business because that decision is based on the average revenue and cost.

12-11. **Suppose the profits of General Foods are on the rise. Why can't you be sure that you will obtain a capital gain if you buy shares of General Food stock?**

The price of the shares already reflects the greater future expected profits. By buying the shares, you can only expect earnings that will compensate you for your time-value sacrifices. To obtain capital gains with certainty, you must have secret information, not public information.

12-12. Why might you produce and sell a marginal pot-scrubber even if it increases the average cost of production? What if it reduces the average rate of return?

As long as the marginal scrubber yields a marginal revenue that exceeds its marginal cost, you would make money by producing it. For example, if the marginal revenue of the next scrubber was $80 and the marginal cost was $70, you would make $10 more even if average cost rose or the average rate of return declined.

12-13. The managers of firms don't seek maximum profits. Once they obtain enough to get by, they are more concerned with either growth or their own welfare. Evaluate.

This is not necessarily true. Growth and the welfare of managers may correspond to maximum profits. It is true that managers want to maximize their personal well-being rather than the profits of the firm. But stockholders can nevertheless motivate managers to focus on profits by using salaries, bonuses, and promotions to link the well-being of managers to profits of the firm.

Of course, substitutability exists and to some extent managers will trade off profits for other goods.

12-14. Do the predictions that a firm will produce if average revenue at least equals average cost and produce the level of output such that marginal revenue equals marginal cost apply to a socialist firm?

Yes. But the gains and costs of production do not take the form of easily observable money earned or sacrificed. Therefore predicting the behavior of a socialist firm is very difficult.

For instance, a socialist administrator in a university making a decision on whether or not to hire another faculty member will, like the manager of a private firm, look at the gains and the sacrifices of various options. But the gains may take the form of prestige from running a larger department, the happiness of students and legislators or the positive reactions of other faculty members. And the costs may take the form of a loss of control over faculty members, the negative reactions of legislators, or the extra work of managing another professor. Nevertheless, if the values of the gains cover the values of the sacrifices, the additional faculty member will be hired.

12-15. If you had to train farmers how to grow potatoes, which farmers would you train if you were concerned with maximum total production?

You would train the farmers who produced more extra potatoes than were sacrificed as the training was occurring.

CHAPTER 13

13-1. Each of the firms producing suntan lotion in the United States have some control over price. Would the recognition of this control improve our ability to understand their pricing and production decisions, or would it only make the theory more complex?

It would probably only make the theory more complex, since the firms behave the same way with or without some monopoly power. That is, when demand for suntan lotion increases, the firms with some price control nevertheless initially increase prices and output a bit in the short run. Then in the long run, they reduce prices toward original levels and raise production further.

Only if we were interested in additional phenomena would the recognition of monopoly power be justified.

13-2. **All farmers producing wheat do so at the same cost. In what sense is this true? In what sense is it false?**

The farmers have the same marginal cost, since they make sure that their marginal cost equals the market price. But they have a different average cost, since the value of the wheat differs from that of the alternative products that their resources could have otherwise produced.

13-3. **When small farmers argue that they can't stay in business because prices are too low or costs are too high, how are consumers valuing the products that the resources of the farmers are producing relative to the products that the resources could have otherwise produced?**

Consumers are valuing the other products that the resources could have otherwise produced more than the agricultural items they are producing. If this weren't the case, the prices of the resources used by the farmers would be low relative to agricultural product prices.

13-4. **Do all monopoly firms earn profits?**

No, the only monopoly firms that earn profits are the ones that have average revenues above average costs. It is possible for a monopolist to break even if demand is such that the demand curve is tangent to the average cost curve so that price equals average cost.

13-5. **How will an increase in the number of firms producing close substitutes for the product of a monopolist affect the demand for the monopolist's product? When will such monopolistic competition tend to occur?**

An increase in the number of firms producing close substitutes for the product of a monopolist will reduce demand for the monopolist's product. The decrease in demand will continue as long as the price prospective producers think they can receive by producing the close substitutes equals or exceeds their expected average cost.

13-6. **Will monopolists continually raise prices to cause continuous inflation? Will they ever be willing to reduce prices during periods of deflation?**

Monopolists will not continually raise prices. Once they raise prices to profit-maximizing levels, they will increase prices further only when demands or costs rise.

Monopolists will reduce prices during periods of deflation. They will reduce prices any time demands or costs fall, and demands and costs tend to be falling during periods of deflation.

13-7. **Graphically show the effects of price discrimination on total revenue.**

Perfect price discrimination allows a firm to obtain all the area beneath the demand curve as revenue, area ADCE, rather than just price times quantity, area BDCE.

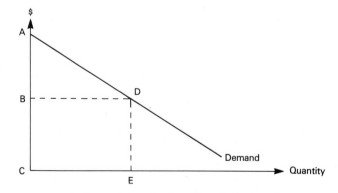

13-8. **When government deregulates the trucking industry, low-cost producers initially flood the market and the price falls. But eventually, most producers be-**

come bankrupt. As a result, only a few monopolistic firms remain and they raise the price above the initial level. Evaluate.

No. Trucking firms consider future as well as present prices and costs. New firms enter the industry only to the extent that their owners expect future prices to cover future costs. Also, firms enter slowly so that prices have a chance to gradually drop to a level just sufficient to cover average cost. When the price hits that level, more firms will not enter. Oversupply will not occur; price won't generally fall below the average cost of efficient producers.

13-9. **When a doctor charges needy people lower rates, is he or she helping the poor or soaking the rich?**

It could be viewed either way. In either case, price discrimination occurs and the doctor obtains more revenue than if he or she had to spoil the market for the rich to sell to the poor.

13-10. **Explain and show graphically the monopoly price and quantity when perfect price discrimination is possible.**

The monopoly price will vary. It will follow the demand curve down to the point at which the curve intersects the marginal cost curve, the point at which price equals marginal revenue. On the following graph, the monopoly price will fall from P_m to P_m' as 0 to Q_m units are sold.

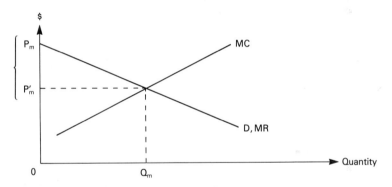

13-11. **What arguments might a dentist give for why dentistry should not be deregulated?**

The same arguments that most regulated monopolists give. The dentist might argue that
a. Quality will fall as quacks enter dentistry and drive quality dentists to other professions.
b. The consumer won't have any information about quality.
c. The price will eventually rise after the supply has fallen because dentists will leave the profession.
d. The monopoly producers will eventually dominate the profession and they will charge much higher prices.
e. The industry will be unstable as supplies and prices fluctuate wildly.

CHAPTER 14

14-1. **How do wage-price controls limit private property rights?**

They limit transferability rights. People are allowed to sell labor and products but only at controlled rates of exchange.

14-2. Suppose consumers value hang gliders more and bicycles less. Explain the effects this will have on the markets for the two goods.

The value changes will cause demand changes which will in turn cause price changes. The prices of hang gliders will rise, whereas those of bicycles will fall. Producers will then respond to the price changes by producing more hang gliders and fewer bicycles. In time, these production changes will change values and cause the prices of hang gliders to fall and the prices of bicycles to rise. Eventually, the value of the gliders will equal the values of the sacrificed bicycles. At that point, prices will be close to their original levels, whereas the production of the gliders will be higher and the production of bicycles will be lower, reflecting the new consumer valuations.

14-3. Suppose producers felt that they have a social responsibility not to produce dangerous hang gliders. Why would it nevertheless be difficult for them to ignore consumer desires?

Market prices would tell them that consumers valued the gliders, despite the lack of safety, and those prices would reward anyone for producing the gliders. The prices would also penalize those producers who chose not to produce the gliders. Prices, by providing incentives as well as instructions, put consumers rather than producers in charge.

14-4. Capitalism is a system of freedom. Since people do anything they want, it is extremely inefficient. Government coordination and control is necessary to prevent arbitrary results. Evaluate.

This is not true. Although people are free to do as they choose, they are told what to do and given the incentive to do it by market prices. In fact, the penalties and rewards for responding to prices are often much more extreme in the private sector of the American economy than the penalties and rewards for responding to government directives in the public sector.

14-5. Adam Smith, the father of modern economics, once argued that the "invisible hand" of self-interest would motivate producers to respond to the desires of consumers. What makes the self-interest of producers match that of consumers?

Market prices. They reflect consumer valuations and also provide instructions, rewards and penalties to producers.

14-6. What prevents producers from selling only to their friends, relatives, whites, and heterosexuals.

Prices in markets tell the producers to sell to those consumers valuing goods the most. The prices are also the rewards. If producers choose to sell only to friends, relatives, whites, and heterosexuals, they will lose money unless those consumers happen to be the ones who are also willing and able to pay the most.

14-7. Parents can't be allowed to make decisions about educational matters because they don't have any information. Evaluate.

One possible reason why parents don't have much information about education is that under present socialist production conditions, the value of information is limited, since choices are limited. For example, if you could buy only a Ford, you wouldn't have much incentive to obtain information about cars. Under capitalist production conditions, information would be more useful since more choices would be available. Also, more information would be produced by private firms wanting to sell their educational services than is produced by socialist monopolies.

14-8. Under a capitalist educational system, would teachers be paid more or less?

It would depend upon what consumers wanted. Some consumers might want more qualified teachers and be willing to pay, whereas other consumers might prefer other educational resources rather than more qualified teachers.

14-9. **Suppose you feel a social responsibility to hire American rather than Mexican labor in your garment factory. How would you and your consumers be affected by your decision?**

Your costs would rise and your profits would fall. You might become bankrupt.

Consumers would be forced to sacrifice the more valuable products that the American workers could have otherwise produced, rather than the less valuable products that the Mexican workers would wind up producing.

14-10. **Do you think that the control of food and drugs by the Food and Drug Administration results in the quality and safety that consumers value most?**

No. If consumers valued that level of quality and safety the most, it would have been produced without government. It isn't that consumers don't want that level, it's just that some of them want other things more.

14-11. **Why is it difficult for socialist administrators to match competitive capitalist results?**

Because they don't have market prices to tell them which goods consumers value most, which resources are least costly to consumers, and which consumers value the products the most.

14-12. **How can religion bring about capitalist results?**

When private-property rights are imperfect or undefined, capitalist results can be achieved by governments. However, religion can also bring about capitalist results and do so at a lower cost. For instance, instead of the government passing a law making stealing a crime, a church can make stealing a sin. While the government must spend money to finance a judicial system to enforce the law, the church can more simply threaten people with hell if they steal.

14-13. **Why do people vote in national elections?**

Since individual votes very seldom count, the benefits to individuals are almost always less than the costs. People vote only because it is considered a patriotic duty to vote. Patriotism is similar to manners, customs, and religion. It is an institution that causes people to consider benefits and costs other than those for which they must pay.

14-14. **The resources of North and South America are similar. Are private-property rights to those resources the same? How does this affect the uses to which resources are put?**

Perhaps South America produces so much less than North America because private-property rights in South America are more limited. South America is more a case of socialism and mercantilism than of capitalism.

14-15. **In the text, a list of things done by governments in the United States is listed below this question. Which ones may be necessary to bring about consumer-orientated results?**

This is a difficult question to answer because the production or consumption of almost every good by an individual affects other people in some way. In almost every case, someone will argue that government intervention is necessary to achieve capitalist results. For example, someone might argue that the government of a university (the administration) should force male professors to wear ties, because this improves the environment for students, or that not wearing ties harms that environment. While you might agree with such a regulation, you're probably not willing to go to the extreme of having government interfere everywhere just because some social benefits or costs can be identified.

You simply have to answer the question using your own values. However, in each case, identify the external effects that you think justify government intervention and be sure that the effects are ignored by markets. Also, try to find ways that markets might be able to take the effects into account.

CHAPTER 15

15-1. **What are some of the characteristics of a commodity that might help it qualify as a monetary form?**

Acceptability, divisibility, identifiability, durability, storability, availability, fixity of supply, weight, and portability.

15-2. **In the hypothetical economy, what major factor determined how many reserves were necessary to back outstanding notes?**

The general acceptability of the notes. That is, had people in all places accepted the notes for trade rather than gold, no demands for gold would have been made and no reserves would have been necessary.

15-3. **In the hypothetical economy, what limited the money supply once you were able to issue notes?**

Three factors:
a. The quantity of gold in existence
b. The percentage of the gold deposited with you
c. The reserve ratio that you had to maintain

15-4. **What two factors determine the extent to which a monetary form is high-powered?**

The quantity of the monetary form that is deposited with creators of private debt money and the ratio of reserves they hold. If more of the high-powered money is deposited or if the ratio falls, then the monetary form will be more high-powered.

15-5. **Why do banks want to make as many loans as possible?**

Reserves are barren assets. Loans generate interest.

15-6. **In early American history, "wildcat banks" were located where the wildcats lived. Why?**

By locating in the bush, fewer demands for reserves were made relative to outstanding notes. The banks were therefore able to keep lower reserves and make more loans.

15-7. **Do banks generally increase the money supply when they grant new loans?**

No. Although the evolution of the hypothetical economy may give the impression that all loans and grants of demand deposits are associated with new money creation, in actuality, most new loans simply replace loans that have been paid off and new demand deposits replace demand deposits lost by other banks. Increases in loans and demand deposits only account for a small proportion of new loans and demand deposits.

15-8. **How much money can the monopoly Honesty Bank shown in the following table create if the reserve ratio is 10%? 20%?**

THE HONESTY BANK

ASSETS		LIABILITIES	
Reserves	$2,000,000	Demand deposits	$2,000,000

At 10%, $18 million (the excess reserves, $1.8 million, times the reciprocal of the reserve ratio, 10).

At 20%, $8 million (the excess reserves, $1.6 million, times the reciprocal of the reserve ratio, 5).

15-9.   The Honesty Bank shown in Question 8 is an individual bank in a multibank system. How much money can it create if the desired reserve ratio is 10%? 20%?

$1.8 million at 10% and $1.6 million at 20%, amounts that equal the excess reserves.

15-10.   Suppose the Honesty Bank represented in Question 9 is a member of a multibank system. How much money can the multibank system create if the desired reserve ratio is 10%? 20%? Why?

At 10%, a total of $18 million. At 20%, a total of $8 million. This is because while the reserves may leave a particular bank, they won't leave the system. At 10%, the excess reserves of $1.8 million can support an additional $18 million in demand deposits. At 20%, the excess reserves of $1.6 million can support $8 million in demand deposits.

15-11.   Why do governments sometimes avoid forcing their government banks to hold reserves?

If government banks don't have to keep reserves, they can create all the money the government wishes. If the nation is at war, this means the government can finance new purchases of war goods by having the treasury sell bonds to the government banks in exchange for new government bank notes. Creating new money is easier than taxing the public or borrowing old money.

Also, if a banking panic occurs and people shift from bank demand deposits into gold, the government may want its bank to prevent a radical decrease in the money supply by issuing more government money. The money supply will otherwise fall radically because in a fractional reserve system, each dollar of gold reserves supports many dollars in demand deposits.

Moreover, if the supply of nonmoney goods is growing because of economic growth, then the government may want its bank to issue new money to facilitate the greater number of exchanges that will occur.

Finally, the government may want the money supply to grow to stimulate the employment of otherwise unemployed resources. More money may indirectly cause the production of more products.

15-12.   The U.S. money supply should be backed by gold to secure its value. Evaluate.

We can't say what should be. We can only identify the effects of a gold standard. If the United States were on a gold standard that required gold reserves, then the money supply would be limited by the supply of gold. With a limited money supply, the value of money in exchange would be relatively fixed. However, this does not imply that the value of money is determined by its commodity value. The value of money is determined by its exchange value and that exchange value is relatively constant when the supply of money is constant.

15-13.   When the Spanish galleons arrived laden with gold found in the New World, did the wealth of Europe increase or was it redistributed?

The wealth of Europe was primarily redistributed. The Spanish gained wealth at the expense of everyone else. This is because an increase in the supply of gold didn't increase the quantities of nonmoney goods.

One qualification is necessary. To the extent that the gold had a jewelry value rather than just an exchange value, the wealth of Europe increased.

15-14.   In what sense are depositors of a bank investing in business firms?

Depositors of a bank are essentially creditors of the bank and therefore entitled to some of the bank's assets. To the extent that the assets include loans to business firms, the depositors have a claim against those firms.

15-15. If banks were totally unregulated, some of them would pay depositors high interest rates and then make loans to risky firms to earn high interest rates. The firms would periodically go bankrupt and some of the banks would then fold. How could depositors avoid losses?

Depositors would investigate banks before depositing their money and would invest in those banks that gave them the combinations of yield and risk that they wanted. Some depositors might want to gamble to earn more on their deposits and would put their money in riskier banks, while other depositors would sacrifice some earnings to obtain security.

CHAPTER 16

16-1. How do people survive in countries where inflationary rates exceed 100%?

High inflation rates increase the prices of resources as well as product prices. Except to the extent that inflation represents a shift of wealth toward the government, people in these countries can pay higher product prices because they earn higher wages, interest, rents, and profits.

16-2. In Canada, many mortgages have adjustable interest rates. That is, the rates change as the economy's prevailing rates of interest change. As a creditor, why might you be willing to accept a lower mortgage rate if the debtor agrees to the adjustable rate feature?

You might accept a lower rate because as a creditor, you wouldn't have to suffer a capital loss if inflation suddenly increased. Higher rates of inflation would increase interest rates to compensate you for the lower value of the money repaid.

16-3. Can a nation have continuous 500% yearly inflation and not suffer a recession?

Yes. All product, resource, and financial asset prices would then rise at 500% per year.
    If the inflation was caused by a constant increase in the supply of money, a redistribution of wealth toward those creating the new money would occur. If the government was obtaining all the new money, the production of public goods would increase relative to private goods.

16-4. Does greed cause inflation?

No. Greed has been around for a long time, but inflation has occurred only when aggregate demand has increased relative to the supply of nonmoney goods.

16-5. Will increases in government spending, decreases in taxes, and decreases in the value of the dollar in terms of foreign currencies cause sustained inflation?

In and of themselves, no. Sustained inflation is caused by increases in the supply of money. If the supply of money remains constant, increases in government spending, decreases in taxes, and decreases in the value of the dollar will at most temporarily increase the velocity of money to cause transitory inflation. These changes will only be associated with sustained inflation if the money supply is simultaneously rising. If the money supply doesn't rise, the changes often only modify the composition of aggregate demand rather than its level, moving money spending from one area of the economy to another.

16-6. What are the economic effects of successful counterfeiting?

Counterfeiting increases the supply of money and causes inflation. It also redistributes wealth toward counterfeiters and away from the public at large.

16-7. Who is responsible for inflation, the president, Congress, or the board of governors of the Federal Reserve System?

Inflation is generally caused by excessive growth of the money supply. Inflation can therefore be eliminated by reducing the growth of the money supply. Since the board of governors of the Federal Reserve System controls the money supply, the board is responsible for inflation. The president and Congress can only apply indirect pressure on the board, so their responsibility is minimal.

16-8.   **What are the economic effects of deflation?**

The reverse of those of inflation. For the most part, unanticipated deflation redistributes wealth toward people on fixed incomes, creditors, and individuals holding money.

16-9.   **Suppose the required reserve ratio is 10%. How much money can the Veracity Bank in the following table create if it is a member of a multibank system? How much money can the system create? If the Veracity Bank buys $50,000 in government bonds from the Fed, how much money can the bank subsequently create? The multibank system?**

THE VERACITY BANK

ASSETS		LIABILITIES	
Reserves	$300,000	Demand deposits	$300,000

The individual bank can create $270,000, an amount equal to its initial excess reserves. The banking system can create $2.7 million, 10 times the initial excess reserves.

After the purchase of bonds, the bank's excess reserves fall to $220,000. It can therefore create only $220,000 and the banking system can create only $2.2 million.

16-10.   **How much money can the Veracity Bank in Question 9 create if the required reserve ratio rises to 20%? How much money can the multibank system create if the ratio rises to 20%?**

The Veracity Bank can then create only $240,000. The banking system can create only $1.2 million, 5 times $240,000.

16-11.   **How much money can the Veracity Bank in Question 9 create if it borrows $100,000 from a Federal Reserve bank? How much money can the multibank system create? If the discount rate increases and the bank borrows only $50,000, how will this affect the bank's money creation? How will the multibank system's ability to create money be affected by the higher discount rate?**

Initially, the bank can create $100,000 since all the borrowed money will be excess reserves. The banking system will be able to create 10 times that amount, $1 million. After the discount rate increases, their abilities would fall to $50,000 and $500,000, respectively, since excess reserves would be $50,000 less.

16-12.   **Why are members of the Federal Reserve System's board of governors appointed to 14-year terms?**

Fourteen-year terms were chosen to insulate members of the board from political pressures and also to make the members focus on long-term effects of monetary policies.

16-13.   **How can your personal rate of inflation be greater than the rate indicated by the rise of the CPI?**

Your personal rate will be higher if you buy large quantities of goods whose prices are rising faster than the price level.

16-14.   **Use the equation of exchange to explain how price searching can cause an inequality between aggregate demand and aggregate supply.**

If aggregate demand rises, price searchers may fail to increase prices even though the quantities of nonmoney goods are the same. As a result aggregate demand will exceed the supply of nonmoney goods and shortages will occur ($MV > PQ$). Also, if the quantity of products suddenly rises and price searchers fail to reduce prices, then aggregate demand will be less than the supply of nonmoney goods, giving rise to surpluses ($MV < PQ$).

CHAPTER 17

17-1. Is unemployment generally caused by too few jobs? Why?

No. As long as we want more products, and labor can produce those products, labor will be scarce. Since labor is insufficient, there are too many jobs to be done, not too few.

17-2. Are people unemployed if they can't find jobs that pay enough to live on?

No. Unfortunately, in some poor nations, people can't find jobs that pay enough to pay for food, shelter, and other goods vital to human survival. Nevertheless, according to our definition, when they turn down such jobs, they are choosing leisure over work and are not unemployed. The problem is low labor productivity rather than a lack of jobs.

17-3. During the early 1970s, demands for engineers decreased drastically causing many to be laid off. Did they become unemployed?

They became unemployed if they refused to work at lower-paying jobs because they thought they could find higher-paying ones. But if their productivity fell 50% and they knew it, and if they still refused 50% pay cuts, then they chose leisure over work and were not unemployed. They simply dropped out of the labor force.

17-4. Would frictional unemployment occur under conditions of unlimited information?

No. Under conditions of unlimited market information, frictional unemployment would not occur. Everyone would know the locations of all jobs and the wages paid. If demands or technology moved jobs to other areas, changes in wages would immediately inform workers and give them incentives to shift to the new jobs.

17-5. Many economists argue that the rate of frictional unemployment in the economy has increased from about 2% to about 4% in recent years. As causes, they cite the entry of women and teenagers into the labor force, the increase in unemployment and welfare benefits, and a higher level of wealth. Explain how these three factors might increase frictional unemployment.

How long someone looks for another job depends not only on how much better he or she expects the new job to be but also on the costs of the extra search. Women and teenagers generally have lower search costs than men and adults, partly because they sacrifice less when their husbands and parents, respectively, work. This explains the statistics showing that these groups change jobs more often and stay between jobs longer. Unemployment benefits, welfare payments, and greater wealth also reduce the costs of job searches and thereby increase the level of frictional unemployment.

17-6. Besides shifts in demands, how can frictional unemployment be caused by searches for better jobs, increases in population, and changes in technology?

Any factor that causes people to want new jobs is going to increase frictional unemployment. Information about jobs is scarce, costly to produce, and less costly to produce when it is produced slowly.

17-7. Structural unemployment occurs when the average length of frictional unemployment is increased by different skill requirements of jobs. Explain how this might happen after demands shift from autos to computers.

People who work on automobiles don't necessarily have the education and skills to work on computers. As a result, their initial productivities while working for computer firms will be low. This will allow them to obtain only low wages. But they may initially demand the same wages they had earned as auto workers, not realizing that jobs don't exist at those wages. They will thus become unemployed and remain so until they discover that they must reduce their wage demands to match their lower productivities. Once they discover that they must accept lower wages, then if they are willing to do so, they will find work. If they refuse, however, they will not be unemployed, they will have dropped out of the labor force, choosing leisure over work.

This explanation may seem brutal, but no matter how much we would like everyone to produce a great deal, productivities are dictated by the innate abilities of resources. Everyone would like to be paid twice what they produce, but there aren't enough products to go around.

17-8. **A decrease in the money supply can cause a reduction in aggregate demand by reducing M and therefore MV. How might a reduction in spending on capital by business firms reduce V, and therefore MV, to cause a recession?**

By not spending money for capital, money may be left sitting, causing a drop in velocity and aggregate demand. People with money may decide that the best use of money is as a store of value rather than as a medium of exchange. In the extreme case, if all money were held, aggregate demand would be zero even if a great deal of money existed.

17-9. **Some economists have argued that monopoly firms and unions cause recessions by refusing to lower prices and wages following a decrease in aggregate demand. How do monopoly firms and labor unions respond when demands for their goods fall?**

When demands for products and labor fall, monopoly firms and labor unions react the same way that competitive firms and workers react: they reduce prices and wages. Monopoly firms and labor unions routinely charge higher prices and wages, but they don't respond differently to changes in demands. If monopoly firms and unions could totally ignore supply and demand, they would raise prices and wages to infinity.

17-10. **If firms owned all the resources they used in production, why would they still cut employment and production rather than prices and wages after a decrease in aggregate demand?**

They would assume that decreases in demands for their products represented a change in the composition of aggregate demand rather than a decrease in the level of aggregate demand. They would cut employment and production and look for other products to produce.

17-11. **Our emphasis has been on labor unemployment. Are other resources unemployed during recessions. Why?**

Yes. In fact, rates of unemployment of other resources are often much higher than the rates of labor unemployment. Nonlabor resources are also generally sold by price searchers who react to lower demands by reducing sales first and prices only later.

17-12. **During the early 1980s, a reporter for the New York Times argued that lower prices and wages signaled the beginning of a recession. Did they?**

No. The lower prices and wages were a signal that recovery from the recession was beginning. The beginning of the recession had been signaled by a previous drop in national production, a drop that wouldn't have occurred had prices and wages fallen fast enough.

17-13. **In what sense are we employed when we are frictionally unemployed?**

We are working to produce information about job locations, wages, and working conditions.

17-14. Why might you be happy if I found a job paying $50,000 per year instead of only $30,000 per year?

A better-paying job would probably represent the production of more valuable products for consumers, perhaps you.

17-15. If people knew the nature of demand decreases during a recession, they could stop the recessions. In what sense is this true? In what sense is it false?

If everyone knew that demand decreases were caused by lower aggregate demand, they would immediately accept lower wages and prices. Production and employment could then stay the same.

However, individuals acting independently could do nothing. For example, you couldn't keep your job just by cutting your own wages. Your employer would have to cut product price and other workers and resource suppliers would have to also agree to cut their wages and prices.

17-16. For simplicity, the chapter discussed sudden decreases in aggregate demands as the causes of recessions. More generally, recessions are caused by sudden reductions in the growth of aggregate demand relative to the growth of the price-wage level. Suppose the money supply, aggregate demand, and the price-wage level are growing at 10% per year. How can a recession be caused by a sudden reduction in the growth of aggregate demand to only 5% per year?

Prices and wages would continue to grow at 10% despite the presence of only 5% increases in aggregate demand. Product and labor surpluses would therefore occur and reductions in production and employment would follow.

CHAPTER 18

18-1. Why don't we aggregate money and all other items into two goods when we want to explain a recession?

With such a high level of aggregation, we would obtain simplicity but have little generality. For example, we wouldn't be able to say anything about demands for labor, consumption commodities, capital, and bonds, nor would we be able to understand the prices of these goods. We would understand only movements from money into non-money goods and back, and the prices of nonmoney goods in terms of money.

18-2. Suppose you purchase a government bond yielding 10% interest on its face value. If the economy's interest rate suddenly rises so that new bonds yield 20%, how can you nevertheless sell your bond?

You can simply reduce the price so that the effective interest yield on the bond rises to 20%.

18-3. When the U.S. Treasury sells bonds, it keeps payments on the bonds the same. The bonds are simply auctioned off to the highest bidders. When the bonds are sold at higher prices, what does this tell you about the economy's interest rate?

When the prices of the bonds rise, the effective interest rates fall. This implies that the economy's interest rate is falling.

18-4. If there is no money market, how can you buy money?

You can buy money when you sell nonmoney goods. Most households buy money by selling labor.

18-5. Why will people hold more money when the interest rate falls and less when it rises?

The interest that could have been earned by owning bonds is sacrificed when money is held instead. Therefore, when the interest rate falls, the cost of holding money falls and people hold more money. Conversely, when the interest rate rises, the cost of holding money increases and people hold less money.

18-6. Explain the relationship between *MV* and money holding.

Money holding shows up in the velocity of money. When money holding rises, money spending falls and the velocity of money falls. Conversely, when money holding falls, money is spent more rapidly and velocity rises.

18-7. How could you reduce the velocity of the money you own?

Hold on to more money and hold on to it longer. This doesn't mean that you lend it to someone else. If you do that, they will spend it and the velocity of money will not necessarily change. You must let the money sit, either in your checking account or in your wallet.

18-8. The price of money is the interest rate. Is this true?

The price of money is what we have to sacrifice to obtain it in trade. That price can be expressed in terms of labor, consumption commodities, capital, bonds, etc. Interest is usually the cost of money since interest is usually the highest valued alternative sacrificed when money is held.

18-9. Are bonds the only things people will sell to obtain money?

No. People can sell labor, products, used goods, land, common stocks, and other goods to obtain money. But when they have bonds, they generally sell them first because bonds are the most liquid of these assets; they can be converted to cash with a minimum loss of market value.

18-10. Does Say's principle imply that the act of demanding a consumption commodity or a unit of capital requires the simultaneous act of supplying some other physical good?

No. Say's principle says only that the act of demanding one good is synonymous to supplying some other good. The other good supplied can be a bond or money rather than a physical commodity.

However, in a barter economy, Say's principle converts to Say's law. Say's law states that the supply of any physical good requires a demand for another physical good.

18-11. Say's principle will hold as long as we neither steal goods nor give them away. Explain.

Demand creates supply only if people can't steal or if other people don't give away goods. If people steal, they can demand without supplying, and if people give goods away, they can supply without demanding.

18-12. How does a shortage of money during the multiplier process differ from the shortage of money that occurs during the beginning of a recession?

During a multiplier process, households want money only as a medium of exchange to buy consumption commodities. That is, if they received more money, they would immediately spend it.

On the other hand, at the beginning of a recession, the households demand money primarily as a store of value. If they received more money, they would hold it rather than spend it.

18-13. Are we as individuals to blame for a recession?

No. A recession occurs because the economic system malfunctions after a decrease in aggregate demand. There is little an individual can do. In fact, individuals throughout the recessionary process act in a rational manner.

18-14. Are recessions a result of monopolistic behavior?

We haven't even mentioned monopoly in this chapter. The problem is limited information, not monopoly. In fact, if the economy contained more monopolists, recessions might be milder, since monopolists know a great deal about their markets and, therefore, respond quickly to reduced demands by reducing prices.

CHAPTER 19

19-1.   Foreigners buy consumption and capital goods in the United States. How does this affect aggregate demand?

Foreigners affect aggregate demand the same way domestic consumers affect it. If we wanted to study these effects in particular, perhaps because we were concerned that they are possible sources of recessionary decreases in aggregate demand, then it might be worth a sacrifice of some simplicity to disaggregate both consumption commodities and capital into two groups, those bought by and sold to domestic buyers and those bought by and sold to foreign buyers.

19-2.   When fiscal policies raise aggregate demand, how is MV affected?

Fiscal policies that don't change the money supply increase aggregate demand only if they increase the velocity of money. They absorb money that wasn't being spent and give it to either the government, households, or business firms who spend it.

　　　　Other fiscal policies increase aggregate demand by causing an increase in the money supply. New money is simply given to the government, households, or business firms who spend it.

19-3.   Antirecessionary fiscal policies don't work. They were tried during the Great Depression and failed. A war was necessary to pull the economy out of that catastrophe. Evaluate.

The policies weren't extensively used during the Great Depression. Although federal government spending increased somewhat, state and local government spending fell.

　　　　During World War II, the first extensive use of fiscal policies occurred. Government spending rose, taxes were only slightly increased, and deficits were financed by borrowing old and new money. An enormous increase in MV resulted and the economy quickly recovered.

　　　　The war was unnecessary. It was government spending and financing that created the recovery.

19-4.   Was the Great Depression caused by overproduction? Explain.

No. Even now, with output far greater than in that period, there aren't many of us who don't want more cars, boats, houses, furniture, clothing, and other items that could be produced if we only had more labor. But labor is scarce; we must do without.

19-5.   What would the government have to do to keep the level of unemployment in the economy below the level of classical plus frictional unemployment?

It would continually have to increase aggregate demand more than would be expected. For example, once prices and wages were increasing 10% per year due to the expectation of a 10% increase in aggregate demand relative to nonmoney goods, the government would have to increase aggregate demand more, say 20%. But in the next round, prices and wages would be increasing 20%, and a 40% increase in aggregate demand might be necessary. In time, aggregate demand would have to be increased exponentially. But even the exponential rates would eventually have to be raised constantly above expectations.

19-6.   How can antirecessionary fiscal policies indirectly cause recessions?

If antirecessionary fiscal policies create inflation because they increase aggregate demand faster than the aggregate supply of nonmoney goods, then to reduce the inflation, a reduction in the growth of aggregate demand might eventually be necessary. But a reduction in the growth of aggregate demand would first cause a recession and only later reduce the growth of prices. Price-searching producers and workers would first cut production and employment in response to a reduction in the growth of aggregate demand and only later reduce the growth of prices and wages.

19-7. In equilibrium, the rents of apartments are at levels where 6% vacancies exist. The vacant apartments provide prospective tenants with apartments that they can inspect and immediately occupy. But landlords are price searchers and when demands increase, landlords don't raise rents immediately. Vacancy rates fall instead, below the normal 6% level. If the government believed that the normal apartment vacancy rate is only 2%, how could it reduce the vacancy rate to 2% and keep it there? Could it do so perpetually?

To keep the rate below the normal level, the government would have to constantly increase demands for apartments at rates faster than landlords expected. However, it couldn't do this forever since landlords would try to anticipate future increases in demands and raise rents before the demand increases occurred.

19-8. Higher taxes won't raise the national public debt but they may increase the national private debt. Explain.

If some households and firms want to maintain consumption and investment, they may simply try to borrow money to pay their taxes. The national private debt will rise although the public debt may remain the same.

19-9. Suppose you presently owe $75,000 on your house and your share of the national debt is $25,000. Had the government raised your taxes in the past, why might it essentially not have affected your total debt or total debt payments?

Had your taxes been $25,000 higher, you might have borrowed $100,000 to buy the house rather than $75,000. Later, you would have had to pay off the bank instead of paying higher taxes to pay for your share of the national debt.

19-10. If the government decided to raise taxes by $25,000 to pay off the national debt, how would you react?

You would probably borrow $25,000 from the bank to pay your taxes, converting the national public debt to a private one.

19-11. Who might want the Treasury to borrow from the public or tax them with inflation rather than raise income taxes?

Borrowing from the public tends to defer taxes to the future. Therefore, older people who anticipate not living much longer might favor debt financing. The inflation is a fairly flat tax. Therefore, people in high tax brackets might prefer inflationary financing.

19-12. Why might political conservatives see deficit spending as a road to socialism?

Deficit spending, to the extent that it allows either the use of the hidden inflation tax or the deferral of taxes to the future, tends to increase government spending and therefore the government's involvement in the economy.

19-13. Because of inabilities to predict, fiscal and monetary policies have done more to cause inflation and recession then to solve it. Is this possible?

This is possible and some economists claim that it has occurred. However, the evidence is unclear.

19-14. If people negate the antirecessionary effects of new money by not spending it, who will spend it?

Politicians. The government is likely to spend all the money it can obtain.

19-15.   **Supply-side theories are narrow in their perspectives. While they recognize that people may work less because of higher taxes, they don't recognize that people will work more when the taxes are spent to buy them public goods. Is this true?**

Although taxes do reduce the rewards that individuals obtain from working, government goods don't increase the rewards individuals obtain from working. This is because the benefits of most public goods accrue to all individuals whether the individuals work or not. Private-property rights to public goods generally don't exist.

CHAPTER 20

20-1.   **What would be the advantage of having only one world currency?**

Transaction costs would fall since exchanges of national currencies wouldn't be necessary before international exchanges of foreign nonmoney goods could occur.

20-2.   **Value differentials may be the basic cause of trade, but production keeps trade going. Explain.**

Trade quickly eliminates most value differentials. It is the introduction of new goods via production that re-creates value differentials and causes trade to occur again.

20-3.   **What would cause the value of the dollar to rise relative to foreign currencies?**

The value of the dollar is derived from the value of the U.S. nonmoney goods it will buy, whereas the values of foreign currencies are derived from the values of the foreign nonmoney goods that they will buy. Therefore, if people value U.S. products, resources, or financial assets more relative to foreign products, resources, or financial assets, then the value of the dollar will rise relative to the values of foreign currencies.

20-4.   **How does a federal budget deficit affect our balance of payments and the value of the dollar?**

The federal budget deficit means that more U.S. government bonds are for sale. If foreigners want to buy these assets, then they must first purchase dollars. This will raise the demand for dollars, increase the value of the dollar, and raise its price in currency markets.

The greater export of financial assets must be matched by a greater import of foreign goods, or by a reduction in the export of other U.S. goods.

20-5.   **Why should we worry if foreign currencies rise in value relative to the dollar?**

It implies that U.S. products, resources, and financial assets are less valuable relative to those sold in foreign countries.

20-6.   **How might you be affected if I can buy products or borrow money from foreigners?**

If I didn't have foreigners to trade with, I might be willing to pay you higher prices for your goods, or I might be willing to borrow money from you at a higher interest rate. To get me to trade with you, you have to match the prices charged by foreigners.

20-7.   **Does a trade deficit that is balanced by foreign purchases of U.S. Treasury bonds have different economic effects than a deficit balanced by foreign purchases of bonds sold by U.S. corporations?**

Not necessarily. The purchases of corporate bonds would help increase U.S. economic growth, since corporations would spend the money to buy capital. However, the same results can occur when foreigners buy Treasury bonds, although the results occur indirectly. By purchasing the bonds, foreigners make it possible for corporations to obtain money from American creditors, money that wouldn't have been available had the Treasury been forced to sell its bonds to only domestic buyers. Since corporations obtain more money for investment, the foreign purchases of U.S. bonds help increase U.S. economic growth.

20-8. **What evidence can you cite to show that international trade doesn't cause unemployment?**

International trade has been occurring throughout history and excessive unemployment has generally been confined to recessions. In fact, periods of greatest growth in international trade have often been periods of maximum employment.

20-9. **How do Japanese regulations that restrict imports from the United States affect the yen price of the dollar?**

The regulations reduce the yen price of the dollar. Since the Japanese can't buy certain U.S. goods, the demand for dollars in Japan falls.

By restricting imports, unilateral restrictions indirectly restrict exports. A lower yen price of the dollar is a higher dollar price of the yen. Japanese goods become more expensive to U.S. buyers and demand for the goods falls.

To balance imports and exports, it isn't necessary for a nation to retaliate against trade restrictions imposed by other nations. The exchange rate will adjust to make sure that the nations imposing the restrictions will find exports more difficult, so that exports will fall as well as imports. Of course, the exchange rate affects all goods while restrictions focus on particular items. A government may want specific trade restrictions if it is concerned about particular domestic buyers and sellers.

20-10. **Who opposed the U.S. Constitution, the creation of the British Empire, and the formation of the European Common Market?**

Those individuals and firms who had to compete with foreign sellers of goods.

20-11. **If you are going to France next year, how can you protect yourself against a sudden increase in the price of francs?**

You can buy francs or franc futures now.

20-12. **What limits the ability of the U.S. and foreign banks when they seek to keep the dollar from dropping relative to foreign currencies?**

They are limited by the amount of foreign currency or dollars that they have available. It is one thing to stabilize exchange rates, for then accumulations of foreign currencies can be matched by decumulations, but when exchange rates are changing to new levels rather than fluctuating, policies aimed at fixing the rates will fail once foreign or domestic currencies are exhausted.

For example, when the government tries to prevent fluctuations in wheat prices, it must buy wheat when prices would have fallen and sell that wheat when they would have risen. But if the prices are falling and are going to remain low, the government will continually have to purchase wheat, year in and year out, accumulating huge surpluses of wheat and gradually spending enormous amounts of money.

20-13. **How could you become wealthy if you knew the value of the dollar was about to fall relative to the Austrian shilling?**

You could buy shillings and sell them later at the higher price.

20-14. **If Japan sells the United States goods at below cost, is this a problem for the U.S. or is it a problem for Japan?**

It is a problem for Japan. I certainly wouldn't complain if you sold me some goods at prices below your costs. Anytime you want to give goods away, you certainly don't benefit. In fact, I might complain if you sold goods at prices far above your costs.

When domestic producers claim that foreign producers sell at prices below costs, the foreign producers are usually selling at prices below domestic costs, not below the costs that the foreigners incur. It would be irrational to sell goods continuously at prices below costs.

Index